## Conflicting Worlds
*New Dimensions of the American Civil War*
T. MICHAEL PARRISH, EDITOR

# WALKER'S
# TEXAS
# DIVISION
## C.S.A.

_To Sam —_
_Best wishes_
_Richard Lowe_
_6/9/04_

## GREYHOUNDS
## OF THE
## TRANS-
## MISSISSIPPI

## RICHARD
## LOWE

LOUISIANA STATE UNIVERSITY PRESS
_Baton Rouge_

Copyright © 2004 by Louisiana State University Press
All rights reserved
Manufactured in the United States of America
First printing
13  12  11  10  09  08  07  06  05  04
5  4  3  2  1

DESIGNER: Amanda McDonald Scallan
TYPEFACE: Minion
TYPESETTER: Coghill Composition Co., Inc.
PRINTER AND BINDER: Thomson-Shore, Inc.

Library of Congress Cataloging-in-Publication Data

Lowe, Richard G., 1942–
    Walker's Texas Division, C.S.A. : greyhounds of the
trans-Mississippi / Richard Lowe.
        p.    cm. — (Conflicting worlds)
Includes bibliographical references (p.    ) and index.
    ISBN 0-8071-2933-X (cloth : alk. paper)
    1. Confederate States of America. Army. Walker's Texas
Division.    2. West (U.S.)—History—Civil War, 1861–
1865—Campaigns.    3. United States—History—Civil
War, 1861–1865—Campaigns.    4. United States—
History—Civil War, 1861–1865—Regimental histories.
I. Title.    II. Series: Conflicting worlds.
E580.5.W34L69    2004
973.7′464—dc22                        2003021052

*For Kevin, Chris, and Mark*

# CONTENTS

# ILLUSTRATIONS

TABLES

# PREFACE

In the late summer of 1862, as Robert E. Lee's Confederate army stalked Federal general John Pope toward the old Manassas battlefield in Virginia, a thousand miles to the southwest another group of Confederates was also on the move. Unlike the men in Lee's Army of Northern Virginia, these soldiers were untested in battle and new to the ways of the military. They were the Texans who would soon be organized into an infantry unit referred to afterward as John G. Walker's Texas Infantry Division. The unit was also known as the "Greyhound Division" for its numerous long, rapid marches across three states. The new soldiers were leaving their "camps of instruction" in Texas with orders to proceed to Little Rock, Arkansas. Traveling as separate regiments, the inexperienced warriors wilted and nearly fainted in the suffocating heat and dust of the piney woods in East Texas. The long columns of farm boys and store clerks and carpenters and lawyers were enveloped in their own special aroma created by mules, horses, sweating men, pine forests, and dust. Too exhausted for the usual banter, the men trudged along to the sounds of creaking wagon wheels, snorting horses, tin cups clinking against metal buckles, an occasional cough, and the rhythmic shuffle of their aching feet.

Who were these men, and what had brought them to this dusty country lane? Why had they joined the army of the Confederacy, and why had they waited until the second year of the war to do so? What adventures and misadventures awaited them in their war against the Yankees, and how would they perform as soldiers? Indeed, what difference would they make, if any, in this bloodiest of all American wars?

Walker's Texas Division, the only one on either side to consist during its entire existence of regiments from a single state, was the largest single body of Texans to fight in the Civil War. The regiments of the division were raised in the winter and spring of 1862, but the Texans' first engagement with Federal forces came more than a year later, during the Vicksburg campaign. The division's most important contribution to the Confederate war effort was its leading role in the struggle to turn back the Federal Red River campaign in the spring of 1864. The

Greyhounds measured up to their reputation that spring, marching nine hundred miles in two months, fighting hard in three important battles, and losing nearly 40 percent of their number in killed, wounded, and missing in only three weeks. The Confederate victory in the Red River valley not only ended further Federal attempts to penetrate Texas, it also prevented Union divisions from joining Gen. William T. Sherman's critical Atlanta campaign and freed up Confederate troops to join the fight against Sherman in north Georgia, prolonging the war perhaps another six months.

The history of the Greyhound Division is worth investigating for reasons beyond the battlefield. Unlike many other divisions, this one remained stable from its formation in 1862 until the last few weeks of the war, marching as one body and allowing the men to identify themselves with the division more than with a particular regiment or brigade. Because the division included several thousand men (as many as twelve thousand at its birth and about three thousand at its dissolution), it left behind more historical evidence (e.g., letters, diaries, official documents, eyewitness accounts by civilians) than most smaller units, like regiments or brigades, enabling later observers to benefit from a richer, more textured view of its history. The division included eleven regiments and one battalion, allowing the interested reader to see how different units were raised, armed, and commanded and how those units behaved under stress. Finally, Walker's division had a fine historian in its ranks, an Irish-born private who wrote a colorful and (mostly) accurate firsthand chronicle of the Greyhounds, sketching out their story for future students to build upon with additional sources and perspective.

The Texas Division served throughout the war in the trans-Mississippi theater, a region that appears only as a general fog in the minds of many readers dazzled by names like Lee, Grant, Sherman, and Jackson, and places like Manassas, Antietam Creek, and Gettysburg. Still, those with serious interest in the American Civil War would do well to shift their gaze westward occasionally, across the Mississippi River, to the hills and prairies and swamps of Arkansas, Louisiana, and Texas. Those who do will find a war fought by smaller armies on a larger geographical stage, but nevertheless a war that influenced events in the eastern and western theaters in important ways and a conflict that involved no less pain, courage, cowardice, nobility, and pettiness. And the single most formidable Confederate fighting unit they will learn about was Walker's Texas Division.

It is customary for authors to thank the people who helped them on their way to a finished book, and it is one of the most pleasant tasks associated with the whole enterprise. Authors know only too well how dependent they are on other writers, archivists, librarians, friends, and family members, and thanking them in a preface is a small gesture of thanks that only begins to balance the books. At one time or another, several colleagues have read parts of the manuscript and provided wise counsel. T. Michael Parrish of Baylor University, Randolph B. Campbell and Jane Tanner at the University of North Texas, Arthur W. Bergeron Jr. of the Pamplin Historical Park, Judith F. Gentry of the University of Louisiana-Lafayette, Steve E. Bounds of the Mansfield State Historical Site, Jane Turner Censer of George Mason University, Gregory J. W. Urwin of Temple University, and independent scholar Noah Andre Trudeau have all improved the book in one way or another. Norman D. Brown of the University of Texas at Austin paved the way for other scholars with his long-standing interest in Walker's Texas Division. The number of librarians and archivists who guided me through their collections is so large that I could not possibly list all of them, but a few deserve special mention: Richard J. Sommers of the United States Army Military History Institute, Michael Musick of the National Archives, Michael T. Meier of the National Historical Publications and Records Commission, and Vicki Betts of the University of Texas at Tyler.

A number of graduate students gathered census and tax data on various Texas regiments and batteries for their own research and generously shared their databases with me: M. Jane Johansson (28th Texas Cavalry), John Perkins (Daniel's battery), Scott Parker and Heather Speed (14th Texas Infantry), and Blake Hamaker (15th Texas Infantry). Clare Austin, Brad Clampitt, Ken Johnson, Matthew Pearcy, Austin Spencer, Lisa Thomason, and Mary Wilson performed similar labors for the usual minimal remuneration. Nelson and Sue McManus helped me to understand the Battle of Bayou Bourbeau, partly out of their own interest in the history of south Louisiana and partly due to family ties. (Who else would hack a path through a sugarcane field to provide a good photograph of part of the battlefield?) Steve Mayeux led me over the walls of Fort DeRussy, even before decades of underbrush had been removed, and educated me about the entire Simmesport–Yellow Bayou vicinity. Gary Canada generously shared his private collection of letters and diaries written by individual members of Walker's Texas Division.

My wife, Kathy, scrambled around Fort DeRussy with me, visited otherwise nondescript sites that meant little to her but much to me, asked unanticipated and pertinent questions about the men of the Greyhound Division, and, in ways too numerous to mention, lightened my burden. My three sons—Kevin, Chris, and Mark—had little or no direct connection with the research and writing, but, because they are my favorites, I dedicate the book to them.

# WALKER'S
# TEXAS
# DIVISION
## C.S.A.

# CHAPTER 1

# Introduction

The state that sent John G. Walker's Texas Infantry Division into Confederate service was a growing, thriving, expanding operation in the fifteen years before the Civil War. The state's population nearly tripled between the federal censuses of 1850 and 1860 (from 212,592 to 604,215), making Texas one of the most rapidly growing areas of the Union. Rich virgin soil, a favorable climate for agriculture, and a ready world market for cotton attracted farmers by the tens of thousands in the 1840s and 1850s. These new Texans agreed with the editor of *De Bow's Review* that "no country in North America holds out such inducements to emigrants as Texas, both for the salubrity of its climate, the fertility of its soil, and the variety of its products."[1]

Immigrants quickly changed the face of the state. They established land claims, cleared forests, plowed soil that had never been cultivated, and planted their first crops, doubling the number of acres improved for agricultural production between 1850 and 1860. Cotton production shot up even more spectacularly, from 58,072 bales in 1849 to 431,463 in 1859, an increase of more than 600 percent. Corn production nearly tripled, and other indicators of agricultural development grew in like proportion.[2] Most of the new Texans were natives of the slaveholding states. Some brought their own slaves to Texas, and others, hungry for cheap labor, prospered enough in the rapidly growing economy to buy bondsmen after they arrived in the Lone Star State. The number of slaves in Texas more than tripled during the 1850s, rocketing from 58,161 to 182,566. Similarly, slaveholders increased in number from 7,747 to 21,878 during the same period.[3]

Thus, Texas was the thriving western edge of the slaveholding South on the eve of the Civil War. Most Texans had ties to family and friends in older southern states and brought the ideas and habits of a slave-owning society with them to Texas. An agricultural economy heavily dependent on slave labor, and on slave owners, connected citizens of the new state with other southerners from Louisiana to Virginia. Southern interests were Texas interests. Nevertheless, the separatist wind that blew across much of the lower South in the 1850s was barely a breeze in Texas. The state's relatively recent annexation to the Union, the federal government's protecting shield against Mexico in the 1840s, the U.S. Cavalry's screen against the Plains Indians, and the blossoming prosperity that seemed so widespread in the 1850s all worked to maintain Texas's ties to the larger Union. Those bonds began to unravel only with the events of 1860.[4]

Indeed, the political atmosphere in Texas was electric in late 1860. Only a year earlier white Texans, along with many other southerners, had been shocked to learn of John Brown's raid at Harpers Ferry, Virginia. For the first time, residents of the Lone Star State began to question their safety in the Union they had joined only fourteen years earlier. Just nine months after the Harpers Ferry scare, some Texans concluded that they too were under attack from northern "Black Republicans," abolitionists, and renegade slaves. On a blistering Sunday afternoon in July 1860—with thermometers registering temperatures near 110 degrees—three unexplained fires in North Texas towns sent another current of fear through the white population. Within days, rumors spread throughout the state and the rest of the South that abolitionist preachers, in league with restless slaves and even nearby Indians, were carrying out a devilish plot to burn, poison, and murder the good citizens of North Texas preparatory to a general uprising of the slaves. Vigilance committees quickly forced "confessions" from terrified slaves and unlucky northern peddlers who happened to be in the area, and before calm and good sense returned, several dozen suspects were hanged for their supposed crimes. Only later did most Texans learn that spontaneous ignition and accidents had caused the fires.[5]

Before fractured nerves and elevated adrenaline levels returned to normal, the presidential election of 1860 stirred up white Texans further. When a northern Republican, Abraham Lincoln, was elected to the White House, the state of South Carolina seceded in December, and five more Deep South states followed South Carolina's lead within a few weeks. Meanwhile, majority opinion among Texas voters shifted to the belief that the Lone Star State, too, would be safer outside the Union than within. Although a few powerful voices—Gov. Sam Houston's, for example—spoke against the growing secessionist din, a special state convention voted, 166 to 8, to separate from the old Union on February 1, 1861. Three weeks later a popular referendum on the convention's action revealed that public opinion was solidly, even enthusiastically, in favor of separation. Only 18 of 122 counties opposed secession, and those who favored a break with the United States piled up more than 75 percent of the popular vote (46,153 of the total 60,900 votes).[6]

Even before the referendum, the secession convention moved quickly to cut all ties with the United States. The delegates sent seven representatives to the lower-South convention that was creating the Confederate States of America in

Montgomery, Alabama. In addition, the Texas convention appointed a Committee on Public Safety that would remain active after the larger body adjourned to await results of the referendum. This committee was given authority to seize U.S. government property in Texas, including munitions and other military supplies. One week before the referendum, and with instructions from the Committee on Public Safety, Ben McCulloch—a legendary Texas Ranger and Mexican War hero—led several hundred Texas volunteers into the streets of San Antonio to demand the surrender of all U.S. military forces in the state. With only 160 U.S. soldiers in the San Antonio garrison, the Federal military commander had little choice but to comply. Very quickly, other Texans commissioned by the Committee on Public Safety seized Federal property throughout the state, from the Red River on the north to the mouth of the Rio Grande on the south to El Paso on the west, all without a shot being fired.[7] In only a few weeks, Texans confiscated about $3 million worth of U.S. Army supplies and facilities, arranged for the removal of more than two thousand Federal troops from the state, and obtained arms for thousands of Texas volunteers. The popular referendum on secession, held in the midst of all this excitement, only confirmed the obvious.[8]

One of the casualties of the secessionist avalanche was the governor himself, Sam Houston. When the old frontiersman refused to take an oath of allegiance to the new Confederate States of America, the secession convention removed him from office and replaced him with his lieutenant governor, Edward Clark, an experienced politician and lawyer from Marshall in the northeast corner of the state. It fell to Clark to raise troops for the Confederate army then being assembled throughout the lower southern states. The new governor transferred the cavalry regiments already formed by the Committee on Public Safety to Confederate service and set about organizing dozens of new regiments. Clark divided the state into recruiting districts and appointed prominent men to head each district, arranged for the acquisition of arms and munitions, set up a system of training camps for new recruits, cooperated with the state legislature to raise taxes, and worked closely with the Confederate War Department to funnel Texas regiments into Confederate service.[9] By the end of the year, the recruiting and training system instituted by Governor Clark had placed slightly more than 25,000 men into Confederate ranks.[10]

Among the units raised in 1861 were some destined to achieve great fame in the war east of the Mississippi River. The 1st, 4th, and 5th Texas Infantry Regiments became the core of what was later known as Hood's Texas Brigade, one of the toughest and most renowned infantry units in Robert E. Lee's Army of Northern Virginia. The 8th Texas Cavalry, more widely known as Terry's Texas Rangers, fought and raided throughout the western theater of the war as part of

Nathan Bedford Forrest's feared cavalry forces. Another well-known contingent of Texas cavalry, Ross's Texas Cavalry Brigade, fought its way from Indian Territory eastward to Atlanta and was considered by some generals the best Confederate cavalry under their commands.[11]

Despite all the early enthusiasm for secession and the rush to join the army in Texas, only about one-third of the approximately seventy thousand Texans who would ultimately serve in the Confederate military signed on in 1861. Most Americans, north and south, believed the war would last only a few months, perhaps a year or so. One soldier in the 3rd Texas Cavalry Regiment recalled that "the eloquent 'stump' statesman did not hesitate to affirm that the end of thirty days would witness the close of the fifth act of the serio-comic drama [of war]." Thus, some men who could not or would not leave a young wife and children to fend for themselves—or leave a farm or business to falter or fail in their absence—resigned themselves to staying at home and missing the excitement. Early Confederate victories at Manassas (Bull Run), Virginia (in July 1861), and Wilson's Creek (Oak Hills), Missouri (in August), only reinforced the idea among many Texans that victory was just around the corner.[12]

Events during the winter and early spring of 1861–1862, however, shook the confidence of many white southerners. A Federal naval expedition seized Port Royal, South Carolina, in November, giving the Union control of an excellent natural harbor on the South Atlantic coast. Other naval and amphibious operations soon grabbed several more toeholds along the Atlantic, from Roanoke Island near the Virginia border to St. Augustine, Florida. By April most major Confederate harbors on the east coast—as well as New Orleans near the mouth of the Mississippi River—had fallen to Yankee sailors and soldiers. In January a small Federal army essentially erased all Confederate presence in eastern Kentucky at the Battle of Logan's Cross Roads (Mill Springs). A few weeks later Brig. Gen. Ulysses S. Grant created a major crevasse in the western Confederacy's line of defense by capturing Forts Henry and Donelson in western Tennessee and opening deeper routes of invasion via the Tennessee and Cumberland Rivers. Less than a month after that Confederate disaster, even more trouble for the reeling southerners developed west of the Mississippi River. The Federal army that had been thrown back from southern Missouri at Wilson's Creek the preceding summer now returned, penetrated into northwest Arkansas, and defeated a Confederate army—including Texans!—at the Battle of Pea Ridge (Elkhorn Tavern), pushing Union lines perilously close to the Lone Star State. Ben McCulloch himself was killed at Pea Ridge.[13]

In short, by early 1862 the war had taken on a whole new character. Federal armies were penetrating the outer shell of the new Confederate nation, seemingly at will; the blockade of the Atlantic coast was now significantly tighter than before; supposedly superior Confederate generals seemed to thrash and fumble about, always a step behind the enemy; and "the iron heel of Yankee despotism" was crunching closer to Texas.

It was in this atmosphere that the regiments and battalions of what would become Walker's Texas Division were organized. Robert S. Gould of Leon County in East Texas, a thirty-five-year-old lawyer and future chief justice of Texas, was one of those who took the new military situation seriously: "When in February 1862 heavy reverses befell our army, I resigned my office of district judge, [and] raised a company of mounted men." In nearby Cherokee County, A. J. Coupland, future lieutenant colonel of the 11th Texas Infantry Regiment, wrote in February 1862 that "our late defeats in Kentucky on the Tennessee River, & in North Carolina has produced considerable excitement & I think by using a little diligence we will be able to raise 2 Regiments." Citizens of Harrison County in northeast Texas formed the "Clough and Hill Avengers," among other new companies, naming their unit after two neighbors killed at Fort Donelson. Texans by the thousands took one last look around the farm or shop, hugged their babies, kissed their wives, and trudged off to join hundreds of new companies signing up recruits in early 1862.[14] This business of whipping the Yankees was proving a bigger job than most Texans had expected.[15]

# CHAPTER 2

# *Joining Up*

The destination of the typical Texan leaving home to join the army was usually a nearby town, often the county seat. A prominent citizen of the county or surrounding countryside—a judge, a politician, perhaps a well-known planter or merchant—normally placed notices in newspapers or printed flyers announcing the formation of a new company. These companies, about one hundred men each, were later grouped by state or Confederate authorities into regiments, usually comprising ten companies each, and rudimentary training began at various "camps of instruction" scattered around the state. Weeks or months after the companies mustered for the first time, military authorities gathered several regiments, usually four, into a brigade, and three or four brigades might then be combined into a division. Thus, a Confederate infantry division normally included twelve to sixteen thousand men when first organized.[1]

While Confederate and state officials scrambled to find enough food, tents, camp equipage, arms, and training sites for them, the men who formed the companies of what later became Walker's Texas Division gathered by twos and threes at the publicly announced places to sign their names to company rolls and become soldiers. Companies generally were drawn from a particular locality, such as the "Clough and Hill Avengers" from Harrison County and the "Yankee Routers" from neighboring Upshur County in northeast Texas. Nearly all (96 percent) of the volunteers in the "Titus Hunters" were residents of Titus County before the war. Indeed, in nine of the twelve sample companies analyzed in this study, more than three-fourths of the soldiers were residents of a single county (see Table 1). Not surprisingly, given this residential pattern, the typical company might include several pairs of brothers and numerous cousins, boyhood friends, and neighbors. James M. Daniel, captain of an artillery battery that was at times assigned to Walker's Texas Division, was assisted by his brother-in-law, Lt. James Wright. Samuel Wright, a cousin of Wright and of Captain Daniel's wife, served in the same battery.[2]

The original rolls of some units had signatures from fathers and sons as well. Perhaps the highest-ranking father-son combination was Dr. Leonard Randal of

TABLE 1

COUNTY ORIGINS OF ENLISTEES IN SAMPLE COMPANIES

| Regiment | Company | County | % of Enlistees |
|---|---|---|---|
| 6th Texas Cavalry Battalion | D | Leon | 96.3 |
| 11th Texas Infantry | D | Titus | 96.0 |
| 12th Texas Infantry | D | Grimes | 87.8 |
| 13th Texas Cavalry | H | Newton | 94.2 |
| 14th Texas Infantry | H | Harrison | 80.3 |
| 16th Texas Cavalry | D | Grayson* | 47.5 |
| | | Collin | 39.3 |
| 16th Texas Infantry | D | 36 counties | scattered |
| 17th Texas Infantry | A | Burleson | 78.8 |
| 18th Texas Infantry | K | Cherokee | 95.5 |
| 19th Texas Infantry | E | San Augustine | 61.0 |
| 22nd Texas Infantry | B | Leon | 82.8 |
| 28th Texas Cavalry | H | Freestone | 92.5 |

*Note:* Soldiers whose county of residence could not be ascertained (568 of 1,557, or 36.5 percent) were not included in these percentages.

*Grayson and Collin Counties are contiguous.

Marshall, a sixty-two-year-old physician, and his son Horace, a West Point graduate and colonel of his father's regiment. Another of the doctor's sons, Leonard Jr., served on his brother Horace's staff. More typical was the Wheeler family of Shelby County on the Louisiana border. The father, Alfred, signed the company roll along with two teenage sons and a nephew, and all were privates. The unit most men identified with first, the company, almost always had a heavy hometown flavor to it.[3]

Life in the military in the first months of the company's existence must have seemed particularly innocent in the memories of hardened soldiers later in the war. Early days in the army were often spent close to home. Family members and neighbors in Rusk County in East Texas held a watermelon supper for the men of Company H, 19th Texas Infantry, when they were mustered into Confederate service in 1862. A young lieutenant in the 13th Texas Cavalry marveled at the hospitality of civilians a few miles away from his home: "Martha I wish you could have been in Jasper & have seen how we were honored by the hospitable people of that place. we reached there on Sunday evening and were shown good stables for our horses. and the Citizens vied with each other in trying to see who could do us the most honor." In fact, he continued, "they took us home with them every one some 95 men and fed us on the best they had."[4]

This early close connection between community and company was also evident in one of the most memorable moments in the history of many units, the presentation to the company of a homemade flag by the ladies of the community. Numerous letters, diaries, and memoirs by Texas soldiers recount these poignant ceremonies. The newspaper in Marshall reported a typical flag presentation:

> On Tuesday evening, Miss CORA SIMS, in behalf of the Ladies of Harrison county, presented a Banner to Capt. Brown's company [Company F, 28th Texas Cavalry]. Miss CORA acquitted herself creditably, eliciting the admiration of those who were present, from her faultless pronunciation and the clearness of her enunciation. It was a flattering position for one so young to be called upon to deliver such an address, and it was gratifying that she performed her part so handsomely. There were five or six pretty, intelligent, little girls who acted as aids upon the occasion. The Banner was received by Lt. T. Perry in an appropriate speech. The affair was decidedly unique and pleasant.[5]

Not only patriotism was in high flower in these early days; respect for matters religious also was on full display. One company, from Upshur County in northeast Texas, marching to join other companies that would form a new regiment in Houston, confronted the cross purposes of war and the Sabbath in April 1862. "Determining not to proceed on the Sabbath day, the company camped in the suburbs of the town" on Saturday afternoon. The next morning the men marched to church, sat in the front pews, heard a sermon delivered by their own captain, then marched back to camp. Such devotion to weekly religious observances, common enough in the soldiers' civilian days, did not survive their first year of service to the Confederacy.[6]

The prominent men who raised these companies sometimes spent as much energy angling to be assigned to a certain regiment as they did recruiting soldiers. Oran M. Roberts, a South Carolina native, East Texas lawyer, and justice of the Texas Supreme Court before the war, was perhaps the most famous secessionist in the Lone Star State. He had been one of the loudest voices for secession before the war and had been elected unanimously as president of the Texas Secession Convention. While raising a regiment in East Texas in early 1862, he was deluged with requests from men who wanted to add their companies to his new unit.[7]

Only three days after Roberts was authorized to recruit his regiment, he received a letter from Shearman Holland of Panola County requesting authorization to organize two companies in Panola and also urging Roberts to consider Holland's brother for "a suitable situation" in the regiment. A few days later M. W. Wheeler of Angelina County offered to raise a company in his neighborhood. Roberts's own nephew, O. E. Roberts of Hopkins County, reported that he was having some difficulty recruiting a company for his uncle because two other companies were also being organized there. "If it was cavalry I could succeed better as Texans dislike to walk." James H. Jones of Rusk County, a lawyer and later successor to Roberts as colonel of the regiment, encountered the same Texas bias against ambulation in his efforts to produce a company for Roberts: "We have some good material for the service yet in our county—men of position and good moral characters—who are willing to go as infantry. We will have some prejudices to remove against walking." Roberts later noted, rather ruefully, that "I could have raised a dozen of Cavalry regiments."[8]

Roberts's correspondence reveals much about the process of forming regiments in the first year of the war. Some of the letters exhibit high zeal for the Confederate cause. Indeed, zeal apparently overcame the good judgment of J. C. Rhea of Cass County in extreme northeast Texas. Rhea recruited a company in 1862 and led it to Arkansas, but he eventually realized he would have to resign, "being too old and very fleshy." W. H. Shotwell, a former schoolmate of Roberts, sent two of his sons to serve with his old friend: "I freely Give you my Boys [for] Your Brigade and shall rest satisfied that when tried they will folow you in to the fire or any where."[9]

Other communications to the judge reported the difficulty of finding necessary arms and equipment for the new companies. A Mr. M. Bolin from Mt. Pleasant in northeast Texas complained that only "from one third to one half of my Company can furnish themselves guns, & the whole of them can procure large Knives [but] . . . it is impossible for more than one half of us to procure a full outfit if any. Our County has been exhausted of arms by the companies that have heretofore left."[10] Roberts's nephew wrestled with a similar problem: "Our county [Hopkins] is destitute of camp equipage tenting &c." The judge himself wrote a few months later that one-fourth of his men had no arms at all, and weapons of the sick had to be passed to those who were fit for duty in order to provide any men at all for actual service. And even those soldiers were outfitted with outdated flintlock muskets, powder flasks, and shot pouches. Four months after joining the army, the men were still severely short of weapons, knapsacks, haversacks, tents, and other equipment.[11]

One by one, the new companies formed in the winter and spring of 1862 marched away from their home communities and gathered in camps of instruction scattered from Austin and Bastrop in south-central Texas to Hempstead and Houston in the southeast to Tyler and Marshall in the northeast piney woods (see Map 1). At these camps the companies were joined with others to form new regiments, and the men were absorbed more fully into the military style of life.

# Map 1
## Texas in 1862

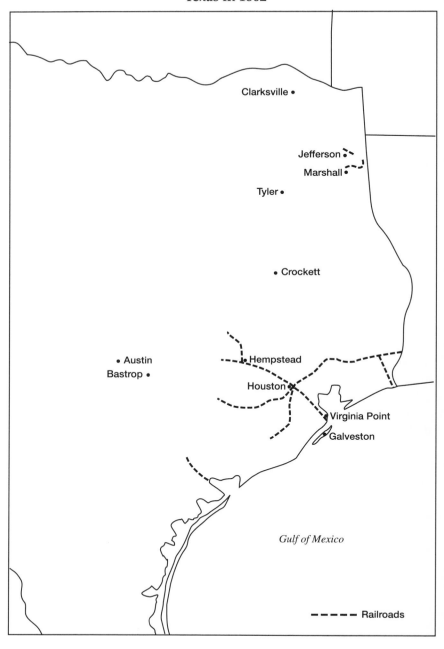

Clarksville •

Jefferson •

Marshall •

Tyler •

• Crockett

• Austin

Bastrop •

• Hempstead

Houston •

• Virginia Point

• Galveston

*Gulf of Mexico*

– – – – Railroads

The camps were usually located near large, open spaces suitable for company and battalion drills, near a water supply, and near major roads, railroads, or rivers.

One of the largest and most active points of rendezvous was Camp Groce, about fifty miles northwest of Houston and three miles east of the small town of Hempstead. The camp abutted the tracks of the Houston & Texas Central Railroad only a few miles from the lower Brazos River. The land was owned by Leonard Groce, a wealthy planter and son of one of the settlers in Stephen F. Austin's original colony of immigrants from the United States in the early 1820s. Groce owned fifty thousand acres in five Texas counties and administered his empire from his plantation house, Liendo, not far from the soldiers' quarters in distance but a world away in its luxuries. A wide verandah with columns, a brick wine cellar, brick outhouses, rose gardens, and a fountain marked Liendo as the home of a major planter in antebellum Texas. Groce provided the Confederacy more than land for this camp of instruction; he also sent four sons to the Confederate army.[12]

The camp centered on several long wooden barracks in a clearing three hundred yards north of the railroad tracks. A Federal prisoner detained at Camp Groce later in the war described the barracks: "They were like most such buildings, long and narrow, with bunks around the sides, and tables for the well and cots for the sick." Nearby was a frame building for officers and a small stream that provided water for the men. Across the railroad was another camp of instruction, named in honor of Brig. Gen. Paul O. Hébert, commander of the Confederate Department of Texas. One soldier remembered that "From this position there was a magnificent view of the hills that gird the place, forming a sort of amphitheatre; looking picturesque with their waving forests of trees, and innumerable white tents."[13]

Other camps of instruction in Texas, while perhaps not so large as the Groce-Hébert complex, were similar in appearance. A civilian visitor to Camp Murrah, several miles northeast of Tyler in the piney woods of East Texas, described neat rows of tents and good water for eight new companies. Like the camps near Hempstead, this camp, known by different names depending on which regiment was in residence, housed the men in barracks as well as tents. In fact, some of the men made their own tents from cloth furnished by inmates at the state penitentiary in Huntsville. Other camps near Austin, Bastrop, Marshall, and Jefferson did not differ significantly from those near Hempstead and Tyler.[14]

Whether stationed in the shadow of a great plantation house or in more humble pine forests, the newly minted soldiers followed similar routines at all the camps of instruction. Their main duty was to master the strange commands and movements required in nineteenth-century armies—how to march in a body, how to change directions without falling over each other, how to deploy from a marching column to a line of combat, how to load their weapons quickly and in unison. (These Texans rarely if ever actually fired their weapons except in combat, mainly due to ammunition shortages.) Most of all, these independent-minded young men had to learn how to take orders. Being ordered about like servants was galling to many of the new soldiers, especially when the commands were barked out by old friends or acquaintances they had known as equals.[15]

A visitor to any one of these camps of instruction would have noted a high level of activity during daylight hours—different companies drilling near each other in dusty open fields, officers shouting commands and shaking their heads in disbelief at the early confusion, other officers poring over drill books to learn which commands to shout, some men standing guard, others policing the grounds, orderlies galloping up to headquarters with orders from superiors. As much as the men grumbled about taking orders and drilling for hours at a time, these initial months of training were essential to turn farm boys and clerks and blacksmiths into soldiers. Drill taught them discipline and obedience to orders and developed unit cohesion and physical stamina. Indeed, almost daily drill was maintained throughout the war because it made them better soldiers. Those units that had the luxury of weeks or months of training before encountering the enemy were better prepared for the shock and confusion of combat. This may partially explain why the companies and regiments that would constitute Walker's Texas Division enjoyed a reputation as good fighters later in the war. These Texans drilled and trained for a full year before firing a shot.[16]

One private in the 16th Texas Infantry, Joseph P. Blessington, an Irish-born Catholic who would, years later, write a firsthand account of the campaigns of Walker's Texas Division, described the daily routine at Camp Groce. The men were rousted from their barracks and tents at dawn, put into line for roll call, then returned to their quarters to prepare for breakfast at 6:00 A.M. "In the mean time two men from each company were detailed to serve in the main-guard, to enforce discipline and guard the camp. A police guard was also appointed, who cleaned up all dirt and filth about the tents, brought water for the company, wood for the cooks, and, in fact, kept everything in order and cleanliness during the drilling of the troops." By 7:00 A.M. the men lined up in the nearby fields for company drill. After lunch they returned to the grounds for more drilling as separate companies. At 3:30 several companies were combined for drilling as a battalion. Dress parade at 5:00 P.M. was followed by another roll call at sundown. The men had a few hours to relax after supper before tattoo at 9:00 P.M. and "lights out," signaled by three taps on a drum, fifteen minutes later. Beginning at dawn the whole routine was repeated.[17]

The drill instructors in these camps were ideally men who had some previous experience as soldiers. Often they had to teach other less seasoned men how to instruct their own companies and battalions, and the sight of former grocers or lawyers thumbing through drill manuals—learning at night in order to teach in the morning—was not unusual. One instructor in the 18th Texas Infantry, Wilburn Hill King, was only slightly more experienced than his pupils. Twenty-two years old when he joined his Texas company, he had served as an officer in the Missouri State Guard in 1861 and fought in the battles of Carthage and Wilson's Creek in Missouri. This made him, though only a private now, a grizzled veteran compared to his charges in the farm fields near Jefferson.[18]

Some drill instructors were much more experienced, and a few had formal training as professional soldiers. Robert Thomas Pritchard Allen, forty-nine years old, had been graduated fifth in the West Point Class of 1834. He had served in the Seminole War, taught at the Kentucky Military Institute, and founded the Bastrop Military Institute in Texas. Unlike many Texans, Allen had serious doubts about the potential combat effectiveness of untrained recruits. "This one thing I fear, more than any other," he wrote while training new soldiers near Bastrop, "the prevalent notion among Texans that discipline is not necessary; that the impetuous valor and devotion of our boys, rushing into the field without drill, will secure them victory. I fear this, because I foresee defeat should our people rest secure under this impression. Let all the companies, and parts of companies, everywhere, drill, drill, drill." Colonel Allen was a man who stood by his convictions, and he drove his charges relentlessly. Indeed, earlier in the war while he was in Virginia, the men in his first regiment, resentful of "Rarin' Tearin' Pitchin'" Allen's hard training and hard discipline, refused to serve under him. Some of the soldiers grabbed the colonel, boosted him up into his saddle, and ran him out of camp "amid the hoots and jeers of the boys." Those rebellious Texans had convinced the colonel to go back to Texas and train still more men, probably with an even stronger determination to drill their civilian ways out of them. The soldiers of his new regiment, the 17th Texas Infantry, were doubtless among the best-drilled units in Walker's Texas Division.[19]

The ranks and files of the new companies gradually began to take on some regularity and precision in the dusty drill fields, but the appearance of the men was decidedly variegated. Some wore homespun shirts and rough work jeans under floppy felt hats; others enjoyed store-bought clothes; a few preened in uniforms made by mothers and sisters. Even a year later Private Blessington noted the lack of uniformity in dress among his comrades:

> Then as to costume, it is utterly impossible to paint the variety our division presented. Here would be a fellow dressed in homespun pants, with

the knees out of them; on his head might be stuck the remnants of a straw hat, while a faded Texas penitentiary cloth jacket would perhaps complete his outfit. His neighbor, very likely, was arrayed in breeches made out of some cast-off blanket, with a dyed shirt as black as the ace of spades, and no hat at all. Then would come a man with a woolen hat made like a pyramid, sitting jauntily upon his head, while, to introduce his style of hat, he had it covered over with assorted buttons; and, to top the climax, had a red tassel sewed on top. Notwithstanding his gaudy hat, a part of a shirt, and occasional fragments only of what had once been a pair of military pantaloons, made up the rest of his attire.[20]

Uniforms were not the only items in short supply in the camps. Governor Lubbock complained to the Confederate War Department in March that Texas was "entirely destitute of means to provide for these camps of instruction. The State is totally unable to make advances. Her treasury is in a lamentably depleted condition, and her people have furnished so much already to the Confederate and State governments on a credit that it is now a very difficult task to obtain supplies on the faith of either." Muskets, rifles, ammunition, knapsacks, haversacks, tents, harness, medicine, cooking utensils—indeed, almost everything necessary to supply a nineteenth-century army—had to be scrounged from a variety of sources.[21]

Most troublesome was the lack of weapons to arm the new warriors. Regiments formed earlier in the war had received the arms seized from Federal troops during the secession crisis. Other regiments had stripped some counties of muskets, rifles, and shotguns. Some of the men brought their shotguns and old flintlock muskets to camp, but many soldiers had no arms at all. General Hébert ordered a census of available arms and gunsmiths in the counties of Texas, but the reports usually indicated that men outnumbered weapons, and those weapons were a varied lot.[22] Brig. Gen. Henry McCulloch, commander of all forces in northeast Texas in the summer of 1862, resorted to appeals to the home folk to provide weapons. His advertisement in a Tyler newspaper indicated how poorly armed the new regiments were.

EDITOR TYLER REPORTER—

Sir:—I desire to say to the people through your paper, that guns are needed by the troops now in the service.

There is a regular Government Agent (Col. John D. Stell) at this place, who will buy double barrel shot guns, muskets and rifles of all kinds, if with reasonably large bores.

The guns must be in good shooting order.

Col. Stell has the cash to pay for these guns at a fair price, and I earnestly hope the citizens of the country will send in every gun they can possibly spare that may be fit for immediate service.[23]

Some company and regimental officers took the initiative and sent details into the countryside to "impress" weapons from the citizens—that is, forcibly take them and provide a receipt for reimbursement. Lt. Edward Cade of the 28th Texas Cavalry wrote his wife about the difficulty his men encountered among some of his neighbors in Smith County: "The two detachments I sent out to press guns have been busy near a week. They pressed two from old Peter Marsh. The men were obliged to take them out of his hands by force. They also pressed a gun from old man Butler near Starrville. He cursed like a trooper." By one means or another, the men were gradually armed for combat, but their weapons were as motley as their raiment.[24]

Women in towns near the camps of instruction sometimes organized community drives to supply the soldiers. The women of Tyler and Smith County were especially active, providing "hundreds of tents, and thousands of knapsacks, haversacks, &c., besides large quantities of clothing and hospital stores."[25] The wives and mothers and sisters of Smith County did not limit their contributions to sewing and knitting, however. They also cared for the sick in camp hospitals. The example of women in Houston was held before them, and they organized in the Christian Church on a Saturday afternoon in July to arrange regular visits to the military hospitals near Tyler. A letter in the Tyler newspaper called on

true-hearted WOMEN, to render such service as is only in the knowledge of the hand of woman. Ladies, those of you who have not visited the hospital, go for a few moments. See yon fair-haired boy, all pale and emaciated as he is—approach him—place your hand tenderly on his brow—ask him if he feels better, and if he will take some nourishment? See his sunken eye fill with tears as he replies quickly, "If you please madam, if you have anything which is not prepared here at the hospital." Listen now to the poor soldier on the next bed. He is dying. He sees you, and thinks of his mother, and asks you in piteous accents to pray that he may see his mother once again.[26]

Tender words and ministrations from feminine hands could not turn away the illnesses that swept through the camps of instruction all across the Confederacy, however. The gathering of so many men in such small spaces, the lack of immunity among farm boys to many childhood illnesses, foul water and contaminated food, filthy quarters, and ignorance of the role of unseen bacteria in causing disease all combined to disable and kill more men than enemy bullets and shells.[27] In his May 1862 inspection report, Dr. Henry P. Howard, medical director of the Department of Texas, reported that "an unusual accumulation of sickness has been reported to me by the Surgeons in charge at Camp Lubbock [near Houston]." He blamed bad water, poor nourishment, and dirty camps. Less than two weeks later, Col. Oran Roberts counted up the costs at the same camp: of 622 men in his regiment and another battalion, 232 (37.3 percent) were unfit for duty due to illness. Another forty or so men "are required to attend to the sick and bury the dying, which is a daily occurrence." Dr. William P. Head, chief surgeon of the 16th Texas Cavalry, reported similar problems at a camp near Clarksville in far northeast Texas: "For the last six days I have had from 30 to 60 patients to visit—daily and sometimes twice a day[.] We have thirty-two in the hospital to day, the most of them are measels cases, and I think the number will be increased for the next few days."[28]

One soldier in Colonel Roberts's regiment at Camp Lubbock described the depressing situation to his wife. "We have a great many diseases here[.] We have the pneumonia tiphoid feaver remitten feaver brain feaver & flux but the most fatal of all is more fatal than balls. It is called the black tongue and is considered contagious or ketching[.]" "Flux" was a word commonly used for diarrhea or dysentery (infectious bloody diarrhea), and "black tongue" was pellagra, a nutrition-deficiency disease that, among other things, turned the tongue black.[29] Conditions were no better at Camp Hubbard near Tyler. A soldier in the 22nd Texas Infantry told his wife, "Susan Camps is the last place that I would go to if I was out of it. It is enough to kill a well man to stay here and see men suffer as they do. There is only about 300 men able for duty in this Regiment. The balance is sick and on detail duty. . . . There is over three hundred sick with the meezles. . . . There has four out of this Regment died. One out of my Company. He taken the diarear and meesles and did not live but a few days. His wife came and wated on him until he died. He said he was willing to die."[30]

Some of the unruly Texans finally decided it was time to flee the sickly camps and march against the Yankees. "We petition to Col Roberts to take us away from here," Private Tamplin informed his wife. "He said [he] would as soon as he could[.] if he does not we will take ourselves away[.] I don't intend to stay here but a few days longer[.] If I have got to die let me die on the battle field[.] I had rather die With a quick pain than a slow feaver any time." In fact, Roberts had to put down a small mutiny in his regiment when some men reacted wildly to an outbreak of diphtheria.[31]

The soldiers generally had little faith in the healing abilities of physicians or hospitals. The misery and suffering that pervaded sick wards filled the men in the ranks with dread. The military hospital at Virginia Point, near Galveston, was a black hole of tribulation, according to one soldier in the 16th Texas Infantry. "It would be a fortunate thing for those who are so unfortunate as to get sick if it should get blown up," he wrote. "I have no doubt that more are killed by being crowded together in small tight rooms where they have foul air to breath continually, and are under physicians who (to judge from the way the sick are treated) are without humanity or conscience" than by being left to their own devices.[32]

Those new soldiers who escaped the misery of serious illness reacted in a variety of ways to camp life. Some, like the ebullient Irishman Joseph P. Blessington, found the whole experience stimulating and interesting: "It was a spectacle both strange and new, to see young men, reared amid the luxuries and comforts of home, whose fair faces and white hands had never been soiled by contact with work, doing soldier's duty, bending over the camp-fire, preparing meals or boiling coffee—tears streaming from their eyes, caused by villainous smoke from those same camp-fires—carrying wood and water, and, when the day's duties were completed, lying down upon a board, with knapsack or a billet of wood for a pillow." Private Blessington, writing a decade after the war, recalled only golden memories of life at Camp Groce: "Everything necessary for the comfort and convenience of the troops was furnished, and laugh, jest, and song attested the general satisfaction and good feeling of the men." Some of the Texans, in fact, gained weight and claimed they had never been healthier. One soldier in the 12th Texas Infantry at Camp Hébert boasted that "I never lived better than since we have been in camp. . . . I go to bed every night by eight o'clock and sleep as much as I did at home which you know was my only fear." A month later he informed his wife that "I have gained five pounds in weight since we left home and am doing as well as it is possible for one to do [away] from home."[33]

At the opposite end of the spectrum—and beyond the ken of Private Blessington—were those who exercised the age-old right of the soldier to complain. A member of the 22nd Texas Infantry advised his father-in-law to keep his son at home: "He has no idea how poor a place the camps are—all manner of diseases, all manner of mean people to contend with, and in fact nothing that is good. My advice to him is, while he has good parents, stay with them and not change a feather bed for the cold ground—mud, water, filth and everything else bad in a camp life, to say nothing of the forty millions of fleas that we are troubled with." One of the most persistent complainers in the entire division was Pvt. Samuel Farrow of the 19th Texas Infantry. A twenty-four-year-old Alabama native, Farrow sent a stream of gloomy letters to his wife, from the month he enlisted until the end of the war. First of all, he was homesick: "I can tell you that I have not learned to love to stay away from you yet. I spend many a lonely hour in camps.

. . . I never shall be satisfied in the Army." Then he expected to get sick: "I expect that I will take the Measles in a few days." Then he was lonesome again: "I have a very lonesome time of it myself. being in a crowd is no company to me." Throughout the war, wherever there was sorrow, there also was Private Farrow.[34]

Why did these twelve thousand men leave their homes and families to risk their lives and futures in the war? Although most of them were literate and many left written records of their experiences, rarely did they spell out specific reasons in their letters and diaries for their decisions to join the Confederate army. A yearning for adventure and the desire to see new places and experience new things doubtless led some to sign the muster rolls. Certainly peer pressure played a role, especially when one considers the large numbers of brothers, cousins, and friends who joined hometown units and the war excitement that gripped nearly every community.[35]

Some, especially among the minority (33.7 percent) who volunteered after passage of the Confederate conscription law in April 1862, doubtless joined the army in order to avoid the ignominy of being drafted. The Confederate national government in Richmond, fearful that early volunteers who had signed up for twelve months' service in the winter and spring of 1861 would go home and reduce Confederate armies to mere skeletons in early 1862, adopted a national conscription law on April 16, 1862. The draft law set up machinery to bring in men between eighteen and thirty-five years of age and extended to three years the terms of enlistment for those already in the ranks.[36] Those Texans who volunteered for the regiments of Walker's division after news of the Confederate draft was splashed across Texas newspapers in late April and early May, compared to men who joined the army earlier in the year, were generally poorer, about two years older, more likely to be married, more likely to be heads of households, and less likely to live with their parents.

In short, the later volunteers were men who could least afford to leave home. More of them had wives and children and separate households to worry about, and they had fewer economic resources to maintain those households.[37] Their later enlistment dates do not necessarily mean they volunteered for reasons different from those of soldiers who signed up in January and February, but the possibility of conscription doubtless pried some of these men away from their homes. Certainly, the draft was not a consideration for the earlier enlistees.[38]

Mostly, though, the soldiers who would form the division, whether they joined in January or June, seemed to identify the Confederacy with home, family, and continuity, and the Union with unwelcome, threatening change. Protection of their families and communities from Yankee domination and from the supposed horrors of slave emancipation was tied up in their minds with the success of the Confederate army.[39] If the Confederacy prevailed, their parents, wives, children, and property (including slave property for the minority who were slave owners) would be safe from marauding Yankee predators and from unruly freed slaves. If the "Black Republican" army of the North overran their states, their homes would be ransacked, their wives insulted, their children left hungry, and a dangerous, servile population let loose on their communities.[40]

Security, stability, and the liberty to live life as they knew it—including white control of the black underclass and freedom from northern meddling—could be guaranteed only by throwing back the Yankee hordes and keeping a firm grip on the black population in their midst. The freedom to live their lives in the usual way, the liberty guaranteed by the Revolutionary generation, could be secured only if the old Union was abandoned and the new Confederacy took its place.[41] They did not separate the ideology of liberty from the practical fear of outside interference and servile insurrection. It was all the same to them.[42]

In their minds, once the war seemed to be getting out of hand and Yankee armies began to draw near to Texas in the winter and spring of 1862, they had little choice but to follow the call of duty. The Confederacy was the means to the end of maintaining life as they understood it. William P. Head, a surgeon in the 16th Texas Cavalry, put it plainly: "if I am to be sacrificed in this war, it will be some consolation to me that I died in defence of my wife and children and to sustain the best goverment that deity ever smiled upon." Edward Cade of the 28th Cavalry was just as explicit: "I have entered this [war] to save my children from vassalage and my wife from what is worse than death." Pvt. B. F. Tamplin of the 11th Texas Infantry expressed the twin themes of home and duty in a letter to his wife, Tinny. About to be released from a twelve-month regiment whose term was expiring, he informed her that he would soon join another unit for the duration of the war. But first he was determined to go home and see his family: "They will not receive any more twelve months men under no consideration. I am truly glad of it[.] if we are disbanded I shall come home as quick as I can and go for the war[.] I bleave it to be my duty to fight for my country but I want to see you before I go in for the war. . . . Take care of my little Baby, Tinny." It was Surgeon Head and Private Tamplin's obligation to fight the Yankees in order to protect their communities from outside interference and unwanted changes in the established order.[43]

What sort of men were Private Tamplin and the thousands of others who joined him in the new regiments of 1862? Wars are generally fought by young men, and this conflict was no different (see Table 2). The mean age of the soldiers in Walker's division at the outset of their military service was 26.9 years (median: 26). One-sixth (16.2 percent) of the volunteers were still teenagers when they en-

TABLE 2

AGE DISTRIBUTION OF MEN IN THE DIVISION

| Age | % |
| --- | --- |
| 13–19 | 16.2 |
| 20–25 | 33.6 |
| 26–29 | 18.3 |
| 30–39 | 25.6 |
| 40 and older | 6.3 |

listed, and one-half (49.8 percent) were twenty-five or younger. One in four (25.6 percent) was in his thirties, and only 6.3 percent were forty years old or older.[44]

Enlisted men (those who were not commissioned officers at the rank of lieutenant or higher) were generally seven or eight years younger than their officers—26.6 years for the privates and corporals and sergeants and 33.2 years for the officers (medians: 25 and 33). This age gap tended to decrease as time passed because younger men usually replaced the officers who first led the companies and regiments. The mean age of enlisted men who became officers during the war was 27.0 years, almost exactly the same age as enlisted men in general. Original officers were not only older than men promoted during the war, they were also wealthier. Median figures for the value of real and personal property owned by original officers were $1,000 and $2,422; the same measurements for men promoted from the ranks were $640 and $1,658; for men who remained in the enlisted group, $168 and $425.[45] The judges and planters and local grandees who raised the troops were not necessarily the ablest leaders on the march and in battle, and they were frequently replaced by younger men more suited to life in the field.[46]

Although two-thirds of the men in the new regiments were in their teens and twenties when they first signed the muster rolls, the soldiers in the division were, on the average, a few years older than their enemies, older than Confederate soldiers in general, older than their comrades who had joined the army in the first months of the war, and older than U.S. soldiers in World War II.[47] The median age of all Union enlistees was 23.5 years; the median for these Texans, 26.0. Two-fifths of Federal soldiers were twenty-one or younger, but only about one-fourth of these Texans were that young. Walker's foot soldiers were also generally older than other Confederates who had joined the army early in the war. The median age of privates in the 3rd Texas Cavalry Regiment, organized in February 1861, was only twenty-three; the median for privates in Walker's division was between twenty-six and twenty-seven (26.4 years). Similarly, the soldiers in H. H. Sibley's

Texas brigade, formed in 1861, were younger than the men who joined Walker's regiments in the winter and spring of 1862. Men in their teens and twenties constituted nearly nine-tenths (86.8 percent) of the earlier brigade; that age group composed only about two-thirds (68.1 percent) of the later division.[48]

Not only were the men in the division older than the typical Confederate or Union soldier, they were also more likely to be married and more likely to be the head of a household. Slightly more than half (50.9 percent) of all men in the new regiments were married and a nearly equal proportion (50.1 percent) were household heads. Studies of Civil War soldiers generally agree that most were unmarried when they enlisted. The men of the Union's 12th Missouri Infantry Regiment, for example, were nearly all (90.7 percent) single. Similarly, only 22 percent of the horsemen in the 3rd Texas Cavalry were heads of households in 1860. The same held true among U.S. privates in World War II: only 27 percent were married when they enlisted.[49]

These figures on age and marital status point up a clear pattern of enlistments in Texas. In general, younger single men from financially stable families volunteered earlier in the war. The wealthy young hotspurs of the 3rd Texas Cavalry are a perfect, perhaps extreme, example of the early group, but other Texas units formed in 1861 fit the same mold.[50] Older men with families and households to worry about, especially those in the middle and lower wealth groups, joined the war effort later. They had more to lose by going off to war, and only an emergency, such as that presented by Confederate reverses in the winter and spring of 1862, convinced them to leave wives and children behind to fight the Yankees. In addition, of course, those who joined after news of the Confederate conscription law reached Texas had an additional incentive to enlist.[51]

Most of the men in the regiments that would become Walker's Texas Division (64.5 percent) were natives of the lower southern states (South Carolina, Georgia, Florida, Alabama, Mississippi, Arkansas, Louisiana, and Texas). Almost half of all the men in the division (47.2 percent) had been born in Alabama, Georgia, Mississippi, or South Carolina. Nearly one-third of all soldiers in the division (30.6 percent) had been born in the upper southern states (Delaware, Maryland, Virginia, North Carolina, Kentucky, Tennessee, Missouri, and the District of Columbia). Only a few were natives of the free states (3.2 percent) and foreign countries (1.7 percent).[52]

These proportions (roughly two-thirds from the lower South and one-third from the upper South) vary widely from those in the general population of the state. Those Texans who were heads of their own households in 1860 (i.e., primarily adult males) were more likely to be natives of the upper South than of the lower (41.1 and 36.6 percent, respectively). Why, then, were men from the lower southern states so vastly over-represented among the soldiers in the division? According to one prominent student of the war, James M. McPherson, natives of the lower South were more likely to express "strong patriotic and ideological motives" for joining the army than men from the upper states, and the lower states seceded earlier than those nearer the free states. Thus, it appears that lower southerners in general were more highly motivated to fight for the Confederacy. Certainly they turned out in disproportionately large numbers in Texas during the winter and spring of 1862.[53]

The overwhelming majority of men in the division, as one might expect, engaged in some form of agriculture to support themselves and their families (see Table 3). "Agriculture" as used in the table is a broad term that includes everyone from planters to farm laborers. More than two-thirds of the men in the agricultural category (56.1 percent of all men in the division) called themselves farmers or stock raisers in the 1860 census. This group included great planters, middling farmers, and small self-sufficient farmers. Another 18.1 percent were listed as farm laborers. The remaining groups (3.9 percent of all soldiers) were either overseers or agents on the one hand (1.5 percent) or tenants or renters on the other (2.4 percent). Men engaged in agriculture were over-represented among the soldiers (compared to their numbers in the general population), and all other groups were slightly under-represented.[54]

Compared to soldiers in the Union and Confederate armies in general, the

TABLE 3
OCCUPATIONS OF MEN IN THE DIVISION

| Occupation | % of Soldiers in the Division | % of Texas Heads of Households* |
|---|---|---|
| Agriculture | 78.1 | 69.7 |
| Unskilled Labor | 7.9 | 9.2 |
| Skilled Labor | 5.8 | 9.1 |
| Professions | 2.8 | 5.0 |
| Commerce | 2.6 | 4.3 |
| Manufacturing | 0.9 | 1.2 |
| Public Service | 0.4 | 0.8 |
| Miscellaneous | 1.5 | 0.7 |

Note: Not all soldiers were heads of households and not all heads of households were adult males, so the comparison of figures in this table could be misleading. On the other hand, the overwhelming majority of individuals in both groups (96.2 percent of the soldiers and at least 95 percent of the household heads) were adult males, eighteen or older.

*Campbell and Lowe, Wealth and Power in Antebellum Texas, 63.

men in the Texas Division were much more heavily involved in agriculture and less involved in skilled or unskilled labor, commercial pursuits, or the professions (see Table 4). This pattern is probably best explained by the more rural and undeveloped nature of Texas, still on the frontier of western settlement in the 1850s, where farming was relatively more important than in older, more established, and more urban areas.[55]

Older, more likely to be married, and more oriented to farming than most Confederate soldiers, and more likely to be natives of the lower South than most Texans, the men of the division were distinctive in another way as well—they were of generally modest means (see Table 5). On average, the soldiers owned only about half as much property as heads of households in Texas and were much less wealthy than the prosperous elite of the 3rd Texas Cavalry Regiment. On the other hand, the Texas foot soldiers were younger than the average head of household in the Lone Star State and had not had as much time to accumulate

TABLE 4

OCCUPATIONS OF MEN IN THE UNION AND CONFEDERATE ARMIES

| Occupations (%) | Union* | Confederate* | Walker's Div. |
| --- | --- | --- | --- |
| Agriculture | 47.5 | 61.5 | 78.1 |
| Skilled Labor | 25.1 | 14.1 | 5.8 |
| Unskilled Labor | 15.9 | 8.5 | 7.9 |
| White-Collar and | | | |
| Commercial | 5.1 | 7.0 | 3.9 |
| Professional | 3.2 | 5.2 | 2.8 |
| Miscellaneous and Unknown | 3.2 | 3.7 | 1.5 |

Note: On the row labeled "White-Collar and Commercial," commerce, manufacturing, and public service were combined for the third column.
*McPherson, Battle Cry of Freedom, 608, 614.

TABLE 5

MEAN PROPERTY HOLDINGS OF MEN IN THE DIVISION, 1860

| Type of Property | Men in Walker's Div. | Texas Heads of Households | Men in 3rd Tex. Cavalry |
| --- | --- | --- | --- |
| Real Property | $1,397 | $2,699 | $12,787 |
| Personal Property | $2,180 | $3,692 | NA |
| Wealth* | $3,484 | $6,393 | NA |

Sources: Campbell and Lowe, Wealth and Power in Antebellum Texas, 116; Hale, "The Third Texas Cavalry," 26.
*Wealth is defined as a combination of real and personal property as listed in the 1860 U.S. census.

property as the typical Texas family head. When wealth is controlled for age (that is, when the soldiers are compared to household heads in their twenties), the men of Walker's division fall into line as average wealth holders ($3,484 for men in the division and $3,091 for household heads of comparable ages).[56]

Not surprisingly when one considers these wealth holdings, soldiers in the division were less likely to own slaves than the average Texas family. Slightly more than one-fourth (27.3 percent) of all families in the Lone Star State owned slaves in 1860, but only about one-fifth (21.6 percent) of the soldiers.[57] Once again, the relative youth of the military population helps to explain the difference: younger men simply had not had as many years to accumulate wealth and slaves. The artillerymen later attached to the division—more urban and slightly poorer than the foot soldiers—were even less likely to own slaves (14.4 percent owned at least one bondsman).

These figures on slaveholdings in the division provide little support for the old argument that the Civil War was "a rich man's war but a poor man's fight." First, the soldiers were about as wealthy as other Texans their age and presumably would have accumulated slaves at the same rate as other Texans. In other words, they reflected the society around them. They were not poor cannon fodder thrown at the enemy by the wealthy. Second, only an analysis of all Texas soldiers—infantry, cavalry, and artillery, and early volunteers as well as late—could determine whether slaveholders joined the army in proportion to their numbers in the general population. Certainly, some Texas units included far more than their share of the slaveholding elite of Texas. More than half of the horsemen of the 3rd Texas Cavalry Regiment, for example, were members of slave-owning households, and planters (those owning twenty or more bondsmen) were greatly over-represented.[58]

The wealthiest families in Texas—the 7.8 percent who owned combined real and personal property worth at least $10,000 in 1860—are another measuring stick for the old charge that rich men started the war and expected poor men to do the dying. In the regiments that would form Walker's Texas Division, owners of wealth worth $10,000 or more constituted 10.5 percent of the original members of the division. In other words, even though the men of this division were not wealthy compared to Texas families in general, the division nevertheless contained more than its share of rich men. Prosperous planters huddled around the same campfires, blinked through the same summer dust, shivered in the same freezing rain, and faced the same enemy missiles as their poorer neighbors. An analysis of all Texans who served in the military would doubtless demonstrate the same pattern: the wealthy families of the Lone Star State pulled more than their own weight in the Confederate war effort.[59]

The "typical" soldier in the new regiments that would form the division, then, was a native of the lower South, in his mid to late twenties, married and the head of his own household, and a non-slaveholding farmer. Compared to his neighbors who volunteered in the first year of the war, the soldier in Walker's Texas Division was somewhat older, more likely to be married, less likely to be a slaveholder, and less prosperous. The electrifying winter and spring of 1861, when Ben McCulloch seized Federal posts in Texas and Confederate artillery opened on Fort Sumter, generally attracted to the cause men whose families could afford to give them up for a while: younger sons from established families, men without wives and children, those whose absence would cause less disruption in the lives of their loved ones. One year later, when the war had turned ominous for the Confederacy, Texas families dug deeper to provide manpower for the army. Men in their late twenties and thirties, men with wives and children, men who worked their own farms and shops, and men whose economic resources were more limited left everything behind and trudged off to the recruiting centers. The soldiers in Walker's Texas Division had much to lose when they marched into the camps of instruction scattered around the Lone Star State.

# CHAPTER 3

# Off to Arkansas

While new soldiers stumbled around drill fields and their captains and colonels searched for arms and equipment, Confederate politicians and generals tried to bring some organization to the scores of new companies created in Texas in the spring of 1862. Confederate officials grouped companies, usually ten at a time, into new regiments while the men were still in their camps of instruction. Higher organization—into brigades and divisions—was still several months in the future. Not until the regiments marched off to central Arkansas and gathered near Little Rock in October 1862 were they arranged into brigades and then into the unit that would later be known as Walker's Texas Division.

Before they left their camps of instruction in Texas, the men received news of the Confederate conscription law of April 1862. In an unprecedented act, the Confederate government resorted to a national draft to keep its armies in the field. Now men from eighteen to thirty-five years old could be conscripted into military service for three years, and those men in that age group already in the army—including the Texans still learning how to march and deploy and take orders—had their terms of service extended to three years. Those younger than eighteen or older than thirty-five, if they had originally signed up for three years' service, were "held to contract," but those beyond the conscript ages who had joined for one year were allowed to leave the army after ninety days if they so chose. The draft law elicited scattered grumbling in Texas, but most civilians and soldiers in the Lone Star State accepted conscription as a necessity.[1]

The new law also allowed men already in the ranks to elect their officers, a time-honored practice in American militia units. In fact, most of the companies had already elected their officers before the passage of the draft law, and now they were allowed to hold a second round of elections. Thus, neighbors and cousins and friends within companies elected their own captains and lieutenants, and all the men in the various companies of regiments selected their colonels, lieutenant colonels, and majors. The newly formed companies and regiments that would later be grouped into Walker's Texas Division held their elections in

May and June 1862. In most cases they reelected the men already serving as their officers.[2]

Only later, after they had marched hundreds of miles and begun to campaign actively, did many of these original officers resign or obtain discharges due to physical disability or other cause, thus allowing younger, fitter men to rise into positions of leadership. Capt. J. C. Rhea, for example, tried the military life but soon resigned. Sixty-three-year-old surgeon Leonard Randal of the 28th Texas Cavalry, for example, reluctantly tendered his resignation to his colonel, his son Horace: "I had hoped to see the end of the war before withdrawing from the service, but advanced age, worn down by protracted Diarrhea, renders it imperative that I should withdraw." One captain blamed his resignation on an act of God rather than on his own weaknesses of the flesh: J. C. Maples of the 18th Texas Infantry resigned due to "almost entire physical prostration, from the effects of a shock of lightning."[3]

Officers were not the only men who left the ranks. The sizes of most companies and regiments dwindled significantly before they left their training camps, partly because of deaths and discharges due to widespread illness and partly because some men beyond the conscript age took the opportunity to go home. Extrapolations from the twelve sample companies indicate that slightly more than 700 men from Walker's future regiments (709, or 6.2 percent) were discharged due to age.[4] The 14th Texas Infantry lost 134 men due to the draft law, including seventeen in Company A alone. Some young boys were too frail for service. Records of the 19th Texas Infantry showed that Jonathan Anderson was of an "immature age and imperfect development. Said soldier is but 15 years of age and of small stature." Thomas F. Hyers of the same regiment was "only 16 years of age and very small in stature weighing 85 pounds." Some cases were almost comical. Inscribed on a company muster roll beside the name of Pvt. W. N. Wallace, age fifteen, were these words, no doubt terribly embarrassing to the fierce young warrior: "Age represented to be 18 years when mustered but since claimed by his mother and discharged."[5]

The diseases that swept through the camps of instruction in the spring and summer of 1862—everything from dysentery to measles to typhoid—reduced the regiments further. Hundreds of men died in the training camps. Others who survived were disabled by prolonged illnesses and discharged only a few months into their military service. Nearly 1,300 men (1,265, or 11.0 percent) died of disease and more than 1,000 (1,045, or 9.1 percent) were permanently discharged from the various regiments due to illness before the end of the summer. In addition, some men were disabled in accidents, others deserted, some were transferred to other units, some officers resigned from the army, and scattered numbers left their

regiments for reasons too unusual to classify.[6] These eroding factors further reduced the strength of the future division by nearly one thousand men (968, or
8.4 percent) before September. When losses due to all causes are added up, it
becomes clear that the regiments of the future division lost about four thousand
men, more than one-third of their total number, before they ever reached their
first camp in Arkansas.[7]

Shortly after the fall of Forts Henry and Donelson cracked open Confederate
defenses in western Tennessee in February 1862, Confederate Secretary of War
Judah P. Benjamin called on General Hébert to send most of the Confederate
regiments in Texas to Arkansas as rapidly as possible. Three months later Pres.
Jefferson Davis's military adviser, Robert E. Lee, reminded Hébert of the urgency
of the move: "I presume those ready for the field are *en route* for Arkansas." By
early August, Hébert reported that a few Texas units were already in Arkansas,
that several other Texas regiments were on the march, and that several more
would soon begin moving toward Little Rock. Brig. Gen. Henry E. McCulloch,
brother of the Texas hero Ben McCulloch and commander of all Confederate
forces in northeast Texas, made arrangements to feed the men and animals as
they marched, establishing subsistence and forage depots along the road to Little
Rock. Finally, it seemed, the new Texas soldiers would be able to do more than
drill and wait, wait and drill.[8]

The men in most of the new regiments packed up and marched out of their
camps of instruction in the summer of 1862. Considerable preparations sometimes attended the departures. Capt. Elijah P. Petty of the 17th Texas Infantry
instructed his wife to "please put my clothes all in a good state of readiness for
marching. Go and see the Cabinet maker Fehr and get him to make me immediately a Camp Chest." Pvt. Volney Ellis of the 12th Texas Infantry wrote his wife
that on the day his company left camp, "I had already loaded my knapsack, filled
my canteen, and shouldered my gun," but Col. Overton C. Young prevailed on
Ellis to stay behind a few days and accompany the quartermaster train. Wagons
had to be put in good order, bags and crates packed, mules fed and watered, and
any number of other tasks completed before all was ready.[9]

One by one, the regiments left their camps. Some reached Arkansas while
others were still drilling in Texas. Maj. Robert S. Gould's cavalry battalion
crossed into Arkansas in the late spring. William Fitzhugh's 16th Texas Cavalry
trotted into Arkansas as early as May and was the first unit of the future division
to see combat. Indeed, the 16th Cavalry was the division's only unit to engage
the enemy in all of 1862. As part of a five thousand–man force sent to parry a
Federal thrust at Little Rock, the 16th Texas Cavalry and seven other Texas and
Arkansas regiments fought a small engagement near Cotton Plant (Cache River),

about seventy miles east of the Arkansas capital, on July 7. Inexperienced and poorly led by Brig. Gen. Albert Rust, the Texas and Arkansas Confederates, after some initial success, were mauled and sent flying to the rear by Maj. Gen. Samuel R. Curtis's Federal Army of the Southwest. Although he won the fight, Curtis was unable to march into Little Rock. His relief and supply flotilla had abandoned him, and Little Rock remained in Confederate hands another fourteen months.[10]

Most of the new Texas regiments left the Lone Star State in June, July, and August. Col. Overton Young's 12th Texas Infantry Regiment, for example, moved out of its camp near Hempstead in late June. About a week later the 16th Texas Infantry boarded trains near Galveston, rode the rails to Hempstead, and then followed in the tracks of the 12th Texas. The first companies of Richard Waterhouse's 19th Texas Infantry left their camp near Jefferson in early August. Col. R. T. P. Allen's 17th Texas Infantry did not begin its march until late August. From the heat of summer until the cold rain of fall, the companies and regiments that would become Walker's Texas Division strung out along the roads from East Texas to central Arkansas.[11]

The journey of the 16th Texas Infantry from Galveston Bay to central Arkansas was described in some detail by the voluble Irish-born private Joseph P. Blessington. At dawn on July 7, "blankets were rolled up, haversacks filled with rations, guns and equipments were highly polished up, awaiting for the regiment to form." After several hours of a swaying, rattling ride on railroad cars, the men detrained at Hempstead and remained at nearby Camp Hébert for more than three weeks to make tents and gather necessities. On July 31 the men, better supplied now, continued on their journey. Blessington noted the sad goodbyes of those soldiers whose families lived nearby and had come to bid adieu. "The warm embrace, the streaming eyes, agonizing expressions of sorrow, loving words of cheer and advice, the whispered prayers for their loved ones' safety, the tokens of love and remembrance, are memories as ineffaceable as the foot-prints of time." Still, the men managed to give "cheer after cheer" for the women of Hempstead as the regiment left town on the Houston & Texas Central Railroad. Near the end of the war, when these same men, now grimy veterans, returned to Hempstead, the greetings on both sides would be much more subdued.[12]

The celebrations continued as Hempstead fell farther and farther behind: "every farm, hamlet, city, and village, poured forth their inhabitants at the roadside to wave an adieu to the men." Blessington was especially pleased with the demonstrations at Navasota, twenty miles north of Hempstead and the end of the train ride. "As we marched through the town to our camp-ground, bouquets of flowers were continually lavished upon us by the fair donors of Navasoto [sic].

We encamped in the rear of the town, and had dress-parade, in order to please the ladies of Navasoto."[13]

Once the men left the flatcars, slung their knapsacks over their shoulders, and hoisted their muskets, the trip turned decidedly less pleasant. August 3, the day of the first long march, was a particularly hard trial for the Texans, more accustomed to riding than walking. "What a day of severe experience it was for all who participated therein! Shoulders grew sore under the burden of supporting knapsacks, limbs wearied from the painful march, and feet grew swollen and blistered as the men marched along the dusty road." By August 8 the regiment reached Madisonville, about sixty-five road miles north of Hempstead, and the hot, weary, dusty men shuffled through town as the regimental band played "Dixie." On August 13, in the piney woods of Houston and Anderson Counties, the new soldiers suffered terribly from extreme heat and humidity: "The heat was suffocating, the thermometer stood at 110°, and the breeze was as refreshing as steam from an escape-pipe." If anything, the next day was worse: "If you wish to imagine yourself in this country, just get into a hot oven, and if there be any difference, it will be in favor of the oven," Blessington complained.[14]

A week later the regiment reached Tyler, headquarters of General McCulloch, the officer in charge of directing troops to Arkansas. The next day the general and his staff reviewed the regiment. "The affair was grand and imposing, and attracted an immense concourse of people," Blessington recalled. Early the following morning the 16th Texas Infantry filed through the streets of Tyler, and the band once again struck up "Dixie" for the onlookers. Two more weeks of heat, dust, and sore feet brought the men to the state border with Arkansas, near present-day Texarkana, on September 6. "The only difference by which we recognized that we were in Arkansas was a sign-board with the learned inscription, 'Ark-Saw,'" Blessington snickered. "The schoolmaster had likely been lately abroad when this was written." The men gave three cheers for Texas as they crossed the state line, some leaving the Lone Star State for the first time.[15]

Later that afternoon they ran upon the rear units of Colonel Waterhouse's 19th Texas Infantry near Rondo, Arkansas, and the two regiments camped adjacent to each other that night. Surviving records do not indicate whether the usually cheerful Blessington encountered the incurably gloomy Private Farrow of the 19th Infantry around a campfire that night, but Farrow was as morose as ever. A few days later he wrote his wife that only forty of the company's men were fit for duty, the other eighty-five being too sick to march. To make matters worse, Farrow grumbled, the road to Arkansas "is a very lonely place to me."[16]

The cavalry units of the future division received bad news in early September: Texas horsemen on the road to Little Rock were ordered to dismount and serve thenceforth as infantry. The 13th, 16th, and 28th Texas Cavalry and Major Gould's 6th Texas Cavalry Battalion (the latter already in Arkansas) were ordered to send their horses home. Forage was scarce in Arkansas, and the state could not support the thousands of new horses arriving from Texas. In addition, the trans-Mississippi Confederacy needed foot soldiers more than cavalry. For Texans, this order not only promised less adventure and more toil, it was also humiliating. Men of the Lone Star State considered themselves natural equestrians, and slogging through dust and mud was not the Texas way of fighting—at least not in the minds of the horsemen.[17]

Thomas J. Rounsaville of the 13th Cavalry spoke for many of his comrades: "When we was dismounted we was sadly disappointed for we was compelled to take it afoot and we walked about two hundred miles and our feet was blistered considerably. Some of our boys gave entirely out." A lieutenant in the same regiment mournfully informed his wife that "time has passed very heavy on my hands since we have been dismounted." The commander of the 28th Cavalry, Col. Horace Randal, appealed to his member of Congress for redress, but all he received was an assurance that his regiment would be remounted first if the various dismounted units were ever returned to their horses. They never were, and from that time to the end of the war the 13th, 16th, and 28th Texas Cavalry Regiments and Gould's 6th Texas Cavalry Battalion served as foot soldiers in the division. They insisted, nevertheless, that they be referred to as "dismounted cavalry" rather than infantry. Dignity, at least, could be preserved.[18]

The soldiers of the 16th Texas Infantry could have told their dismounted comrades a thing or two about marching. On and on they tramped, northeast toward Little Rock. They crossed the Red River on an oxen-powered ferry on September 8 and reached Arkadelphia, about midway between the state line and Little Rock, eight days later. The next morning, as they marched up the left bank of the Ouachita River, these raw troops could not have known that nine hundred miles away, more experienced Confederate soldiers were gripped in a death struggle with a Union army in the bloodiest single day of combat in the war, along Antietam Creek in western Maryland. Neither could the Texans know that leading one of the Confederate divisions on that gory field, and winning laurels for his efficiency, was their own future commander, John G. Walker.[19]

On September 23, after washing their clothes and dressing their lines in preparation for a public review in the capital city of Arkansas, the men finally reached Little Rock. "As we marched through the city we did full justice to 'Hardee's Tactics,'" Blessington boasted, referring to the standard manual on military training. Maj. Gen. Theophilus H. Holmes, commander of all Confederate forces west of the Mississippi River, and Arkansas governor Henry M. Rector observed the passing of the regiment from the steps of the state capitol as the regimental flag bearer dipped the colors in salute. It was a golden, glorious moment for Blessington and his fellow Texans: "They attracted universal attention and received a perfect ovation, the streets being crowded with men, and fine ladies, who greeted them enthusiastically. There was the fluttering of innumerable handkerchiefs, and showers of bouquets greeted us on our march."[20]

After walking nearly five hundred miles through piney woods and nondescript villages, the Texans were delighted with the sights of Little Rock: "It is hard to conceive a city more beautifully situated or more gorgeously embellished, with splendidly shaded walks and drives, with flowers, shrubberies, and plantations. Most of its stores and public buildings were of brick, while most of the private residences were framed, neatly painted, with piazzas hanging with plants and creepers. A spell of ease and voluptuous luxury seemed to pervade the place." Unfortunately for Blessington and his comrades, the regiment lingered in these pleasant surroundings only two days before pushing east thirty miles to Brownsville, where many Texas regiments were camped after their long journeys.[21]

Six days later the 16th Texas and numerous other regiments left Brownsville for De Valls Bluff and Clarendon, about twenty-five miles east on the White River in eastern Arkansas. General Curtis's Federal Army of the Southwest had raided through that neighborhood earlier, and the Confederates were determined to fill the vacuum left when Curtis withdrew to Helena on the Mississippi River. This excursion proved another hard trial for the bone-weary Texans. The weather had turned wet and cold, and much of their clothing and all their tents had been misplaced when their baggage trains were diverted to other uses in Little Rock. After a few days spent building fortifications at Clarendon, the whole force, teeth chattering, reversed directions and began a rapid march back toward Brownsville. Rumors that a Federal river fleet was steaming up the Arkansas River, threatening to cut them off from Little Rock, sent the men back through their own muddy footprints from the week before.[22]

On the return march a heavy hailstorm thrashed the exposed troops. But that was nothing compared to their miseries on the muddy Arkansas prairies the next day, October 10. The same men who had gasped for air in 110-degree heat a few weeks earlier now shivered, some of them barefoot, in a freezing blast of premature winter. "It rained, sleeted, and froze," Blessington moaned. "Men lost their step, and, swerving from the line, dropped by the wayside, to rest on the few mounds in the prairie that were not covered with water. Completely chilled through—even their senses were benumbed—they would beg to be left behind, to sleep and to perish. A stupor, a perfect indifference for life, came over many of them." No bands played "Dixie" and no frilly ladies threw bouquets on the freezing march from Clarendon. According to Lt. Sam Wright of Paris, the whole expedition "was a wild goose chase and will kill more men than a hard fought battle would have done." After two days of warming themselves and drying out around campfires near Brownsville, the soldiers of the 16th Texas joined dozens of other Texas and Arkansas regiments in winter quarters at Camp Nelson near Austin, about thirty miles northeast of Little Rock.[23]

From the day the regiment began its march from Navasota (August 2) to the day they settled into their winter camp at Austin, Arkansas (October 14)—seventy-four days—the men walked at least 594 miles (see Map 2). That was about as far as the distance from Boston, Massachusetts, to Richmond, Virginia, or from Washington, D.C., to Chattanooga, Tennessee.[24] The soldiers actually marched on forty-eight of the seventy-four days, resting or washing clothes or building fortifications between jaunts, and averaging about 12.5 miles per day.[25] The regiment traveled eight straight days in one stretch and nine in another and covered nearly sixty miles per week from beginning to end. Modern world-class athletes in some Olympic distance events may average fifty to seventy miles of training per week—without heavy brogans, muskets, and knapsacks to slow them down. On this one long march, the Texans sweated through blistering temperatures and debilitating humidity on the dusty roads of East Texas and shivered against driving sleet and freezing rain in Arkansas before they found rest in winter quarters. Few, if any, units on either side in this war traveled so far afoot under such trying conditions simply to reach their first assigned camp. Little wonder that in later years old men would boast that they had fought with Walker's "Greyhound Division."

Winter quarters, a few miles east of the village of Austin, were nothing short of depressing for most of the soldiers. Located between long, rocky ridges on the north and south, Camp Nelson proved to be a dreary home for the next several weeks—cold, wet, far from home, and far from the attractions of any large population centers. The smoky campfires of the various Texas regiments stretched several miles in the long gray valley, and forests in the vicinity gradually disappeared to provide firewood for the men.[26]

Some of the Texans came to hate everything about Arkansas, even the people.[27] Capt. Elijah Petty wrote his wife back in Bastrop, Texas, that "this is an awful Arkansas. The most forlorn and God forsaken Country under the sun." After a serious illness that sent him into delirium, Petty was relieved that he had survived: "I did'nt come to Arkansas to die—I think that God would never resurrect me here." Indeed, he continued, "it is an awful country and an awful population here in Arkansas, ignorant, selfish, hoggish and almost despicable. They are a curse to any country." The captain hoped that the hundreds of refugees he saw

# Map 2
## The Road to Arkansas, 1862

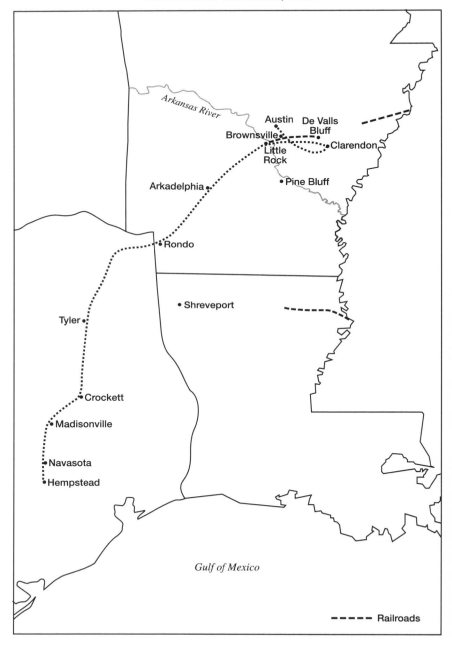

*Arkansas River*

Austin

De Valls
Bluff

Brownsville

Clarendon

Little
Rock

Pine Bluff

Arkadelphia

Rondo

Shreveport

Tyler

Crockett

Madisonville

Navasota

Hempstead

*Gulf of Mexico*

- - - - - Railroads

on the road to Texas would stop before they reached his neighborhood: "I am afraid that our country and people will be ruined by the admixture of such a population." Dr. Edward Cade of the 28th Cavalry agreed that Arkansans were a particularly rough sort of people: "I have not seen a woman in a long time that had shoes on and when I did see them with shoes they had no stockings." A fellow officer in the same regiment, Theophilus Perry, was somewhat more sympathetic. "This is one of the poorest country [sic] I have ever seen," he wrote his wife. "The poor people live as poorly as Job's Turkey."[28]

Col. Richard Waterhouse of the 19th Texas Infantry wrote his wife that his men were not impressed by Arkansans and admitted that he had some doubts himself: "I do not think them as pure and patriotic in evry respect as Texians." Lt. Sam Wright of Paris repeated a joke going through the camps, a story sometimes applied to other states by soldiers on both sides: "Lincoln and Jeff Davis had met on the Potomac and made peace; had bid each other goodby and got off some distance, turned and said that they had forgotten to 'assign' Arkansas. 'You take it' said Lincoln, 'I don't want it'. 'Damned if I do either' said Davis. 'But you shall take it', said Lincoln, whereupon Davis refused again, and they immediately pitched into fighting each others' armies and have been fighting ever since. The Texans 'cuss' Arkansas from the bottom of their hearts."[29]

The Texans might have formed a better opinion of Arkansas if so many of them had not come down with serious illnesses. The various diseases that had struck down so many in the camps of instruction returned with even greater intensity at Camp Nelson. Again, close quarters, ignorance of disease-causing bacteria, the careless placement of "sinks" (latrines) too near water supplies, exposure to the winter weather, inadequate diets, lack of immunity to childhood diseases, and filthy conditions among the tents and cabins turned the camps into one large valley of affliction. Some of the men were especially repelled by their squalid surroundings. "A man gets indifferent to cleanliness very soon in camp," Lt. Theophilus Perry discovered. In fact, the camps even smelled dirty: "There is an odor about camps, that is sickening after one has been absent," he reported to his wife. "And any thing that is cooked taste[s] like the camps smell." A captain in the 19th Infantry identified another benefit of cleanliness: "I tell you iff a man don't keep clean he will get full of Boddy lice. some of my company have had lots of them."[30]

Soldiers from southern states tended to be less healthy than northern men, and camp life struck Confederates particularly hard. Their warmer, wetter climate exposed southerners to more diseases during their lifespans and reduced their ability to fight off sickness and recover from wounds. In a given year, about half of all northern-born soldiers suffered from some type of intestinal illness.

By contrast, nearly all southern-born soldiers experienced the same infirmities. Diarrhea and dysentery were the most serious and widespread maladies, but typhoid, pneumonia, and childhood diseases like measles brought many men low during the war. The common gag among U.S. army surgeons in the trans-Mississippi theater applied to the Confederate army as well: "It was a standing joke in our department that to be a good soldier here bowels are of more consequence than brains."[31]

Some of the men occasionally, and unintentionally, made themselves more vulnerable to digestive ailments. Dr. William P. Head, surgeon of the 16th Cavalry, described a typical encounter with a careless soldier in gastric distress: "Some fellow will come grunting around my tent and say Dr. I am suffering mighty bad with cramp in my stomach, and bad headache an the most general complaint is the same old military song; I am in mighty bad fix, & have got the Diarrhaea desperate bad, can you do anything for me Dr. I am getting mighty bad and would like to get some relief!" Dr. Head then began taking the groaning patient's history. What had he eaten?

> not much of anything. I just eat my rations, which is a pound and half of beef the same of meal, and 1/4 lb of bacon. Did you eat any peas? Yes I eat about a quart but I thought they would not hurt me. Do you think they did? What else did you eat tell me all? They had some green apples and I eat some of them. How many do you suppose? About a dozen. Anything else? Yes they had some fish in the mess and I eat some, a piece about as big as my hand. Did you eat anything else? Yes we had some polk sallet, and I eat some; and we had a big turtle and I eat a good deal of that and drank some of the soup. You certainly don't think Dr. that I have eat anything that has hurt me? I hardly ever eat very harty. I see sir you are . . . very moderate in your diet I think sir you have eat enough for a small company and I will soon show you the contents of your stomach. David [the surgeon's assistant] gives this gentleman about thirty grains of Ipecac [i.e., double the usual dose] in the usual way, and by the time he gets through I think he will be convinced that he has been very extravigant for these hard times.[32]

Self-induced health problems were unusual, but illness in general was all too common in the cold and muddy winter camp. Almost every surviving letter from Arkansas back to Texas mentioned the sick and dying. John S. Bryan of the 16th Texas Cavalry wrote his wife that "the helth of the redgment is not verry good. thair is 6 or 8 in our company that is sick with the fever." Bryan finished his missive several days later and reported that "thair is more sickness in camps now than thair was when I commensed this letter." Illness in military camps, especially diarrhea and dysentery, was particularly troublesome for the unfortunate victims, who had to coordinate their visits to open-air sinks with the weather. Capt. H. A. Wallace of Rusk County, suffering with diarrhea, missed his timing: "everything I eat just Run off like Water. Friday night was so clear I took a portion of Blue Mass & opium but it came on Rain by midnight. I had to be out in the Rain."[33]

Sylvester Kirk described the troubles of the 17th Infantry in his letters back to Bell County, Texas: "the helth of the army is verrey bad. the boys are dying verrey fast. wee have lost out of the bell County company five men. . . . Nick Dority will dy to day. he is delaric [delirious] and has been so for twelve hours and it takes too men to hold him on the bed." Private Kirk blamed exposure for most of the sickness. "we march so harde coming out her[e] and was so exsposed coming out her[e] and then when wee got her[e] the snow and cold wether and us unprepard for the winter and in a difernt climate from what wee have bin use to and I think if [we] have to stay in this contry twelve months I don't think wee will be able to get home with more than half of the men that wee got her[e] with."[34]

Disease killed twice as many men during the Civil War as enemy fire, so it is not surprising that reports of illness were soon followed by accounts of dying. "At almost all hours of the day you can hear the guns firing the salute over some soldier gone to his long home far away from friends & home," Capt. Elijah Petty wrote his daughter. In almost identical phrasing, John C. Porter of the 18th Texas Infantry recalled that "there was scarcely an hour in the day, but what there could be heard plattoons firing over the dead . . . Oh! what an army of Texas soldiers are lying at old camp Nelson." One of the generals at the camp finally ordered an end to the firing of salutes at grave sites. It was too dispiriting to patients in the hospital. David Ray, a schoolteacher from Grayson County, wrote his sister that the army had run out of coffins for all the dead men: "The last two men that died had to be buried without coffins. I saw them carrying two men to day tied up in a blanket and swung to a pole." Even holes in the ground were becoming scarce, according to Theophilus Perry of Harrison County. "Some men of one company went out to dig a grave for one of their company, & when they carried the corpse out to be burried, another man had been burried in it by another company." William E. Stoker of the 18th Infantry was appalled by the death all around him: "There is so much sickness & so many dyeing. They just dye all the time." Edward Cade summed it all up: "The Army [is] dying up like rotten sheep."[35]

Watching hitherto healthy young men like themselves die was painful and depressing, but eventually some of the soldiers became accustomed to the sight of corpses. For others, the hardening process was almost as distressing as the dying. Captain Wallace of the 19th Infantry wrote his wife that "you cant tell how hardened men get. Just to give you an Idea last night Tomy Easley was lying in the tent a corps[e]. not more than fifty yards off in another company the fiddle was a playing and the men a dancing a Reel. even in our own Company they don't mind it. Bury the poor men without shedding a tear and [with] their poor wives and children at home." Another soldier expressed similar sentiments to his sister. The sights we see, he wrote, "would look horrible [at home] but men become accustomed to anything here. they will even play cards while perhaps a man is dying in the next tent." The war in the trans-Mississippi, like wars for thousands of years, stripped away some of the layers of humanity and sympathy more common in peaceful times.[36]

Although general comments about the numbers of dead men were pitiful enough, accounts of individual deaths doubtless were even more disturbing to families and friends in Texas. A soldier in Private Kirk's company from Bell County was lost in delirium before he finally died: "one of the pore boys hallowed all night las night." A lieutenant from Lamar County recounted the more peaceful death of a close friend: "Tyler is dead—calmly and peacefully he breathed his last about two hours since. . . . He was perfectly resigned to his death, and conscious to the last of his approaching dissolution." Captain Wallace reported sadly to his wife that "John Ray poor fellow now lies cold in Death in my tent beside me. he died last evening at dusk. was taken the evening before at four oclock with a chill . . . about twelve [noon] he grew worse. it took four men to hold him in bed. he was the worst deranged man I ever seen. he never new anything more[,] just grew weaker and died about dusk perfectly easy. has as pretty a smile on his countenance as you ever seen." As usual, Private Blessington was most expressive in remembering the long gray valley: "How mournful thus to die, among rough but sympathizing comrades, with no soft hand to wipe the death-damp from the clammy brow; no loved one's voice to whisper words of hope and consolation to the departing spirit!"[37]

Surviving records do not indicate the total number of men who died at Camp Nelson that winter, but Private Blessington estimated the figure at 1,500.[38] A soldier in the 17th Infantry guessed that "this division lost more men from measles and pneumonia in one winter at Little Rock than in all the battles in which it was engaged."[39] Extrapolations from the twelve sample companies indicate that at least 1,290 men of the division either died or were discharged due to illness between September 1, 1862, and April 30, 1863. In view of the sometimes incomplete evidence on which these extrapolations are based—the military service records for individual soldiers—it is quite possible that 1,500 of the Texans were buried in Arkansas that winter. Another 326 men left the division for other reasons from September to April. Considering the fact that roughly four thousand men of the future division never reached the camp near Austin and remembering the hundreds who died in Arkansas, it becomes clear that the division was only about half its original size by the time it began its first campaign in the spring of 1863.[40]

The division may have been only half its original size by spring, but it was also younger and fitter. Three-fifths (59.8 percent) of all soldiers who left service before May 1863 were at or above the median enlistment age (twenty-six) for all men in the division. Many of the weaker soldiers had died or been discharged due to illness, some of the older officers had been replaced by younger men, and hundreds of men beyond the draft age had gone home.

In late November the Texans left Camp Nelson, with few regrets, and moved about fifteen straight-line miles southeast to a large prairie near Bayou Meto. The new camp, roughly twenty-five miles east of Little Rock, was nearer their supply line, the Memphis & Little Rock Railroad, which ran from Little Rock eastward to De Valls Bluff on the White River. The transfer from Camp Nelson required three days to move only fifteen miles, mostly because men, animals, and wagons sank into the cold Arkansas mud every step of the way. A sergeant in the 17th Infantry described the ordeal: "I knew an army was fourced to move verry slow but I had not the least Idear of its moveing as slow as we came to this place. we was three days comeing from Austin hear not exceeding fifteen miles. but amagine one thousand wagons traveling the same wet boggy road in one day[,] mireing up[,] priseing out[,] and you will conclude that it would be slow traveling."[41]

Colonel Waterhouse found the new site satisfactory: "We are encamped in a very pretty place on the edge of a prairie in a skirt of timbers in full view of the railroad where we can see the cars of an evening and morning arriving and departing." There were others, of course, who disagreed. A lieutenant in Waterhouse's own regiment complained that "the country is generally low & marshy, the prairie is very level, low & wet. I don't like our present Camp." A captain in the same regiment seconded that opinion: "this is the disagreeables[t] wet country I ever saw. the ground is perfectly level and wet and swampy . . . we are on the edge of a large Prairie. not a stick of Timber on it."[42]

Whether at Camp Nelson or Bayou Meto, those fortunate enough to avoid the hospital or the cemetery could usually be found on the drill fields. "At 5 o'clock the Reveille is beat when all get up and the roll is called," Ned Cade wrote his wife. "At 5 1/2 the Surgeons call when all the sick go before the Surgeon. At 7

Guard mounting. From 7 to 8 officers drill. From 8 to 10 Company drill. At 12 dinner call is beat. From 2 to 5 Battalion drill. At 6 dress parade. at 8 the Tattoo at which time all must prepare for bed and 9 1/2 the Taps are beat at which time all lights must go out." Like countless soldiers before them, the Texans found drill boring and tiresome. Private Blessington noted an "alarming increase in sickness" when orders were read to the men specifying a minimum of four hours of company drill a day. The schoolteacher David Ray resented the mind-numbing routine: "my mind seems barren of anything interesting as you might imagine for we are penned up by strong guards with no chance of seeing anything scarcely but what is going on in camp which is principally drilling." J. T. Knight of the 22nd Infantry found military life more demanding than he had predicted: "I thought that I had seen hard times but I did not no anything about hard times. We live hard and drill hard and the officers are hard on us and by the by it is hard all the time."[43]

The sameness of this daily cycle was occasionally relieved by a grand review of dozens of regiments, battalions, and batteries. On a sunny, windy Thursday in late November, several thousand men—those, at least, not too ill to march—put on a review for General Holmes, commander of the entire trans-Mississippi Confederacy, on the prairie near Bayou Meto. A band played "Hail to the Chief" as Holmes rode along two miles of lines, and citizens of the neighborhood pointed and exclaimed as the Texans went through their paces and flags snapped in the sharp breeze. Orange Cicero Connor of the 19th Infantry thought the whole event "was really a *Grand* sight. . . . I think this line of men, standing in 2 ranks, that is, two men deep, touching elbos in both Ranks, must have been 2½ miles long. It was so long that I could not distinguish the men at either end of the Line (I was near the Center) but could just see the solid Row across the Prairie." The foot soldiers were fascinated by the drill of the batteries attached to the division. A Grayson County man thought the maneuvers of the gunners were "quite a pretty sight the men being uniformed and their cannon shining like gold."[44]

Teenagers and young men far from home could always find other ways to entertain themselves, of course. Lt. Sam Wright of Daniel's battery described one camp adventure: "Last night some fellows blindfolded a horse, tied a bundle of fodder to his tail and turned him loose in the camps. He kicked up the very devil—tore down about 50 tents, killed one man, and wounded several others, finally butting his brains out against a tree."[45] The soldiers of the 28th Cavalry were less destructive in their fun but just as inventive. One night Horace Bishop scolded his tent mate, who was howling because he could not sleep.

Then he yelled all the louder. I joined him and in ten minutes there were 10,000 soldiers yelling at the top of their voices. At sunrise an old citizen came, and asked about the good news that had brought on the yelling. We told him that England and France had recognized the independence of the Southern Confederacy. He replied, "How did you hear it?" "A fellow brought a paper in at midnight," was our answer. "Where is it?" he asked. "Why, he just now passed by Gen. Randall's tent," we said. We kept him looking for that paper all day long, going from tent to tent. Of course, the poor, gray-haired, old citizen never did find it. This was a sample of the recreation in which we sometimes indulged between drill hours.[46]

While some of the men lay in sickbeds and others drilled on Camp Nelson's muddy fields, their higher officers had kept busy organizing the regiments into brigades and divisions. In late October, under orders from General Holmes, Brig. Gen. Henry McCulloch had arranged the fifteen regiments and one battalion of Texas infantry and dismounted cavalry at Camp Nelson into four brigades.[47] The new brigades were known at first as McCulloch's division of the 2nd Corps of the Army of the Trans-Mississippi Department. The 4th Brigade, commanded by Col. James Deshler, was soon detached and never rejoined the command.[48]

Thus, the division consisted of three brigades for most of the war (see Table 6). It was the largest body of Texans in the Civil War and the only division on either side to serve throughout its existence with regiments from a single state. The eleven regiments and one battalion in the division numbered somewhere between 11,500 and 12,000 men when first mustered in the spring of 1862. By the time they were organized into a division, however, the various units were rapidly dwindling down to about half that strength.

The higher officers of the new division were men of some distinction, well educated and accomplished in public affairs. Of the ten who served for any significant length of time as brigade commanders, five were natives of the upper South, four of the lower South, and one was born in Pennsylvania.[49] Most had been professional men before the war. Four (George Flournoy, Wilburn H. King, William R. Scurry, and Thomas N. Waul) were attorneys, three (James M. Hawes, Horace Randal, and Robert P. Maclay) were professional army officers, two (Henry McCulloch and Richard Waterhouse) were merchants, and one (Overton C. Young) was a large planter (Waul combined the law and planting). Three (Flournoy, McCulloch, and Scurry) had held statewide public offices before the war, two (King and Waul) would hold statewide offices after the war, and one (Waul) served in the Provisional Congress of the Confederacy. Several had significant military training or experience. Three (Hawes, Maclay, and Ran-

TABLE 6

UNITS OF THE TEXAS DIVISION, OCTOBER 1862–MARCH 1865

---

*1st Brigade, Col. Overton Young*
12th Texas Infantry, Col. Overton Young
18th Texas Infantry, Col. William B. Ochiltree
22nd Texas Infantry, Col. Richard B. Hubbard
13th Texas Cavalry (dismounted), Col. John H. Burnett
Capt. Horace Haldeman's Battery

*2nd Brigade, Col. Horace Randal*
11th Texas Infantry, Col. Oran M. Roberts
14th Texas Infantry, Col. Edward Clark
28th Texas Cavalry (dismounted), Col. Horace B. Randal
Maj. Robert Gould's Texas Cavalry Battalion (dismounted)
Capt. James M. Daniel's Battery (Lamar Artillery)

*3rd Brigade, Col. George Flournoy*
16th Texas Infantry, Col. George Flournoy
17th Texas Infantry, Col. Robert T. P. Allen
19th Texas Infantry, Col. Richard Waterhouse
16th Texas Cavalry (dismounted), Col. William Fitzhugh
Capt. William Edgar's Battery

---

Sources: *Official Records*, vol. 22, pt. 1, pp. 903–4; Blessington, *Campaigns of Walker's Texas Division*, 46–59.

dal) were graduates of the U.S. Military Academy and veterans of the Indian Wars, and five (Hawes, Maclay, McCulloch, Scurry, and Waterhouse) had served in the Mexican War.[50]

Some officers at the regimental level were at least as distinguished as their brigade commanders. Oran Roberts of the 11th Infantry was a former justice of the state supreme court and a future governor of Texas. Edward Clark of the 14th Infantry had succeeded Sam Houston as governor in 1861. Col. Richard B. Hubbard of the 22nd Infantry, a graduate of Harvard College, would serve as governor in the 1870s. Robert T. P. Allen of the 17th Infantry was a West Point graduate, a veteran of the Seminole Wars, and founder of the Bastrop Military Institute. George Washington Jones, lieutenant colonel under Allen, would be elected lieutenant governor of Texas in 1866 and would serve in the U.S. House of Representatives for two terms in the late 1870s and early 1880s. William B. Ochiltree of the 18th Infantry was a judge in the Republic of Texas, a state legislator in the 1850s, and briefly a member of the Confederate Provisional Congress. Col. John H. Burnett of the 13th Cavalry had stormed the castle of Chapultepec during the Mexican War, served in the Texas House of Representatives in the 1850s, and resigned his seat in the Texas Senate to raise his regiment. William Fitzhugh, colonel of the 16th Cavalry, was a veteran of the Seminole Wars, the Mexican War, and the antebellum Indian Wars. If public service and military experience were guides to success, the officers were very well equipped to lead the new division.[51]

One of their most urgent needs was arms for their men. Upon his regiment's arrival at Camp Nelson in early September, Pvt. William Stoker of the 18th Infantry reported that "we havent been armed yet; there is but verry few regaments hear that is armed." A comrade in the same unit described the firearms the men had brought from Texas: "shot guns and squirrel rifles that we had carried from home. Some had [flint]locks, some none, some without any hammers." Private Blessington recalled that "many of our troops were armed with the old flint-lock guns, with a buckskin pouch, resembling the backwoods hunter." Even if they had weapons, the inexperienced soldiers were not yet accustomed to military procedures regarding firearms. A soldier in the 18th Infantry recounted a telling incident when his unit was sent to De Valls Bluff in October: "Camped, stacked our arms after a fashion, but they soon fell down, whereupon Col. Culberson ordered them taken to a large gate fifty yards distant, and stacked against that, for fear some one might get shot."[52]

Finally, in early November, seven thousand stands of arms arrived at government depots in Little Rock. Within a few days the men were writing home that at long last they could consider themselves soldiers now that they had military weapons. "We are now armed with plain Muskets (a pretty fair and efficient arm) and are quite busy cleaning up and drilling the Manual [of arms]," Capt. Elijah Petty wrote. "We feel and look now like soldiers." Most of the men received old, outmoded .69-caliber percussion smoothbores, effective at less than one hundred yards. A few companies—reportedly, one in every regiment—shouldered one of the most popular firearms of the war, the .577-caliber English Enfield rifle, effective at five hundred yards or more. An inspection report the following spring found the division armed with 3,581 muskets, 916 Enfields, 47 .54-caliber "Mississippi rifles," 80 notoriously unreliable .70-caliber "Belgian rifles," and 48 Colt repeating rifles, also unreliable. Thus, about three-fourths of the soldiers began their first campaign with outdated smoothbores, and some of the remaining one-fourth, who carried rifles, found them undependable as well.[53]

Although the Texans were happy finally to be armed with military weapons, they were not as excited about another feature of army life. Their officers demanded more discipline than Texans found dignified. Sylvester Kirk was a private in the 17th Infantry commanded by Col. R. T. P. Allen, the West Pointer widely known for his insistence on strict observance of regulations. Such fussiness did not sit well with the independent-minded private. It appeared to Kirk and some of his comrades that enlisted men were treated no better than slaves.[54]

> wee have about one half of liberty of a negrow in this plase. wee have to get apass from the captane and then from the Co[lonel] and then have to go to the generl and get him to sine it and you have [to] get their to him befoure nin oclock. if [you] don't he wont sine it for you and if you happen to put your hands in you pocket of acold morning when in line they will put you under garde and kepe you under garde for twnty four hours. and if you have one speck of rust on you gun it is the same thing. and when you are on garde you have to salute the offiser of the garde and if he comes by the garde fire when you out on garde and you are sleepe you have to bewok up and get up and put on your cloth[es] and get in to line and get you gun and present arms to him to plese him.[55]

John T. Knight of Colonel Hubbard's 22nd Texas Infantry chafed under the discipline in his regiment as well. "The officers are hard on us," he wrote his wife. "There is two men in my sight diging up a stump for disobeying their officers." John Simmons found Colonel Hubbard to be a hard man, especially after a request for a furlough was denied. "A great many of [us] could have come home this spring if we had the right sort of a *Colonel,* but he is mean in every respect. . . . I hope the day will come when we can point our fingers at him and tell him of it, and not be afraid of being put under guard." After recounting more indignities, Simmons concluded, "It is too bad that a man must, after being born in a free country, cease to be a freeman for the demagogues of our country." Pvt. John Porter's resentment extended all the way up the line to the brigade commander, the West Pointer James M. Hawes: "Gen. Hawes came down upon us with a vim, with his old army discipline, which was very coarse for us new soldiers, and we kicked right sharply, and laid a plan to run him off, but like all other soldier plots, it failed."[56]

The long-suffering Private Farrow of the 19th Infantry made way for no man when it came to complaining. "We have inspection every Sunday and every man has to have on a clean shirt. if he does not he goes to the guard house for a day or two," Farrow groused. "Our officers are very strict. We cant get out side of our Brigade guard lines unless we have a written pass from our Captain and signed by the Colonel and Brigadier Gen. McCulloch[,] the same as a Darkeys pass. what few Negroes there is here has more privileges than the privates do."[57]

The most severe form of discipline, death by firing squad, was reserved for the most serious crimes, usually aggravated cases of desertion.[58] Conditions in

Arkansas during the winter of 1862–1863—poor rations, inadequate clothing, widespread disease, camp restrictions, boredom—convinced some of the Texas and Arkansas soldiers to steal away home. To set an example for the rest of the men, the generals sometimes ordered executions for deserters and required the men in the ranks to witness the punishments. As early as mid-August 1862, a trooper in the 16th Texas Cavalry reported, five Arkansas soldiers "were brought out in an open field in presence of the whole army drawn up in line; and at the command fire they were fired on by about 60 men; one was not killed by this and another Platoon was brought up which finished him. another one was not dead when they put him in the coffin." At another execution, the condemned man fainted several times before he was shot. John C. Porter of the 18th Texas Infantry described the usual ritual at such events: "Their grave is generally dug in some old field, where the army may be assembled, and they and their coffins are hauled there in a wagon, followed by the band playing some mournful piece; the doomed man then kneels or sits on his coffin, when twelve men are drawn up in a line, whose guns are loaded by other parties, six having balls in them and six none. The squad is commanded by a Lieut. and at his command, they all fire, and none knew who killed him."[59]

One of the batteries attached to the division, commanded by Capt. Horace Haldeman of Bell County, had a particularly bad reputation for desertion. A rival in Capt. James Daniel's Lamar Artillery contrasted his own battery's record that winter—no desertions—with that of Haldeman's unit, forty-seven desertions.[60] In an open field near Pine Bluff on March 12, 1863, two of Haldeman's gunners, German Catholics from Houston, were executed. Several soldiers in Walker's division recounted the sad spectacle in their letters to Texas.[61]

Capt. Elijah Petty of the 17th Infantry set the scene: "The Division was drawn up in 3 sides of a hollow square fronting the river[,] the open side on the river in a large field just in the lower edge of Pine Bluff." A band playing the "Dead March" led a procession into the square. Then came twenty-four men (the two firing squads) followed by a priest and the two condemned men. Behind them was a wagon carrying two coffins and then two companies acting as guards. The melancholy parade proceeded slowly before each side of the square and then turned to the center, where two open graves were waiting. While the two firing squads stood about ten paces away, an officer read the sentence of death, and then the priest prayed with the two condemned deserters kneeling by their graves. Edward Cade of Smith County learned that "one was a married man whose family consisted of a wife & 3 children. The other was a young beardless lad." Finally, a lieutenant barked out the order to aim and fire, twenty-four sharp reports echoed across the river, and "the poor fellows fell over on their faces, gasped a little and were gone," Petty wrote. "The boys says that they was shot all to pieces," one of the witnesses in the square recalled.[62]

The men in the division almost always found these scenes repulsive, but they described them in dozens of letters during their service. Captain Petty thought the whole affair at Pine Bluff was "a melancholly and tragic end" but also "the just doom of the deserter." Still, it seemed a waste: "I had rather see a hundred killed in battle than these poor devils here." Private Farrow thought it was "a painful sight" that "I hope to God I never will see again. it looks like cold Blood murder to me." Edward Cade agreed with Farrow: "My feelings were such as I never again wish to experience." Unfortunately, Farrow and Cade would see more executions before they returned to civilian life.[63]

All things considered, the men of the division found their first winter away from home less than satisfactory. Arkansas was cold, gray, and wet, and its people were not up to the mark that Texans expected. Drill was boring after countless repetitions, officers were apparently determined to humiliate the enlisted men, and hundreds of friends and relatives had been lowered into untimely graves far from home. Besides, their sacrifices seemed pointless since most of the men had not even seen a Yankee yet. To make it all worse, the Texans were lonesome for their wives and children. It was an awful Arkansas.

# CHAPTER 4

# The Folks at Home

Most of the men in Walker's Texas Division had been farmers and stock raisers before the war, occupations that required their steady presence around the farm and home. They were not accustomed to long separations from their fields and pastures, and they certainly were not accustomed to extended absences from their wives and children. Of course, shopkeepers, clerks, and lawyers—married or single—were not immune to loneliness, either. Arkansas seemed unpleasant to the Texans in the fall and winter of 1862–1863 partly because they were lonesome for familiar faces and voices, the comforts of home, and the affection of their women and children. Their diaries and letters from Camp Nelson and Bayou Meto were filled with yearnings for home and family.

For many of them, probably most, the fall and winter of 1862–1863 were the first time this loneliness closed in on them. The spring and summer of 1862 had been spent in Texas, in many cases near enough to their homes to visit or be visited. The military life was new then, and the novelty of the whole experience was at first distracting. Watermelon suppers organized by their families and neighbors, Sunday services in neighborhood churches, visits by citizens from nearby communities, and the buzzing activity around the camps of instruction kept their minds busy and engaged. But when the men marched five hundred miles away, when the drilling and newness of army life had become old business, and when they were forced to sleep long winter nights in cold tents in muddy, filthy camps far from home, their thoughts turned to loving wives and children far away—a warm embrace, a giggling infant, a home-cooked meal, a bright fireplace. Once they were thrown into active campaigning in the spring of 1863, they marched and fought and maneuvered on a steady basis, seeing new places, setting up new camps, facing the terror of combat, and generally remaining active soldiers for the remaining two years of the war. That first winter in Arkansas, though, was their dark night of loneliness.

The division included more than the usual share of married men, and letters to wives flowed in a steady stream from Arkansas to Texas. William E. Stoker, a farmer from the Coffeeville community of Upshur County in northeast Texas, wrote his wife even before winter set in that he was aching for home: "Betty, I cant express my feelings when I think of you and Priscilla [his young daughter]. My heart leaps, but at the same time being so fare off and cant come home and see you it almost makes my heart break." Stoker kept his wife's letters, but when he looked at them in moments alone, "I cant keep from weepping about you, feeling so loley bye your self." To make matters worse, he had to face the possibility that he would never see her again: "I want to see you so bad, I am nearley ded but I don't know wether I will eveer be blessed with the pleasure of seeing you any more or not. . . . If I ever get the chance to come [home], I am a comeing like a feather in the wind."[1] When the winds brought no furloughs, Stoker thought about sneaking away to Upshur County: "I am great mind to come, if it want [were not] for the name of a deserter, I would come home & see you once more," he wrote. "I can doo verry well all the week but when Sunday morning comes, I think of loely [lonely] Betty & how I would like to be at home with her to spend the day—not only the day but the balance of my life. Kiss priscilla for me & Ile kiss you the next time I see you." Desertion stayed on Stoker's mind for several more weeks. In December he wrote, "Tongue cant express, nor I cant write with this pen how bad I want to see you. If it want [were not], for the after clap [consequences] I would of ben home to see you before now, but if I desert and come any how, Ile hav to keep a going untill I get over in to mexico."[2]

By February, Stoker had steeled himself to reality and given up on the idea of running off to Upshur County: "I was fretted a long time & wrote to you like I had as leav come home as not, but I studdyed the matter over & I found out it wasent good polacy, but thare was several just wanted me to say the word & they was readdy, but I told them no, I loved my rib [wife] as well, & would do as much as any boddy to see them [his family] on honerable terms."[3] Stoker asked his wife to assure his mother that he would not desert: "Tell her not to be uneasy; I aint going to come home untill I can come like a white man." Although he gave up the idea of desertion, he still preferred farm life to army life. "The harness don't fit me in the ware; there is no place that would soot me so well now as well as to be there [at home] between a pare of plow handles, following Jarrel [his mule]."[4]

Private Farrow of the 19th Infantry likewise felt the first pangs of loneliness shortly after leaving his home in Panola County, also in northeast Texas. "I wish I was with you this evening and would like very much to eat supper at home with you," he wrote while still in Texas. "Josephine when you write to me write what is going on and how the Folks is generally throug the neighborhood generally." Two weeks later Farrow continued on the same theme and repeated Stoker's fear that he might never see his wife again: "Men never know what Pleasure a home [is] until he is compelled to leave his wife and children. . . . But if I never see you anymore you must remember your ever loving husband." Like Stoker, and at about the same time, Farrow considered sneaking away to his wife and children. "If they don't let me come home I shall go pretty soon anyhow for I am tired of this place and want to go somewhere," he warned her. Also like Stoker, Farrow eventually pushed aside the idea of desertion in order to preserve his good name. Still, he ended one of his letters in the spring of 1863 with these pitiful words, "Home Sweet Home. Where I ought to be."[5]

A captain in Farrow's regiment demonstrated that longings for home were not limited to the enlisted men. "I know I am hard but I cant read your letters with out shedding Tears," H. A. Wallace wrote to his wife in Rusk County. Jonathan T. Knight of the 22nd Infantry had similar feelings: "Susan its enough to kill any man that thinks any thing of his family to stay away from them so long for my family is all that I can study about night or day." A sergeant in the 17th Infantry fought the same demons. John Holcombe wrote his wife, Mandy, "if I could erace the thauts of home from my mind I could make myself contented but the thauts of home makes me spend many disagreeable hours & if it was not for the cause of freedom stimulating me I could not stand it." When he received his first letter from home, Holcombe was overcome with emotion, even in front of his fellow soldiers: "I never was so proud in my life though I could not suppress my tears to of saved my life. some of my friends asked me if any of my family was dead. when I told them they were all well & doing well they laughed at me but it was not funny to me." Like many of his comrades, Holcombe gained a new appreciation for family life as a result of his absence. "If I ever git home I expect to be a better husband and farther than I ever was," he assured his wife.[6]

One of the most interesting features of these letters is the emotion and affection that flowed so freely from the pens of these Texas men. Some scholars of family life have maintained that nineteenth-century American husbands were remote, cold, and distant from their wives—insensitive and overbearing patriarchs. Other writers have detected a very different sort of husband: affectionate, loving, and sensitive to his wife's emotional needs. The hundreds of letters from Walker's Greyhounds that have survived the generations since the Civil War clearly fall into the second category. Some haughty patriarchs doubtless walked among the soldiers in the division, but they left little evidence of their presence in letters back to Texas.[7]

Edwin P. Becton of Hopkins County in northeast Texas, a surgeon in the 22nd Infantry, indicated that he and his messmates often talked about their wives around the campfire. "We have a fine time talking about our Mary's. There are six married men in my mess & four have wives named Mary." When his wife neared the time for delivery of another child, Becton assured her of his love and affection: "It would be to me the greatest happiness to attend you in your confinement, to stand around your bed side, mitigate your sufferings, give to you that comfort & kind assurance of heartfelt sympathy which an affectionate husband only can give."[8]

Captain Wallace of the 19th Infantry clung to physical reminders of his faraway wife: "you are in my mind through the day [and] often through the night. when I wake you are the first one I think of. I often look at your and Mattys [his daughter's] likeness. I would not part with them for anything. don't forget to send me a bracelet of your hair." Orange Cicero Connor of Cass County, a man whose unusual given name was matched by that of his wife, told her, "My dear America I know not how to express my heart's desires and wishes for you. I can find no language strong enough[,] for you, of all the world alone sustain the relation of *wife* to me."[9]

John Samuel Bryan of the 16th Cavalry was so happy with his wife that he decided to bind her to him again when the war was over: "I told the boys I thought I would marry you again when my three years are served out as three years absence intitles a woman to a divorce." Sadly for Bryan, he was mortally wounded during the Red River campaign, a year before his scheduled remarriage. Cicero H. Spears of the 18th Infantry boasted fifty years later that marital affection in his family was mutual. When he fell ill with typhoid and pneumonia in Arkansas, "My wife left home with a year old baby in her arms and rode horseback in the dead of winter with the roads bad, bridges washed away, and rivers out of banks; after many delays and passing through many dangers reached me on the 4th of March, 1863."[10]

Healthy young men in their twenties and thirties thought about more than home-cooked meals and other comforts of home, of course. Their almost total separation from women for months inevitably stimulated their imaginations in other directions as well. Their letters and diaries rarely mention their sexual longings—nineteenth-century American men generally kept those thoughts private—but occasionally their urges were expressed in indirect language.[11] Capt. H. A. Wallace spoke of sleep: "I spend many an hour thinking about you on my bed. it would be a great pleasure to sleep with you on my arm one night." On another occasion he mentioned cold nights and hugs: "oh what a pleasure it would be to me to hug you up to my bosom these cold nights." Such thoughts were not limited to Captain Wallace. Indeed, some wives winked and hinted at their own sexual loneliness. In a letter to his wife, Surgeon Edward Cade described his pleasant stay in a Louisiana home while he cared for his patients away from the army, but he also indicated that he had been eager to return to camp.

His wife let him know that things would have been different had she been there: "If I could only have spent the time with you while at Natchitoches in that nice house how differently the time would have passed to you. Your desire to get back to camps wouldn't have been quite as strong."[12]

Some soldiers felt compelled to assure their wives that, unlike some of their comrades, they remained faithful to their wedding vows. Private Stoker of Upshur County was appalled by the women of Arkansas and the men of Texas. "Betty, I must tell you something about the women in arkingsaw. As we came along, I can say there is but verry few vertious ones along the road we travailed. There husbands had gone to the ware and they [the wives] have for saken them. The men [in Stoker's regiment] would go way on be fore & some would stay behind and go [to] their houses and get all around them and such talk you never hea[r]d among straingers." In fact, Stoker continued, "there was so many [soldiers who] would croud up on the women that it was enough to scare them to do any thing but such as that was just as lots of them wanted. I can speak for my self—I hav ben jus as virtious as I could be but, all of the boys cant say it."[13]

Theophilus Perry, a lawyer from Harrison County, likewise assured his own wife that, despite all the temptations, he would remain faithful. "I have always been lucky so far as the girls are concerned," he wrote in February 1863, but "I shall behave properly towards the Ladies & the lasses that enliven the society of the White Sulphur Springs [near Pine Bluff]. Every Pretty woman will but serve to transport me in sweet fancy in to the presence of her, that makes the sun to shine & the skies to look Blue over my head. And my Dear so long as I cultivate the society of the girls, just for the purpose of thinking about you, I shall be within the bounds of Taste & Duty."[14]

Capt. Elijah Petty's joking references to his own fidelity probably elicited few smiles around his wife's kitchen table back in Bastrop County. In one letter he recounted a recent dream in which, upon his return from the war, his wife had refused to kiss him and accused him of having kissed Arkansas women. "Now was'nt that funny but the funniest thing of all will be that I intend to kiss some of them before I do leave for it shall never be said that I left Arkansas where kissing is so cheap and did'nt take any stock at all but you know this is all a joke and if a man cant joke his own wife who can he joke." A month later, perhaps in response to a good scolding from his unamused spouse, Petty reassured her. "My Dear Wife let me assure you that I shall never be guilty of any thing that if known would tinge the cheek of her I love best and of my dear little children. No Never Never. This is enough on the Arkansas girl question."[15]

Whether Perry and Petty stuck to their vows cannot be known, of course, but it is clear that many of the Texans found the women of Arkansas and Louisiana irresistible. Captain Wallace could see the signs: "I am surrounded by wickedness where men are alone and none of the sacred influences of women to constrain them. they become perfectly Reckless. here there is Thousands of us men some times never see a woman in weeks." Private Stoker, worried that soldiers still in Texas might have similar ideas about his own wife, could rest easy, remembering that he had left her armed with a Mexican *pistola.* "There is some men mean enough to do any thing. They go too or three miles off of the road to pester the women [whose] husbands has gone to ware . . . if any boddy pesters you, just to take your pistole and blow their trotters from under them." Mr. and Mrs. Stoker were not a couple to be trifled with.[16]

If unfaithful Arkansas wives were not available, more professional aid was never far away from Civil War soldiers. Theophilus Perry of the 28th Cavalry, appointed temporary provost marshal as his regiment was traveling to Arkansas, had to rummage through Shreveport's brothels to find all his missing charges: "I was sent into Shreveport yesterday evening with 16 men and 3 lieutenants to scour the town out, and carry the soldiers into camp. We got a long string of them before we were done. I had to go to some places, a gentleman ought never to be caught at, and take them out of the embrace of their amours." Prostitution became such a serious problem in Shreveport, in fact, that the city government finally passed an ordinance to shut down all "houses of ill fame," much to the disappointment of the soldiers.[17]

Faithful or not, the Texans in Walker's division worried about their wives. Could they handle the farm in the absence of the man of the house? Could they raise the children without the presence of a father? In general, the soldiers believed there was no substitute for a man when it came to running the farm or business. Although he could not be home in Cass County to run his farm, Lt. Orange C. Connor assured his wife that other adult males were available to help her. "I am not able to tell you what to do but I know [your father] will advise you well."[18] Despite their concerns, the Texas soldiers generally gave way to necessity, accepted their situations, and placed their faith in the intelligence and competence of their wives.

Typical of many soldiers, Sergeant Holcombe of Bastrop County in central Texas advised his wife on crops and animals and money:

> write how you are gitting on generaly & how mutch land you have broke up. I think it would be best to plant but little cotton but probaly you had better plant afew acres to buy sutch things as you will be forced to have next fall. you must bear in mind that you will have to pay your tax again soon & will have to have some gold or silver. you had better git it and lay

it by and have it ready. I would allso like to know [how] your corn is holding out, how your shoats looks & if you have any more pigs & how many and especialy how our children are gitting on.[19]

Capt. Elijah Petty, a pre-war lawyer in the nearby town of Bastrop, likewise advised his own wife about business affairs: how much salt to store, how much sugar, how to keep the frost of winter off sweet potatoes, etc.[20]

Despite their attitudes toward women and business, some husbands were pleasantly surprised by their mates' common sense and business acumen. "I am proud to learn that you are so provident that you manage the affairs of a family so well," Petty wrote, "and I hope that by the time I return home you will be such an adept in these matters that I will have no trouble of the sort on my hands[,] that you will do it all." His suggestions, Petty assured her, were only that: "I only suggest—I am not now the head of the family and don't pretend to dictate." Surgeon Edwin P. Becton of Hopkins County, a man with traditional ideas about women in general, was fully confident in his own wife's ability to handle the family's affairs: "you have managed my business in every particular to my entire satisfaction. You have exhibited more judgement & business qualification tha[n] most women possess."[21] In the minds of the Texans, farming and business were best left to men in normal circumstances, but many of them were proud that their women could stand up to necessity when the times demanded.

Family communications to and from the camps in Arkansas were normally civil and often tender. Occasionally, however, intentionally or not, some letters only intensified the anxiety felt by soldiers far from home. Expressions of loneliness by wives were particularly troublesome for the Texans. Private Farrow of Panola County, already given to fits of despair, must have sunk even lower when he read some of his wife's letters. "Sam you don't no how bad I feel," she wrote in one letter shortly after he left home. To drive the point home, she signed her letter, "Your wife until death." Pvt. Sylvester P. Kirk of the 17th Infantry read a similar complaint from his wife in Shelby County: "oh! How I long for the time to come when you can come home. I miss your company so much sometimes I think I cannot wait on this tedious war to close to see you." Volney Ellis of Lavaca County in south-central Texas admitted he had been brought low by a recent missive from home: "I must confess that my heart sinks with sadness, my dear Mary, when I peruse your last letter, burthened as it is with sorrow."[22]

Such letters were not at all uncommon in the camps of the Texas Division. None of the men had more to contend with than Lt. Theophilus Perry of Harrison County, though. His wife, Harriet, bucked and strained against his absence, and she never hesitated to scold him from afar. Less than two months after he left his home in Marshall in the summer of 1862, she wrote, "Oh me—when will it end & let my husband come back to me." In the next few weeks, she signed her letters, "At home All alone" and "At Home Alone." Pregnant and unhappy, she continued her protests in December. "I don't think it possible for me to go on any longer, for I am almost *entirely* helpless, it is all I can do to get in & out of the bed. I do hope & pray I never shall be in this condition again, death is nearly preferable. You don't know how I feel & never can . . . I don't think any *man* can." If Lieutenant Perry was not reeling yet, she finished him off with a broadside of defeatism: "I don't feel confident of our success by any means. I think the South is nearly exhausted." Ten days later, more gloom: "I am dying to see you, but I will not write my feelings, for I will only make you unhappy & will do no good. There is no pleasure in life to me, having to live separated from you as I do. I don't care to live." When at last she delivered her baby, her mood remained the same. In fact, she warned her husband to forget about any new conceivings anytime soon: "While I was in labor & bemoaning my separation from you Mrs. Marshall said she would tell me *for my encouragement* that you would come in about a year just time enough *for me to start again,* she termed it. Well I told her if you did come now, I did not want you to come for that."[23]

Harriet Perry feared that her husband preferred his new military life to their pre-war domestic arrangements. He seemed not to appreciate her trials and her efforts to support him. When he did not acknowledge receipt of some packages she had sent him, she reprimanded him sharply. "If you do not [acknowledge the packages] I shall feel *slighted & unappreciated.* . . . I can't bear to be treated with indifference & especially by you. I set too much value on *my labor* to let it go without being appreciated." Reports that her husband was thriving in his new profession of arms elicited more subtle scolding. "All the accounts I have of you my darling are that you are an incessant talker & the bussiest man in Camp & *very cheerful & happy.* Now, husband you must devote some of your 'talking time' to writing to your wife." Nor was Mrs. Perry happy about her husband's prospects in the army. When he informed her that Col. Horace Randal would soon reassign him from less demanding staff work to field duty, she complained. "I think I never will like Randall nor do I thank him for the way he has acted." Colonel Randal's orders must have seemed the least of Lieutenant Perry's troubles.[24]

Some women, in contrast to Harriet Perry, took pride in their ability to stand up to hardship and separation. At least, their husbands took pride in their wives' stoicism. Edward Cade of the 28th Cavalry instructed his pregnant wife that she must not complain that he was not there to help her through her ordeal: "In the trial of your confinement you must show yourself a *soldiers* wife." Five weeks later, after delivering a healthy son, Allie Cade assured her husband that she had met his expectations: "The ladies all say they never saw greater forbearance. You may say you have got a *soldier* wife." Surgeon Becton of Hopkins County boasted that his wife's letters "have the ring of the pure metal. A friend read me his wife's letter a short time ago. I was tired long before she closed. 'Oh do come home darling. Oh for one hour with you. I would come to you if I could &c &c.' Now isn't that childish? Thank God you have more sense than that." Two months later Becton complimented his sturdy companion again: "I am truly glad my dear Mary that you appreciate my contentedness—for nothing would make me more unhappy than to receive 'whining, homesick epistles' from you. . . . You talk like a woman of sense & not like a sixteen year old girl."[25]

Mary Becton was at least as tough as her husband. No crying about loneliness or hints about desertion entered her letters. "My own dear Edwin my feelings in respect to your being a soldier are just yours precisely. I have thought just as you said often but never expressed it before that I would not have you at home if I could[,] dearly as I love you. I had rather you were just where you are than lying round at house [as a deserter] and then it would not only be visited on you but on your children." And if he died on duty, so be it. Honor before comfort. "Nothing would do me more good than to know of your standing firm and doing your duty even if you died. let you die at your post." In a completely unnecessary reassurance, she promised, "I do not intend to be a draw-back to you if I can help it with my whining."[26]

Mary Cheek, wife of Tolbert F. Cheek of the 12th Infantry, went beyond stoicism to outright aggression. Shortly after learning that, contrary to earlier news, her husband had not been killed in action or captured, she described her reaction: "I'll tell you when I heard you were killed or taken prisoner, it made my blood boil for revenge and I felt like if it was in my power I would go and have it if I lost my own life in the attempt. Sometimes I long to be a man, so that I could go and help you fight the infernal Yankees. I do think I would [love] to kill them, for they have caused us women so much trouble." Mrs. Cheek had no illusions about an early peace settlement and had no use for Abraham Lincoln: "I have no hope for [peace] as long as old Lincoln is in office. It was rumored here a few days ago that he had been killed but that news is too good to be true." And she had nothing but contempt for some men from her neighborhood around Weatherford who reportedly had skulked during a recent battle at Galveston: "That sort I think they would do well to send home to make bread for those that can stand." Considering these letters from home, Private Cheek had no choice but to be a good soldier.[27]

Most surviving letters from Walker's division were written to or by wives, so spousal relationships are a leading theme in these records. Almost as prominent, though, were discussions of children. Similar to the view of nineteenth-century American husbands as cold and distant patriarchs is the related notion that they were also forbidding "enforcers of discipline and arbiters of family morals," men who left child-rearing to women and expressed little affection or tenderness toward their children. If their private thoughts expressed in letters home are any indication, that theory is as wrong-headed as the first. The rough-handed farmers and stock raisers who marched away from Texas in 1862 frequently, almost constantly, expressed affection and tenderness toward their children.[28]

Soldiers often requested that their wives "kiss the children for me." John S. Bryan of Collin County, a man who had worked in the rough gold-mining camps of California and now soldiered in the equally rough military camps of Arkansas, asked his wife to "kiss my boy for me. tell him of how I would love to see him and you." No sentimentalist, Surgeon Becton wrote his equally tough-minded wife, "write to me all about the children. Kiss them for me." Jonathan T. Knight reminded his wife to "kiss my beloved little Jony for me for I am a long ways from him and soon will double the distance." Captain Petty instructed his daughter to "kiss all the little rats for me and tell them to think of Pa who thinks of them very much." Lt. Orange Connor enclosed a note to his children in one of his letters: "Willie, Egg, Orange, Marion & Lee my dear boys I send my love to you all 'tis [all] that I can now do. I will come to see you all as soon as I can, & I want you all to be good boys obey your Ma & try to help her along the best you can." Even colonels were not immune. Richard Waterhouse, commander of the 19th Infantry Regiment, asked his wife to "kiss my little boyes for me." Expressions like these are too numerous to count.[29]

The Texans did more than add a line or two about kissing their children to the ends of letters. Some of their missives were truly tender. Pat Martin of the 28th Cavalry celebrated his young son's progress at home. "Bless the sweet little boy. I feel so rejoiced to hear of his proficiency in singing and counting and Papa will send him a ballad of 'Nellie Grey' and he must learn to sing it all and if Papa comes home in January he will assist his little [boy] to sing it." Adopting language that he would have used in speaking to his son, Martin asked his mother-in-law to "tell Jimmie that Papa will come home this winter to see his boy, if he can get off, and then he wants to find a big fat boy and a good boy and then Papa wants to sleep with him on a bed."[30]

Sergeant Holcombe was just as proud of his daughters. "Marthy Pa will be verry proud to hear you and Lina read for him when he comes home," he wrote. "God bless your little souls." The sergeant could barely wait to return to his children: "tell the children I often think of how mutch I used to pride in making their little swings [and] playhouses and go haw [berry] hunting & to go abraud with them & tell them if I ever git home again I will never tire in trying to add to their pleasure."

D. E. Young of the 17th Infantry likewise looked forward to the day when he could enjoy his wife and children: "I hope that Pease Will Soon com and We Will get home and then We can eat drink and Be Merry With our litle Children." Private Stoker mentioned his five-year-old daughter, Priscilla, in virtually all his letters. In the fall of 1862, he did the best he could to talk to her, at least indirectly: "Get Priscilla to say some thing and write it. You wrote that she was as smart & as pretty as ever." Hoping for some clever reaction, he wrote, "Betty, Shew Priscilla my ampletipe [ambrotype] and write what she says about it."[31] Texans may have had rough reputations in the rest of the country, but many of them were affectionate and loving fathers in their homes.

As much as they missed the pleasures of home, however, many of these foot soldiers preferred to prolong their absence rather than dishonor their wives and children by deserting. Private Stoker was sorely tempted to desert from the cold, gray camps in Arkansas, but to desert, in his words, "would throw a stigmey on me & her [his wife] to[o] & it would be thrown up to [daughter] Priscilla for years that her par deserted the armey [and] wouldent fight for his cuntry." Surgeon Edward Cade expressed the same fear in a letter to his wife: "Did you see the Marshall Republican [newspaper] that contained a list of deserters from this Division. Dr. Cox of Belleview and Lee Wiley of Starrville were both published. A stigma that will last them for ever and their children & children's children."[32]

Like his fellow soldiers, John S. Bryan of the 16th Cavalry was determined to uphold the honor of his children. For a man "to withdraw his servis from the confedracy at this the darkest hours that our little republic has ever seen will brand him with a name that he will carry to his grave[.] nor will it stop thair[.] he has even disgrased his family if he has one[.] perhaps when he is dead and gon it will be thrown in his childrens fase that thair father deserted from the army." Volney Ellis of the 12th Infantry, answering his wife's plea that he come home any way he could, scolded her in flowery Victorian prose: "The service of the country has demanded the sacrifice of our separation, and without dishonor I could not come to you. Dishonor. Oh! how my dear Mary would have turned from me at my own door with this foul blot upon my brow; how reprovingly would have shone upon me the dark eyes of my little daughter and how guilty, guilty, thrice guilty would I have been to see the noble face of my infant son." Those Texans who did desert, obviously, managed to control their fear of dishonor, but a significant number of others worried themselves to distraction over society's good opinion of their families.[33]

What they feared most—other than the possibility that they might never see their wives and children again—was that their young children would forget them while they were away. Dozens of letters pleaded with wives to remind the children of their father, to show them a portrait. Other messages asked whether the children "have forgot me yet." Lt. E. Steele of the 12th Infantry expressed this fear almost as soon as he left home, even before he left Texas. "You must not let Manny forget me," he pleaded in February 1862. A month later: "tell all the children to learn fast and not forget me." Lt. Edward Cade of Smith County also worried while still within easy traveling distance of home in June 1862: "Kiss Henry—Don't let him forget his papa." Ten days later: "Don't let Henry forget papa."[34]

Private Farrow of Panola County was of course among the chief worriers. "I am very anxios to see you and my sweet children. Please do not let them forget me in my absence," he begged. Private Stoker could not bear the thought that his beloved Priscilla might drift away from him: "Write if Priscilla has forgot me or not." Five months later the possibility still gnawed at him. "I want to see you so bad I am nearley ded & the thoughts of Priscilas forgetting me, hurts me." Only a few weeks away from his home in Bastrop County, Sergeant Holcombe repeated the same theme. "Has the children quit talking of me?" he asked pitifully. "Has John & Charley forgotton me[?] kiss them for me."[35]

Images of wives and children swirled through the minds of the Texans during the long nights in Arkansas—bittersweet images. The pleasant memories of warm embraces, intimate conversations, and laughing children mixed with pangs of loneliness, worries about the farm, alarm that their children might forget them, and dread that they would never see their homes again. Some of the men finally could stand no more and stole away for Texas during the night. Most of them, though, remained in their tents, wondering why they were in the army, so far from home. After all, they had not yet fired a shot—or even heard a shot fired—against the Yankees.

# CHAPTER 5

# Walker's Greyhounds

While the Texans drilled in their Arkansas camps, the war continued all around them. In late November 1862, Confederates under Maj. Gen. Thomas C. Hindman attempted to push two small Federal armies in northwest Arkansas back into Missouri. The two sides fought to a tactical standoff at Prairie Grove, about 140 miles northwest of Little Rock, but Hindman's army, short on ammunition and supplies and plagued by desertion, retreated, solidifying the Union hold on northern and western Arkansas. Meanwhile, Major Generals Ulysses S. Grant and William T. Sherman drove toward one of the Confederacy's last strongholds on the Mississippi River, Vicksburg, 180 miles southeast of Little Rock.[1]

Thus, in the late fall and early winter of 1862, the Texas Division occupied a quiet corner of the war, about midway between two Federal campaigns and not involved in either. Confederate commanders in the trans-Mississippi region fumbled and dithered with the Texas troops, sending them first toward Vicksburg, then reversing them toward northwest Arkansas—and then compounding their indecision by reversing the march three more times. Then, on the heels of this confusion, command of the Confederate Trans-Mississippi Department changed from Theophilus H. Holmes to Lt. Gen. Edmund Kirby Smith. Smith continued the almost comical redirections of the Texans by sending them off to deal with still a third Federal campaign, this one under Maj. Gen. Nathaniel P. Banks in faraway central Louisiana. The division, sent east and then west—and then east and west and east again before turning south to Louisiana—traveled a thousand miles in these various marches and countermarches before it ever encountered the enemy. The men honestly earned the nickname attached to their unit ever since, the Greyhound Division.[2]

Rumors of a movement to engage the enemy began circulating in the camps on Bayou Meto on December 7. One story had the division headed back to Texas, another to relieve General Hindman in northwest Arkansas, and a third, to reinforce Vicksburg.[3] The reports of a transfer to Vicksburg, on the east bank of the Mississippi River, elicited some interesting and revealing comments from the men, especially when those comments are compared to their reaction to similar rumors nearly two years later. In the later case, many of the Texans flatly refused to cross the river, and hundreds deserted rather than put the river between them and their homes. In December 1862, on the other hand—when the men were still new to military life—they accepted the idea of a transfer east of the Mississippi with considerable equanimity.

Captain Petty admitted that "my feelings, inclinations and all my yearnings are to be in Texas if she is invaded . . . but I belong to the Confederacy and where ever the Authorities think it best for me to go I submit to." Theophilus Perry of the 28th Cavalry agreed. "I shall be glad to go," he told his wife, Harriet, doubtless to her dismay. Indeed, all the men seemed eager for the transfer, according to Perry. "The Men are in fine spirits. They expect hard fighting, but believe that the most good can be done on the Mississippi." John S. Bryan joined in the chorus: "if we can serve our country better on the other side of the Missippi than we can hear I am perfectly willing to go." Dozens of letters and dispatches referred to the rumored movement east of the Mississippi in late 1862, but none of them mentioned desertion or refusal to cross the river.[4]

The expected orders to move to Vicksburg arrived at Gen. Henry McCulloch's headquarters on December 10. The Texans packed up their clothes and tents and cooking utensils, stuffed their haversacks with whatever food they could scrounge, and tramped out across the wet prairie for Vicksburg on December 12 and 13. "It was the awfullest march I ever saw," Captain Petty wrote. "The water and mud was about from shoe mouth to half leg deep. The men fagged and broke down from heft of load and distance of march." Among the fatigued was Petty himself: "I [was] road foundered, foot sore, leg weary, hip shot and as near broke down as a man could well be." On the evening of the 13th, just after the men set up camp, a courier brought new dispatches from Little Rock ordering the division to abandon the move toward Vicksburg and begin a hike in the opposite direction toward Van Buren, 140 miles away in northwest Arkansas. Now the Texans were marching to reinforce General Hindman, retreating after the Battle of Prairie Grove. A few miles after they bypassed Little Rock on their westward jaunt two days later, new orders arrived, directing the division to reverse course toward Little Rock and await further instructions. After three sets of orders directing them to three different destinations in five days, some of the men understandably wondered exactly what was going on. "Our Generals it seems to me, are confused," Theophilus Perry grumbled. "It may be strategy but it looks to me like confusion."[5]

The Texans spent their first Christmas away from home on the Arkansas River across from Little Rock. Even the normally cheery Private Blessington had to admit it was "anything but a merry Christmas." No home fires, no wives, no children—not even a respectable Christmas dinner. Instead, they gnawed on "a piece of corn bread and some blue beef." At least the citizens of Little Rock could look to the left bank of the river on Christmas night and see thousands of camp-fires twinkling in the cold night air.[6]

The next day the division was put on the road again, this time toward Pine Bluff, forty straight-line miles southeast of Little Rock on the Arkansas River. Confederate authorities, worried that Federal gunboats might make a dash up the river toward Little Rock, had determined to strengthen the river's defenses. Some regiments left on the 26th, and others trailed a day or two behind. Considerable time was spent ferrying the men across to the right bank of the river, and the lead regiments proceeded only a few miles down the Pine Bluff road before establishing their camps for the night. At dress parade on the evening of the 26th, officers read an important order from General Holmes: Maj. Gen. John G. Walker had come from Robert E. Lee's army in Virginia to command the Texas Division. General McCulloch, the division's less experienced original leader, would assume command of George Flournoy's brigade.[7]

General Walker, forty years old, had been born in Jefferson City, Missouri, and educated at the Jesuit College in St. Louis (now Saint Louis University). His family had a distinguished record of public service. His grandfather had served on George Washington's staff during the War of Independence. His father, after marrying a niece of Andrew Jackson, had served for several years as Missouri's state treasurer. Walker enlisted in the U.S. Army during the Mexican War and fought with Gen. Winfield Scott's army from Vera Cruz to Mexico City, receiving a wound at Molino del Rey and a brevet rank of captain for gallant service. After the war he was promoted to captain and served at various army posts in Oregon, California, New Mexico, and Texas. Between assignments, he made a grand tour of Europe, visiting the great capitals of London, Paris, and Rome, at least part of the time with Sen. Stephen A. Douglas of Illinois. In short, on the eve of the Civil War, Walker was well equipped to lead. His prominent family had prepared him for great things; he was well educated and highly experienced and accomplished in his chosen field; and his travels across the United States, Mexico, and Europe had given him an unusually wide perspective on public affairs.[8]

Walker took his profession seriously. He studied George B. McClellan's reports on the Crimean War and demonstrated a sophisticated understanding of military procedures and concepts. After the Civil War erupted, he resigned from the U.S. Army and was appointed a major of cavalry in the regular army of the Confederacy. By September 1861 he was a colonel of infantry, and five months later he was promoted to brigadier general. His brigade was under heavy fire at Malvern Hill during the Peninsular campaign near Richmond, and he led a division during Stonewall Jackson's capture of Harpers Ferry. His division's skillful performance in the thick of the fight near the Dunker Church and Bloody Lane at Antietam brought him another promotion, to major general, in November 1862. Shortly afterward, the War Department ordered Walker to the Trans-Mississippi Department. Gen. Robert E. Lee regretted the reassignment of such a fine officer. "I feel that I am much weakened by the loss," Lee wrote Pres. Jefferson Davis, "but I hope the general service will be benefited." Walker was given command of the new Texas Division when he arrived at Little Rock in late December.[9]

Walker would lead the Texans for the next year and a half, through all of their wartime combat, and his name has been associated with the division ever since. The men took to the Missourian right away and in their old age always referred to their unit as "Walker's Texas Division," even though three other men also commanded them at one time or another. Newspapers reported his "unbounded popularity with his men," and individual soldiers and officers spoke highly of him. The comments of Capt. Harvey Wallace of the 19th Infantry and Private Blessington of the 16th Infantry were representative of many such evaluations: "our whole Army loves Gen Walker," Wallace wrote. "He is the best Gen. on this side of the Miss. sure treats his men best." Blessington remembered years later that Walker's "presence was always hailed with the wildest enthusiasm by both officers and soldiers." Douglas French Forrest, a Confederate naval officer who served on Walker's staff late in the war, confirmed the general impression. "The Genl. is the most popular General in the Trans Mississippi & has acquired his popularity by gallant service in the field & an equal & regular, but very rigid discipline."[10]

After his division was once again ordered to reverse directions and backtrack forty miles to Little Rock (because of reports that the Federals in northwest Arkansas were moving toward the state capital), the new commander joined his regiments on the road on a bitterly cold New Year's Day 1863. At dress parade that afternoon, under windy and darkening skies, officers read Walker's General Order No. 1, taking command of the division and announcing the names of his staff officers. General Walker himself, mounted on an iron-gray horse, circulated among the shivering troops, receiving introductions to their officers and making short talks to the men. On one of the coldest days he could remember, Pvt. John C. Porter of the 18th Infantry divided his time between getting warm and sizing up the new general. "The men, when allowed to break ranks, would pile up like logs to keep from freezing to death," Porter recalled. As for Walker, "he was a small man, weight about 140 lbs., height about 5 ft., 10 in., auburn hair, very large blue eyes, long bunch of beard upon his chin, and a mustache; in all a handsome man." If this new general could point the division in one direction—and keep it pointed—he would doubtless gain a great deal of respect from the soldiers.[11]

Finally, on January 5, the alarm from the northwest having proved false, General Walker turned his brigades around and marched them toward Pine Bluff once again. In the four weeks since December 10, the men had been ordered east to Vicksburg, then west to Van Buren, then east to Little Rock, then southeast to Pine Bluff, then back to Little Rock, and now to Pine Bluff again. "It was generally believed amongst the troops that General Holmes was advised by the Medical Board to give Walker's Division enough of exercise," Private Blessington joked. The regiments reached their camps a few miles west of Pine Bluff on January 8, 1863. Blessington found Pine Bluff, like Little Rock, much to his liking: "Some of the residences were very fine, and built of brick. Delightful gardens, tasteful lawns, and spacious streets, give the whole place an air of comfort and elegance." The men in Captain Petty's 17th Infantry agreed that the town was "quite a [busy], flourishing and pretty place."[12]

Some of the men, tired of tough army beef and hungry for their pre-war diet of pork, had become quite skillful at pork procurement, no matter where the hogs roamed or to whom they belonged. Virgil Rabb, a farmer from Fayette County before the war, took some pride in the ingenuity of his fellow soldiers. "The Government tries to feed us Texians on Poor Beef, but there is too Dam many hogs here *for that,* these Arkansaw hoosiers ask from 25 to 30 cents a pound for there Pork, but the Boys generally get it a little *cheaper than that.* I reckon you understand how they get it," he wrote his brother.[13] General McCulloch took the opportunity to establish firm discipline in his brigade by punishing a few of the less nimble-fingered men for their ham-handed hog hunting. "At this camp the division was formed in line of battle to witness three soldiers belonging to McCulloch's Brigade, drummed out of camp for 'hog-stealing,'" Private Blessington recalled. "The bands played 'The Rogue's March' along the line. The three soldiers marched along the entire line, followed by a file of soldiers, with fixed bayonets. This kind of punishment . . . seemed to be a novelty to the Texas boys, and it created roars of laughter amongst the troops."[14]

While the Texans set up their new camps near Pine Bluff, about fifty miles downriver other Confederates were sliding into a deep hole. Brig. Gen. Thomas J. Churchill and forty-nine hundred men, assigned to block the river against Federal thrusts toward Little Rock and central Arkansas, occupied a fort on the left bank at Arkansas Post. On the night of January 9, a Federal fleet of gunboats and troop transports approached the Confederate position. Union major general John A. McClernand's combined army-navy force, about thirty thousand men, had little trouble surrounding the outnumbered Confederates on January 10.

That night, dispatches from the beleaguered General Churchill reached Walker's division upriver at Pine Bluff. Send reinforcements, Churchill pleaded, and he would hold off the Federals as long as possible.[15]

Walker rousted his men out of their tents early the next morning and pushed them down the road toward Arkansas Post. The prospect of facing fire for the first time was chilling to some of the men. Captain Petty noted that some soldiers made the unusual request of being sent to the hospital. "Unwilling to face the music," he surmised. As for himself, "I don't know how I will stand the fire but I have made this promise to and request of my men that if any of them show the white feather I will shoot them with my own hands and if I show it for them to shoot me instantly." The captain was proud to say that his regiment was ready: "The news of a prospect of a fight was received by the regiment with cheers. . . . We will receive them *'with bloody hands to hospitable graves.'* "[16]

As his men—the courageous and faint-hearted alike—raced along, Walker received more dispatches from Churchill indicating that his situation was deteriorating rapidly. Having covered twenty-five miles on the 11th, the Texans resumed the push at daylight on the 12th. After marching only a few miles, Walker received word that Churchill had surrendered his men and the fort the previous afternoon after a furious Federal infantry assault and naval bombardment. The Texas Division's first opportunity to confront the enemy had slipped away. The Greyhounds were probably more fortunate than they realized. An extra six thousand Confederates, on the wrong side of the river, were more likely to be gobbled up by the victorious Federals than to provide a dramatic rescue of their comrades inside the fort.[17]

Having failed to turn back the enemy at Arkansas Post, the Confederates determined to set up a new strong point where Walker had halted his advance, about halfway between Pine Bluff and Arkansas Post, on the right bank of the river. If the Federals continued upriver, Generals Holmes and Walker wanted to contest the advance. Detachments from each company were sent with axes into the nearby woods to cut down timbers for breastworks. Other men were set to digging entrenchments in the cold, wet soil. All the while, the men glanced downriver, expecting any minute to see Yankee gunboats bearing down on them.[18]

The Texans were accustomed to hard physical labor, but not in these conditions. During their first night on the riverbank, freezing rain, sleet, and snow began falling, and the snow continued well into the next day. "The snow was from 4 to 6 inches deep, ground froze, tents froze so hard they stood alone," Surgeon Becton wrote his wife. Private Blessington remembered that even the clothes on their backs stiffened with ice. Then, to lighten the men's loads and protect the division's baggage in case of a battle, the generals sent most of the wagons upriver. "Each man to keep one blanket, each man a skillet or frying pan and axe. Sent off everything, tents and all," Captain Wallace wrote in his diary. Lt. Samuel Wright of Paris described the wretched conditions in a letter to his father. "I hauled on five shirts, three pairs of pants, and socks in proportion, and away went everything else with all of our baggage, tents and transportation. . . . I never saw men suffer so before. It felt kinder cold to lie down in snow and ice and try to sleep at night."[19]

Snow, sleet, and freezing rain continued to fall on the exposed troops over the next several days. Walker's foot soldiers had no choice but to shiver through the wet misery at the site they called "Camp Freeze Out." Pvt. John Porter of the 18th Infantry had to stand guard one night, an experience he never forgot: "it seemed the two hours never would pass. I could hold up my hand, and the water would run from the elbow of my sleeve in a stream; and when my time was out, the fires in camp were all drowned out, and I really felt fears of freezing to death before I could start one up." Without their tents, some men did freeze to death, and their icy bodies were buried in the cold mud beside the river. Surgeon Becton of the 22nd Infantry, the man whose wife had instructed him to die at his post rather than disgrace his name, labored through the whole experience with a longer perspective than most of his comrades: "I frequently tell the boys when they complain that this will do to tell our boys about when we are old."[20]

After a week of cutting and hauling trees, digging earthworks, and sleeping in ice and snow, the Confederates learned that General McClernand's Federals had leveled the defenses at Arkansas Post and returned downstream to the Mississippi River. General Grant had plans around Vicksburg for the victors of Arkansas Post. Their labors now meaningless, the Texans packed up the few belongings they still had with them—muskets, blankets, skillets, and axes—and prepared for a return march to Pine Bluff, happy at least to leave Camp Freeze Out behind them. The return trip was nearly as miserable as their week-long stay on the riverbank. "The roads from shoe mouth to knee deep in mud and water, some snow still on the ground, the ground still frozen underneath in places," Captain Wallace scribbled in his diary. Edwin Becton tried to describe the experience to his wife: "Now imagine 12 regiments & a great many wagons & ambulances going over the same ground the same day & you will have some faint idea what a time we had." The artillery batteries attached to Walker's column had a particularly hard time slogging through the mud. "The roads in some places seemed to have no bottoms," a lieutenant in Daniel's battery wrote. "The gun carriages would go under sometimes nearly out of sight." Some of the teamsters ahead of the column had lightened their wagons by throwing away the men's baggage: "Our tents, pots, ovens, and clothing were strewed for thirty miles," a private in the 22nd Infantry wrote his wife. The road along the river was such a quagmire, in fact, that some of the men had their shoes sucked off their feet by the mud, and the columns were soon detoured off the road through the nearby fields. On they squished and sloshed for two days, blinking against the rain in their faces, until they reached Pine Bluff on January 20.[21]

Despite their failed rescue attempt, their useless construction of earthworks along the river, and the unspeakable conditions in which they labored, the Texans rediscovered their usual high spirits on the road back to Pine Bluff. Some of the men sang "'The Bonnie Blue Flag,' and other patriotic songs" and others joked about their miserable plight in Arkansas. "I frequently passed crowds of men & boys hollowing laughing, singing, swearing &c &c.," Becton wrote. "I remember passing a crowd & one fellow, in answer to some question, remarked 'there are no boys & plow horses in Texas—all *men & race horses*." Even the perennially upbeat Blessington marveled at his comrades' resilience: "It appears almost incredible that men could exhibit such reckless indifference, such strength of will and determination, after such a week of bitter experiences as these men underwent. The war, however, developed and decided some strange theories as to the amount of physical powers which the human frame contained."[22]

Soldiers were not the only people caught up in the war, and, as usually happened when a Federal army penetrated into Confederate territory, civilian refugees flooded the roads, seeking safety deeper in the interior. John T. Knight of the 22nd Infantry noted the flight as early as January 12: "The planters are runing their negroes today every direction. Some of them are going to the cane brakes. Some of them are going to Texas. The people are the worst scared people that I ever saw." An officer in the 13th Cavalry described the panic in Pine Bluff: "I never saw so much excitement in my life, as there is now in this town. All of the citizens, are leaving as fast as they can get away, & taken all of their furniture out of the place. Gen. Holmes has ordered government property to be removed from the river & all negro to be taken out of the country & they have been sending them several days to Texas." Lieutenant Perry agreed: "The people are running in every direction down here. I have met hundred[s] of negroes, many of them endeavoring to make their own escape from the common enemy of them & mankind. They come in all styles, in wagons, carts, water carts, on horses & mules."[23]

Samuel Wright of Lamar County was struck by the forlorn appearance of previously prosperous plantations along the river. "It is all abandoned now and looks deserted. The roads are lined with fugitives—little niggers—people of all sorts, dogs, pigs, all promiscuously mixed up. Old homesteads are being hastily abandoned, magnificent residences are closed and little groups of sad women, weeping children, and old servants with such belongings as they can carry walk along the roads, seeking safer refuge farther south from the dreaded federals." Volney Ellis of the 12th Infantry summed it all up: "everything looked like the besom [i.e., broom] of destruction had passed over the very best country in the world." The citizens of Arkansas were learning the hard lesson that war extends far beyond the battlefield.[24]

The Texas Division remained at Pine Bluff for three months, first at Camp Mills northwest of town and then at Camp Wright directly north of town on the riverbank. In almost every way, army life during those weeks improved for the men. First, General Walker arranged sixty-day furloughs for two men in each company, to the "general satisfaction" of the whole division. In addition, the men were reunited with their tents and a sufficient number of blankets to keep them warm at night. Then the hard Arkansas winter of 1862–1863 gave way to "bright, clear, and pleasant days," and the health of the men improved along with the weather. "Fields lately luscious with vines are drooping with amber-colored corn, all of them covered over [with] white tents, arranged with street-like precision, with regiments or battalions on parade or review, with martial music echoing along the river-bank, from splendid bands," Private Blessington recorded. "Add to this the Arkansas River, flowing on in majestic grandeur, on its bosom numerous transports steaming up and down. Such was our encampment at Camp Wright." Fair weather, better health, and a fine campground lifted Texas spirits and seemed like a dream compared to their recent tribulations.[25]

For the first time, the Texans began to encounter enemy soldiers, but usually they were deserters from the Yankee army. Elijah Petty of the 17th Infantry noted that "since the fall of the Arkansas Post desertion has been the order of the day with the Feds. They have been pouring into . . . Pine Bluff & to Little Rock by ones, twos, in squads and by Companies to be paroled and sent home until I am informed near 1000 have been paroled." President Lincoln's recent proclamation freeing the slaves offended some western men, and many Union soldiers willingly surrendered (in order to be paroled) rather than fight a war to end slavery. "They say that they will no longer fight under Lincoln's proclamation and the people at home will sustain them," Petty explained to his wife. David Ray, a schoolteacher from Grayson County, gave the same reports about the Yankees to his mother: "They represent that Lincoln's Emancipation proclamation is having a very demoralizing effect on the Federal army, that numbers of them are going home swearing they will fight no longer for Abraham."[26]

John Knight confirmed the stories told by others in Walker's division. "The feds are deserting daily and coming to Pine Bluff to get paroles," Knight wrote. "They make an average of 10 per day. . . . They say that they are not fighting to free the negroes nor dont intend to. They say that they have been fighting to restore the union but never intend to fight any more." Pvt. William Stoker of the 18th Infantry discerned the same motives among the Federals: "They say they want it [the war] to close so they can go back home & liv like white folkes. There has ben 1100 of them deserted & come over since the fight at the post. They said they [set] out to fight for the union, but it has run into the negro question & they aint going to hav any thing to do with it." Volney Ellis, a Lavaca County attorney before the war, saw favorable signs in all these desertions. "We have some excitement relative to Lincoln's emancipation proclamation. . . . We all hope that it may have the effect to produce an explosion in his own magazine."[27]

These Texans noted a serious problem in the western Union army in the winter of 1863, a problem that Federal soldiers confirmed in their own letters and diaries and campfire conversations. An Ohioan near Vicksburg wrote his sweetheart about the uproar in Federal camps: "It would give you some amusement to listen to the profound discussions carried on in each tent—all the time, the Negro question predominating. . . . Lincoln's proclamation was not very well received by this portion of the army, they holding that it has come down to be a nigger war, fighting for the Blacks etc." An Iowa private, still in his camp of instruction, noted the same attitudes among his comrades. "The Proclamation is not endorsed by a majority here. The boys in the union brigade do not like it. They say the army below [near Vicksburg] is also opposed to it."[28] The Texans doubtless hoped that all these signs pointed to an early end to the war, but of course the war would grind on for another two years.

Despite the comparatively pleasant conditions in the camps near Pine Bluff, desertion worked its way through some of the units in Walker's division that spring. The men were not discouraged about the cause or defeatist—the Confederacy was still vigorous, and victory was still seemingly within its grasp. Rather, their long absence from home without furloughs, their loneliness, the poor rations and high prices for civilian food, and the lack of any movement or activity in this backwater of the war led some of the Texans to slink away in the darkness of night. One Texan blamed the unhappiness in the ranks partly on the lack of furloughs: "We have a great deal of dissatisfaction through out our regiment simply because our time is about to expire, & no prospect of going home very soon just raving and pitching about it & swore they will not stand it." A soldier in the 22nd Infantry wrote that "the men are still deserting from our Regt, 8 men left night before last. It is supposed that they all rode off as there was several mules and horses missing." Col. Richard Waterhouse believed the dullness of camp life drove some of the men to desert: "This division of the army are getting very tired and restless on account of the great inactivity that seems to prevale."[29]

A member of the 22nd Infantry laid the blame primarily on poor rations. John Knight wrote his wife that "the way that we have been fed is enough to kill the last one of us." In fact, he continued, "if I had what we throad away last year I could live fine. Yes if I had them old line peaces of meat and hock joynts & joles [jowls] I could make it get further." John Simmons of Smith County growled, "We live horrible. We have nothing but bread to eat. We scarcely ever get any meat to eat at all—probably one pound in ten days. I am thinking all the time of my empty stomach and when I can get some meat to eat. We are mad all the time, and the cause is we are hungry, and the government won't feed us. You need not be surprised to see us all coming home before they get ready for us to come, some of these days."[30]

Enlisted men, paid only eleven dollars a month—when pay was available—often could not compensate for their inadequate diets with purchases from civilians. "The army has been so long on this river that everything a soldier desires has reached the most enormous prices, anything in the way of luxuries such as chickens, eggs, butter, &c. are becoming entirely beyond their reach on account of the prices placed upon them," one member of the 12th Infantry complained. Private Stoker of the 18th Infantry grumbled about high food prices and dreamed of a good meal: "If I get to come home [on furlough], youl see some of the powerfulest eatting you ever saw, for I am nearley perrished out for something good to eat. I havent had any milk since last summer." Some of the officers sympathized with their men and half excused their rebelliousness. "Since we have been in Arkansas the men have spent half their wages in provisioning themselves when it was the duty of the government to do it," Captain Petty wrote. "It is hard for the private to serve for $11 per month and buy his own clothes and board himself. It is becoming unbearable and the men will not submit much longer."[31]

More of Walker's Texans were shot for desertion—a dozen or more—in the winter and spring of 1863 than during any other comparable period of the war, if comments from the men are any indication. Dozens of letters and diary entries written at Pine Bluff mention these executions by firing squads. The witnesses generally recoiled at the sight of their comrades kneeling on their coffins and slumping over into their graves. Some of those who flinched nevertheless understood the military necessity. Even though he sympathized with their plight, Captain Petty would not countenance desertion: "I hope the scoundrels will be caught and shot. I dont want our Southern society disfigured with the slime of deserters or traitors." After the names of some deserters were published in Texas newspapers, Edward Cade of the 28th Cavalry shuddered at the stain on the rep-

utations of those men. It was a stigma that would mark their families for generations.[32]

While the Texans had been marching back and forth across Arkansas in the
winter of 1862–1863, all to no effect, the Confederate high command in Richmond made a fundamental change in the leadership of the trans-Mississippi
army. On January 14 Pres. Jefferson Davis appointed Lt. Gen. Edmund Kirby
Smith to command the troops west of the Mississippi River. Smith was one of
the Confederacy's brightest stars in early 1863. A graduate of the U.S. Military
Academy and a veteran of the Mexican War, he had led a brigade at the First
Battle of Manassas (Bull Run) and played an important role in the Confederate
victory there. While the Texans were marching to Arkansas in the fall of 1862,
Smith had led an army north into Kentucky, almost to the Ohio River, and had
commanded his troops at the Battle of Perryville. Because Generals Hindman
and Holmes had seemingly made such a hash of affairs in Arkansas and the
trans-Mississippi theater, President Davis sent Smith west of the river to establish
order and infuse new life into the military there. The general did not arrive in
the Trans-Mississippi Department until early March, and he made few immediate changes when he did reach his new command, but he would bring some system to the Confederate war effort west of the Mississippi River and lead the
department for the remainder of the conflict.[33]

Few of the men in Walker's division noted the change in their high command,
but those who did were happy to see someone of Smith's stature replace Theophilus Holmes, the general who had seemingly botched their war so far. Captain
Petty was "truly glad" of the change. "I look upon Genl H as a dilapidated old
Granny and a drunkard besides. He has done no good nor ever will here," Petty
wrote his daughter. "The confidence of the soldiery and people have departed
from [him]. Genl S has a world wide reputation, has won it deservedly at
Mannassas and other battle fields and will beget a confidence and impart an energy that will result in good to the Confederacy." Colonel Waterhouse claimed
that his men were pleased with the change in command and blamed Holmes's
mismanagement partly on the general's advanced age (fifty-eight): "It seems that
the management of this Dept has not been very skillful for a man of age, skil,
and ability at the head of affairs. General Holmes can at least lay claime to the
1st named qualification as he is an old man."[34]

General Smith and his staff toured Louisiana and Arkansas upon their arrival
west of the Mississippi River and found conditions in the trans-Mississippi below
acceptable standards. Although Smith was kind in his comments about Holmes,
he found that "there was no general system, no common head; each district was
acting independently." In addition to "a great deficiency of arms and equip-

ments," Smith also discovered that he had far fewer troops in Arkansas than he thought—only two infantry divisions of about five thousand men each and scattered cavalry units. His chief of staff, William Boggs, complained that "there was no system of communication between the different district headquarters," so events along the Mississippi River were unknown to commanders farther inland. Smith and his staff set about immediately to provide better integration of the Confederate war effort west of the Mississippi.[35]

When they began connecting the pieces of the Trans-Mississippi Department, they discovered that the Federals were marching an army right through their territory. Maj. Gen. Ulysses S. Grant, having failed to get at Vicksburg by marching overland from the north or by cutting canals or by navigating the Yazoo swamps, determined in the late winter of 1863 to land his army on the west bank of the Mississippi River, march down the Louisiana side, and recross the river to the higher, drier terrain south and east of the river city. Accordingly, on March 29 he ordered General McClernand, conqueror of Arkansas Post, to march his corps south from Milliken's Bend (about twenty-five miles upstream from Vicksburg) to New Carthage (about thirty miles downstream from the city). The remainder of Grant's army would follow in the footsteps of McClernand's corps and then, with the help of the Federal river fleet, cross to the Mississippi side.[36]

In mid-April, when General Smith learned of Grant's push, he also discovered another Federal penetration into the Trans-Mississippi. Maj. Gen. Nathaniel P. Banks was driving his Union army from south Louisiana north toward Alexandria in the central part of the state. By this time, every Confederate regional commander was calling on every other for help. Lt. Gen. John C. Pemberton at Vicksburg wanted reinforcements from west of the river, Smith wanted reinforcements from Vicksburg and Texas, and Maj. Gen. Richard Taylor, outnumbered and falling back before Banks, wanted reinforcements from anywhere. Facing major threats on the river around Vicksburg and in central Louisiana, General Smith reacted on April 14–15 by ordering Walker's Texas Division to move quickly from Pine Bluff to Monroe, Louisiana, seventy miles west of Vicksburg and ninety miles north of Alexandria (see Map 3). From Monroe, Walker could strike at Grant's army strung out along the river or rush to the aid of Taylor near Alexandria. Finally, it appeared, a year after their original muster, the Texans would have a chance to contribute something to the war effort.[37]

General Holmes, now commanding forces in Arkansas, took his time sending Walker's division to Louisiana. On April 19 Smith pleaded with Holmes to get Walker's Texans on the road to Louisiana as soon as possible and to arrange for river transports to meet the Texans on the way. They could march part of the journey and then board the transports for a quicker dash to Monroe. Not until

# Map 3
## Arkansas and Louisiana, 1862–1863

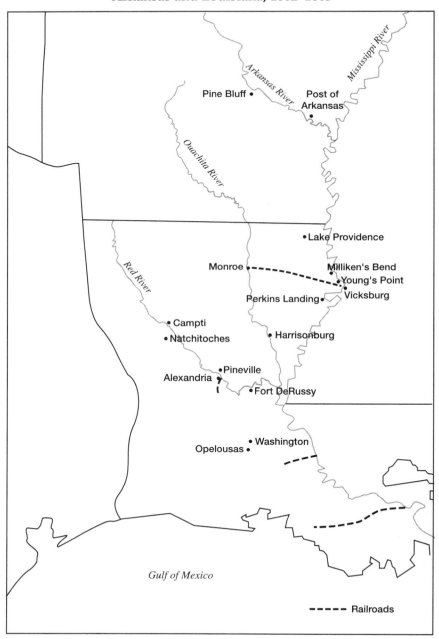

Mississippi River

Arkansas River

Pine Bluff •

Post of Arkansas

Ouachita River

• Lake Providence

Red River

Monroe • — — — •Milliken's Bend
•Young's Point
Perkins Landing• •Vicksburg

• Campti

• Natchitoches

• Harrisonburg

•Pineville
Alexandria •
•Fort DeRussy

• Washington
Opelousas •

*Gulf of Mexico*

- - - - - Railroads

the evening of the 23rd, nine days after Smith issued his orders, were Walker's regiments officially informed of their mission to move to Monroe, 120 straight-line miles to the south. Meanwhile, General Grant's divisions were sloshing down the west bank of the Mississippi River and concentrating below Vicksburg for their river crossing.[38]

Walker's Texans were happy finally to have a sense of purpose. A lieutenant in the 11th Infantry wrote that "all is joy at the move. I hear a thousand voices shouting now over the news—all is bustle in making preparations." Samuel Wright, a lieutenant in Daniel's battery, agreed: "I never saw such enthusiasm in my life." At 5 A.M. on April 24, the first regiments marched out of their camps at Pine Bluff, south toward Monroe, and the last units of the division moved the next morning to the music of military bands.[39] The advance to Monroe must have reminded some of the Texans of their early days in Texas when civilians cheered them at every village and crossroads. Captain Petty was delighted at the response along the way: "The ladies in perfect swarms were on the road side at every house. At points the whole neighborhood would assemble and such waving of handkerchiefs and throwing boquets I havent seen hardly in my life."[40]

A soldier in the 16th Infantry also noticed the large numbers of women along the road. "Crowds of women (and there are more women in this part of the state than any place I ever saw) collect on the sides of the streets and roads and wave their handkerchiefs and throw bouquets of flowers into the ranks," he wrote. "Some old ladies prayed aloud for us as we passed through Monticello, while some middle-aged ones wept as if some near and dear relative had died." Lt. Samuel Wright noted that the men loved the attention. "Every soldier has his hat ornamented with many varieties of roses and carries boquets in his hands," he informed his father. "We have visitors to the camp every night, and I do the honors to the best of my ability, telling the old women some of the biggest lies imaginable, which they swallow like a plain unvarnished tale, and which they repeat next day."[41]

The Texans proceeded more in the fashion of basset hounds than greyhounds on this march, averaging only about thirteen miles per day. Spring rains had turned the roads to mush, and the wagons and men found the going slow. "Sections of road for miles would have to be laid down, or 'corduroyed', with logs to permit the passage of the baggage and subsistence trains, and bridges, carried away by the floods, [had to be] reconstructed by engineer and pioneer corps," General Walker complained. After eight days of road building, the division crossed the state line into Louisiana on May 1, still about forty straight-line miles and nearly ninety road miles from their destination at Monroe. Four days later the Texans had pushed as far as Ouachita City, a nondescript port on the Ouachita River, about thirty-five miles directly north of Monroe. Waiting for them there were a dozen riverboats, ready to carry the lead brigade the rest of the way. After zipping along at the breathtaking speed of eleven miles per hour, the transports landed the men at Trenton, two miles upriver from Monroe, and then returned to bring down the rest of the division.[42]

The Texans remained at Trenton four days as the transports deposited the men, regiment by regiment, on the riverbank. Even before they left Pine Bluff, General Smith had decided to send Walker's Texans to the relief of Richard Taylor, retreating before Banks's superior numbers near Alexandria, ninety air miles south of Monroe. Interference with Grant's brigades, pushing down the Mississippi River only seventy miles to the east, would have to wait. In an inspired moment of strategic understanding, Brig. Gen. Paul O. Hébert, commander in northeast Louisiana, suggested to Walker that he send at least part of his division to cut the vulnerable Federal lifeline along the river. Walker, already smarting from Smith's reprimands for his slow movement from Pine Bluff and Smith's peremptory orders to hurry to Taylor's aid, could only shake his head in disappointment. In his postwar memoirs, General Walker lamented Smith's strategy: "if Gen. Smith had thrown his whole force at this period upon Grant's communications . . . it would, undoubtedly, have forced the Federal General to open up his communications with the upper Mississippi at the expense of suspending operations against Vicksburg." But Smith was in charge, and Walker could only regret the lost opportunity.[43]

To complicate matters, Smith and Taylor had already been forced out of Alexandria and had retreated up the Red River toward Shreveport in the northwest corner of Louisiana. After some initial confusion about how best to link the forces of Walker and Taylor now that Taylor was retreating up the Red River, Smith concluded that Walker could reach Taylor more quickly by water than by marching overland. Smith therefore ordered Walker to use the riverboats at Trenton to move his division south, down the Ouachita River and connecting waterways, to within twenty miles of Alexandria. Once the Texans reached the vicinity of Alexandria, they could cast about until they found Taylor's retreating army somewhere to the northwest. The advantage of the water route was that it was quicker. The disadvantage was that it would put Walker's Texans perilously close to Banks's much larger army.[44]

At sunrise on May 9, two days after General Banks's sixteen thousand Federals occupied Alexandria, Walker's division of about six thousand Confederates boarded transports to steam downriver toward the same city. Theophilus Perry of the 28th Cavalry was optimistic about the advance: "Our Division is in high spirits, and seem to speak and feel as if it will be the main dependence and stay of an army. We are composed of Texans alone & are about six thousand five hundred fighting men with three batteries—16 guns. It is a right pretty little army of itself, and as it seems to expect great things of itself I am in hopes they will do themselves honor."[45]

At 8 A.M. the signal whistles sounded, and the convoy of fourteen transports pulled away from the riverbank, chugging south past Monroe on the three-hundred-yard-wide stream. Private Blessington, as usual, found the experience exhilarating: the people of Monroe "appeared to have turned out in mass to witness us passing by. The ladies waved their handkerchiefs as a token of friendship, and the bands played some of their favorite pieces of music, to please the ladies." Captain Petty was just as excited: "It presented a grand scene to see us steaming one after another down this beautiful river with banners fluttering, bands playing, men huzzaing and cheering, with the bank lined with ladies with palpitating hearts and fluttering handkerchiefs." This was the way to travel—no marching, no dust, no mud, no knapsacks to lug, just floating down the stream. On they steamed for several hours, down the winding course of the Ouachita.[46]

About halfway to Alexandria, as the convoy approached Harrisonburg, a courier from Taylor's retreating army hailed the lead boat and informed General Walker that Banks had already occupied Alexandria, that part of the Union army was now moving north toward Harrisonburg, and—most important—that Federal gunboats were steaming upriver toward Harrisonburg and Walker's own convoy. The transports carrying the Texans were not designed or armed for hostile action, and the possibility of being blasted off the river by the big guns of the enemy navy (including eleven pieces of heavy artillery) had to be faced. Walker therefore ordered the riverboats to turn around and steam back to Trenton. Pvt. John Porter of the 18th Infantry was on Walker's lead vessel when it turned back upriver. "We had gone but a little way when we came in sight of the first boat in rear, which, as soon as they saw us in retreat, began to turn around, without waiting [for] any information or orders, and so did the whole fleet, which were wild with excitement, both soldiers and boatsmen; but after many threats from Gen. Walker, he got them quiet enough to explain the cause of our retreat," Porter recalled.[47]

Captain Petty was on one of the transports farther back in the convoy. When they saw the lead boats coming upriver, the pilots of the other transports "turned and commenced steaming back up the river each one trying to get ahead of the others and all running seemingly for life. No one knew the cause of our retrograde movement. All supposed that the gun boats were after us. Men were excited to a high pitch—some got their guns, some loaded pistol and some did one foolish thing and some another." Finally, General Walker's lead boat came alongside, and the general explained the about-face and assured the men that there was no cause for alarm. Walker's calming words were not totally effective on some of the Texans. Private Porter recalled that "many ludicrous stories were afterwards told upon the officers of other Brigades and Regts., such [as] a Col. Filpots [Benjamin A. Phillpot of the 12th Infantry] ordering his men to throw their rations of bacon into the furnace for fuel, and when told that the bacon was all exhausted, told them to heave in their greasy haversacks. And offering his services to the pilot to help turn his wheel, which, when rejected, he mounted the chicken coop on the hurricane deck with his spurs to urge the boat forward."[48]

The Texans did not know, as they looked over their shoulders for smoke from the pursuing gunboats, that the pursuers were far behind them. In fact, the Federal fleet was stopped cold at Harrisonburg the next day by the spirited resistance of a small force of Louisiana infantry manning a two-gun battery of 32-pounders. Walker's nervous convoy finally reached the camps at Trenton at 3 A.M. on May 10, nineteen hours after they had steamed away to the sounds of music and cheering civilians. It had been an exciting if fruitless excursion.[49]

Having failed to reach Taylor by water, Walker's division was now directed to move overland to the Red River valley and link up with Taylor at Natchitoches, about 120 road miles southwest of Monroe. Two of Walker's three brigades started immediately after leaving the riverboats on the morning of May 10. General Walker and McCulloch's brigade remained at Trenton for nearly a week, preparing to meet the Federals if they came up the Ouachita River to Monroe. While they waited, Walker and McCulloch and their staffs were entertained by the citizens of Monroe and the vicinity. One of the young ladies of the community, twenty-two-year-old Kate Stone, was a refugee from her family's plantation, about forty miles east of Monroe. She and her friends found the smartly uniformed staff officers irresistible. "All of the staff made themselves agreeable, and the girls went wild over them and so flattered and complimented them that I think another week of it would have ruined the young officers," she wrote in her diary. "We went over to see the drill, and the compliments heaped on the officers were enough to turn the heads of so many Solomons. It was about their first experience with soldiers, and the girls ran wild." Such pleasant diversions were temporary, however, and the Texans at Monroe were soon on the road again.[50]

When the Confederates realized that Banks's penetration had been stopped at Harrisonburg and that Monroe was safe, McCulloch put his own men on the road on May 16, following in the tracks of their comrades toward the Red River. As they tramped out of Trenton and Monroe, the men received one last gesture of support from the Stone family. "The children, headed by Sister [thirteen-year-old Amanda]," Kate wrote in her diary, "were in a great state of excitement and spent most of the day perched on the fence with buckets and gourds of water, offering it to the hot, tired soldiers, who every now and then hurrahed for the little girl in red. Sister was a blaze of scarlet in her Turkey-red calico." The soldiers had found Arkansas excessively muddy, but on this journey Louisiana seemed to be clouded in dust. Still, dusty or not, the march toward Natchitoches was accompanied by cheering and flowers. "We have been treated with every Kindness & respect by all of the citizens in our Route both in Arkansas & Louisiana," Theophilus Perry wrote. "The ladies come to see us in crowds at every cross road & public place. They strew our path with flowers and cheer us on our way in all the ways they know how to use." Indeed, "in Mount Lebanon the ladies came out, and took the lame & sore footed soldier by the hand & carried them in to their houses to dinner."[51]

After seven days on the road, McCulloch's brigade caught up to the rest of the division on May 22 at Campti, on the left bank of the Red River ten miles north of Natchitoches. While the division had been moving from Trenton to Campti, General Banks had packed up his army and turned it around, leaving Alexandria and central Louisiana and moving back toward the Mississippi River to cooperate with Grant's army. Gen. Richard Taylor's small Confederate army had left Natchitoches on May 20 to reclaim the territory they had lost when Banks advanced from south Louisiana. Thus, Walker's division once again missed the action, and the Texans had to move down the Red River to catch up with Taylor. The Greyhound Division may have marched more steps per shot fired than any other division on either side in the entire war.[52]

Walker's soldiers were shocked by reports of the ruin Banks's army had spread up the Red River valley. Samuel Wright of Lamar County wrote his father that Banks "robbed the country of everything and utterly devast[at]ed it as he passed, burning houses and plantations entirely up and taking all horses, mules and live stock." Captain Petty informed his wife that the Federals had left central Louisiana only after "laying waste farms, breaking sugar kettles, destroying farming utensils, household furniture, beds, clothing, etc., stealing all the negroes & other transportable property and carrying it away with them." The stories were essentially correct. General Banks informed the War Department in Washington that "the destruction of foundries and shops, and the seizure of horses, carts, & c., throughout the whole of that district . . . has made it impossible to organize and supply a large force from that country." In fact, Banks had piled millions of dollars in confiscated property in two thousand wagons when his army left Alexandria for the Mississippi River.[53]

The Texans, eager to finish their endless marching and see some action, had to wait four more days at Campti before steamboats arrived from Shreveport to carry them downriver to join Taylor. Finally, on May 26 the tardy transports huffed up to the landings, and the men crowded aboard for the trip to Alexandria, about one hundred river miles to the southeast. By the next morning the men were trotting down the gang planks and setting up a new camp near the falls of the Red River, about two miles above the town of Alexandria. Horace Randal's brigade continued downstream, hoping to catch trailing units of Banks's army before they reached the Mississippi River, but Banks was gone, and Randal's regiments rejoined the other two brigades the next day.[54]

In the month after they left their camps at Pine Bluff, Walker's Texans had marched 250 miles through Arkansas mud and Louisiana dust and steamed 260 miles up and down the Ouachita and Red Rivers. And still they had not fired a shot at the enemy. In other theaters during the same period, Generals Lee and Jackson had stunned a Federal army at Chancellorsville in Virginia and Grant had fought his way to the outskirts of Vicksburg. The Texans may be forgiven for wondering whether their generals would ever get it right. "Why all this boxing the compass[,] this marching and countermarching I can hardly form a conjecture," Captain Petty grumbled on May 27. The lawyer from Bastrop was only eleven days away from his first battle.[55]

# CHAPTER 6

# Milliken's Bend

While the Texans traveled from Trenton to Campti to Alexandria, their superiors in the Trans-Mississippi Department were discussing what to do with them next. Now that General Banks's Federal army was slipping away to besiege Port Hudson on the Mississippi River near Baton Rouge, General Smith thought Walker's division should be aimed at Grant's supply line along the west bank of the Mississippi near Vicksburg. Smith was under considerable pressure to reinforce or somehow relieve the garrison in Vicksburg, now virtually surrounded by Grant's army and the U.S. Navy. If Walker's division could snap the long Federal supply line on the Louisiana side of the river, Grant might be forced to turn away from Vicksburg and perhaps even abandon the whole campaign. A similar strike at his communications by only thirty-five hundred Confederate cavalrymen at Holly Springs, Mississippi, the previous December had accomplished that very purpose. Grant seemed even more vulnerable now because his supply line was longer and on the other side of a great river from his army.[1]

The general assigned to sever those Federal communications was thirty-seven-year-old Richard Taylor. The son of former president Zachary Taylor and former brother-in-law of Confederate president Jefferson Davis, Richard Taylor was one of the most colorful and interesting figures in the Confederate army. Educated in one of the best preparatory schools in Massachusetts and at Yale College, he easily acquired the social graces his military father never mastered. One of his Yale classmates described him as "handsome, always finely dressed, popular, generous, talented, and rather easy-going." A close friend, future Confederate general Dabney Maury, recognized Taylor's outstanding qualities as early as the 1840s. "Even then Taylor was self-reliant and brilliant in conversation; all he said was terse, and illustrated by vivid and classical metaphor," Maury recalled. "Keen sarcasm and ready wit abounded in his talk, and in a circle of gentlemen educated in the highest social associations of this country he was pronounced by all of them the most brilliant young man they had ever met." Taylor at first managed for his father and then owned a sugar plantation thirty miles upriver from New Orleans, joining in the highest circles of southern plantation society in the 1850s.[2]

When war interrupted his life as a planter, Taylor threw his considerable support to the Confederacy. He took command of a Louisiana infantry regiment in the summer of 1861 and led one of Stonewall Jackson's finest brigades during the brilliant Shenandoah Valley campaign of spring 1862 (while the regiments of Walker's division were just being organized in Texas). In his postwar memoirs, Taylor provided some of the most revealing and colorful accounts of his Valley commander. Promoted to major general in the summer of 1862, Taylor was sent west by his former brother-in-law, Jefferson Davis, to command the Confederate District of West Louisiana.[3]

In the late spring of 1863, the Louisiana general was in a foul mood. His home had been sacked and plundered by Federal soldiers several months earlier, two of his beloved children, refugees in north Louisiana, had recently died of scarlet fever, and he had been forced to retreat up the Red River by General Banks, a man for whom Taylor had little respect. Now Smith was ordering him on a mission that, Taylor believed, was foolish and useless. Sloshing around the swamps west of Vicksburg—unapproachable from the Louisiana shore, according to Taylor—could accomplish little if anything, and General Pemberton, refusing to come out of his Vicksburg defenses, was beyond aid. The Confederacy's best strategy, Taylor was certain, was to use his small army and Walker's division to cut through southern Louisiana and threaten New Orleans in a campaign of misdirection. General Banks, besieging Port Hudson 150 miles upriver, would be forced to raise the siege and rush back down to protect the Crescent City, too valuable a prize to lose. That in turn would allow the garrison at Port Hudson to rush north in aid of the defenders of Vicksburg. Marching north into the flooded lowlands west of the river, as Smith proposed, would be utterly useless, a waste of time and resources.[4]

If Taylor, 120 miles away and preoccupied with his own theater, had known all the particulars of the military situation around Vicksburg, he would have been even more adamant in his opposition to operations in that vicinity: the Federal supply line he was supposed to cut was no longer there. While Walker's division had been marching south from Pine Bluff in late April, General Grant had crossed his army to the east bank of the Mississippi River south of Vicksburg. For the next few weeks, the Federal army on the east bank of the Mississippi depended on supplies shipped down the west bank and then delivered over the river. For part of that time, the Federal wagon road on the Louisiana shore stretched as far as sixty-three miles, from Milliken's Bend, upriver from Vicksburg, to Hard Times, downstream from the city. Thus, Grant's army was most vulnerable to a slashing attack on its communications during the first three weeks of May. But the nearest body of Confederate troops capable of cutting the Federal lifeline at this golden moment, Walker's Texas Division, was sent in other directions—to Monroe, then down the Ouachita River, then southwest to Natchitoches—all to counter Banks's less threatening campaign in central Louisiana.[5]

Indeed, by the time Walker's Texans boarded the river transports at Campti to steam downriver to Alexandria on May 26, their opportunity to cut Grant's communications already had passed. Beginning on May 21, food, munitions, medicine, and other vital supplies were being shipped to Grant's army in large quantities via the Yazoo River and a connecting road north of Vicksburg, all on the east side of the Mississippi. After the war General Walker could only regret the lost possibilities: "The golden opportunity had been allowed to pass, Grant had completed the investment of Vicksburg, brushed away the obstructions to the navigation of the Yazoo River by his supply vessels, and thus rendered his line of operations and supply secure from attack."[6]

Taylor, unaware yet that Grant no longer depended on the old supply route, proposed his alternative strategy to Trans-Mississippi headquarters because he believed his plan was more practical. But Smith would not budge. "Remonstrances were of no avail," Taylor sighed. "I was informed that all the Confederate authorities in the east were urgent for some effort on our part in behalf of Vicksburg, and that public opinion would condemn us if we did not *try to do something*. To go two hundred miles and more away from the proper theatre of action in search of an indefinite *something* was hard." Nevertheless, Taylor bowed to his superior's orders and made arrangements to lead Walker's Texans back to northeast Louisiana, whence they had just come. Because time was pressing, Taylor decided to ship the Texas Division by water rather than have the men tramp overland for two weeks. A short march north of Alexandria would put the Texans on riverboats that would then ascend a series of waterways to the neighborhood between Monroe and Vicksburg.[7]

While the Texans milled around the north bank of the Red River just above Alexandria on May 27, an officer from the Confederate Inspector General's office filed an inspection report on Walker's division. The report counted 3,661 old large-bore muskets and 1,011 rifles of various types, mostly the highly effective and popular Enfields. Thus, the Texas Division, halfway through the war, was still armed primarily with outdated shoulder arms effective at less than one hundred yards. The three batteries attached to the division were equipped with nine bronze 6-pounders and five bronze 12-pounder howitzers. None of the batteries had the most effective artillery weapons of the war, the famous 12-pounder Napoleons. For the Greyhound Division, pride and a year of drill would have to compensate for second-rate arms.[8]

With new orders to return to northeast Louisiana, the lead regiments of the division left the Red River behind them on May 28 and marched north toward a landing on the Little River, where side-wheel steamboats were waiting to rush them northeast toward Vicksburg. After a hastily cooked meal on May 29, the men of McCulloch's brigade once again bounced up the gangplanks and crowded on board. Accompanying the brigade were Generals Taylor and Walker and their staffs. The other two brigades, commanded by Horace Randal and James M. Hawes, remained near the landing until other transports arrived over the next twenty-four hours.[9]

Theophilus Perry, waiting with Randal's brigade near the riverbank, scribbled a quick letter to his wife, Harriet, back in Marshall, Texas. Perry saw the signs of a coming battle: "We have freed ourselves of all encumbrance except a change of underclothes and a blanket." He warned Harriet that he probably would be under fire for the first time very soon. "I am hopeful. You must be so too," he wrote, but he admitted that "I feel awfully solemn." Perry ended his letter with words that must have sent a chill through his wife: "Farewell Harriet / Farewell Sugar Lumpy [his daughter] / Farewell Theophilus [his infant son]." Captain Petty, already aboard one of the lead transports, had the same nervous feeling. "I am told by those who know that in battle life is uncertain and that bullets and balls are wreckless & blind. One by chance might hit me and stop my writing & thinking process." Fearing that he might never see his daughter again, Petty felt obliged to instruct her on the proper way to conduct herself as she grew up—"be respectful to age, dignified & courteous to your equals. . . . Take a high & digni-fied stand in society," he wrote. "This may be my final parting advice to you."[10]

Along the Little River and through Catahoula Lake they chugged, and then farther north up to the Black River, where it fed into the Tensas. The latter stream paralleled the Mississippi River, about twenty miles to the east, from cen-tral Louisiana to the lowlands west of Vicksburg. Because of the scare three weeks earlier, when the men were certain that Federal gunboats were racing up behind them, and because enemy pickets were known to be scattered throughout the country between the Tensas and Mississippi, General Walker placed light artillery pieces in the bows of the steamboats and stationed lookouts on the upper decks of the transports to warn of approaching gunboats. No hostile smoke was spot-ted, though, and the three river convoys wound their way 250 miles to the head of navigation on the Tensas, about twenty-five miles southwest of Vicksburg. On the afternoon of May 30, the men of McCulloch's brigade trotted down the gang-planks, set up camp on the east bank of the Tensas, and began cooking their supper. Randal's brigade arrived late that evening, and Hawes came ashore a day later.[11]

Only a few hours after they left the transports, McCulloch's men were roused from their sleep, put into ranks, and sent trudging off through the thick night-time air of Louisiana. A small body of Federals was camped about ten miles away, at one of the points along the recent supply line on the Mississippi River, and General McCulloch wanted to bag them. To the music of frogs and insects in the surrounding darkness, the Texans moved eastward toward the river, passing the dark silhouettes of deserted farmhouses and empty barns and hoping to surprise the enemy in their tents. After pausing to bridge an unfordable bayou, the men resumed their march near dawn.[12]

The last plantation they reached, just as first light was creeping into the east, was Somerset, owned by the wealthy Perkins family and managed by Judge John Perkins Jr. The judge, an alumnus of Yale and the law department at Harvard, had served as a representative in the 33rd Congress (1853–1855), was chairman of the committee that drafted Louisiana's ordinance of secession, and was a Confederate senator in Richmond when the Texans marched onto his property. His neighbor directly across the river on the Mississippi side was Jefferson Davis, president of the Confederacy. To deprive the Federals of the use of his Somerset plantation, about one mile from the river, Judge Perkins himself had torched his home and two thousand bales of cotton, together worth hundreds of thousands of dollars, before the Yankees arrived in his neighborhood. An Illinois soldier who had recently passed this way was impressed by the layout: "There is a very fine garden about where the house used to stand; a beautiful grove of live-oaks stands between the garden and the river."[13]

Camped near the right bank of the Mississippi on the Perkins property was Col. Richard Owen's 60th Indiana Infantry Regiment. Fifty-three years old, Owen was a son of the famous British social reformer Robert Owen and brother of Robert Dale Owen, the American reformer and former congressman. An educated man of science, Colonel Owen had earned a medical degree and served as state geologist of Indiana in the 1850s. After the war he would earn a reputation as an eminent scholar of natural sciences at Indiana University, and he later served as president of the college that eventually became Purdue University. In late May 1863, however, he found himself in a tight spot. His pickets informed him early on the morning of the 31st that a large force of Confederate infantry (McCulloch's brigade of about fifteen hundred men) was bearing down on his regiment of three hundred, and reinforcements were nowhere near. Owen immediately hurried his men out of their camp, about a half-mile from the river. He ordered them and about three hundred fugitive slaves who had come into

Union lines to build breastworks of cotton bales atop the levee beside the river. Working quickly, the Hoosiers and their black co-workers built a three-sided fort of cotton bales, the open end of the works facing the river.[14]

While McCulloch's brigade closed in on Owen's regiment, a nearby Federal ironclad ship, the *Carondelet,* steamed down the river. Commissioned in early 1862, the 512-ton *Carondelet* bristled with heavy armament: four 8-inch smooth-bores, three nine-inch smoothbores, one 42-pounder smoothbore, one 32-pounder, a 30-pounder rifled gun, and a 50-pounder rifle. Heeding frantic signals from shore, the *Carondelet* edged over to the right bank of the river and agreed to provide cover for the Federal infantry until a transport could arrive and take them off the levee. To counter the heavy guns of the Federal behemoth, General McCulloch had only one light field battery of two 6-pounder and two 12-pounder smoothbores, barely enough firepower to dent the iron sides of the *Carondelet.*[15]

While the Federals were withdrawing toward the river and throwing up cotton bales, McCulloch's Texans came into view in the distance. Spying the enemy's tents between his brigade and the river, McCulloch put his regiments into line and charged across an open field and into the camp. The Texans were pleasantly surprised to find the camp empty, and they rummaged around the tents, liberating Yankee hardtack and coffee and finding the Indiana beverage much superior to their poor coffee substitutes. General McCulloch then reformed his lines and continued his advance toward the river, still several hundred yards away. By this time the Confederates could see that the Indiana regiment had taken refuge behind the cotton bales on the levee and under the wide muzzles of a Federal ironclad. McCulloch sent three of his four regiments into a nearby skirt of timber for concealment and placed two 6-pounders and his fourth regiment, the 19th Infantry, in the open for a duel with the *Carondelet,* a bold gesture considering the contrasting armaments.[16]

Capt. William Edgar's 6-pounders quickly unlimbered and threw their undersized charges in the direction of the cotton fort and the ironclad, already firing its big guns. The *Carondelet* sprayed some shells toward the Confederate field-pieces and some into the woods concealing the infantry. "The intervening valley was one dense cloud of smoke, which rose in floating canopies over it," as Private Blessington described it. "We could behold the sheets of flame, followed by volumes of smoke, jump out from the mouths of the brazen monsters, while the loud reverberating sounds echoed through the river valley." Captain Petty, standing with his company in the nearby timber, was relieved to observe that nearly all of the *Carondelet*'s shells flew high and wide: "They did'nt know where to find us & hence sent them out generally some exploding high in the air, some as they struck & some not [at] all." Edgar's fieldpieces threw ninety-six shot and shell toward the Federals, and the *Carondelet* responded with twice as many, but neither set of gunners won marksmanship medals that morning.[17]

While shells flew back and forth, a Federal transport, the *Forest Queen,* came downriver and pulled over to the landing near the cotton-bale fort. Colonel Owen's Hoosiers scrambled aboard, the *Forest Queen* chugged away from the levee, and McCulloch's prey slipped away from him. Not yet realizing that the Federal infantry were gone, General McCulloch ordered two more field pieces into action and formed his remaining three regiments into line in the open near his battery. Captain Edgar's gunners and the *Carondelet* continued to blaze away until McCulloch's skirmishers reported that the enemy had left aboard the transport. By this time Generals Taylor and Walker had arrived on the scene with Randal's brigade. Realizing that the game was over, Taylor ordered Edgar's battery to cease firing and set the Texans to destroying the Federal camp and any supplies they could not take with them. Elijah Petty reported that the Confederates "got 2 wagons, 6 mules, a lot of clothing, blankets etc and about 100 beeves with one fed[eral] prisoner & 5 negroes."[18]

In the end, this little scrape at Perkins Landing had little impact on the campaign around Vicksburg. A brigade of Confederates chased a regiment of Federals off the levee, destroyed some tents and supplies, and carried off what they did not burn. Colonel Owen and naval officers alerted their superiors that Walker's division might be marching toward other Federal camps on the Louisiana shore, but Grant's main supply line was now safe on the other side of the river anyway. McCulloch's report of the incident indicated that he had lost only one man killed, two wounded, and two missing. Capt. Gallatin Smith of McCulloch's staff, a lawyer from Tyler, was hit by shrapnel during the artillery exchange and fell dead from his saddle, the division's first battle casualty of the war. One of the missing men was a gunner from Edgar's battery, captured by a landing party from the *Carondelet* when he lagged too far behind his comrades after the fight.[19]

On the other hand, the confrontation at Perkins Landing was very significant in the history of the Greyhound Division. More than a year after they first mustered in Texas and more than halfway through the war, the Texans—or one brigade of them, at least—had stood fire for the first time. By the time Captain Edgar's gunners pulled the first lanyard at Judge Perkins's plantation, Confederate armies in the east had fought at Manassas, the Peninsula, Cedar Mountain, Manassas again, on the banks of Antietam Creek in Maryland, on the heights behind Fredericksburg, and in the tangled woods of Chancellorsville. In those engagements alone, the Confederacy had lost more than seventy thousand soldiers. Confederate armies in the western theater had fought at Fort Donelson,

Shiloh, Corinth, Murfreesboro, Champion Hill, Big Black River Bridge, Port Hudson, and dozens of smaller engagements. Walker's Greyhounds doubtless marched more miles than almost any other infantry unit in the war, but they were fortunate to escape the grinding slaughter east of the Mississippi River.

Some of the Texans, pumped up by adrenaline and deceived by the off-target shells and low casualties at Perkins Landing, were almost giddy with excitement after the fight. Captain Petty, who had extended "final parting advice" to his daughter, could now report to her that he was fine: "Well I have been in one battle at last. I stood it finely not a nerve twiched or muscle trembled—not a palpitation of the heart, not a misgiving. I was as cool, quiet & self possessed as you ever saw me. I thought no more of it than going to a frolic." The men around him were just as unconcerned, he wrote. "Co F was all right[,] so was the regiment—every body cool. Jokes & cute remarks about the shooting etc passed freely. If this is all the fear I don't mind a battle." Theophilus Perry, who arrived with Randal's brigade after the fight, thought some of the men in McCulloch's brigade were not quite so imperturbable as Petty and his comrades: "The first firing of Battle to raw troops, all confess[,] makes them feel very strangely."[20]

After the Federal camp was destroyed, Generals Taylor and Walker led the Texans back to their own camp on the Tensas. The men spent the next day crossing their wagons, animals, and artillery to the opposite bank of the river, and on June 2 the brigades resumed their voyage toward Vicksburg. This was swamp country, and some of the Texans marveled at the exotic sights. Canebrakes, sluggish brown bayous, mosquitoes, alligators, and snakes seemed to surround them: "On our march through the swamps we beheld several large rattlesnakes, that had been killed by our advance guards. Very frequently, in the swamps of Louisiana, a soldier wakes up in the morning and finds that he has a rattlesnake for a sleeping partner; but there is one excellent trait in the character of these reptiles: they never bite unless disturbed, and will get out of the way as soon as possible," Private Blessington observed. If the soldiers managed to avoid snakebites, they still had to contend with heat, suffocating humidity, and tainted brown water. "We are drinking Bayou water . . . hard necessity forces us to drink. It preserves life but does not quench thirst. Oh for a cool drink of Water," Lieutenant Perry complained.[21]

After five days and fifty miles of hacking their way through the swamps, the Greyhound Division reached the little village of Richmond, about twenty straight-line miles west of Vicksburg. General Taylor had arrived there a day earlier, on June 5, to hear reports from Louisiana cavalry familiar with the vicinity and to plan the strike on Grant's communications. For the first time, Taylor learned that the main Federal supply line had been moved to the other side of the Mississippi River, bolstering his conviction that the whole expedition from Alexandria was a waste of time. Nevertheless, he had his orders, and he rolled out his maps and mulled over his options. The commander of the Louisiana cavalry battalion in the area, Maj. Isaac F. Harrison, informed Taylor that only scattered small detachments of Federal troops defended the enemy camps along the river. Unfortunately for Taylor, Harrison's report seriously underestimated the strength of the Union posts, and Taylor assumed that quick strikes by separate brigades of Walker's division could break up the Federal camps very easily.[22]

When the Texas brigades tramped into Richmond on June 6, Taylor outlined his plans to General Walker. A detachment of Louisiana cavalry was instructed to attack the Federal post at Lake Providence, about thirty miles directly north of Richmond. Taylor ordered Walker to send one of his brigades to reduce the Union outpost at Young's Point, thirteen miles upstream from Vicksburg and about twenty miles from Richmond. Another brigade would destroy the Federal camp at Milliken's Bend, thirteen miles upriver from Young's Point and about ten miles from Richmond. Walker and his third brigade would take position between the two points and be prepared to rush reinforcements to either. If the intelligence Taylor had received from the cavalry had been accurate, the plan might have been more feasible, but the Confederates were mistaken about the strength of the enemy.[23]

By now Federal commanders were aware of the presence of General Taylor and Walker's division in the vicinity of Vicksburg. The duel at Perkins Landing had warned them a few days earlier, and they sent out probes early on June 6 to locate the menace. A clash between one of these probes and Harrison's cavalry near Richmond put the camps at Young's Point and Milliken's Bend on high alert. At Young's Point four infantry regiments and soldiers from a large quartermaster depot—more men than the Confederates were sending against them—could be put into line immediately. At Milliken's Bend were an Illinois cavalry regiment, three regiments (and part of another) of recently recruited black soldiers, and a detachment from an Iowa infantry regiment, a force about equal in size to the Texas brigade assigned to attack them. In addition, the Federal defenders at Young's Point and Milliken's Bend had the support of heavy naval guns on the river directly behind them.[24]

The Union commander at Milliken's Bend, Col. Hermann Lieb, was particularly diligent in his preparations for the expected attack. His regiments of black soldiers (the 9th and 11th Louisiana Infantry Regiments and the 1st Mississippi Infantry), only recently organized and not yet well trained, at least had the advantage of being on the defensive behind solid works, although their old smoothbore muskets were no better than the weapons Walker's Texans carried. About

150 yards from the river, an eight-foot-high levee ran parallel to the riverbank for about a quarter of a mile. The Federal camp was situated between the river and this manmade embankment. Twenty-five yards beyond the levee, a fifteen-foot-high bois d'arc (Osage orange) hedge, bristling with evil-looking thorns, paralleled the dike. A gap in the hedge, about thirty paces wide, had been cut on the Federal left the day before. The opening gave the defenders a clear field of vision, but it also gave the Texans an open path to that part of the levee. Farther out, other hedges and ditches cut the open ground into a maze of obstacles, and briars and vines were everywhere in between. To reach the enemy camp, the Confederates would have to cross the outer ditches and hedges, slip through narrow openings in the big hedge next to the levee, and then storm the levee itself. Lieb placed his men, about thirteen hundred strong, on the levee at 2 A.M. on June 7. The Federals had dug a trench along the inner edge of the embankment, enabling them to stand and fire with some protection. Cotton bales placed at various points on the levee provided additional cover, and pickets and videttes ranged several hundred yards in the direction of the expected attack.[25]

Shortly after Walker's brigades reached Richmond on June 6, they received orders to cook rations and prepare for a night march. General Taylor wanted to spare the men the hardships of a forced march in the extreme heat of day, and he hoped that an attack before dawn would destroy the enemy camps before Federal gunboats could bring their heavy armament to bear. After four hours of rest, the officers put their men into column on the little road leading toward the river. "All the troops realized the hardship of a night-march, and the forthcoming battle," Blessington recalled. "Many of the men delivered letters to those detailed to remain with the wagons, for the loved ones at home, in case they died on the battle-field. In sections four abreast, and close order, the troops took up the line of march . . . not a whisper was heard—no sound of clanking saber, or rattle of canteen and cup."[26]

Five miles down the road, the division reached Oak Grove Plantation, where the road forked, the right branch leading southeast to Young's Point, fifteen miles away, and the other northwest to Milliken's Bend, five miles away. In the warm, humid darkness, General Hawes directed his brigade (minus one regiment on detached duty) onto the right fork. General McCulloch motioned his regiments onto the left fork, and the men of Randal's brigade threw off their knapsacks and assumed their position as the reserve. General Walker and the artillery remained at Oak Grove with the reserves, and General Taylor remained in Richmond, waiting expectantly for the news that Walker's Texans had destroyed the Federal posts.[27]

The closer they approached the enemy camp, the quieter McCulloch's Confederates became, hoping to catch the Federals asleep in their tents. They were unaware that the soldiers in blue were already in line, staring into the darkness and waiting for them. A soldier in the 17th Texas Infantry, an itinerant Methodist preacher before the war, glided nervously through the night. "It was so dark that I could not see our skirmishers, about one hundred yards in advance of our line of battle. We marched with bayonets fixed and guns loaded and capped. Such feelings I never had before or since," he recalled. "No word was spoken louder than a whisper. Every order was in a whisper as it passed from officer to man."[28]

By 3 A.M. McCulloch's Texans had drawn within a mile and a half of the enemy camp, and a detachment of Louisiana cavalry moved ahead to locate the outer picket lines of the Federals. Suddenly, without warning, muskets blazed from behind one of the hedges, sending the horsemen spinning into confusion. Colonel Lieb's pickets, stationed far outside the main line on the levee, had fired into the darkness toward the sound of approaching horses and alerted everyone on both sides that the engagement had begun. "The effect of so sudden and terrible a fire, from an invisible foe, was very startling and disheartening," one Confederate remembered. "No wonder the simple-minded cavalry scouts were broken, and that many of them hurried to the rear, in utter confusion, with and without muskets, hats, or coats!" They jerked their horses around and galloped away from the hedge, only to be greeted by shots from their own skirmishers, who nervously assumed that Yankee cavalry was bearing down on them in the darkness. McCulloch's inexperienced skirmishers bagged three horses, but the Louisiana scouts survived the fright.[29]

McCulloch now ordered his skirmishers forward, and they steadily forced Colonel Lieb's pickets back, from hedge to hedge, until the Confederates approached within a few hundred yards of the fortified levee. At this point McCulloch and his colonels ordered the Texans to deploy from marching column to line of battle, preparatory to the final charge. The 16th Texas Cavalry, the 17th Infantry, and the 19th Infantry lined up, left to right, on the left side of the Richmond road. Slightly behind them was the 16th Infantry, held in reserve and placed on the right of the road (see Map 4). "As soon as it was light enough to see the further hedge, we got glimpses of the enemy forming his line of battle," a Federal lieutenant remembered. "His front covered the field from hedge to hedge, double rank, elbow to elbow . . . they had the appearance of a brigade on drill." The months of drill that Texans had complained about so often were now yielding dividends. "We had no line of retreat here except to swim the Mississippi, and were evidently up against something this time that was extra-hazardous," the Federal officer realized. Another white officer in one of the black regiments remarked on the precision of McCulloch's advance: "On came the fore

# Map 4
## The Battle of Milliken's Bend, June 7, 1863

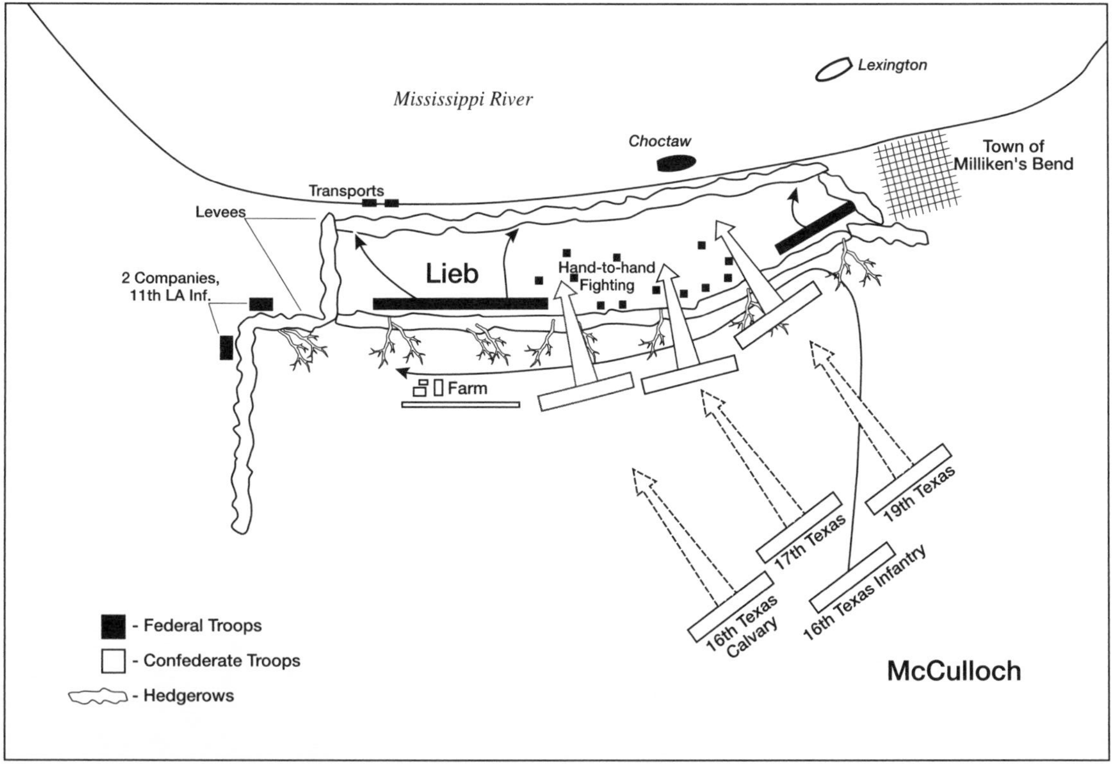

[line], with all the pomp of a field-day show; they came easily, at right-shoulder-shift arms; the commands of their officers became more and more distinct" as they neared the levee.[30]

Just as first light began to color the eastern horizon, McCulloch's line pushed forward, but it soon lost symmetry when the Texans were forced to cross ditches, stumble through vines and briars, and filter through gaps in the hedges. Ironically, the openings in the hedges had been cut by the Federals themselves, to provide easy access to their targets during earlier target practices. Forty years later, one soldier in the 16th Texas Infantry still remembered losing a young German friend early in the advance. "My friend and I were . . . side by side and he was killed by the first volley. He pulled a small bible out of his bosom and told me to send it to his mother in Washington County." Over the last two hundred yards, the Texans moved at the double-quick, all the while reforming their lines and forcing Lieb's skirmishers to fall back to the last hedge. "With yells that would make faint hearts quail, on double-quick they charged our little band," wrote one Yankee.[31]

The Texans, trotting toward the Federal position from an oblique angle, had to halt when they reached the fifteen-foot-high hedge only twenty-five yards from the levee. The only way to get at the enemy was to file through a few gaps in the hedge and re-form on the other side. This stopping and filing and re-forming exposed the men right under the blazing muskets of the Federals, and many of the Confederate casualties that morning fell near the hedge. Captain Petty's 17th Infantry suffered more casualties than any other Confederate regiment at Milliken's Bend, and most occurred at the hedge. Petty himself fell with a wound to the shoulder. "I don't See how We kept from All Being Kill," Pvt. D. E. Young of the 17th Infantry wrote later that day. "Wee Wair expose to all the fire[.] the Yankeys and the negro Stood 5 deepe Behind thair Breast Works." Despite their losses, the Greyhounds poured through the openings, hurried into line again, and then scrambled up the levee in the dim morning light, bayonets forward. The former Methodist preacher in the 17th Texas recalled the moment: "We rushed through the hedge, driving the foe before us, and they fell behind the levy, thus making their ranks four lines deep. We mounted the embankment and turned loose our war dogs, and I tell you . . . they howled!"[32]

At this point the conflict became something rare in the Civil War, a hand-to-hand fight with bayonets and clubbed muskets. An Iowa captain near the center of the Union line recalled how "one member of the regiment and a rebel met and at the same instant plunged their bayonets into one another, and both fell dead on the works, with their bayonets in that position. . . . It was a very hot place." An Iowa private wrote that "Colonel [Samuel L.] Glasgow was bespattered with the blood and brains of his slaughtered men, beaten out with the clubbed muskets of the enemy." One Iowa soldier, John Virtue of Polk City, more than six feet tall and weighing more than two hundred pounds, crossed bayonets with one of the onrushing rebels. "After a few parries," one witness recalled, "each pierced the other through. They stood thus struggling when another soldier of the 23rd Iowa, named Thomas McDowell, rushed on the rebel and beat his brains out with his musket." Both Iowans and the Texan died of their wounds. According to another Union account, "upon both sides men were killed with the buts of muskets. White and black men were lying side by side, pierced by bayonets, and in some instances transfixed to the earth. In one instance, two men, one white and the other black, were found side by side, each having the other's bayonet through his body."[33]

About two hundred yards from the Iowans, on the left end of Colonel Lieb's line, one of the African American regiments, the 9th Louisiana, was taking the worst of the Confederate assault. The hedge that had slowed the Confederate wave along most of the line had been cut down for a span of thirty yards in front of the 9th Louisiana, giving Col. Richard Waterhouse's 19th Texas Infantry a clearer path to the levee, especially after the Federal soldiers fired too high and too soon. "Where the hedge was down [the Confederates] sailed up the exterior slope of the levee to meet our thin line on the top with empty guns and lowered bayonets," Lt. David Cornwell, a white officer of the 9th Louisiana, wrote. "Their guns being loaded [the Texans] shot the men in their front and slowly moved down the interior slope, loading their pieces as they came."[34]

Lieutenant Cornwell was directly in the path of the oncoming Texans, and he waved his reserve line forward: "I . . . ordered my men to keep their loads and not shoot a man if he could bayonet him, and not to pull off his gun until the muzzle was against a rebel. They were intensely excited and could not stand still. I guess I was a little excited myself, for instead of saying [the correct order to charge, "double quick, with bayonets"] . . . , I simply said 'Now bounce them[,] Bullies.' " When the two lines collided, one of the lieutenant's best soldiers, called "Big Jack" by everyone who knew him, showed his mettle. Big Jack was very recently a field hand on a nearby plantation, but his obvious talents had earned him a promotion to sergeant. "Big Jack Jackson passed me like a rocket. With the fury of a tiger he sprang into that gang and smashed everything before him." Soon, "there was nothing left of Jack's gun but the barrel, and he was smashing in every head he could reach. . . . On the other side [of the levee] they were yelling, 'Shoot that big nigger, shoot that big nigger,' while Jack was daring the whole gang to come up there and fight him. Then a bullet reached his head and he went full length on the levee." Another officer in the 9th, a veteran of much larger battles east of the Mississippi, admitted that the carnage at Milliken's Bend was awful. "It was a horrible fight," he said, "the worst I was ever engaged in, not excluding Shiloh." An Iowa veteran of Port Gibson, Champion Hill, and Big Black River Bridge agreed: "It was a hard fight for the number of men engaged; the hardest one we have been in yet."[35]

While the three front-line Texas regiments assaulted the levee, McCulloch's fourth regiment (Col. George Flournoy's 16th Infantry), following behind, filed through the last hedge, fixed bayonets, and began moving toward the embankment. While they were still at the foot of the dike, a courier from General McCulloch rushed up with orders for them to halt and then double-quick to the left end of the Confederate advance. McCulloch feared the Federals might attempt to turn his left because black soldiers were seen milling around some farmhouses in that area, and several Confederate officers had come under fire from that direction. Colonel Flournoy, a thirty-one-year-old Austin lawyer, former attorney general of Texas, and leading secessionist in 1861, preferred to go straight ahead. But he redirected his regiment in the noise and smoke at the bottom of the levee and led them along the foot of the embankment to the far left. When his companies reached the end of the line, Flournoy put them into line of battle, ready once again to advance. General McCulloch then rode up and instructed Flournoy to station some of his men on the top of the levee as sharpshooters. The advance of Flournoy's regiment, the harassing fire of his sharpshooters, and the general course of the fight succeeded in driving the Federals from the upriver end of the levee. The 16th Texas Infantry thus missed most of the close-in fighting at Milliken's Bend and thereby suffered the fewest casualties among the four Confederate regiments that day.[36]

While Flournoy's regiment solidified the Confederate left and the battle raged along the rest of the line, one of the musicians in the 16th Texas Infantry gained a measure of fame for his quick wits. Pvt. Anton Schultz, like band members generally, was assigned to work with the surgeons during the fight. Sent by a physician to fetch water for the wounded from a farmhouse to the rear of the Confederates, Private Schultz walked right into a company of black soldiers who were separated from the main Federal line and found himself a prisoner. As the white captain of the company interrogated Schultz, the officer, confused about the disposition and location of the nearby Confederates, asked where the rebel line was. Schultz pointed to the southwest, exactly opposite the real location, and offered to lead the captain and his isolated company to the safety of Federal transports on the river. In the words of General McCulloch, "The Yankee suffered himself to be humbugged by our German youth, or young man, and he led him and his entire company of 49 negroes through small gaps in thick hedges until they found themselves within 60 yards of Colonel Allen's [17th Infantry] regiment, who took them all prisoners without the fire of a gun." Reflecting the attitude of many Confederates toward black soldiers, McCulloch recommended to his superiors that Private Schultz "should have a choice boy from among these fellows to cook and wash for him and his mess during the war, and to work for him as long as the negro lives."[37]

Meanwhile, after several minutes of hand-to-hand, skull-splitting fighting, the 19th Texas broke through the last line of the 9th Louisiana and set off a wave of Federal withdrawals from the levee, beginning on the Union left and running along the line finally to the 11th Louisiana on the far right. "They poured a murderous enfilading fire along our line, directing their fire chiefly to our officers who fell in numbers," Colonel Lieb reported. "Then, and not until they were overpowered and forced from their position, were the blacks driven back, when numbers of them sought shelter behind wagons, piles of boxes and other objects [in the camp between the levee and the river]. The others sought shelter behind the river bank." Within minutes the wave reached the 23rd Iowa in the center of the Union line. "We had been in the ditch about three minutes, when the negroes gave way on our left and let the rebels in," an Iowa captain reported. "They fired a terrible volley on us, right down the ditch, and were preparing to give us another, when the Colonel ordered us to fall back to the . . . [camp between the levee and the river]. We did so, when they flanked us again and we had to fall back to the river bank." Another Iowan claimed that the retreat to the river was the worst part of the battle: "We were ordered to fall back to the shelter of the bank, and while retreating was the time we were cut up so badly." The white Federals, although more experienced than their black comrades, were just as quick on the retreat.[38]

The whole Federal line soon peeled back, from the levee to the camp to the riverbank, with the yelling Texans following close behind. Some retreating soldiers panicked and leaped into the river to swim out to nearby transports, but most jumped down behind the riverbank. The river happened to be low, and the riverbank provided a natural earthwork. One Texan admitted to his wife that "we suffered much in the assault of the inside Levy, which was strengthened by Cotton Bales, and the skill of engineers." The strong new defensive position of the Union line finally halted the Texas advance. While some Confederates carried off the wounded, others ransacked the Federal camp, searching for food and other plunder. The busy rebels gathered up several dozen stands of arms, two hundred horses and mules, and a herd of cattle, and sent everything to the rear.[39]

Now that the sun was well up and the two lines were separated somewhat, the heavy guns of the Federal river fleet came into play. Rear Adm. David Porter had sent the monstrous 1,000-ton ironclad *Choctaw* to Milliken's Bend the day before to buttress the camp's defenses, but until the naval gunners had daylight to see by and space between friend and foe, they could do nothing. Now they had an opportunity to unleash their firepower. A 100-pounder rifled gun, two 30-pounder rifles, a nine-inch smoothbore, and two 24-pounder smoothbores far overmatched anything the Texans had in the vicinity. Not even the 6-pounder field guns McCulloch had thrown at the *Carondelet* at Perkins Landing were available; the artillery had been left behind with the reserve brigade.[40]

It is not clear from surviving accounts how much actual damage the naval guns inflicted on the Confederates, but it is certain that the Texans were awed by the more than one hundred heavy shells thrown their way. Because the river was so low and because the *Choctaw* therefore had to fire over the fifteen-foot-high riverbank, the naval gunners were forced to fire blindly. Spotters on shore sent signals out to the *Choctaw* to help direct the fire, but many shells apparently created more dust than damage to the rebels, and some rounds fell among Federal soldiers who had not yet reached the protection of the riverbank. Lt. Col. Cyrus Sears of the 11th Louisiana had a firsthand encounter with friendly fire: "The gun-boat men mistook a body of our men for rebels and made a target of them for several shots, before we could signal them off. From the fact that I was very unpleasantly splattered with blood, brains and flesh of one of our men, who there had his head shot off from one of our gunboats, I shall never forget that our navy did some real execution at Milliken's Bend."[41]

Federal bayonets and musket balls spilled more Confederate blood than did gunboats at Milliken's Bend, but the big naval guns made the desired impression on the minds of the Texans. They scrambled back over the levee and had to settle for firing potshots at the Federals behind the riverbank. The two lines, now separated by the 150 yards from the river to the outer levee, with the Federal camp in between, continued to exchange fire for two or three hours until further developments convinced the Confederates that the battle was over. First, they could see more riverboats steaming toward the scene, including the timberclad *Lexington,* which immediately joined the *Choctaw* in throwing shells at the rebels. Some concluded that even more ironclads were about to enter the bombardment, and others figured that heavy reinforcements were arriving by transports. Either way, the tide seemed to be turning. In addition, the Confederates had marched all night and fought all morning, and fatigue began to slow them down, especially in the muggy 95-degree heat. The stiffened Federal resistance along the riverbank, the heat, the arrival of more riverboats, and the monstrous shells falling all around them—but especially the shells—finally convinced General McCulloch that his brigade had accomplished all that was possible. Around noon, he turned the Texans around and ordered them back to Oak Grove Plantation.[42]

The brigade that shuffled back toward Oak Grove at midday was very different from the one that had passed in the opposite direction twelve hours earlier. On their way to the river, most of the Texans had never been in a real battle. Now they had seen and heard the worst of war—the sudden, violent deaths of friends and relatives, grunting hand-to-hand combat, torn bodies, the smoke and confusion and overpowering din, the pitiful moans and gasps of the wounded. Driving their prisoners and captured animals before them and hauling their wounded in wagons, McCulloch's regiments trudged past scenes as grisly as those on the battlefield. Several trenches, fifty feet long and three feet wide, had been dug during the battle to receive the dead. Coffins were not available, of course, and the corpses of brothers and neighbors were wrapped in their blankets, lowered into the trenches, and covered over with soil. The men walked right by the brigade's field hospital, set up in some slave cabins fronting the road. Some of the wounded were conscious, and they greeted their more fortunate comrades as they marched by. One soldier with a musket wound in the face hailed a friend: "Well, they have popped me this time . . . but I will be at them again."[43]

Other sights at the hospital stayed with Private Blessington for the rest of his days: "so fearful, so horrible are the scenes, that, long after you leave the place, perhaps haunting you to the verge of life, the screams of the wounded, the groans of the dying will ring in your ears, or some form, cold and stiff in death's icy embrace, be present to your mental vision." Peter Gravis of the 17th Infantry, the itinerant Methodist preacher, could only shake his head when he remembered the bloody cabins by the roadside: "it was a horrible sight after the battle to see the arms and legs amputated at the field hospital, and the suffering wounded pleading for help; the dying praying for mercy; the living weary and battle worn, seeking to raise and relieve their comrades, though they themselves were worn out and almost ready to fall from exhaustion." Few of the Texans, grimy and stinking with sweat and dust and gunpowder, thought about bouquets and cheering ladies and bands playing "Dixie" on the march back to Oak Grove. Their foes in blue were also traumatized by the nightmare on the levee. Lieutenant Cornwell, recuperating in a Federal hospital from a gunshot wound to his arm, could not chase the memories from his mind, even in sleep: "That infernal Milliken's Bend fight got into my dreams, and I suddenly awoke with an exclamation and a start that brought a sharp twinge of pain to my wounded arm."[44]

After the Union and Confederate adjutants had counted out the cost of the battle, Colonel Lieb and General McCulloch made their reports. The Federals lost 101 killed, 285 wounded, and 266 men captured or missing—a total of 652, or about half the entire garrison. These numbers are somewhat misleading because most of the missing eventually came straggling back into camp. One of the regiments, the 9th Louisiana, took the brunt of the assault and sustained far more losses than the other units: 62 killed and 130 wounded of 285 engaged (67.4 percent). McCulloch's losses were much lighter: 44 killed, 131 wounded, and 10 captured or missing, a total of 185, or about 12 percent of those engaged. The 17th Texas lost 92 men, about 20 percent of its total manpower. Despite the combat inexperience on both sides, the Yankees and rebels of Milliken's Bend had fought one of the bloodiest small engagements of the war.[45]

The large number of killed and wounded men among the soldiers of the 9th Louisiana raises the possibility that many of the black soldiers were massacred, killed after they were wounded or captured. On the other hand, the overall number of deaths among black soldiers at Milliken's Bend (95 of 1,223 engaged, or 7.8 percent) was far less proportionally than the 63.9 percent of African American soldiers killed at a widely acknowledged massacre, Fort Pillow, Tennessee, in April 1864, raising serious doubts about Milliken's Bend as a massacre.[46]

Certainly there were reports after the battle that the Texans had shouted "no quarter" as they came over the outer levee. Some Union accounts even claimed that the Confederates fought under a "black flag" or a "skull and crossbones flag." Three reports by Federals who actually fought in the battle are damning at first glance, but their inconsistency raises some doubts. Lt. Col. Cyrus Sears of the 11th Louisiana Infantry claimed forty-five years later that the Texans "fought us under the skull, coffin and cross bones (black) flag." Since Sears wrote nearly half a century after the fact and since some of his comrades claimed that he had spent the better part of the fight hiding behind the riverbank, his account seems insufficient in itself to settle the matter. Colonel Lieb's detailed official report of the battle, written the day after the engagement, seems much more reliable. According to Lieb, when the Confederates reached the levee, "they came madly on with cries of 'No quarters for white officers, kill the damned Abolitionists, but spare the niggers &c.'" Captain Miller of the 9th Louisiana wrote only that some rebels shouted "no quarters."[47]

Although the excited nerves and pulsing adrenaline of men in their first combat—especially men who recoiled at the very idea of black soldiers—may well have led some individual Confederates to shoot wounded black soldiers or others who had thrown down their arms, the Texans apparently had no prearranged plan or order to massacre the African American soldiers in blue at Milliken's Bend. Colonel Lieb's specific and contemporary recollection indicates that the Texans were shouting that black soldiers should be spared (for return to their masters), and General McCulloch on the day after the battle discussed how black captives should be returned to slavery. If the Texans had had a prearranged plan to massacre the African Americans, there would have been few if any prisoners to worry over. Pvt. B. G. Goodrich of the 16th Texas Infantry scoffed at later reports of a massacre: "With their usual disregard of truth, the Yankees accused us of shouting 'No quarter,' but the Sixteenth Infantry captured an entire company of negroes."[48]

In fact, in their planning for the battle, the Confederates seem not even to have considered the question of black soldiers—their officers were confused after the battle about what to do with the African American captives.[49] Confederate survivors boasted of several dozen black prisoners taken during the fight, and later newspaper reports indicated that those prisoners were turned over to army authorities in Monroe several days later.[50] Colonel Sears of the 11th Louisiana, no friend of the rebels, reported that the African American prisoners were taken to Texas, put to work for the Confederacy, and released by Gen. George Custer at the end of the war.[51] It seems certain that the ragged Texans, some of them barefoot and most of them without uniforms, had no special flags for such occasions. Stories of black flags and skulls and crossbones were circulated later, almost entirely by men who had not been on the gory levee at Milliken's Bend.[52]

Although an organized and predetermined effort to massacre black soldiers probably did not occur at Milliken's Bend, it appears that Confederate authorities in Monroe may have executed two captured white officers of black regiments. When General Grant heard rumors about executions of prisoners taken at Milliken's Bend, he wrote General Taylor, asking for an explanation. The gentlemanly Taylor huffily denied the allegations and swore that he had given no such orders, and Grant let the matter drop. Nevertheless, a careful examination of the affair concludes that 2nd Lt. George L. Conn of the 9th Louisiana Infantry and Capt. Corydon Heath of the 11th Louisiana may well have been executed days after the battle by officers not under Taylor's command.[53]

As often happened in this war, the men on both sides claimed to have whipped the other. Rank-and-file Texans remembered that they had broken the blue line at the point of the bayonet and chased the Federals back to the water's edge. J. H. Pillow of the 17th Texas sneered at Federal claims of victory: "The truth is that we ran them to their gunboats and held our ground till all our wounded were taken off the field. If that is counted a victory for the Federals I can't wonder that it has been said that he never lost a battle." General Taylor was not so happy with the result. He considered the whole exercise a waste of time and resources that should have been focused on south Louisiana. The men in blue concentrated on the bottom line of the day—the ultimate retreat of the Confederates and the survival of the Federal camp.[54]

In the larger context of the war, of course, the battle at Milliken's Bend had little strategic importance. As General Walker recognized, even if his Texans had pushed every last defender into the river, the Federal river fleet's heavy guns still would have forced the Confederates to abandon their prize. Moreover, the original purpose of the Confederate strike at Milliken's Bend—to break Grant's supply line—could not have been accomplished even if the Texans had wiped out the entire Union garrison. Grant's main line of communication was secure on the other side of the river. In short, the Confederates had lost the battle before the first shots were fired from behind that outer bois d'arc hedge.[55]

Although the struggle on the levee had no significant impact on the Vicksburg campaign, it did loom large in the overall history of the Civil War: for only the second time in the history of the United States (the first had been about two weeks earlier at Port Hudson), black regiments fought in a general engagement and earned new respect for the whole idea of using African American soldiers in the Union army. Assistant Secretary of War Charles A. Dana, traveling with Grant's army during the drive on Vicksburg, reported to Secretary of War Edwin Stanton that "the sentiment of this army with regard to the employment of negro troops has been revolutionized by the bravery of the blacks in the recent battle of Milliken's Bend. Prominent officers, who used in private to sneer at the idea, are now heartily in favor of it." Confederate officials too recognized the significance of the fight at Milliken's Bend. General Walker later wrote that "this was the first [sic] instance during the war in which negroes in the service of the Federal government came into collision with the troops of the Confederacy, and the obstinacy with which they fought, and the loss of a hundred and twenty killed and wounded of McCullough's men, opened the eyes of the Confederates to the consequences to be apprehended by the Federal employment of these auxillaries."[56]

While McCulloch's brigade struggled on the levee at Milliken's Bend, General Hawes's brigade of fourteen hundred men was still tramping toward Young's Point. The men in Hawes's regiments would have fewer stories to tell their comrades and their grandchildren. First, the brigade was halted nearly six hours in the middle of the night because a bridge they expected to use had been destroyed by the Federals. The Louisiana cavalry scouts, supposedly very familiar with the neighborhood, did not realize the bridge was down, nor did they know that another bridge a few miles away was easily available. When Hawes finally put his men back on the march to the second bridge, it was 4 A.M., and McCulloch's troops were already hard at work at Milliken's Bend. Not until 10:30 did Hawes reach the vicinity of Young's Point. Then the cavalry scouts gave him more erroneous information, assuring him that the Federal camp was only one mile away and that the infantry could advance unseen under the cover of heavy woods to the edge of the camp. After hacking their way through the woods, the men emerged, not into the Federal camp, but into a level clearing still one and one-half miles away from the Federal tents, in full view of the waiting enemy. To top it all, the Texans, expecting to find only a few defenders at Young's Point, could see heavy lines of blue infantry forming in the distance.[57]

General Hawes, a West Point graduate and veteran of the Mexican War, deployed his regiments and started them across the open plain, driving Federal skirmishers back toward the river. But the sight of menacing gunboats directly behind the enemy infantry brought him up short. Realizing the futility of an advance across open ground against equal or superior numbers backed up by the wide muzzles of the navy, Hawes finally halted the advance and pulled his men back into the woods. The withdrawal from the open field was accompanied by considerable confusion in the 18th Infantry. Pvt. John Porter reported that his comrades reversed direction only "after a great many awkward and confused commands from Col. [David B.] Culberson to his Regt." Then, "after we had gained the woods, the gunboats shelled at a terrible rate in the direction of our retreat, but with no damage. The day was extremely warm, and the men suffered severely from the heat."[58] In fact, regimental officers discovered that nearly half the men were suffering from heat exhaustion and could not fight, even if they had surprised and outnumbered the Federals. Hawes concluded that his reduced command could not succeed at Young's Point, and he ordered his brigade to return to Richmond.[59]

The return march through the stifling heat and humidity drained away what little energy the men had in reserve. After tramping several miles, the Texans were halted to rest a few hours. Then their officers urged them back on their feet and led them down the road to Oak Grove, where they joined the other two brigades at 5 A.M. on June 8. Private Porter remarked that the men had nothing left "after marching two days and nights without sleep, and maneuver[ing] in line of battle several hours; and besides, our rations, like all other three day rations, grew short." From Oak Grove they turned west to Richmond, but finally Hawes's Greyhounds gave out. "We yet had four miles to go, to reach our supplies, and the officers seeing the complete exhaustion of the men, ordered the train back to haul the most of the army to camp."[60]

The third Confederate thrust along the river, aimed at the Federal camp of instruction at Lake Providence, upriver from Milliken's Bend, accomplished no more than the first two. Col. Frank A. Bartlett, commander of all Confederate forces near Lake Providence, led nine hundred men (the 13th Louisiana Cavalry Battalion and the 13th Texas Cavalry, detached from Hawes's Texas brigade) toward Lake Providence on June 7. Bartlett frittered away whatever surprise might have been possible by marching first in one direction, then backtracking and approaching from a different angle, and ended up reaching the enemy forty-eight hours behind schedule on June 9. That afternoon Bartlett's Confederates and Union brigadier general Hugh T. Reid's eight hundred Federals skirmished across Bayou Tensas for about two hours before Bartlett gave up on his idea of bridging the stream. Near sundown the colonel withdrew his men and turned back south, abandoning the whole project. Thus, only one of General Taylor's assaults actually closely engaged the enemy (McCulloch's advance at Milliken's Bend), and none accomplished its overall objective.[61]

In the six weeks since they left their camp at Pine Bluff, Walker's Texans had marched 350 miles and steamed up and down four rivers and a lake for another 510 miles—all to reach the vicinity of Vicksburg, only 150 miles from their original starting point. If Smith had sent them directly to the west bank of the Mississippi River to break up General Grant's communications, they would have arrived at the crucial point at exactly the right time, early May, to catch the Federal army at its most vulnerable moment. Instead, the Texans were sent to Monroe, down the Ouachita River, then to Natchitoches, and finally to Alexandria, far from the Federal supply depots on the Louisiana shore of the Mississippi River. Nearly a thousand miles of wasted motion brought the division to Milliken's Bend and Young's Point, too late for any useful purpose. As Private Blessington observed on an earlier occasion, "if ever there was an army that had been harassed and 'used up' to accomplish nothing so far, it was this army."[62]

CHAPTER 7

# The Dismal
# Summer of 1863

The four months following the affairs at Milliken's Bend and Young's Point proved to be some of the most difficult of the war for the officers and men of Walker's Texas Division. They were the object of a tug of war between E. Kirby Smith and Richard Taylor and were ordered first one direction then another by those two generals. They succumbed by the hundreds to fevers and intestinal disorders in the steamy, disease-ridden lowlands of northeast Louisiana. Left without adequate cavalry support, General Walker was forced to campaign almost blindly against superior numbers west of Vicksburg. Then, when things seemed perfectly awful, they got worse—Vicksburg fell to General Grant's besieging army on July 4 and Port Hudson to General Banks a few days later. Virtually all of the Greyhounds were discouraged by the loss of Vicksburg, and some of them concluded that the whole war was lost. When they finally emerged from the swamps, their situations did not improve: rations were shorter and poorer than ever, their pay was a year or more in arrears, promised furloughs were slow in coming, and they seemed to be stuck in a quiet backwater of the war, useless to the Confederacy and to their families. Many of the men turned to religion to soothe their troubled souls. Scores of others, angry and disappointed, simply went home, with or without benefit of furlough papers. It was a dismal summer.

The troubles began almost before the smoke from the last musket shot at Milliken's Bend drifted away. In his official reports on the recent campaign, Gen. Richard Taylor blasted his subordinates for failing to destroy the camps along the Mississippi River. In Taylor's opinion, Walker and his brigadiers had botched the attacks at Milliken's Bend and Young's Point. They had approached the enemy too slowly, losing the element of surprise; they were not sufficiently aggressive when they did attack; they were too intimidated by the Federal gunboats; and they were simply too green for their assignments. "General McCulloch appears to have shown great personal bravery, but no capacity for handling masses," Taylor sniffed. Ignoring the fact that the Federals were alerted to the Confederate presence before the assaults and unaware that Union positions were stronger than originally reported, Taylor blamed the failures on the officers and

men of the Texas Division: "Nothing was wanted but vigorous action in the execution of the plans which had been carefully laid out." Besides, Taylor grumbled,
the Texans were overawed by the naval fire. "Unfortunately, I discovered too late
that the officers and men of this division were possessed of a dread of gunboats
such as pervaded our people at the commencement of the war. To this circum-
stance and to want of mobility in these troops are to be attributed the meager
results of the expedition."[1]

While General Hawes's stumbling, fumbling approach to Young's Point
might have deserved censure, the mercurial Taylor's criticisms in general were
too harsh and probably reflected his frustration at being ordered on a mission
he thought useless. Federal officers along the river had been alerted that a strong
Confederate force was lurking nearby at least a day before McCulloch and Hawes
advanced against them. Thus, Union infantry and gunboats were in line and
ready for the Texans well before the first shots were fired. Contrary to Taylor's
assumption, the element of surprise had not been frittered away—it had never
existed. In addition, the camps at Young's Point and Lake Providence were considerably stronger than Taylor originally realized. Rather than having surprise
and superior numbers on their side, the Texans had neither. It is true that neither
McCulloch nor Hawes had ever led a brigade in battle, but if Taylor doubted
their abilities, he could have led the men himself. Instead, he remained behind,
miles away, in Richmond. He certainly did not lack physical courage, as his previous experience amply demonstrated, but he did seem to lack much commitment to this campaign.

Finally, Taylor gave too little credit to the Federal navy. The heavy artillery of
the gunboats could easily have obliterated the attacking infantry ranks if the Texans had remained in the open spaces at Milliken's Bend and Young's Point. Although General Taylor was not impressed by the danger from the gunboats,
Confederate generals in other theaters would have agreed with McCulloch's and
Hawes's men that infantry simply could not stand against heavy naval armament.
Gen. Robert E. Lee, mulling the possibility of assaulting Federal lines on the
James River after the Seven Days' Battles a year earlier, concluded that such an
attack would be suicidal: "I fear [the enemy] is too secure under cover of his
boats to be driven from his position." Pres. Jefferson Davis readily agreed: "I fully
concur with you as to the impropriety of exposing our brave and battle-thinned
troops to the fire of the gunboats."[2]

Stung by Taylor's critique, Walker expressed pride in the behavior of McCulloch's brigade at Milliken's Bend. His brigadier had "gallantly attacked" the
enemy on the levee. "The impetuousity of McCullough's Texans . . . could not
be resisted, and the levee was carried and almost the entire negro force was either

killed, captured, or driven into the Mississippi River and drowned," Walker later wrote. Only when the heavy fire of the Federal gunboats came into play did the battle turn against him, and then McCulloch "very properly retired beyond the range of the enemy's guns." Walker, like Taylor, found Hawes's performance on the Young's Point expedition far below standard, but McCulloch's brigade had done all that could be expected.[3]

When one of Walker's staff officers, recently returned from Richmond, informed him that Taylor's report had raised doubts in the Confederate capital about Walker's abilities, Walker confronted Taylor and asked for an explanation. By that time, four months later, Taylor's frustrations had passed, and he gave Walker a ringing endorsement. "Nothing in the report was intended to reflect, directly or indirectly, on General Walker. The plan was mine, and the position held by General Walker was strictly in accordance with my orders. The misconception existing at Richmond is calculated to injure unjustly a meritorious officer, and I ask that this communication be forwarded."[4]

Although Walker ultimately received the credit he believed he and his division deserved, General Hawes's military career was tarnished by his wandering night march toward Young's Point. Hawes rightly complained that his orders had been based on faulty intelligence about the Federal camp and that the Louisiana cavalry guides assigned to him were "inefficient and useless." Hindsight may forgive Hawes for not subjecting his exposed infantry to naval gunfire on an open plain in broad daylight, but he had no good explanation for why he arrived at Young's Point several hours after—not before—sunrise. A more aggressive and resourceful officer would not have taken six hours to find a bridge, despite the inefficient and useless guides. His failure to engage the enemy was noted disapprovingly by both Walker and Taylor. President Davis himself indicated that "such failure to execute orders . . . should not be overlooked." Secretary of War James A. Seddon raised the possibility of a court-martial or removal of Hawes from command but left the decision up to General Smith at Trans-Mississippi headquarters. Smith apparently found no good reason to bring charges against Hawes, and even General Taylor's attitude toward the unfortunate Hawes eventually softened. All the same, Smith later reassigned Hawes to the less volatile district of Texas.[5]

The Texas Division remained at Richmond for a week after the action at Milliken's Bend. General Taylor at first decided to take Walker's brigades down to south Louisiana, where some real damage could be inflicted on the Federal war machine. Randal's brigade actually moved to Monroe, boarded steamers, and proceeded downriver, but Taylor soon changed his mind and ordered them back to Richmond—there was still work to do along the Mississippi in the event that Grant was forced to retreat from Vicksburg. By June 15 Walker's numbers at

Richmond included possibly no more than fifteen hundred effectives. Randal's brigade had not yet returned from its abortive trip down the Ouachita River, and McCulloch's and Hawes's brigades were "terribly reduced by sickness." General Walker blamed the misery on the "excessive heat of the weather, the deadly malaria of the swamps, [and] the stagnant and unwholesome water." In short, the Texans were in no condition to take the offensive and posed no immediate danger to Federal outposts along the Mississippi.[6]

Nevertheless, the presence of Walker's brigades just west of Vicksburg was worrisome to General Grant, and he instructed his subordinates to flush the Confederates away from the western approaches to Vicksburg: "They should not be allowed to remain about Richmond." Admiral Porter, too, was concerned about the rebels lurking west of the river. He ordered all his vessels to stay away from the west bank of the Mississippi after nightfall in order to prevent Walker's Texans from boarding them. In addition, Porter instructed one of his units, the Mississippi Marine Brigade, to cooperate with the army in shooing the Confederates farther away from the river. Thus, one week after their attacks at Milliken's Bend and Young's Point, the feverish remnants of McCulloch's and Hawes's brigades became the targets of General Grant and Admiral Porter.[7]

On the morning of June 14, Brig. Gen. Joseph Mower's Federal brigade of twelve hundred men left Young's Point with orders to clear the rebels out of Richmond. Early the next morning, again on the move, Mower's infantry was joined by Brig. Gen. Alfred Ellet's thirteen hundred men of the Mississippi Marine Brigade. Nervous Confederate scouts, exaggerating the size of the Federal column of about twenty-five hundred men and two batteries, reported to General Walker in Richmond that seven or eight thousand Federals and three batteries were bearing down on him. Without competent cavalry to feed him reliable intelligence or screen his movements, and believing that his reduced division was outnumbered five to one, Walker quickly barked out orders to save his command. He placed the 18th Texas and Captain Edgar's four guns one mile out toward Young's Point to slow the Federal advance, ordered his supply wagons and ambulances to hurry west toward Monroe, and kept the remainder of his command behind Roundaway Bayou, on the north edge of town, to protect the only nearby bridge.[8]

Col. David B. Culberson of the 18th Texas, the officer whose confusing commands had embarrassed his regiment at Young's Point, redeemed his reputation when the Federal column neared Richmond. The thirty-two-year-old lawyer from Marion County had resigned his seat in the Texas legislature because he opposed secession, but he helped recruit his regiment once war was inevitable. Concealing his five hundred soldiers in a ditch fronted by a willow hedge, Culberson waited until General Ellet's first line of marines advanced within thirty yards of the ditch. Suddenly the Texans rose and poured a volley into the stunned Federals. A quick countercharge drove the marines back temporarily, but superior numbers and firepower soon forced Culberson to withdraw slowly toward the main line behind the bayou. Captain Edgar's gunners then opened with grape and canister shot, initiating an hour-long duel with General Mower's two batteries and delaying the Federal advance long enough to allow Walker to move his men and trains to safety.[9]

The Confederates were overmatched, and Edgar's battery eventually joined Culberson's infantry in the withdrawal behind Roundaway Bayou. By the time they retreated across the muddy stream and set fire to the bridge, General Walker's other regiments were following the wagon trains westward to safety. Culberson and Edgar had accomplished their mission. Brought up short by the burned bridge, the Federal infantry halted, but a detachment of Illinois cavalry swam their horses across the bayou, galloped after the retreating Texans, and collared about two dozen stragglers. While Walker's division limped away in the distance, Generals Mower and Ellet burned every building in the village of Richmond and carried off the few women and children still cowering there, leaving only blackened ruins that were never rebuilt.[10]

Walker's retreat from Richmond toward Monroe was one of the most painful of the war for the Texans. "My division looked like a vast moving hospital," Walker wrote. "We had sick men in wagons and carts, wounded men on litters, borne by soldiers, and a crowd of enfeebled and emaciated men for whom no transportation could be had."[11] Pvt. John Porter of the 18th Texas described the methods the men used to move their wounded comrades:

> Eight men were detailed to one wounded man, he was placed upon a litter, which is a light frame work, the side pieces being long enough that cloth is tacked from one to the other, that a man may lie upon it, then extend two feet at either end, beyond the cloth, so that these pieces serve as handles, something like a hand barrow; then two cross pieces to keep the cloth in proper place—the whole thing being set upon four legs, like a bedstead. Then four men carried it by the four handles, and the other four carried two guns each, occasionally exchanging.[12]

Some of the sick and wounded died on their litters before the sickly column reached its destination, and the corpses were lowered into makeshift graves along the roadside. Pvt. Peter Gravis of the 17th Texas, the Methodist minister who had mounted the levee at Milliken's Bend, noted that civilians too joined the sad procession: "The inhabitants [of Richmond] fled in wild confusion. Our wounded were scattered all along the road to De[l]hi where they were sent by rail to Monroe. Such distress I never witnessed. Women and children flying in wild disorder from an insidious and unscrupulous foe." After thirty miles of this misery, the Texans set up camp on June 17 at Delhi, thirty-five miles east of Monroe, on the Vicksburg, Shreveport & Texas Railroad.[13]

After five days of recuperation at Delhi, Walker's Texans, now including Randal's brigade and reinforced by an Arkansas brigade under James C. Tappan, spent the next three weeks crisscrossing the swamps and bayous of northeast Louisiana. At the request of Confederate generals east of the Mississippi and under instructions from E. Kirby Smith, General Walker made it his mission to range up and down the Mississippi River from Lake Providence to Milliken's Bend, disrupting operations on the cotton plantations leased by northern businessmen from the federal government, returning the black workers on those plantations to slavery, and interfering as much as possible with enemy communications. If possible, he hoped also to place his batteries on the west bank of the Mississippi to harass Federal riverboats supplying Grant's army at Vicksburg. The Texans had considerable success on this campaign, burning cotton gins and slave quarters, chasing the lessees from their plantations, capturing hundreds of black workers, and generally creating havoc among two dozen federal leases. Two regiments of Texas cavalry (the 12th and 19th), recently arrived from Little Rock, joined Walker's infantry in spreading ruin along the Mississippi.[14]

An Arkansas surgeon in Tappan's brigade provided graphic descriptions of the destruction: "The torch was applied to *every* building: Gin houses, cotton, fences, barns, cabins, residences, and stacks of fodder. Mules were taken from the plows where the Negroes had left them at the approach of danger, and driven off to the rear of our lines." Some of the Texans were appalled by the flaming, smoking waste: "it's an awful thing to think of destroying things in such a manner," Pvt. John Simmons of the 22nd Texas Infantry wrote. "It looks like destroying the country forever." Capt. John Stark of Newton County could only sympathize with the civilians in the area. "War is a dreadful thing. . . . The enemy burns awhile then some of the planters take [the] oath of allegiance then our men [burn] them out and the plunderers and robbers end by sweeping what is left and the country once in the highest state of cultivation and pride of the South is nothing but a desert." The whole experience left Captain Stark with a dim view of human nature. "When I look on and see the many depredations committed even by our own men[,] as tight as our rules are[,] my soul sickens at the utter depravity of man when turned loose from the restraints of society & the genial influences of home."[15]

The Arkansas surgeon noted that "the result of Walker's raid out there was the capture of a hundred mules and horses, fourteen hundred Negroes, and the destruction of several million dollars worth of property. The country from Milliken's Bend to Lake Providence has been pretty well rid of Yankees and Negroes. It is very certain that their farming operations will not amount to much." Federal officials agreed that the summer raids along the river had ruined a year's work on the government leases: "fully one-half of the crops were not worked at all, and in other cases, when some work was done, the weeds and plants had to grow up together, the ill weeds overtopping the cotton plant." Indeed, according to an observer for the *New York Herald*, "some of the plantations were not restocked after the raid, and speedily ran to waste."[16]

Admiral Porter was furious that the rebels were operating with such impunity and inflicting such damage so close to Federal lines: they have committed "an almost total destruction of houses and property along the river front in that vicinity," he fumed. Porter sent General Ellet's marines to smash the marauding rebels, but the Confederates slipped away from him after a brief skirmish. The admiral noted that the roads were strewn with "all their plunder, splendid furniture, pianos, pictures, etc." Evidently, some of Walker's Texans—given the appropriate target—were just as capable of pillaging and wanton destruction as any Yankee unit. Frustrated at his failure to punish the rebels, Porter could at least insult them: "They are a half-starved, half-naked set, and are in hopes of capturing some of the transports with clothing and provisions."[17]

Some of the Texans might have agreed with Porter that they were a tattered bunch that summer. Their weeks in the swamps had certainly done nothing to improve their appearance. Lt. Theophilus Perry of the 28th Cavalry wrote his wife that "some of the men have not changed suits in four weeks. They remain naked while they wash their clothes. A number of our men have been left at Monroe on account of being barefooted." Private Farrow of the 19th Infantry grumbled that "our clothing is in an awful condition[,] some is perfectly rotten. My bed clothes are damaged badly. I will throw all of them away when we leave here but my blanket." Private Blessington laughed that "Falstaff's ragged regiment was well uniformed in comparison with our troops. No two were costumed with any attempt at uniformity." Not only were they shabby in raiment, they were scruffy and filthy beyond recognition. "But few of the troops had shaved for weeks, and, as a consequence, there was a large and general assortment of unbrushed black, gray, red, and sandy beards, as well as ferocious mustaches and whiskers—enough to rig out an army of West India buccaneers. A more brigandish set of Anglo-Saxon forces has never been collected," Blessington wrote. "So completely disguised were we all, that I doubt whether our anxious mothers would have recognized us."[18]

While the hirsute Texans burned their way up and down the west bank of the Mississippi in late June and early July, they could hear the heavy artillery booming downriver at Vicksburg. Day after day, the distant rumbling continued. "We still hear the big guns at Vicksburg like thunder in a clear sky," Captain Stark of the 13th Cavalry wrote his wife. "Still the brave defenders hold out and show an undaunted front to the enemy." General Grant and Admiral Porter, still casting a wary eye toward Walker's command west of the river, took measures to seal the besieged city off from any possible aid. Grant placed some of his infantry on the narrow peninsula across the river from Vicksburg, thus shutting off the only conceivable approach from the west. Porter placed a "strong force of gunboats" in the same vicinity to guard against any attempts to relieve the city from that direction.[19]

Ignoring the Federal defenses, General Smith asked Walker to find a way to reach the city from the west. Walker, understanding the terrain and the forces arrayed against him, could only shake his head and explain that a march up a narrow, heavily defended peninsula, under the guns of the enemy navy on right and left, would be suicidal: "I consider it absolutely certain, unless the enemy are blind and stupid, that no part of my command would escape capture or destruction if such an attempt should be made." The men in the ranks agreed with Walker. Private Farrow of the 19th Infantry predicted that "we will have a warm time in getting there." In the end, Vicksburg would receive no relief from the west. Gen. Joseph E. Johnston, hovering around the rear of Grant's army with his own Confederate "Army of Relief," saw no way to rescue the Vicksburg garrison from the east, either. By late June and early July, civilians and soldiers on both sides could only wait for the inevitable result of the siege.[20]

On the last night in June, General Walker was happy to receive Richard Taylor's orders to take his division out of the swamps and join Taylor in south Louisiana, leaving the depressing situation at Vicksburg behind. Just as Walker waved the first of his three brigades down the rails from Delhi toward Monroe, Smith countermanded Taylor's orders and directed Walker to hold his division in place. Finally agreeing that a direct approach up the peninsula to Vicksburg was unwise, Smith then instructed Walker to take his Texans back into the swamps to interfere with Federal transports steaming down toward Vicksburg. On the morning of July 7, while on the march from Delhi to the Mississippi River, Walker received the news everyone had dreaded: Vicksburg had surrendered on July 4. At first he did not believe the reports, but confirmation from other sources and new orders from Smith to abandon the whole Vicksburg enterprise convinced him that the river city was lost.[21]

The news spread quickly through the regiments and set off a round of excited and worried speculations. Some of the men lost hope, at least temporarily. "The army is in low spirits since the fall of Vixburge," John T. Knight of the 22nd Infantry wrote, "and a great many of the boys say they will not fight any longer but I do not know what they will do." Pvt. Samuel Farrow of the 19th Infantry was, as usual, among the gloomiest: "Since the fall of Vicksburgh the men are very low spirited. it is the opinion of a great many that the war will soon close. . . . it seems that we had as well give up all for lost. they have got full control of the Mississippi river from its fountain head to where it empties into the Gulf and the Northwestern states now will pour down their forces upon us in such number that we will be compelled to retreat before them as far as they choose to follow." James B. Rounsaville of the 13th Cavalry matched Farrow's pessimism: the surrender of Vicksburg "has caused deep gloom among our officers and arms on this side [of the river], cut off from all communication, for the Feds can soon take Port Hudson, then Richmond and we are gone up [the spout—i.e., ruined] I fear. Very near that now." Capt. Volney Ellis of the 12th Infantry, usually more upbeat than some of his comrades, minimized the damage to morale: "The fall of Vicksburg had somewhat the effect to depress the spirits of the men. It has, however, worn off with the patriotic, but with the croakers and the milk-and-cider fellows, they still refer to it quite ominously."[22]

Like Ellis, others in the division were deeply disappointed but not ready to give up the fight. John S. Bryan of the 16th Cavalry wrote his wife back in McKinney that "the p[o]ssession of vicksburg will give the fedrels free navigation of the Missisippi River. it will also discurage meny of our soldiers, but tis no use to get discuraged for we must fight it out." Theophilus Perry, recently promoted to captain, took the news as evidence that the Confederacy should redouble its efforts: "I am far from disparing. I met the news of the fall of Vicksburg with more equanimity than any body I have seen. I have endeavored to cheer up all that are in low spirits. Our armies are yet in the field and they are the hope of the country. . . . Every man between 18 & 50 that is able to shoulder a gun ought to be put in the field. . . . Every little Editor and stump speaker ought to be put under a musket & knapsack." Surgeon Edward Cade of the 28th Cavalry admitted that the loss of Vicksburg was a setback, but he could detect "no feelings on the part of any one to abandon the struggle." Far from giving up, Private Blessington was angry. He saw no flagging spirits among his comrades. Instead, "a perfect storm of indignation burst forth among the troops. What! surrender, and that too on the 4th of July, above all other days? Impossible. The men broke forth in bitter denunciation of Lieutenant-General Pemberton, boldly proclaiming that he had sold it to the enemy." Blessington still was convinced long after the war that Pemberton had sold out the Confederacy when he surrendered. The loss of

Vicksburg certainly disappointed the men of the Texas Division, and some of them muttered about giving it all up. In the end, though, nearly all of them stuck to the colors, and the Greyhounds continued their war for nearly two more years.[23]

General Walker was happy at least to pull his sickly, sallow, bedraggled brigades out of the low country along the Mississippi River. "The ravages of disease have fearfully weakened my force," he reported, "and I consider it essential to its future usefulness that it should be removed from here as early as practicable." The surgeon for the 14th Infantry recorded 260 illnesses among the 319 men in his regiment in July, most due to various fevers or digestive disorders. The stagnant bayou water the men had been drinking—the only water available—was alive with dangerous microscopic organisms and doubtless was the source of much of the sickness. Capt. Harvey Wallace of the 19th Infantry complained that "we had to drink Bio [bayou] water with a perfect green scum on it."[24]

Edward Cade marveled at the endurance and persistence of his fellow Texans during this campaign:

> Men may sit at home and talk of what soldiers and armies could do or should do but no one can conceive of what a soldier suffers in an arduous and active campaign like ours. Could they see men marching all day through the broiling sun with the thermometer over a hundred degrees carry a load of forty pounds and suffering the intense thirst that is caused by heat dust and perspiration and no water to drink for hours at a time and when night comes camped upon some surface with water *thick* with insects and warm as water can be made by sun . . . , they then would show more sympathy for their condition. . . . I have seen a hundred fall upon the ground incapable of moving hand or foot completely exhausted from heat on a hot days march.[25]

By the second week of this steamy July, E. Kirby Smith was preparing to send Walker's Texans, finally, to join Richard Taylor in south Louisiana. After Milliken's Bend, Smith had turned General Taylor loose to follow his own plan: make enough noise and thrust close enough to New Orleans to force Nathaniel P. Banks's Federal army to abandon the siege of Port Hudson. Taylor's little army of three thousand had swept south in late June and captured Brashear City (present-day Morgan City), the key to any western approach to New Orleans. The loss of Brashear City along with the only railroad in the vicinity (the New Orleans, Opelousas & Great Western), twelve heavy guns, thousands of rifles, and millions of dollars in supplies shocked Federal officers in New Orleans, and they appealed to Banks for protection. Taylor had immediately sent orders to Walker to lead his Texans to Brashear City, which would more than double the size of the Confederate army in south Louisiana. With Brashear City in his pocket and Walker's Texans swelling his ranks, Taylor believed he could pry the Federals away from Port Hudson by appearing in force on the right bank of the river opposite New Orleans. When Smith countermanded Taylor's instructions to Walker and held the Texas Division near Vicksburg in early July, Taylor proceeded without Walker's reinforcements. His army of Louisiana and Texas troops cut and thrust from Brashear City eastward to the banks of the Mississippi River and advanced within sixteen miles of New Orleans, sending Unionists in the Crescent City into a panic. On the very edge of seeing his plan work to perfection, Taylor received the news on July 10 that both Vicksburg and Port Hudson had surrendered. "A few hours more, and the city would have been wild with excitement," Taylor groaned.[26]

The Louisiana general blamed Smith for the failure to relieve Port Hudson. "The plan I had arranged for an attack on New Orleans fell through as soon as I was advised that Walker's division would not join me," Taylor informed Smith's adjutant. "That the plan referred to would have succeeded . . . I do not entertain the slightest doubt." Taylor continued that theme in his postwar memoirs. General Smith had unwisely kept Walker "and his fine division" idle around Vicksburg. "The time wasted on these absurd movements cost us the garrison of Port Hudson." Whether the addition of Walker's Greyhounds to his army would have enabled Taylor to raise the siege of Port Hudson can never be answered with any certainty, of course, but Taylor was not alone in thinking his plan would succeed. Federal soldiers in Louisiana and later historians agreed that Taylor, if reinforced, probably would have disrupted the entire Port Hudson campaign. A Massachusetts infantryman wrote that "there can be little doubt that had Walker's division been sent to Taylor, as he requested, he would have captured New Orleans, though he would have been unable to hold it for more than a short time. In regaining it, however, Banks might have felt obliged to raise the siege of Port Hudson."[27]

Walker's Texas Division might have made a significant difference in the war along the Mississippi River on two occasions in the spring and summer of 1863. In the first instance, when General Grant's almost unprotected supply line lay within easy reach of the Texans, E. Kirby Smith sent them off in the opposite direction—to Natchitoches and Alexandria. By the time Smith redirected them to the west bank of the Mississippi, Grant had moved his once exposed communications to the opposite bank. On the second occasion, when New Orleans was virtually unprotected and vulnerable from the west, Smith held Walker's division in the swampy lowlands near Vicksburg. By the time Smith released the Texans to reinforce Taylor, Port Hudson had fallen and New Orleans was no longer a target. When Walker's soldiers could have made a difference at Vicksburg, they were in western Louisiana. When they could have made a difference at Port Hudson, they were in north Louisiana. Smith, a fine military leader in some ways, certainly squandered good opportunities to disrupt Federal operations along the Mississippi in 1863, and his misjudgments contributed to the Confederacy's loss of control of the Mississippi River.

Beginning on July 11 and continuing for several days, General Walker began shuttling his regiments and brigades from Delhi to Monroe, thirty-five miles to the west, via the Vicksburg, Shreveport & Texas Railroad. Higher ground, better water, and proximity to the hospitals in Monroe, Walker hoped, would restore his men to marching and fighting trim. Within a few days Walker received E. Kirby Smith's belated instructions to join Richard Taylor in south Louisiana. The division would follow the same route it had taken two months earlier: an overland march to the vicinity of Natchitoches, 120 miles to the southwest, and then a riverboat ride down the winding Red River to Alexandria.[28]

The march to the Red River was hot and dusty—and unusually slow. Roughly one thousand of the Texans were too sick to march and had to be transported in wagons and ambulances. Because Walker had only twenty wagons and twelve ambulances to carry the sick, he was forced to rig up a system that slowed the march enough to allow the weaker ill soldiers to keep up: "The plan adopted was to take the worst cases early in the morning by ambulances and wagons, and transport them say, five, six, & at most seven miles, to the encampment for the next night. The ambulances, etc, then returned for the next worst class of cases, whilst the stronger ones and the convalescents would take their own time, resting frequently under the shade of the forest through which they were passing, and reaching camp before dark." The surgeons and quartermasters thus "succeeded in moving this camp and all it's sick over one hundred miles in sixteen days." By the time the division reached the Red River, the great majority of the sick were able to shoulder their muskets once more and resume their places in the ranks.[29]

The only event worthy of note on this march—other than the back-and-forth movements of the ambulances—was the departure of Gen. Henry McCulloch from the division he had organized and once briefly commanded. On July 22, at the overnight camp near the village of Vernon, McCulloch packed his bags, made his farewells, and prepared to assume new duties in Texas. He would spend the remainder of the war as military commander of the Northern Sub-district of Texas, dealing with conscripts, Comanches, deserters, and outlaws of various stripes. Although he never rose to the legendary status of his brother Ben, the quiet and unassuming Henry McCulloch was among the first prominent Texans to join the Confederate army, and he served his state and the Confederacy in a number of thankless positions. Replacing him in command of his brigade until a more senior officer could be appointed was George M. Flournoy, the young colonel of the 16th Texas Infantry who had led his men along the base of the levee at Milliken's Bend to shield McCulloch's left flank.[30]

One by one, the regiments reached Campti, several miles upriver from Natchitoches, in late July. A few days later they marched down the left bank of the river, ferried across to the small river port of Grand Ecore, and then boarded transports sent down from Shreveport to transfer them to Alexandria. By now the Texans were old hands at loading and boarding riverboats. Pvt. John Porter was one of the men detailed to guide wagons and mules up the gangplanks. "We worked all night," Porter wrote. "After all the wagons were aboard, we began to lead the mules, one by one, aboard over the stage plank, and very soon, one seemed a little scared, and the boys began a Texas yell, which caused it to fall a distance of twenty feet into the river. He swam down about two hundred yards and landed on the opposite side. We took a yawl, and went and swam him back." Soldiering involved considerably more than mere battles.[31]

After several hours on the river, the lead transports puffed up to the landings at Alexandria on August 4, and the rowdy Texans moved down the gangplanks to set up camps near the town. The last time Walker's division had been in the vicinity—in late May—local citizens had welcomed them as saviors from the clutches of General Banks's Federal army. This time, Private Porter observed, the reception was noticeably cooler: "We landed here with less welcome than we received a few months before; no enemy now being in their country, they feared for their commissaries and forage of their fruitful farms." A son of one of the local citizens wrote later that "Walker's troops were about as welcome as the Union Army to the citizens of the part of the State in which they operated. They committed almost as many depredations as the enemy. . . . These Texas men were good soldiers, brave and daring, and as fearless as one could desire, but they would confiscate property as badly as any Union soldier who ever served in this section." Some of the men, convinced that the " 'Commissary Department of the C. S. Army' was nothing more than a myth," offered to buy food with discounted Confederate currency. "I have tried to buy [necessities] and cannot for these big planters wont sell nothing they have got because they have to take Confederate money, but you ought to see me taking watermelons and sugar cane," Jonathan Knight laughed to his wife. If the Confederate military bureaucracy could not provide adequate food for the Greyhounds, they knew how to supplement their diets.[32]

After several days under the suspicious eyes of local planters, the Texans marched off on August 10 to a new camp in the pine forests about twenty-five miles southwest of Alexandria. If the soldiers thought they would be allowed to rest after their labors in the swamps, they soon learned otherwise at the new site, which they named Camp Green. "The health of the troops at this camp was very good," Blessington wrote, "owing, I suppose, to the *morning exercise* we took before breakfast, in the way of marching five miles. . . . This kind of exercise was considered rest for 'Walker's Greyhounds.'" At another camp in the vicinity, called Camp Texas, drill proceeded as usual. Pvt. John Porter of Upshur County remembered later that "Camp Texas was a beautiful pine slope, with the prettiest clear creek in rear of the camp that I ever saw. We cleared off a large drill ground in front, and spent a great deal of our time in drilling, and in addition to our Reg't drill, we were marched to the woods, and drilled in Brigades, and the entire Division occasionally." Even on the hot, dusty training grounds, Porter could find something entertaining: "While here, Col. [Wilburn] King was thrown from a horse on the drill field. Here, also, to the great amusement of the [18th Infantry] Reg't., while on the drill field, he stepped into a hole (where a pine stump had burned out) almost to his armpits." There was always time to laugh at officers.[33]

From early August to late September, the division had little to do, and the inactivity began to wear on the men. The lack of any immediate military threat, inadequate rations, delayed wages, and a stingy furlough policy combined to produce another rash of desertions in the late summer and early fall of 1863. Poor and insufficient rations—and no pay to supplement the fare—were particularly troublesome in the piney woods that summer. In fact, pay was more than a year in arrears for some units. "There are a great many deserted. There have been twelve or fifteen that left this regiment," Pvt. John Simmons of the 22nd Infantry observed. "The men are very badly dissatisfied here. They ain't treated like white men ought to be. They won't half feed them, nor pay them what is due them."[34] Private Knight, also of the 22nd, was just as angry: "Yesterday they [the men] never got any beef and today they refused to go on guard but the officers talked them all out of that but two of Comp. (A). They went under guard and I heard today they was going to ball and chain them but that will not do for I don't think this Division will ever bare it."[35]

At one point in early September, General Walker had to call some of his troops into line to quell the mutinous actions of others. On the night of September 4, apparently under some prearranged plan, scores of men walked away from camp and dared anyone to stop them. "About dark the men commenced the War hoops and Fireing signal guns all over the Division," a soldier in the 19th Infantry wrote. "I was at church at the time. The Parson was requested to close the service and send the men to their camps." Before their officers could talk sense to the mutinous soldiers, "the men loaded their guns and then they all collected together and then they marched off in good order for Texas. . . . The regiment was called out in line. Company H turned out to a man all present and ready for action but we was on the line at least 20 minutes before any other Company, and consequently the gard house is full today." David M. Ray, the former Grayson County schoolteacher, was struck by the brazenness of the troublemakers. "A few nights ago a crowd of them came by our regt and hallooed for all men who wanted to go to Texas to fall in," Ray told his mother. "I think they will have to bring back and shoot a few of them." The unauthorized absences in the late summer of 1863 were different from those in Arkansas the preceding winter: the later leave-takings were loud and public, very unlike the quiet disappearances at Camp Nelson, Bayou Meto, and Pine Bluff.[36]

Capt. Elijah Petty, now returned to his unit after a long recuperation at home for a shoulder wound suffered at Milliken's Bend, noted that morale had deteriorated in his absence. The men generally had not given up on the idea of fighting the Yankees, but they did believe they were being mistreated: "Dissatisfaction and mutinous feelings exist to a considerable extent mostly however on account of rations etc and not against the Cause." Other comments by the Texans, including references to "Spanish furloughs"—absences without leave followed by a voluntary return to the army—buttress the idea that most of the men were not giving up on independence and certainly not deserting to the enemy. They were just hungry, lonesome, and resentful, and they wanted to go home for a while. The four Lakey brothers of the 19th Infantry (Noah, J. V., S. H., and W. C.), all in their twenties and thirties and close neighbors in San Augustine County before the war, walked away from camp on September 3, but all were back in their tents by February. Pvt. Samuel Farrow of the same regiment noted a few months later that "all the boys that deserted our company last summer has returned, and have been pardoned, so we have a larger company by 13 men than [earlier]. . . . Men that have been absent a good while without leave are dropping into the regiment every day."[37]

In the gloomy late summer of 1863, though, their officers and comrades could not foresee the return of these prodigals. Even the ever-cheerful Private Blessington noted dark mutterings among the men. When captains in the division requested the authority to furlough two men at a time from each company, General Walker forwarded the request to General Taylor, but Taylor refused.

There was much excitement and dissatisfaction in camp. After long months of severe service, enduring untold hardships and trials, fighting several battles with a courage and bravery which had made their name distinguished everywhere, the only boon asked, the only favor which could have been conferred on them as a recompense for their deeds, was refused. Now they could look forward only to a life in the army until the termination of the struggle. The disappointment was most bitterly felt, and it is not surprising that it found expression in still more bitter words.[38]

By late September the number of desertions dwindled and whispers of mutiny faded away. Arrests of the most outspoken troublemakers, a general pardon for those who returned to their units by September 30, and the threat of firing squads for those who continued to resist military authority all seemed to get the attention of the men. "I think it will go no farther as some of them have been caught, tried, and are sentenced to be shot before the command on the 25th," Col. Richard Waterhouse wrote his wife. Captain Petty informed his daughter that "the desertion furor has about ceased the prospect of getting shot having detered some and the bad material having most been expended."[39]

The Confederate government's inability to feed its soldiers adequately and pay them on time, and its reluctance, given its numerical disadvantage, to provide a generous furlough policy explain most of the Texas Division's desertions and unauthorized absences through the summer of 1863. Nearly all the Texans were discouraged by the fall of Vicksburg, and a small proportion apparently gave up on the war effort as a result. But the great majority suffered no sudden failure of will or inadequate nationalism or class anger. They resented the Yankees as much as ever, they still believed they were protecting their wives, children, and communities from northern tyranny, and they remained in their tents. But they also thought they had been treated shabbily—especially after their Herculean labors in the swamps near Vicksburg—and some of them simply would not stand for it. Instead of thanks and rewards for their recent sacrifices, they received scanty rations, no pay, and no furloughs. A visit home would mean decent food, reunions with loved ones, and attendance to personal business. The Confederacy owed them that at least. The war could wait for a while.

Rather than take "unofficial furloughs," many of the men turned to religion in the late summer and early fall. Civilian ministers roamed through the camps in the piney woods near Alexandria, preaching in open-air services to the restless soldiers. Religion had generally been relegated to a very low priority once the men left their home communities in Texas, but now—having been buffeted about by the misfortunes of war and military life—hundreds of soldiers found comfort once again in the Protestant traditions they had learned as children. A private in George Flournoy's brigade, David Ray of the 16th Cavalry, wrote that "there [has] been a protracted meeting going on in camp with considerable success[.] about 50 were baptized beside a good many which joined other churches[.] the preaching was all by baptist ministers I believe; I was surprised at the interest manifested by the soldiers as they had previously cared but little for preaching." In another letter Ray described the success that visiting preachers were having in the army: "while we were at Alexandria . . . I heard the Rev. Mr. Howard of New Orleans preach a very good sermon after which we repaired to the water where six subjects were buried in baptism by Parson hay, beneath the turbid waters of old red river." Edward Cade of the 28th Cavalry also was struck by the shift from sin to sanctity: "You never Saw such Scenes in your life. The woods are filled day and night with men praying and singing. You seldom hear an oath or see men playing cards when before oaths saluted your ears on every side and cards were played by near every one day and night."[40]

In early October, Ray reported that the revival had also reached into Horace Randal's brigade: "There is a protracted meeting going on in Randalls Brigade which is camped near ours. I saw seven baptized yesterday evening and they are now baptizing again. in the last two months there have been a great many conversions among the Soldiers." One of the preachers in that brigade, Martin Smith, had resigned from the army in order to serve as a chaplain to his comrades. In the camps during the fall of 1863, he wrote his sister, he had "nothing to do but preach." Even after several weeks, he wrote, "our meeting still goes on. Have baptized 92 & had two baptized for me while I was sick." Chaplain Smith's brother-in-law, Surgeon Edward Cade of the 28th Cavalry, agreed that a new attitude was spreading through the army, including the third brigade commanded by General Hawes: "The spirit of the Lord is in the army here," he wrote.[41]

Historians have long remarked on the religious revivals that swept through Civil War armies. Among some armies in the eastern and western theaters, where thousands of men were killed and torn apart in colossal battles, religion often served as soothing consolation for personal losses. It reassured terrified or grief-stricken men of their spiritual immortality. In the case of Walker's Greyhounds in the late summer and fall of 1863, religion provided a sense of community in shared suffering. The Texans were not so much terrified by war as they were bored and angered by the inefficiencies and injustices of a military life that seemed to be accomplishing nothing. They might be able to stand their problems if they felt they were achieving something. But here they were, almost always sent to the wrong place at the wrong time, doing no good and languishing in the piney woods of central Louisiana, far from home and far from the enemy. It all seemed such a waste.[42]

In the midst of the grumbling about rations, pay, and furloughs, General

Walker received word in late August that Federal troops had crossed the Mississippi River and occupied Monroe, that other Federal columns were bearing down on Little Rock, and that still another Federal expedition had crossed the Mississippi from Natchez to reduce the small Confederate fort at Harrisonburg, about forty miles northeast of Alexandria. Confederate gunners at this strong point, Fort Beauregard, had turned back pursuing Federal gunboats four months earlier when the transports carrying Walker's division had reversed course and raced up the Ouachita River in a mad scramble for safety. It was now the Texans' turn to rescue Fort Beauregard.[43]

On September 1 Generals Taylor and Walker, apparently misinformed about the strength of the Federal raiding party, sent Col. Horace Randal's lone brigade, about eleven hundred men, to confront a Federal column of roughly four thousand. Randal, a young West Point graduate (Class of 1854) and veteran of the frontier Indian Wars, had neither artillery nor cavalry on this assignment, and he therefore moved blindly through the piney woods north of Alexandria toward a much stronger foe. Pvt. William Oden of Leon County wrote his wife that the Texans "got in to a very ticklish place" on this trip. When the Confederate commander inside the fort, Lt. Col. George W. Logan, realized that the enemy was closer to his works and much stronger than Randal's relief expedition, he destroyed everything his forty effectives could smash and abandoned the earthworks early on September 4. Randal's Confederates skirmished with lead elements of the Federal raiding party the same morning, but the young colonel, informed that Logan was abandoning the fort and retreating to join him, broke off the engagement and turned back toward Alexandria with a loss of only two men captured. The Federal raiders destroyed as much of the fort as they could and then returned to Natchez with two cannons and twenty prisoners. They thus accomplished their mission to reduce Fort Beauregard and distract trans-Mississippi Confederates from focusing on Little Rock, which fell under Union control on September 10.[44]

While Randal's brigade was on its fruitless errand, the rest of the division moved to Alexandria and Pineville, directly across the Red River from Alexandria. Some of the restless Texans almost immediately got themselves into trouble in Pineville. "This place was filled with a great many low characters of the fair sex, and it was a difficult matter for the officers to keep the men in camp," John Porter of the 18th Infantry remembered. "One of these women struck one of our men on the arm, with a large knife, and inflicted a very serious wound. Many others suffered the penalties of military law, for being caught in their company by the patrol." Prostitutes, brawls, and unauthorized absences may have combined to convince officers to move the men back into the forests, where they might be more easily controlled. When Randal returned from his expedition toward Harrisonburg, he found the Texans back in the countryside, drilling and muttering under their breath.[45]

Taken altogether, the months from June to September had been most disappointing for the Texas Division. Although the men in McCulloch's old brigade counted their bayonet charge at Milliken's Bend as a victory, still, the affair at Young's Point had been a bust, and neither action accomplished the overall goal of disrupting the Federal supply system. Hundreds of men had been disabled by swamp maladies of one type or another, reducing the division to the strength of a brigade for much of the summer. The fall of Vicksburg and Port Hudson disappointed everyone and convinced a few of the men that the whole cause was lost. Even when the Texans escaped from the steamy bayous near Vicksburg, they felt mistreated. Their pay was far in arrears, their rations were poor and scant, their furloughs were past due, and they had nothing much to do in the piney woods, far from the enemy. In fact, they felt useless, both to the Confederacy and to their families. October would bring cooler weather, more action, and better attitudes to the Texas Greyhounds.

Major General John G. Walker at the end of the Civil War.
*Courtesy Lawrence T. Jones III Collection, Austin, Texas*

Major General Richard Taylor, Confederate commander at Mansfield and Pleasant Hill.
*Courtesy Hill College History Center, Hillsboro, Texas*

General Edmund Kirby Smith, commander of the Confederate Trans-Mississippi Department.
*Courtesy Hill College History Center, Hillsboro, Texas*

Colonel Edward Clark, former governor of Texas and
commander of the 14th Texas Infantry Regiment.
*Courtesy Hill College History Center, Hillsboro, Texas*

Colonel Oran M. Roberts, president of the Texas
secession convention and commander of the
infantry at the Battle of Bayou Bourbeau.
*Courtesy Hill College History Center, Hillsboro, Texas*

Brigadier General Horace Randal and his wife.
*Courtesy Hill College History Center, Hillsboro, Texas*

Brigadier General William R. Scurry, veteran of the New
Mexico campaign and the recapture of Galveston and
commander of a brigade in Walker's Texas Division.
*Courtesy Hill College History Center, Hillsboro, Texas*

Brigadier General Thomas N. Waul, commander of a brigade in
Walker's Texas Division, photographed after the war.
*Courtesy Hill College History Center, Hillsboro, Texas*

Colonel Wilburn H. King, commander of the 18th Texas Infantry.
*Courtesy Hill College History Center, Hillsboro, Texas*

# CHAPTER 8

# Bayou Bourbeau

While Walker's Texas Division sweated from camp to camp around Alexandria in August and September 1863, Gen. Nathaniel P. Banks launched another Federal expedition from New Orleans. Banks's objective this time was Texas. Powerful textile mill owners in the northeastern United States had been lobbying in Washington for a military offensive into Texas, partly to redeem the Lone Star State for the Union and partly to feed Texas cotton to the hungry maws of their mills. Joining the New England and New York manufacturers in their political campaign was a group of Texas Unionists. The most prominent among them was Andrew Jackson Hamilton, an Alabama-born lawyer, former member of Congress from Texas, and staunch Unionist. Hamilton's allegiance to the United States had prompted his neighbors to chase him out of Texas in 1862, and he had taken refuge in Washington, where President Lincoln appointed him a brigadier general and military governor of Texas. Hamilton and other refugee Unionists hoped to accompany a military expedition into Texas and set up a state government loyal to the United States.[1]

President Lincoln had another motive for a takeover of Texas. In June 1863 a French army of thirty-five thousand men marched into central Mexico, occupied Mexico City, deposed Pres. Benito Juárez, and established a French-made government. This obvious slap at the Monroe Doctrine—a U.S. warning to European powers to keep their hands off the Western Hemisphere—and the potential for cooperation between the French and the Confederates convinced Lincoln that the United States needed a military presence in Texas. After the fall of Vicksburg and Port Hudson in July, Lincoln turned his attention west. Federal occupation of the Lone Star State would satisfy the insistent textile mill owners and the impatient refugee Texans and put the impertinent French on notice to avoid any flirtations with the trans-Mississippi Confederacy.[2]

General Banks first tried to penetrate Texas along the Gulf coast. By landing near the mouth of the Sabine River, the state boundary with Louisiana, Banks hoped to march the short distance to Houston and Galveston to establish a Federal presence in the Lone Star State. From this base in the state's trade and transportation center, Banks's army could provide a protecting umbrella over the new Unionist government to be established by Hamilton, gradually extend Federal control into other parts of Texas, give New England and New York textile magnates a chance to acquire cotton, and shake a warning finger under the noses of the French in Mexico. Accordingly, on September 4 Banks sent five thousand infantry under Maj. Gen. William B. Franklin by steamer from New Orleans. Four gunboats accompanied the expedition along the Gulf coast to the mouth of the Sabine River. And then the unthinkable happened. On September 8 forty-seven Confederate artillerists—outnumbered one hundred to one and commanded by a mere lieutenant, Richard Dowling—drove away the entire Federal expedition after disabling two of the gunboats and capturing three hundred prisoners. The one-sided Battle of Sabine Pass became one of the most embarrassing defeats of the war for the U.S. Army and Navy.[3]

After the humiliation at Sabine Pass, General Banks shifted his efforts toward an overland expedition into Texas. Banks's superior in Washington, Maj. Gen. Henry W. Halleck, urged Banks to move up the Red River through Alexandria, Natchitoches, and Shreveport and then jump directly into East Texas near Marshall and Jefferson. The advantages of this route were very attractive: the Red River would provide a valuable supply line from New Orleans, Banks could break up the headquarters of the Confederate Trans-Mississippi Department and the war plants at Shreveport, and cotton bales by the thousands could be gathered in the Red River valley and in East Texas. Banks agreed that, under normal circumstances, the Red River route would be best. But the river in the late summer of 1863 was unusually low, he reported, too low for Federal gunboats and supply vessels. Since the Confederates were alert to any coastal landings after the Sabine Pass expedition and since the Red River route appeared impractical, the best alternative might be an overland dash across the sparsely settled prairies of south Louisiana to Texas. An eighty-mile train ride from New Orleans westward to Brashear City, followed by a short jaunt up Bayou Teche to the vicinity of Vermilionville (present-day Lafayette), would put Banks's army in a position to follow either route into Texas: up the Red River if the water was high enough or directly west across the prairies to Niblett's Bluff on the lower Sabine River.[4]

General Banks's army of thirty thousand men began crossing from New Orleans to the right bank of the Mississippi on September 13. While Banks remained at headquarters in New Orleans, General Franklin, the ill-starred general of Sabine Pass, took field command. The New Orleans, Opelousas & Great Western Railroad took the men westward to Brashear City over the next several days. On October 3 the long blue columns of the Federal army began snaking their way up the narrow roads along Bayou Teche, from Brashear City toward Vermilionville, about sixty miles to the northwest. The only Confederates in the vicinity were Richard Taylor's forty-four hundred veterans of earlier campaigns along Bayou Teche—about twenty-four hundred Louisiana and Texas infantry commanded by Brig. Gen. Alfred Mouton and two thousand Texas cavalry led by Brig. Gen. Thomas Green. Grossly outnumbered once again, Taylor ordered General Walker in late September to lead his Texas Division down to south Louisiana as soon as possible. Even with the forty-two hundred lean and road-toughened Greyhounds in his ranks, Taylor's army would rise up to only one-third the strength of Franklin's advancing column.[5]

One day after a grand review of the whole division on September 23, Walker started his brigades down the roads to meet General Taylor's army. Leaving the scenes of their recent troubles seemed to buck up the spirits of the men. Private Farrow admitted that "we are all better satisfied while moving than when we are stationed." Another Texan, W. B. Hunter, noticed the change: "Our men have quit desirting and seem to be better satisfied than they have been for some time. I believe we can whip any number any where. what men we have now are the true grit." J. T. Knight in Wilburn King's brigade detected the same quality: "Our army is in the best spirits now that it has ever been. I think it has whitled down to the pure grit at last." After zigzagging through the country south of Alexandria, the Texans settled into camps a few miles from the old bayou village of Washington on October 17. Camped nearby were Taylor's infantry and cavalry, and General Taylor himself arrived from Alexandria a day later, happy, finally, to have Walker's Texas Division where he wanted it. "Released at length from the swamps of the Tensas, where it had suffered from sickness, Walker's division of Texas infantry joined me in the early autumn, and was posted to the north of Opelousas," he wrote in his memoirs. "Seconded by good brigade and regimental officers, he had thoroughly disciplined his men, and made them in every sense soldiers; and their efficiency in action was soon established."[6]

Now that they were joined with Taylor's army and directly under Taylor's control, the Texans expected to fight. "Owing to his [Taylor's] arrival in camp, the troops anticipated being brought into action every day," Blessington wrote. Besides, Washington was only seven miles north of Opelousas, and General Franklin's Federal army, slowly grinding north along Bayou Teche, was only eleven miles south of Opelousas. Somewhere and soon, there in the heart of Louisiana sugar country, Taylor was determined to engage the enemy, no matter the numerical odds. He ordered Walker on October 11 to "have all your surplus baggage and the wagons not actually needed and indispensable sent to a camp at some eligible point." In addition, Taylor wrote, "hold your command in light marching condition and ready at a moment's warning to move toward the enemy, fully prepared for action." Captain Petty got his company ready for a fight. "Our trains & sick have been sent back," he wrote his wife. Like any good officer, Petty also had to deal intelligently with personnel problems: "Tom Irvine is sick again & has been sent to the rear. This is according to his Mothers wish which was that he should get sick before every fight."[7]

Like soldiers for thousands of years, Walker's Texans hurried to their stations, anticipating some excitement, and then waited—and waited. General Franklin's advance was very slow and cautious, and the overmatched Taylor could not afford to strike until conditions were exactly right; thus, little happened for more than two weeks. Some of the Greyhounds, remembering Perkins Landing, Milliken's Bend, and Young's Point, suspected that the Federals were not willing to fight unless their gunboats were nearby. Capt. Virgil Rabb of the 16th Infantry observed that the Yankees "place implicit confidence in their Gun Boats. They hate like the D——l to get on dry land, so I think they will wait for the rivers to get up before they try to invade this country." John S. Bryan of the 16th Cavalry agreed that the Federals "generly stay close to thair gun boats so thair is no getting at them unless by a great disadvantage on our side." If General Taylor could entice the Yankees into a scrap, Captain Petty was certain, the Texans would be prepared: "We are ready, eager and anxious for a fight and aint at all particular when or how it comes. Our army is in good health, fine spirits and good moral[e], better than it has been in three months and if the fight does come off the federal fur will fly."[8]

While they waited for the Federals to approach, the Texans marveled at the richness of the sugar country all around them. They had seen the swamps of northeast Louisiana, they had steamed up and down the rivers of north Louisiana on several occasions, and they had marched across the sandy hills between Monroe and Natchitoches, but never had they seen such lush vegetation and refined homes and neighborhoods. Captain Petty wrote his daughter that this "is the finest & richest country I have ever seen. It looks like the garden spot of the world." Captain Rabb was equally impressed: "The whole country through here is the richest I ever saw. Its just one Sugar farm after another. In fact, the whole country is covered with them." Rabb was particularly impressed by the yards and shrubbery around plantation homes. "They have trees here growing in almost every shape you can mention. Some in the shape of large rocking chairs, others in the shape of tables, perfectly round with a level surface, and then beautifull Arbors of all discriptions with doors and windows to them and hedges of all sorts. . . . Oh, I tell you, they are beyond discription."[9]

The Greyhounds also noted the scars of war on the countryside, even the scars they cut. David Ray of Grayson County wrote his mother that "this is the finest country I ever saw in my life but the war has nearly ruined it. very few of the plantations are cultivated and the homes are entered by the soldiers and every thing of value carried off that they want." Captain Rabb also mentioned the deserted plantations: "Most of the owners have gone to Texas and left their plantations here to go to destruction. Very often our Army has to use their [fence] rails for firewood, and the Yanks never use anything else when they are convenient. So between both armies, if the war lasts much longer this country will be a complete wreck." In fact, Rabb concluded, it did not matter much which army was in the neighborhood: "There is nothing worse than a friendly army except the army of an enemy. . . . I will give you one instance. There was a fine Piano left in a house near where we are now camped, and I am told that some of the Boys from this Division went up there and tore it all to pieces." Sadly, Rabb conceded, "there is always men along in an Army mean enough to do almost anything in the world." Louisiana's civilians must have prayed at times for protection from their protectors.[10]

After a week of anticipation, the Texans finally had a chance for action. On October 24 General Franklin's cavalry division trotted north out of Opelousas, through Washington, and then approached Taylor's army near the village of Moundville. General Taylor was kept well informed by his cavalry scouts, and he prepared a large-scale ambush for the Federal horsemen. Six batteries of artillery were concealed in the edge of some timber, Walker's Texans and Mouton's infantry were hidden in drainage ditches and behind outbuildings of a sugar plantation, and all Confederate eyes were trained on the road leading from Washington. "Every minute seemed like an hour to us, till the ball should be opened," Blessington remembered. While waiting in the ditch, Captain Petty noticed that "citizens were flying by us to the rear. Our Cavalry were driving back all the cattle and other stock left by the Citizens in their flight to keep the feds from getting it. The sick, the halt, the maimed, the blind with the wagons were sent to the rear. The horns (brass band) were sent away and the musicians transposed into an infirmary corps to pack off the wounded. The guns were furnished, ammunition inspected, cannons planted, sharp-shooters and skirmishers thrown forward, every officer and man at his post and on the lookout." After some sharp skirmishing with the Confederate cavalry, though, the Federals turned their horses around and returned to Washington. There would be no battle that day.[11]

The only other event that sparked much interest during this waiting game was the arrival in Walker's camp of Brig. Gen. William Read Scurry in late October. Forty-two years old, the Tennessee native had moved to Texas in his teens, practiced law while he was still only twenty, and served in the legislature of the Republic of Texas in his early twenties. Scurry had fought in the Mexican War, owned and edited an Austin newspaper, and served in the Texas Secession Convention before entering Confederate service in July 1861 as a cavalry officer. He was a personal and political enemy of Sam Houston, who smeared Scurry with a nickname that has stuck to him ever since—"Dirty Neck Bill." Scurry's hard-hitting military style had served the Confederacy well during the ill-fated New Mexico expedition of 1862 and the recapture of Galveston from Federal control on January 1, 1863. In both campaigns Scurry had distinguished himself as a skillful, daring, and aggressive military leader. On September 17 Gen. Edmund Kirby Smith had appointed Scurry to replace Henry McCulloch as brigade commander in Walker's division, and Scurry relieved the interim commander, Col. George Flournoy, while the Texans were camped north of Washington. The men in the brigade were quite happy to welcome so famous a commander to lead them. Captain Petty of the 17th Infantry wrote that Scurry "is a fighter and those who follow him will go to the Cannon's Mouth." The regimental bands in his new brigade serenaded General Scurry upon his arrival.[12]

General Franklin could have used a forceful and clever leader like Scurry in his own army. Because of poor intelligence gathering by the blue cavalry, Franklin and his subordinate officers believed that Taylor's army was in full flying retreat toward Alexandria in late October. Maj. Gen. Cadwallader C. Washburn, commander of the Federal 13th Corps, believed that the Confederates had withdrawn and were no closer than twenty-five or thirty miles to the north. Actually, Taylor's men were primed for combat only three miles from Federal sentries. Brig. Gen. Albert L. Lee, the Federal cavalry commander, told Franklin that Taylor's "whole force is retreating as fast as it can march toward Alexandria." Generals Washburn and Lee clearly did not understand Richard Taylor. Rather than retreating, he was searching for some way to strike at the larger Federal army.[13]

General Franklin edged back south of Opelousas in early November to secure better forage and provisions for his twenty-five thousand men.[14] That gave Taylor his opportunity. Franklin incautiously left his rear guard—part of his cavalry and an infantry brigade of westerners from the 13th Corps—isolated about three miles from the main body of the army. This was exactly the sort of error for which Taylor had been waiting. The commander of the Federal infantry brigade, Col. Richard Owen, was the same officer who had faced McCulloch's Texans at the Perkins plantation five months earlier, and one of his five regiments, the 60th Indiana, was the same one that had scrambled aboard the river transport at Perkins Landing. The veterans of Owen's brigade, about 1,250 strong, were experienced, tough, and confident. They had helped to turn back Confederate invasions of Kentucky in the fall of 1862, had borne the brunt of the fight at Arkansas Post in early 1863, and had fought with Grant's victorious army at Port

Gibson, Champion Hill, and Big Black River Bridge during the Vicksburg campaign. They represented the cream of the western Federal army, and they had no fear of Taylor's scruffy Confederates.[15]

Brig. Gen. Tom Green's Texas cavalry had been flitting around the edges of the Federal army for weeks, scooping up stragglers, burning bridges, counting regimental flags and artillery pieces, and generally making life miserable for General Franklin. General Taylor had been assigning two or three different infantry regiments from Walker's and Mouton's divisions to support the horse soldiers every few days. In early November the three regiments were Col. Oran Roberts's 11th Texas Infantry from Randal's brigade, Col. Wilburn H. King's 18th Texas Infantry from Hawes's brigade, and the 15th Texas Infantry from Mouton's division, temporarily commanded by Lt. Col. James E. Harrison of Waco. All three units were stationed just north of Washington while the rest of Taylor's infantry camped several miles to the northwest. Several hours before sunrise on November 3, General Green sent a courier to shake the foot soldiers of the three advance regiments out of their blankets. By 2 A.M. they were hurrying south through Washington toward Opelousas, where Green and his cavalry were waiting. Armed with fresh information from Federal deserters, Green was ready now to come crashing down on Franklin's exposed rear units, camped several miles south of Opelousas near Bayou Bourbeau.[16]

One hour before daylight on Tuesday, November 3, the three Texas infantry regiments pulled into the north edge of Opelousas and filed off the road to cook their breakfasts on the grounds surrounding the local Catholic church. General Green gathered his officers around him and handed out instructions. Col. Oran Roberts of the 11th Infantry, the former Texas supreme court justice and future governor, was the senior officer among the three regimental commanders and was therefore placed in charge of the infantry. His lieutenant colonel, James H. Jones, would lead the 11th Texas in its first fight of the war. Up to now the regiment had always been held in reserve. Col. Wilburn King's 18th Infantry was nearly as inexperienced. Their only time under fire had been their rearguard defense at Richmond, Louisiana, five months earlier. They were still armed with old .69-caliber smoothbore muskets, effective at less than one hundred yards. The 15th Texas of Mouton's division had taken part in the later stages of Taylor's summer campaign in south Louisiana and had recently fought well under General Green at Stirling's Plantation on the Atchafalaya River. In addition, the 15th was armed with highly effective Enfield rifles. Compared to the soldiers in the 11th and 18th, the men of the 15th were veterans. As a group, the three infantry regiments numbered only 950 men. With Green's two thousand horsemen and the gunners from two sections of artillery, the little army counted about three thousand men altogether.[17]

As soon as the foot soldiers had gulped down their morning meals and the cavalry and artillery were lined up, the whole column moved south on the road from Opelousas to Vermilionville. One of the two artillery sections rolling down the dirt road toward the enemy was from one of the batteries originally attached to Walker's division, Capt. James Daniel's Lamar Artillery. None of Daniel's gunners in the two-piece rifled section had yet fired a shot at the enemy. Like Colonel Roberts's infantry, they had always been held in reserve up to now. Their comrades in the other section were experienced veterans from the famed Valverde Battery who had been fighting with General Taylor in his south Louisiana campaigns. Camped seven miles down the road, near the village of Grand Coteau, were Colonel Owen's westerners. Supporting them were a six-gun Ohio battery, a section of a Massachusetts battery, part of Albert Lee's cavalry, and detachments from various other units—nearly two thousand men altogether. Owen's tents were on the western edge of a belt of woods that skirted Bayou Bourbeau, about two hundred yards to the east. As far as the eye could see west of the camp were the open grasslands of south Louisiana. The Federals were, as usual, preparing for yet another day of skirmishing with Green's cavalry out on that prairie. All eyes scanned the horizon to the north and west. No one in the Federal camp had any idea that close-packed Confederate infantry would be thrown against them this time.[18]

When the Confederate column approached within a few miles of the Federal camp, General Green halted the advance, gathered his colonels around him, and explained how the attack would be made. Oran Roberts's three infantry regiments would form the left, Col. Arthur P. Bagby's cavalry brigade and the two artillery sections would take the center, and Col. James P. Major's cavalry brigade would constitute the Confederate right. These arrangements were announced in the vicinity of some enlisted men, and Pvt. John Porter overheard the fiery Green end the meeting with an oath: "D——n them, they will retire." Colonel Roberts then issued instructions to his foot soldiers. His own 11th Infantry would file off the road to the left and anchor the far left of the entire line, starting at the bayou. The 18th, because it was armed entirely with short-range smoothbore muskets, would line up between the other two regiments. The 15th, because it had the advantage of Enfield rifles and more experience, would be nearest the enemy, extending from the 18th on its left to the road from Opelousas on the right. Bagby's horse soldiers and the artillery would form on the infantry's right, from the road into the prairie, and Major's cavalry would trot over to the far right.[19]

While the Confederates halted, made their arrangements, and then resumed the march, Federal soldiers went about their usual morning duties. They had been hauled into line on the prairie at 4 A.M. to keep an eye out for Green's pesky horsemen, but when nothing happened they had been allowed to return to their tents to cook breakfast. By late morning some of the Wisconsin men were receiving their pay and voting in state elections at a table set up near their campfires. The Indiana soldiers also lined up to pocket their pay and cook the midday meal. The 83rd Ohio had left the scene entirely, accompanying a wagon train to do some foraging in Grand Coteau, a few miles east of Bayou Bourbeau. As far as anyone could tell, this was just another day on the Louisiana prairie.[20]

About 11 A.M., only two miles north of the pay lines and voting boxes in Colonel Owen's camp, General Green gave orders to deploy for battle. The most advanced Federal scouts, having spotted the gray column coming down the road from Opelousas, began throwing long-range rifle shots in Green's direction. It was not clear to them yet that this body of Confederates included infantry. Roberts's foot soldiers filed off the road to the left and took the positions assigned: the 11th Texas stretching from the bayou on the far left, the 18th next to the 11th, and the 15th continuing the line to the road. Bagby's and Major's cavalry brigades meanwhile moved out onto the prairie, and the artillery unlimbered and prepared for action (see Map 5). Colonel Roberts scattered three companies of skirmishers forward, and the line of nervous Texans began its approach through a series of farm fields. Although the firing from skirmishers on both sides intensified after an advance of about three hundred yards, still the Federals did not understand that enemy infantry was closing in on their right. The pickets could see Green's horsemen deploying on the open prairie, but Roberts's men were hidden. "The cornstocks and weeds served considerably to conceal from view our numbers," Roberts wrote in his after-action report.[21]

"After getting our ammunition, we were ordered forward," Private Porter wrote later. "Scarcely a word was spoken by the men, after we began the march, each silently thinking of the anticipated battle." Hoping the Yankees might oblige them by just retreating, but knowing better, the Greyhounds followed their officers through the dried-up cornstalks. Porter admitted that "there were many pale faces and palpitating hearts" moving through the farm fields.[22]

The neat lines and textbook maneuvers the Confederates may have envisioned when they planned their assault soon gave way to reality. The men of the 11th Texas, jammed between the bayou on their left and the 18th Texas on their right, discovered that the terrain would not permit drill-field precision. The muddy bayou looped and twisted in front of them, forcing some of the Texans to wade through the waist-high water in order to keep up. Then, before they could dress their lines, the bayou looped back again, and they plunged in once

# Map 5
## The Battle of Bayou Bourbeau, November 3, 1863

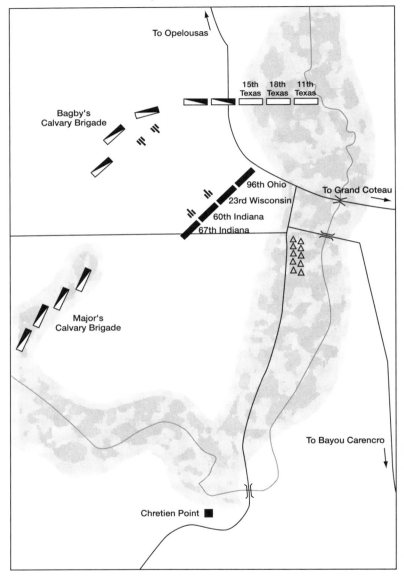

To Opelousas

15th 18th 11th
Texas Texas Texas

Bagby's
Calvary Brigade

96th Ohio

23rd Wisconsin

60th Indiana

67th Indiana

To Grand Coteau

Major's
Calvary Brigade

To Bayou Carencro

Chretien Point

more, all the while falling farther behind their comrades. After a couple of these baptisms, the men avoided the problem altogether by slanting toward their right and falling in behind the advancing ranks of their friends, creating a thick mass around the center of the line. Adding to the mass were some of the men in the 15th Texas, who instinctively edged away from Federal skirmishers and gunners on the prairie. Even those soldiers who had no bayous to cross found other obstacles that threw their lines into crooked approximations of their original symmetry. A thick bois d'arc hedge forced the men to break ranks, file through a few openings, and then re-form on the other side, much as their comrades in McCulloch's brigade had done at Milliken's Bend.[23]

The farm fields soon gave way to the skirt of woods along the bayou, forcing the men to maneuver through the trees and around and over fallen logs, tangling vines and briars, and thick underbrush. All the while, enemy skirmishers and eventually Federal artillery threw lead and iron in their general direction. Private Porter remembered the advance vividly: "On the march, the men would stoop, when the shells would pass over us, whereupon Col. Roberts would cry out 'They will not hurt you, my men.' Then after a moment's reflection, he would add, 'Provided they don't hit you.'" On they struggled for a mile and a half before Roberts halted them for a few minutes' rest in a ravine, only five hundred yards from the Federal tents. The men had been marching since 2 A.M., the day was growing warmer, and the Texans were thirsty. Indeed, some of them had gone beyond their limits. "Here several stalwart men fainted," Private Porter reported.[24]

By the time Roberts's infantry reached the woods along Bayou Bourbeau, the skirmishers on both sides were fully engaged. At first these distant gunshots went almost unnoticed in the Federal camp. Skirmishing had become a daily occurrence on this campaign, and Federal officers wrote the noise off as the usual ritual both sides followed when Green's bothersome horsemen approached too close to friendly lines. "During all this time, and until the final clinch," the Wisconsin paymaster reported, "we all supposed it to be a mere guerrilla annoyance, that no serious attack was contemplated—and felt quite as safe as if in the streets of Madison." The Wisconsin men continued to vote, the Indiana Hoosiers continued to sign for their pay, and the Ohio regiment continued on its foraging trip to Grand Coteau. As the Texans drew nearer and nearer, tramping through the timber with bayonets forward, the skirmish fire grew louder and closer—so loud and so close, in fact, that some of Colonel Owen's officers on the prairie and in the camp began staring at the woods off to their right. Surely, they thought, Green's cavalry would not attack through the woods. The open grasslands were their natural environment. Col. Joshua Guppey of the 23rd Wisconsin reported that "up to this time no one supposed that the enemy had any infantry within striking distance of us." But when the firing grew so intense that no one could doubt what was happening—the enemy's infantry somehow were slipping around their flank—Federal officers saw a possible disaster unfolding. They began shouting and gesturing for their companies and regiments to drop their ballots, forget their pay, abandon their cooking pots, and form up in the trees over to the right.[25]

At about this moment, after ten minutes of rest in the ravine, Roberts's foot soldiers were ordered to their feet for the final charge. Colonel King of the 18th Texas suggested that Roberts redeploy the mass of men away from the middle of the line. The soldiers of the 11th had piled up behind the 18th Texas to avoid the bayou, and the veterans of the 15th had likewise edged toward the middle to reach the concealment of the woods. It was too late now to make changes, Roberts believed, and "to the astonishment of all, the old Col. Replied, 'Just let me give one command, forward, forward, forward, march!'" As the crowded Texans came over the lip of the ravine, many of them were gunned down by storms of rifle fire from the rapidly gathering Federal infantry. Private Porter of the 18th Texas dodged the destruction near the ravine, but he thought later that the enemy missed a perfect opportunity for a countercharge right at that moment.[26]

As Roberts's yelling infantry double-quicked toward the Federal camp, Colonel Owen's division commander, Brig. Gen. Stephen G. Burbridge, rode back and forth between the Federal tents and the prairie, waving his hat for attention and redirecting his regiments toward the woods on the right. Men on both sides were now falling in significant numbers. Capt. Richard Coke of the 15th Texas, a future governor of the Lone Star State, fell near the Opelousas road with a wound to the chest. Not far away, a Pvt. P. Alonzo had his trigger finger shot off and a Private Story doubled over when a minie ball ripped apart his scrotum. On the Confederate left, near the bayou, Capt. J. L. H. Stillwell of the 11th Texas was hit twice before he could take cover, and he died four days later. A Private Wimberly in the same regiment pitched forward gushing blood when a ball tore through his neck; he lived three more days. Christopher Koonce of Company A staggered when he was hit in the leg. He survived the battle, but he spent the rest of his days with a stump where his good leg had been.[27]

In the center of the Confederate infantry line, the men of Col. Wilburn King's 18th Texas were taking the worst of it. Pvt. J. M. Elkins had his elbow split open in the woods near the Federal camp and lost his arm to the surgeon's saw after the battle. A Cpl. E. Willingham was hit in the face, and Pvt. Jesse Steelman of Company H somehow survived a head wound from Federal shrapnel. Five successive color bearers for the 18th Infantry were killed during the charge, and the sixth was blinded by a minie ball through his temple. Colonel Roberts himself was thrown to the ground when his horse was wounded, but the forty-eight-year-old judge regained his feet and pointed his regiments forward in the smoke and noise among the trees.[28]

Across the way Federal soldiers too were falling rapidly. Cpl. Charles McGarvey of the 60th Indiana, caught in a beehive of missiles, was hit three times. Sgt. Henry Endicott of the 60th was shot through the left eye. Charles Standfield of Ohio whispered one last call to his mother before a chest wound stopped his heart. Wherever they looked, Federal officers saw their men pitching forward to the forest floor or sinking down with wounds. Their main problem was that their own regiments were arriving on the scene one at a time, and they could not hold back the onrushing tide of yelling Confederate infantry. Colonel Guppey of the 23rd Wisconsin noted that the rebels bearing down on his men were "10 or 12 deep," far too much mass and momentum to resist for very long. Guppey doubtless was in the path of the center of the Confederate line, tripled up with men from all three Texas infantry regiments. When the 18th Texas approached within about eighty yards of Guppey's last line, close enough for the regiment's old smoothbore muskets to take effect, Colonel King's Texans fired a terrible volley that dropped about forty of Guppey's men. Guppey himself was hit below his left knee and soon taken prisoner. This volley was apparently the proverbial last straw, and the Federal foot soldiers who had survived so far gave up the battle for lost and scrambled to the rear to save themselves. What had been a hurried and poorly organized defense gradually turned into a running rout.[29]

Roberts's infantry had broken General Burbridge's line, but now Gen. Tom Green's Confederate cavalry joined in the mayhem. After waiting thirty minutes for Roberts to do his work, Green unleashed his two cavalry brigades, and the Texas horsemen swept down at full gallop on an already reeling and confused enemy. A surgeon in the 96th Ohio looked up from his work long enough to see "clouds of cavalry . . . deployed on the flanks of their infantry, scattering like wild Comanches, and enveloping our camp." The 67th Indiana, still on the edge of the prairie, formed into a hollow square to receive the cavalry charge, but it was no use, the surgeon wrote: "The fierce cavalry sweep like a whirlwind among them with gleaming sabres. The swift riders enfold them, and, almost without resistance, march them away captive before our eyes."[30]

One of the Hoosiers in the hollow square seemed to think resistance was useless: "they came sweeping over the prairie like an avalanche," George Chittenden wrote his wife two days later. The Ohio and Massachusetts gunners near the 67th did their best to halt the gray landslide, but they too were engulfed. "Gen Burbridge moved one cannon himself and worked it with terrible effect until the enemy were all around the guns, and some of their horses jumping over them, when our artillery men took their gun rammers and knocked rebs off their horses and drove them away," Chittenden recalled. "But the enemys name was legion, and the odds was too great." Those Federals not captured were chased off the prairie, past the Federal tents, and through the woods bordering Bayou Bourbeau. "In the end," an Ohio soldier wrote, "our men were outnumbered so much, they had to run for dear life through the camp, leaving everything behind, the enemy cutting down the wounded with their sabers. Tom said he made one fellow tot[t]er in his saddle who had buried his sword in the head of one of [our company], after throwing up his hands for mercy. These Texans are very blood thirsty in the heat of battle."[31]

Bloodthirsty and persistent. Green's cavalry galloped through the Federal tents, knocking over anything in their way, and plunged into the woods, slashing at the heels of the retreating westerners. Isaac Jackson of the 83rd Ohio was one of those running for safety through the trees. "Now every man (after we got in the woods) ran and fought for himself. The rout was in earnest," Jackson wrote. "I ran until I got through the woods [on the other side of the bayou] when I caught hold of the spare wheel of a caisson and drug along for several yards on the ground, when I managed to get up on top . . . they would a had me sure if I had not grabbed hold of that fifth wheel." All around him, other wild-eyed soldiers ran among the trees, flailed through the muddy stream, and then ran again, hoping to dodge the hooves, sabers, and pistols of their pursuers. Fortunately for the pursued, not all of the horsemen joined in the chase. Some preferred to celebrate their victory rather than follow it up, and they wasted valuable time wandering through the abandoned Federal camp, rummaging through tents, rifling through knapsacks, and gobbling down recently cooked meals. "To the famished Confederates the sight of our beautiful rations was terribly demoralizing," an eyewitness newspaper correspondent wrote. Before their officers could get them fully under control, many of the Texans rode away with new overcoats, boots, pistols, rifles, knapsacks, cigars, whiskey, and other detritus of the U.S. Army.[32]

While Green's horsemen galloped into the timber along the bayou, Colonel Roberts's infantry had to deal with a threat from the Federal cavalry. Albert Lee had taken part of his blue horse division to the east side of the bayou when the battle opened and then re-crossed behind the Confederate infantry, planning to gobble up the rebels when they retreated. As it turned out, Roberts did not retreat, and as soon as Federal resistance in his front had broken down, the judge turned his men around to deal with Lee's troopers in the rear. Lee's men were suddenly not only outnumbered; their carbines and sabers were no match for the massed firepower of the Texas infantry. Lieutenant Colonel Harrison of the

15th Infantry described the cavalry's quick reversal once the Texas foot soldiers fired a volley and charged: it was "a scene of wild confusion, Men tumbling from Horses, screaming, Others throwing up their hands for mercy, Horses running wildly over the field without riders, others reeling and tumbling." Within a few minutes the Federal horsemen were scattered and chased back across the bayou. Not all of them managed to escape. "Just at this point," Private Porter wrote, "three Cavalry of the enemy mistook us for their men, I suppose, and came within fifty paces, when they discovered their mistake; two of them faced right about and fled, the third one undertook to pass the end of our line, which was a right angle to his route, when fifty perhaps of our men, ran out of the line and fired on him—his horse turned a complete summersault, after which, I don't think either ever moved."[33]

General Green, flushed with apparent victory and adrenaline, mistook his infantry's about-face for a retreat, and he came storming and cursing up to the scene, waving his sword in the air and demanding an explanation. When he was satisfied that the foot soldiers were in fact not retreating, Green ordered them to follow the cavalry and artillery through the woods and onto the prairie across the bayou. The pursuit must be maintained as long as possible, regardless of the numbers of Yankees "this side of Hell or Halifax." Colonel King of the 18th Texas resented Green's scolding for the supposed retreat, and he dismissed the cavalry general's behavior as "a very common and cheap sort of bravado."[34]

Green may have been posturing, but his determination to press the pursuit was creating mayhem among the retreating Federals. Surgeon J. T. Woods of the 96th Ohio described the hasty withdrawal of the supply wagons through the belt of timber and across the only nearby bridge: "At the summons of the long-roll, the stores of the brigade had been promptly loaded, and started pell-mell for the rear. In mad haste some dashed into the deep ravine, to find their wagons instantly mired. Others, with more coolness took their places, rapidly flew over the bridge, and, with lavish whip and spur, escaped." The paymaster and election commissioner of the 23rd Wisconsin, Maj. H. A. Fenney, slammed his cash box shut, left some of his poll lists behind, jumped into the back of an ambulance, and hung on while the ambulance raced through the woods at "its highest speed." The Texas cavalry sent a swarm of balls in his direction, but the paymaster and his cash made it across the bayou and through the woods. "As we emerged on the [other] side, the prairie was a moving spectacle of teams and stragglers, going at the highest speed," Fenney related.[35]

A relief column of two divisions, alerted to trouble and coming up from General Franklin's main camp three miles south of the battleground, encountered the remnants of Owen's brigade and Lee's cavalry streaming out of the timber east of the bayou. "The whole of their Wagon Train came out of the Woods onto the Prarie running for dear life, a regular Stampede[,] the Drivers lashing their mules, men running others riding, like it was their only chance[,] Helter Skelter with the Rebel Cavalry in their rear coming at a full Charge," according to a soldier in one of the reinforcement regiments. The commander of one of the relief brigades, Col. James R. Slack of Indiana, was disgusted by what he saw. General Burbridge's "wagon train came on the prairie in a perfect stampede, wagons filled with great healthy men with their guns in their hands, teams in a full run, negroes eyes nearly all white, looking back over their shoulders. I abused the cowardly pups as much as I had time and ability to do, but they took no offence at it. Our boys jeered them a great deal. It was a novel sight indeed."[36]

The heavy blue infantry columns coming up from the south and a few well-placed volleys by the rapidly arriving Federal infantry and artillery brought the Confederate pursuit up short. General Green knew this would happen eventually, and he called his units back to the west side of the bayou, burned everything in the enemy camp that could not be hauled off, and backtracked up the road to Opelousas. On the march away from the battlefield, many of the foot soldiers showed off the new Enfield rifles they had picked up in the enemy's wake, weapons far superior to the old smoothbore muskets the Texans had been using. The Federals in the relief column did not follow much farther than their burning tents, and by mid-afternoon, three hours after it began, the Battle of Bayou Bourbeau was finished.[37]

Now that the excitement was past, some of the Texans suddenly were overcome by exhaustion. On the march to Opelousas, Private Porter of the 18th Texas lost his strength when he stopped for a drink of water.

> Up to this time, I had not felt tired, notwithstanding we had marched near twenty miles, without rest, and fought three hours and ten minutes. . . . After I had quenched my thirst, I resumed my march to overtake the Company, which was but a little way ahead, but to my astonishment, I could not gain the distance. I was completely exhausted. I soon overtook a wagon, and pressed it into service, or myself into it, and rode to camp, which was near Opalousas, ten miles distant from the battlefield. Here I slept the sweetest night's sleep of my life.[38]

General Franklin had to admit that the whole affair had been "a discreditable surprise on our part" and that his rear units had been "severely handled" by the enemy. Some of his regiments had been badly crippled on the prairie and in the strip of woods along Bayou Bourbeau. Nearly every man in the regiment that had formed the hollow square, the 67th Indiana Infantry, had been wounded (nine) or captured (two hundred). The regiment essentially disappeared from the army, and its commander, the Prussian-born Lt. Col. Theodore Buehler, was later dismissed from the service, probably unfairly, for cowardice and incompetence. The 60th Indiana, the unit that had escaped from McCulloch's brigade at Perkins Landing several months earlier, did not fare as well this time, losing 4 men killed, 30 wounded, and 97 captured or missing. Altogether, General Franklin lost 25 killed, 129 wounded, and 562 captured or missing, a total of 716, nearly half of those engaged. In addition, the Federals lost a great store of rifles, clothing, camp equipment, and one cannon.[39]

Confederate casualties were similar in some respects and very different in another. The numbers of killed (25 Federal and 22 Confederate) and wounded (129 and 103) were not far apart, but the number of Federal missing (562) was ten times greater than the Confederate total (55), an indicator of how quickly General Burbridge's lines crumbled under the surprise infantry assault from the woods and the avalanche of cavalry from the prairie. Colonel Roberts's infantry had taken most of the casualties on the Confederate side—all but one of the deaths, three-fourths of the wounded, and three-fourths of the missing. Some infantry officers were not above pointing this out. Capt. Joshua Halbert of the 15th Texas boasted to his wife that "Green's . . . cavalry brigades were both with us on the occasion, and did good service in taking prisoners after the infantry routed the enemy—but nothing more. They did no good in the fight." General Walker himself regarded the battle as an infantry affair: "The Confederate cavalry took but little part in the engagement save to bring in the prisoners when the rout became general."[40]

General Franklin had originally intended to pull his army back only a few miles south of Opelousas. After the embarrassment at Bayou Bourbeau, however, and after Green's cavalry continued to dart aggressively around his flanks over the next several days, Franklin withdraw his army all the way back to prepared earthworks at New Iberia, about fifty road miles south of Opelousas. The Federals eventually gave up on the whole idea of an overland march to Texas. The unhappy prospect (especially after the fight at Bayou Bourbeau) of a long march across mostly unoccupied prairies while Confederate infantry and cavalry swarmed around his flanks, the difficulty of supply in the wilds of southwest Louisiana, and a lack of specific instructions from General Banks must have discouraged General Franklin. Besides, by the time Franklin's army reached New Iberia, Banks had led a small army of seven thousand men from New Orleans and made a landing on the Texas coast at the mouth of the Rio Grande. Not only was an overland march extra hazardous, now it was not even necessary.[41]

On the march south from Bayou Bourbeau, the men in Franklin's army muttered darkly about the recent fight. The westerners in Burbridge's division, conquerors of Vicksburg and accustomed to victory, blamed their defeat on eastern generals: "The blame of the disaster lies on Gen. Franklin's shoulders," according to Isaac Jackson, the lucky Ohio soldier who had escaped by grabbing onto a passing caisson. A comrade in his regiment, Frank McGregor, nodded in agreement: "There was poor generalship somewhere. Our boys neither like the eastern troops or their Generals, having but little confidence in Banks, Washburn or Franklin." Besides, defeat also brought discomfort. "Since the rebels had burned up all our tents and camp equipage, we were left here upon this bleak prairie without blankets, tents or food," an Indiana Hoosier complained. Similar protests circulated around Ohio campfires: "It is really laughable to hear some of the boys bemoan the loss of their clothing, saying every once in a while, that some dirty rebel is strutting around in his parade suit, or while he is shivering by the fire, some rebel rascal is snug and warm wrapped in stolen blankets." But worse than the discomfort was the embarrassment of being chased off the battlefield. Henry Watts of the 24th Indiana was humiliated: "This was the first time the 13th Army Corps ever turned its back to the Foe," he growled.[42]

While the disappointed Federals grumbled, some of the more voluble Confederates were congratulating themselves for their victory and stretching the facts considerably. One officer on General Green's staff wrote a Houston newspaper that the Texans had "rout[ed] and scatter[ed] their boasted '13th Army Corps' to the four winds." Not a brigade, not a division, but an entire corps had been chased across the bayou, according to this account. In fact, the staff officer boasted, "The men and their officers are confident that we can whip Gen. Franklin's entire force with the greatest ease." Another Texan, who had met with some Federal officers under a flag of truce after the battle, was just as proud of besting the cream of the western Federal army. "They compliment our boys for their fighting qualities in very high terms," he wrote. "Some of them said they had fought in seven States, and had never before met our equals. This was putting it on rather thick, but was intended to be in extenuation for their own defeat."[43]

General Walker himself later referred to the battle as "this brilliant little affair." An officer in one of Green's horse regiments, in presenting a drum captured during the fight to Colonel Roberts's foot soldiers, shook a finger at those Yankees who had eyes on Texas: "this battle fought by Texans alone is another warning to the enemy as to what he may expect to suffer should he ever dare to meet the sons of Texas upon their own soil." A Houston newspaper sent a more lighthearted message to the embarrassed General Franklin: "Adoo [adieu] Yankee General, Adoo, and next time you come, bring along your knitting."[44]

The Confederate wounded from Bayou Bourbeau, laid out in the parish courthouse in Opelousas, received close attention from local citizens. "The ladies of Opelousas and its vicinity, young and old, Catholic and Protestant, came crowding in, and waited upon our men just as if they had been their husbands and brothers," Private Blessington recalled. "Indeed the kindness of the ladies of that place to our wounded braves exceeds anything I ever saw and is worthy of all praise," Capt. Joshua Halbert wrote his wife. "On the evening they were carried to town although it was night, these noble women hurried to the hospital with beds, blankets, lint etc etc, threw aside all false modesty[,] stripped them, bathed and dressed their wounds, put them to bed, sat up by them during the night and nursed them with all the fondness of mothers. And such quantities of soups and other good things as they sent in next day you have not seen in a long time."[45]

Understanding that a full-scale assault on Franklin's much larger army was useless, especially once the Federals reached the earthworks at New Iberia, Taylor redistributed his forces after Bayou Bourbeau. Green's cavalry followed Franklin's long blue columns, rounding up stragglers by the dozen, threatening to charge, withdrawing, and generally continuing the torment Green had been dishing out for several weeks. Walker's and Mouton's infantry divisions, on the other hand, were sent to the region around Simmesport, about forty road miles northeast of Washington, to watch for Federal incursions up the Red River toward Texas. General Walker and his men must have smiled on the march to Simmesport. After the engagement at Bayou Bourbeau, General Taylor praised Walker's regiments in his official report and went further in a special congratulatory address to Walker: "the conduct of the two regiments from your division . . . has responded to [my] highest hopes and expectations. They pressed the veterans of Vicksburg with a coolness, resolution, and perseverance that was irresistible." That was the sort of commendation the Texans expected from their generals.[46]

# CHAPTER 9

# Winter on the River

The war in the trans-Mississippi theater settled into a lull in the winter of 1863–1864. Federal armies and gunboats had taken control of the Mississippi River during the summer, another Federal army had finally pushed its way into Little Rock in September, and Nathaniel P. Banks had put a small Federal force ashore near the mouth of the Rio Grande in November, but military activity slowed almost to a halt during this unusually cold winter in Louisiana and Arkansas. Confederate authorities were not sure what the Federals might try next, but the possibility of an enemy push up the Red River toward Confederate headquarters in Shreveport and toward barns bulging with Texas cotton always worried General Smith and his lieutenants. Partly to guard against that threat, Gen. Richard Taylor moved Walker's Texas Division to the area where the Mississippi, Red, and Atchafalaya Rivers converged in central Louisiana. Federal mischief aimed at the Red River valley and Texas would probably go through that region, and Walker's Texans would be there to blunt any offensive. In addition, the Texas regiments could provide infantry support for Confederate artillery aiming to disrupt commercial and military traffic along that stretch of the Mississippi.[1]

Some regiments of the Greyhound Division began moving out of their camps near Washington the day after the fight at Bayou Bourbeau, snaking forty miles to the northeast to a point where the Mississippi, Red, and Atchafalaya Rivers met. Other units struck their tents and followed over the next several days. After two or three days on the road, the regiments reached Simmesport, situated on the west bank of the Atchafalaya in Avoyelles Parish (see Map 6). At that small river town, burned to the ground by the Federals the previous June, the Atchafalaya ran parallel to the Mississippi River (only eight miles to the east). Along the Mississippi, Taylor's artillery companies were digging emplacements and sighting their guns for a campaign against Federal shipping. Engineers sent ahead of the infantry to build a pontoon bridge across the Atchafalaya had not completed their labors when the earliest regiments arrived, however, and some of the Texans dropped fishing lines into the river while they waited to cross.[2]

When the engineers were still not ready by November 12, officers began cross-

## Map 6
## The River War of 1863–1864

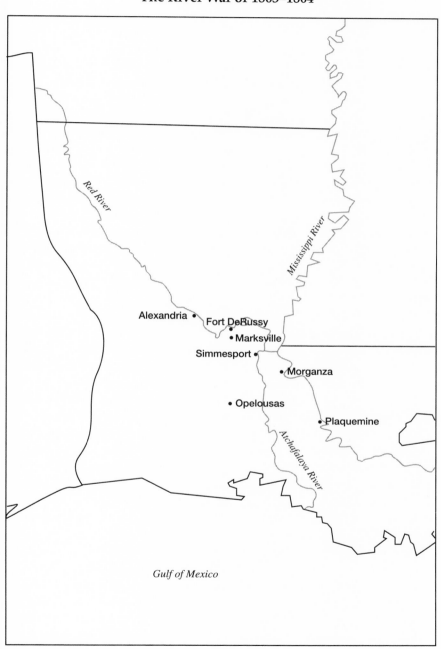

Red River

Mississippi River

Alexandria •
• Fort DeBussy
• Marksville
Simmesport •
• Morganza

• Opelousas
• Plaquemine

Atchafalaya River

Gulf of Mexico

ing their men on flatboats. Trailing regiments arrived at Simmesport to find the bridge complete, and their companies shuffled across the shaky span for more than two hundred yards, only a few inches above the dark waters of the Atchafalaya. Private Porter of the 18th Infantry thought it was a novel sight: "When the army was crossing, it looked at a distance, precisely like they were marching upon the surface of the water." By mid-November the various regiments of the division had spread across the neck of land between the Atchafalaya and the Mississippi, ready to receive whatever attentions the Federals might pay them.[3]

Walker's Texans spent their first few days in this vicinity belly down on the Mississippi River levee, watching their artillery companies prepare gun emplacements and take sightings on passing vessels. Taylor's officers had selected an ideal position to harass river traffic. Just south of the point where the Red River flowed into the Mississippi, riverboats were forced to slide over near the west bank because of sand bars. Moreover, levees at that point were high enough to shield the Confederates from enemy eyes and artillery fire. Federal navy officers had heard from informants that Walker's division was on its way to the river to disrupt traffic, but the Texans stayed low enough to avoid detection. The newly arrived Greyhounds were eager to open up on the slow-moving river targets. John S. Bryan of the 16th Cavalry wrote his wife, Nancy, that "the boyes hear now are all in good fix for a fight and in fine spirits[.] we have our canon planted along the bank of the Mississippi ready to anoy boats as thay pass and to prevent fedrel troops from passing up or down the River." Capt. Elijah Petty of the 17th Infantry informed his daughter that he and his men had been peeking over the levee at enemy gunboats near the opposite bank. "They don't have any idea that we are here notwithstanding we have been at work night & day in their vicinity. The levy is so high they cant see us," he boasted. "Oh how anxious we all are to hear the music. We are like gallants at a ball waiting for the fiddler who is seemingly late in comeing."[4]

The fiddler arrived two days later. On November 18 the 190-ton gunboat *Signal,* towing a flatboat with a heavy naval gun upriver, chugged unknowingly under the Confederate cannons and rifles concealed on the western shore, about one mile south of the Red River. At a signal from their officers, Confederate gunners quickly ran their pieces up to their firing positions and let loose on the sternwheeler with a sudden barrage of shot and shell. Lt. Comdr. James P. Foster, commander of the squadron that included the *Signal,* reported that the gunboat was "badly used up" in this fight. "She received nine shots, most of them directed at her boilers. One shot came in her after port, striking her port sill, and one deflected upward, passing through her plating near the boilers, just grazing her steam drums, through the deck of the steerage, and out forward through the bulkhead and smokestack. Another shot came in the port beam, penetrated a mess chest, exploded, and wounded 5 men and cut up the decks considerably. The other shots were mostly through the wardroom, just over the boilers." The commander of the *Signal*, Lt. C. Dominy, believed he had been fired on by six guns and hit eight times. "We returned the fire and kept on up the river. This vessel was struck eight times, several balls going entirely through her. We had 5 men wounded, 4 slightly and 1 severely; his leg has since been amputated. Our upper works are somewhat shattered."[5]

Steaming nearby was the 1,000-ton ironclad *Choctaw*, the same behemoth that had scattered McCulloch's brigade with heavy shells at Milliken's Bend five months earlier. To suppress fire from the light Confederate field guns, the *Choctaw* turned its big muzzles against the western shore and blasted ninety-one rounds of shrapnel toward the levee, forcing the gunners to jerk their artillery pieces back down the levee and throw themselves against the embankment. The *Choctaw*'s commander was satisfied that he had quieted the rebel battery, but Walker's infantry was not as cooperative. "It was impossible to see the effect of our shell, but we succeeded in driving the enemy away. Not a shot was fired at us from the battery, but the sharpshooters behind the levee gave us several volleys." Veterans of Milliken's Bend must have grinned as they peppered the *Choctaw*'s gun ports with musket and rifle balls.[6]

Another riverboat, the transport *Emerald* with five hundred soldiers aboard, was fired on from the same vicinity the same day. Just as a morning fog was lifting, the men aboard the *Emerald* noticed that "the opposite shore was . . . alive with gray-backs." Before the transport could steam out of range, three Confederate shells tore into the wooden superstructure of the vessel. Capt. William Edgar, commander of one of the batteries normally attached to Walker's division, reported that even though the fog obscured his target, he could hear "the crashing of the timbers" when his projectiles struck the *Emerald*. An Indiana soldier aboard the beleaguered riverboat wrote that "the shot in the pilot-house was a twelve-pound shell, and in exploding, tore it to pieces and knocked over the pilot, who, considerably stunned and bewildered, ran below, the boat in the meantime running ashore, and making prodigious efforts to climb the bank. A soldier of the Seventeenth Kentucky threatened to blow the pilot's brains out, and drove him back to his post, when the boat was headed down stream and steamed off, making better time than she ever made before."[7]

Taking note of the two attacks, Lieutenant Commander Foster, naval commander on this stretch of the river, steamed up to the mouth of the Red River to learn what he could about Confederate forces in the area. He gathered from various sources that the rebels had at least eighteen field guns along the riverbank and that the batteries were supported by several thousand infantry. Taking the threat seriously, he informed his superior, Rear Adm. David D. Porter, that "while the enemy are in this immediate vicinity I will convoy all passing vessels."[8]

Some river captains, impatient and on tight schedules, ignored Foster's warnings and offers of help and tried to run past the Confederate guns without an escort. The transport *Black Hawk* made that mistake only three days after the *Signal* and *Emerald* were raked over by General Taylor's gunners. At 4:10 P.M. on November 21, the *Black Hawk* steamed downriver and into the sights of the gunners of Capt. William Edgar's Texas battery, the Alamo City Guards. Captain Edgar reported that he

> immediately opened on her, with my 6 pdrs [pounders], using solid or Round shot, directed at her hull machinery and boilers. My Howitzers [were aimed] on her upper works with shell, canister, & Sphe [spherical] case shot. With the shell I succeeded in setting fire to her upper works, the fire breaking out in the neighbourhood of the Ladies cabin. The Canister shot was directed at the Pilot House killing the Pilot, & shattering the House. The boat by this time had reached a point opposite Hog Point when she was discovered to be on fire by the Crew, & using her Engines she rounded too [*sic*] and made for land on the East side . . . as soon as she struck [the bank,] the passengers got ashore, some one hundred & fifty or two hundred of them, and broke for the woods abandoning the boat to her fate.[9]

Walker's infantry cooperated with the artillery to compound the Federals' troubles. Captain Edgar urged "the Sharp shooters to keep up a constant fire in order to prevent the crew & passengers from extinguishing the fire, but the Gunboat [*Choctaw*] soon arrived, & we were compelled to retire." When the guns of the ironclad were leveled on them, the Texas infantrymen firing from the top of the levee scattered once again, just as they had at Milliken's Bend. One Texan wrote his mother and sister that "they throw some shells at our men that weighs over a hundred pounds but they hardly every touch any of our men[.] they are so large that they almost jare [jar] the earth." A soldier in the 13th Infantry had ample respect for the big naval guns: "the Yankees opened fire on us from the gunboats at a short distance above and below, and we then made for the swamp [behind the levee]—and old Rebels' coat-tails stood out behind." Private Blessington laughed that when the gunboats opened fire on the levee, " 'Rats, to your holes!' was the cry among the troops." The Greyhounds apparently made good rats, for only one man was hit: "He was killed while playing cards, near the top of the levee. A round shot ricochets, and strikes him, with a dull, heavy sound, and bounds over him. He is stone dead." The scene on the *Black Hawk,* burning and riddled by twenty hits, was much bloodier. Captain Edgar reported that "the passengers suffered a good deal from the fire of the Howitzers, as many were seen being removed, either dead or in a helpless condition."[10]

The captain of the *Black Hawk* gave a newspaper reporter a detailed account of the smothering fire from shore. "The first shot from the enemy was followed by another and another, and as the boat proceeded other guns opened on it, and it was soon discovered that the enemy had guns at intervals over a line of two miles, during which the boat was attacked in front, flank and rear. In addition to this, there was a perfect storm of Minie balls from squads of sharpshooters, who acted as supports to the guns." The Confederate shot and shell quickly ignited fires aboard the transport: "The deck and staterooms on the starboard side of the boat, forward of the wheel[,] also the pilothouse, were soon enveloped in flames, which spread with such rapidity as to threaten a quick destruction of the boat. In the midst of this threatening aspect of affairs, which could not have been seen by the enemy, they kept up a terrific cannonade and fusillade, the twelve pounder balls and shells perforating the boat, rending into fragments the saloons of the boat." The reporter inspected the *Black Hawk* shortly afterward and wrote that "there is hardly an imaginable direction in which solid shot, a piece of shell, a grapeshot or a Minie ball has not passed through the steamer, and she is splintered and scarred in all parts."[11]

Some Confederates believed that because they were not sinking riverboats on a regular basis, their harassment was having little effect. In fact, the light field guns and Walker's muskets and rifles created exactly the sort of anxiety and dread behind Union lines that Confederates had hoped to produce. Charles H. Farrell, a *New York Herald* reporter writing from New Orleans, testified to the fright along the Mississippi: "The increasing audacity of the rebels in interrupting the free navigation of the Mississippi river, by firing on unarmed steamboats traversing its waters, has created much serious alarm and uneasiness in the minds of the merchants and citizens of this city, and, indeed, of all the towns below Vicksburg. . . . So extensively have the rebels carried on their guerrilla warfare on the river that commerce and trade on its waters will soon be cut off, and New Orleans, which is now depending on the West for supplies, will be commercially isolated from the upper country."[12]

Another civilian, a famous Texas Unionist and federal judge, Thomas H. Duval, was more worried about being captured by the "guerrillas" on the river than being hit by their fire. Traveling downstream from Natchez toward New Orleans in late December, he scribbled in his diary that he would have to destroy all papers identifying him as a Unionist and federal judge if his riverboat was boarded: "I am not so much afraid of being shot and killed in the boat, as I am of being made a prisoner, identified and carried back to Texas." Judge Duval, anticipating only cruelty and barbarity from his fellow Texans, predicted that "hanging, drawing & quartering in the presence of my family would be the least I could expect." Civilians were not the only ones worried about General Taylor's "guerrillas." Rear Adm. David D. Porter wrote General Grant on December 15 that "I must tell you that the guerrillas are kicking up mischief on the river. . . . Dick Taylor has come in with 4,000 men and 22 pieces of artillery, and has planted them behind the levee to great advantage. He does not trouble the gunboats, which have driven him away twice, but the transports get badly cut up, even when they are convoyed."[13]

All things considered, Walker's Texans found the harassment of Federal river traffic much more interesting than their usual diet of marching and drilling. Certainly, Federal sailors on the Mississippi discovered that Walker's Texans "were at times more demonstrative than agreeable in their attentions to us."[14]

After a few days of this novel activity, General Walker sent some of his regiments several miles farther south to find additional locations for artillery emplacements overlooking the river. This proved to be wasted motion for the most part, however. At least one regiment and accompanying artillery and cavalry misunderstood their orders and wandered too far south, almost running up against superior Federal forces. By late November the Texas regiments were once again concentrated along the banks of the Mississippi, just south of the Red River.[15]

A few days later General Taylor sent Walker's division on another march downriver, this time to strike suddenly at the supposedly undermanned Federal garrison at Plaquemine, on the right bank of the Mississippi and about sixty air miles southeast of Simmesport. Walker doubted the worthiness of the objective, but he dutifully led his division downriver on December 1. The Greyhounds kept away from good roads along the river because of the exposure to Federal gunboats, but that required them to slog through muddy lanes and cross numerous bayous farther inland, slowing their progress. After three days and forty miles of heavy going, the Texans reached the vicinity of present-day Livonia, where General Walker "received the most exact and entirely reliable information" about the enemy's defenses at Plaquemine, still forty more road miles away. Those defenses were apparently much stronger than earlier believed. At the same time, he learned that a spy had alerted Federal officers at Plaquemine that Confederate infantry was moving downriver for an attack. Having lost the element of surprise, Walker believed the whole expedition was now compromised. His fellow division commander, General Mouton, and brigade commanders from both divisions agreed completely, and Walker abandoned the enterprise. After all, Walker reported to Taylor, Plaquemine was "a position of no strategic importance" and therefore not worth the blood it would cost to take it.[16]

Even though the move toward Plaquemine had produced nothing except more marching through more mud, it did afford another opportunity to observe the waste that accompanied war. During the march the Texans came upon the site of a small battle fought by other Texas infantry and cavalry several weeks earlier, the Battle of Stirling Plantation. Although the Confederates had won the little engagement, neither side had tarried afterward to give proper burial to the dead. Private Blessington wrote that "we beheld several corpses exposed to the rays of the sun, some of them apparently only half buried." Other Greyhounds detected the odor of death as well. Capt. Harvey A. Wallace of the 19th Infantry wrote his wife that "there was dead lying every direction." Some of his men walked over for a closer look, and "they said one mans foot was sticking out[,] anothers chin[.] Our men covered them over." Blessington noted that the waste and destruction extended to homes and plantations, too. "This section of the country might have been termed the 'Paradise' of Louisiana before the war; but alas, what a change has befallen it now! The houses are all deserted; occasionally you meet with a few old, faithful negroes, left by their owners to take care of their place until their return. Here you can behold mansion after mansion, including costly sugar-houses, now going to decay." An officer in Mouton's division noted that "Morganza, formerly a little village which had sprung up there [on the Mississippi River], on account of its being a convenient landing, is now entirely burnt down; smouldering ruins only tell of its former existence & bear testimony to the vandalism of the enemy." The smell of destruction and rot seemed to hang over every neighborhood the war visited.[17]

On the division's return march to the vicinity of Simmesport, the 16th Infantry and artillery from four batteries were detached and sent over to the river to create whatever mischief they could. Commander of the temporary consolidated battery was Capt. James M. Daniel, a railroad surveyor before the war. He was the brother of John Moncure Daniel, the fiery editor of the *Richmond (Virginia) Examiner,* and the nephew of Peter V. Daniel, a justice of the Supreme Court that had decided the controversial Dred Scott case in 1857. While Captain Daniel's detached artillery quietly dug in along the levee upstream from Morganza, a few miles below that little river port other Confederate artillery surprised the steamer *Henry Von Phul,* chugging slowly upriver from New Orleans with a cargo of salt and sugar and a few passengers bound for St. Louis. Before the riverboat could react, the Confederates perforated the entire port side of the vessel. According to the *New York Herald,* one of whose reporters was wounded in the barrage, "the boat was completely riddled with shot."[18]

The reporter, Thomas Knox, found the whole experience extremely unsettling: "A sheet of wet paper would afford as much resistance to a paving-stone as the walls of a steamboat cabin to a six-pound shot." The pilothouse was even more vulnerable than the cabins, according to Knox: "The floor was covered with blood, splinters, glass, and the fragments of a shattered stove. One side of the little room was broken in, and the other side was perforated where the projectiles made their exit. The first gun from the Rebels threw a shell which entered the side of the pilot-house, and struck the captain, who was sitting just behind the pilot. Death must have been instantaneous." A passing riverboat took the crippled *Von Phul* in tow and accompanied her upriver until the USS *Neosho,* an ironclad sternwheeler, could provide some protection.[19]

The naval convoy was a very porous shield, however. Captain Daniel's gunners, now dug in and waiting for prey, soon spied the crippled *Von Phul* limping slowly upstream. Ignoring the *Neosho,* the Confederate consolidated battery poured more shot and shell into the unfortunate transport when it chugged within range a few miles above Morganza. According to the commander of the *Neosho,* in this second encounter the *Von Phul* "was struck twenty times, three of the shot passing through her hull below the water line, one cutting off her supply pipe, another penetrating her port boiler." The nerve-wracked *Herald* reporter could find safety nowhere. "One [shell] exploded under the portion of the cabin directly beneath my position. The explosion uplifted the boards with such force as to overturn my table and disturb the steadiness of my chair." When he later had time to think about his ordeal, he concluded that a river cruise in wartime was not a good idea: "I can hardly imagine a situation of greater helplessness, than a place on board a Western passenger-steamer under the guns of a hostile battery." A passenger stood a good chance of being hit directly by artillery or rifle fire from shore, but "added to this, you may be struck by splinters, scalded by steam, burned by fire, or drowned in the water. You cannot fight, you cannot run away, and you cannot find shelter. With no power for resistance or escape, the sense of danger and helplessness cannot be set aside." General Walker's Texans probably never realized the distress they helped to create along the river in late 1863, but it was considerable.[20]

The next day, December 9, the detached infantry and artillery left the levee and rejoined the main column under General Walker on the return march to the vicinity of Simmesport, still twenty miles to the northwest. The Greyhounds were accustomed to Louisiana mud by now, but this trip truly tested their reputation for mobility. One Texan wrote that "the rain fell in torrents; many of the troops were unable to get to camp [that night]; our train and artillery had to remain in the swamps, the roads through them being impassable in the black darkness of a cloudy night." If anything, the next day was worse. When finally ordered to halt for the day under wet gray skies, "the troops quickly put up their blankets in tent form, on their arrival, for the purpose of making a shelter for the night. The roads were knee-deep in mud, oftentimes holding the men fast, who, in the struggle, left their shoes behind, or fell into some hole, out of which they were dragged coated over like a pie-crust."[21]

Those who assume a steady decline in morale and commitment among Confederate soldiers after Vicksburg and Gettysburg might do well to consider the truly miserable conditions these men endured while yet staying true to their cause, even after the defeats of the summer of 1863: little or no pay, inflated currency when they were paid, poor food, inadequate clothing, a stingy furlough policy, and a bitterly cold winter. And yet, there the Greyhounds were, caked with mud and shivering under wet blankets in the watery space between the Mississippi and Atchafalaya Rivers, still a threat to Federal ambitions in the trans-Mississippi theater. In their own words, they had whittled down to the true grit. The way they saw it, their wives and children and communities still needed a shield against invading enemies, maybe now more than ever, and no amount of Confederate bureaucratic bungling or shortages would change that. And the growing Federal tendency toward a "hard war" policy seemed to stiffen the Texans' will to resist rather than weaken it. Even a chronic complainer like Private Farrow, a man who seemed to suffer more than anyone around him, preferred to stick it out in the ranks: "I had rather stay here than for the Federals to get into Texas[.] it makes my blood run cold to see how they have laid waste the country they have passed through."[22]

By the time the Texans squished back to the vicinity of Simmesport on December 13, General Walker had received intelligence that Federal gunboats were preparing to come up the Red River and then turn south into the Atchafalaya to break up Confederate forces interfering with river traffic. Since the rivers were rising, making a raid by enemy gunboats more likely, Walker crossed his brigades west of the Atchafalaya for the first time in a month. If enemy vessels had reached Simmesport and destroyed the pontoon bridge there before Walker crossed, the Greyhounds would have been stranded in the neck of land between the Atchafalaya and Mississippi, useless for their primary mission—protecting Alexandria and the Red River valley from Federal penetration. Walker then scattered his three soggy brigades along the lower Red and upper Atchafalaya Rivers, two areas where the Federals might begin any push toward Shreveport and East Texas. In that triangle of land between the Red River, coming down from the northwest, and the Atchafalaya, flowing straight south, the Greyhounds settled into winter quarters.[23]

One year earlier the Texans had begun their first winter in the army in the dreary, sickly environs of Camp Nelson and Bayou Meto in central Arkansas. They were tougher now, physically stronger, healthier, more accustomed to military life, and less expectant of civilian comforts. The weakest among them, physically and ideologically, had fallen out of the ranks, some by resigning, some by dying, some by being released from service due to chronic illness, some by deserting. In short, Walker's Texas Division was a more formidable obstacle to Federal ambitions in the trans-Mississippi region in the winter of 1863–1864 than it had been when first organized in early 1862. General Walker, who must have noted the difference in his men, sent two of his brigades, those commanded by James M. Hawes and Horace Randal, to the right bank of the lower Red River, near the small town of Marksville and about twenty road miles northwest of Simmesport. The third brigade (formerly McCulloch's), now commanded by William R. Scurry, settled into slave cabins on the Norwood plantation near Simmesport.[24]

The Texans near Marksville began chopping down trees in mid-December to build their winter cabins. Capt. Theophilus Perry of Randal's brigade wrote his wife back in Marshall, Texas, that "we have a little Shanty made of slabs and a great big chimney filling up one end of it. The regiment have built good houses, and are in what may be called winter quarters, about two miles from Marksville." John C. Porter of Hawes's brigade recalled later that his regiment had no pretensions when they threw together their little huts near Marksville. "Here we were ordered to build winter quarters, which we soon did, in a rude way." Another soldier in the same brigade, Volney Ellis of the 12th Infantry, expected to settle in for the winter: "We have gone into winter quarters here and are making ourselves pretty comfortable building huts, and the Red River is still low, and there is no prospect of a enemy here soon, and they are not expected until the river gets up."[25]

The Texans soon had reason to wish they had built tighter, snugger cabins because the winter of 1863–1864 was one of the coldest on record in Louisiana. Some longtime residents of the Marksville area claimed it was the coldest season since 1822; others, the worst ever. Virtually everyone who commented on the weather—Texans, natives of Louisiana, and even visiting Yankees—agreed that it was one of the coldest winters they could remember. General Taylor himself complained about "the formation of ice, to an extent previously unknown in this latitude." Captain Wallace wrote that "the ground froze like a Rock" along the Red River in December. William Quesnell, a German native in Horace Haldeman's battery, kept a running account of the weather in his diary and complained on December 20 that "the ice has not thawed for 3 days." Edwin Becton, a surgeon in the 22nd Infantry, wrote his wife that "we have had three days & nights of the coldest weather that I have experienced in many a day." Becton, a man with little use for a comb, worried about the frosty air keeping him up at night: "though I have not slept cold as yet, that prairie on the top of my head got cold one night."[26]

Pvt. Joseph Blessington of the 16th Infantry remarked on the piercing cold of late December: "The men retired under their blankets, and into their huts. The wind howled above us, and the snow fell thick and fast." Arthur W. Hyatt, a captain in Mouton's division, noted the same bitter weather near Monroe: "All the ponds are frozen over, and our boys are sliding over them on the ice; every now and then one of them gets a heavy fall. This is the coldest weather I have ever seen. . . . The ground is too cold for them to lie down on, and their one blanket is not warm enough for them to cover with. This is soldiering, this is."[27]

Even Federals from northern climes noted the bitterness of this winter in Louisiana. As far south as New Iberia, Harris Beecher, a surgeon in a New York regiment, wrote that "among the oldest inhabitants it was generally conceded that such cold weather had never before been experienced in that region." The *New York Herald* reporter who had narrowly escaped death on the steamer *Von Phul* only a few weeks earlier recovered enough from his fright to go hunting in the countryside north of the Red River that winter. He later recalled his experience with a frisson: "In that day's ride, and in the night which followed, I suffered more than ever before from cold. . . . I was thickly clad, but the cold *would* penetrate, in spite of everything."[28]

The Greyhounds had spent Christmas of 1862 on the left bank of the Arkansas River at Little Rock. Now they were scattered along the lower Red and upper Atchafalaya Rivers, huddling in their little winter huts and warming their hands by their crude fireplaces. Back in Texas on Christmas Eve, Surgeon Edward Cade's wife could muster little holiday cheer. "I could get nothing suitable to put in their [the boys'] stockings tonight," she wrote. "Henry says he reckons Santa Claus has gone to the war, & the Yankees have stolen all his toys." Two hundred miles east of that sad scene, some of the Texans in Randal's and Hawes's brigades attended church services in the open air on Christmas night. Those of a more secular nature constructed a brush arbor where two fiddlers from the ranks entertained the men. Some of the Greyhounds were "dancing jigs, reels, and doubles," Private Blessington observed. "Even the officers' colored servants had collected in a group by themselves, and, while some timed the music by slapping their hands on their knees, others were capering and whirling around" in the flickering light of the campfires. Pvt. John Porter celebrated more than he should have. To mark the day, he recalled later, "many of the soldiers got drunk, and with shame, I confess that I was among the number, and again I confess, it was not by accident. . . . I began early in the morning and in a few hours, I had experienced fully the effect of Louisiana rum."[29]

Even in the icy months of December and January—whenever freezing rain or sleet let up for a few days—officers of the division tried to keep the soldiers busy. Idle minds and hands were always trouble among the Greyhounds. As they had done so many times before for nearly two years, captains and majors and colonels put the men through their paces on the drill field. Now that the war seemed farther away than usual, the generals even cooked up competitions and games to keep the men occupied. Porter, only a few weeks away from his twentieth birthday, wrote that "we spent the best weather in drilling, which we followed for some days, when Gen. Walker offered a flag as a prize to the best drilled Reg't. The Reg'ts. were all to drill, and the two best were to be selected by the inspector Gen., as contestants." In Randal's brigade the contest was eventually narrowed to the 28th Cavalry and the 11th Infantry. The men of the 11th, veterans of the charge at Bayou Bourbeau, eventually represented the brigade against the champions of Hawes's brigade, the 12th Infantry, on February 13. After some snappy movements by both groups before a large audience of officers, civilians, and fellow soldiers, General Walker himself presented the prize flag to the men of the 12th. One soldier in the champion regiment, Lavaca County attorney Volney Ellis, proudly informed his wife that "we now claim to be the banner regiment of the division."[30]

At about the same time that one of his regiments won the drill contest—seemingly an appropriate outcome for a brigadier trained at West Point—Hawes himself was preparing to leave the division for a new assignment in Galveston, Texas. In mid-February, Taylor received an order reassigning Hawes, a change requested by Hawes himself. Although he might have jumped at the chance to replace him right after the botched affair at Young's Point the previous summer, Taylor had come around to the view that the Texas Division was a first-rate unit and Hawes was a competent commander. "General Hawes' brigade is in splendid order and a change would be very unfortunate," Taylor informed Trans-Mississippi headquarters, perhaps worried about a change in leadership on the eve of spring campaigning. Despite his urging, the orders stood, and Hawes packed his bags in late February for the trip to Galveston. Before he left the winter camp near Marksville, the officers and men of his brigade adopted resolutions expressing "not only the esteem, but the unfeigned affection of every officer and soldier of his command." Although Hawes's men had apparently put aside any hard feelings from the bungled night march to Young's Point, Gen. E. Kirby Smith believed Hawes would be most useful as a drill officer in Texas. Someone with a brighter record as a field commander was needed for the coming campaign.[31]

Replacing Hawes was Brig. Gen. Thomas N. Waul. Recently turned fifty-one, Waul was a native of South Carolina, a former attorney in Vicksburg, and a migrant to Texas by 1850. He had established a cotton plantation on the Guadalupe River in Gonzales County and dived into politics as a strong southern rights proponent. The Texas secession convention appointed him to the Confederate provisional congress in Montgomery, Alabama, in February 1861, where he served until November of that year. While the regiments for Walker's division were being formed in the spring of 1862, Waul raised a legion (i.e., a unit composed of infantry, cavalry, and artillery) of two thousand men, known thereafter as Waul's Texas Legion. Although he had no formal military training, he ably led the infantry companies of the legion at Fort Pemberton, Mississippi, in March 1863 and in the fighting around Vicksburg in the summer of 1863, but nearly all, including Waul, were captured when the river city fell on July 4. After being exchanged, Waul served a few months under Gen. John B. Magruder in the Department of Texas before taking command of Hawes's old brigade near Marksville.[32]

While generals and their adjutants shuffled official papers, the men in the ranks continued as usual. One compensation for the bitter weather that winter was a more generous furlough policy, which gave "general satisfaction to the troops," according to Private Blessington. In the letters they scrawled in their little winter huts, the Texans were excited to inform their wives and families that a sixty-day leave would be the reward for any man who could recruit a new soldier for his regiment. Private Farrow of the 19th Infantry had mixed feelings about the policy: "I would not advise any one to go into the army if they can help it, but if either of [two friends] would come a sixty days Furlough would be very acceptable with me at present." In Hawes's old brigade the men drew lots for eight furloughs in each regiment. Pvt. John Simmons of the 22nd Infantry was especially eager to draw one of the prized furloughs. He was one of fourteen married men in his company who had not been home since leaving Tyler in the summer of 1862.[33]

When the men were not shivering on the drill fields or otherwise occupied, they gathered in tight knots around the fireplaces in their huts. A major topic of conversation around those hearths was what appeared to be illegal trade with the enemy. Both the Federal and Confederate governments winked at such trade on occasion during the war; northern textile mills needed cotton, and southern armies needed hard money, arms, and medicines. In the winter of 1863–1864, Generals Smith, Taylor, and Walker sold tons of cotton through the lines in order to purchase needed supplies for the trans-Mississippi army. In their correspondence during January, the generals mentioned that cotton was selling for $250 per bale in Liverpool, about four times its pre-war price.[34] Agents of the Metropolitan Bank of New York alone, according to Taylor, had offered to buy $500,000 worth of cotton (in gold or sterling) and haul it through the lines themselves if the Confederates could supply it, and the Trans-Mississippi Department had already gathered twenty-five thousand bales for sale to speculators who could come through the lines.[35]

Texas soldiers in central Louisiana made note of the heavy flow of cotton moving from the backcountry toward the Yankees in January and February. William Quensell of Haldeman's battery recorded his observations in his diary in late January: "Every day, wagons loaded with cotton pass on their way to sell their loads to the Yankees." Two weeks later: "Government trains are still continually passing here loaded with cotton." Private Farrow also watched the cotton parade. "I saw about 100 bales going to the river today," he wrote his wife on January 18. The Federal navy too had detected the sudden surge of cotton pouring through the lines. Thomas O. Selfridge, commander of the timberclad *Conestoga,* informed his superiors in February that "there is at present a large contraband trade going on with the rebel army under Walker through the agency of cotton buyers. These men obtain the goods at New Orleans or Baton Rouge, under the head of family supplies, when, if the barrels were inspected, they would be found to contain most everything else. They are landed at Waterloo [on the Mississippi River], and on being hauled to Walker's lines, he returns them cotton at 25 cents per pound to the amount of goods delivered."[36]

Many trans-Mississippi Confederates were puzzled by this sudden cooperation with the enemy and by the new policy of protecting cotton that they normally would have burned. In the absence of any explanation from their superiors, some suspicious soldiers concluded that generals and government officials were siphoning off cotton from Louisiana plantations to sell through the lines for bribes, whiskey, cigars, and other luxuries for themselves. Even those Texans who doubted that their own officers were benefiting from such distasteful activity resented the trade because the civilians buying the cotton were apparently making great profits while southern soldiers lacked adequate food, clothing, and other necessities. Capt. Elijah Petty, the Bastrop attorney serving in the 17th Infantry, could not decide whether to blame the whole mess on civilians, especially Jewish merchants, or on high officials who might be profiting while poorly fed and inadequately clothed soldiers shivered in their winter cabins. Petty laid the blame on both groups. First, the civilians:

The government is winking at a considerable cotton trade here. A lot of Jews are running the blockade and bringing out goods and some medicines for the army. I look upon it as an infamous trade contrary to law and demoralizing in its consequences and if I were in command a little while I'd rid the country of both the trade and the Jews that carry it on. They take the oath of allegiance (I suppose) to both governments so that they can pass in & out and smuggle and steal. They care nothing for obligations or any thing else but the almighty dollar. They have neither country, character or honor.[37]

Then Confederate officials: "I fear that there is something rotten in Denmark and that government & other officials are quite deeply interested (privately) in the trade. I am glad the Yanks steal it from them when they can. . . . I am glad that we burn it sometimes. . . . So you see we trade and steal and burn all in good harmony. Fine times these. If the country is'nt cursed it will not be for the want of rascals to bring down the ire of God almighty upon it."[38]

John Simmons, a Smith County farmer before the war, was certain that he and his fellow enlisted men were being duped by higher-ups. "For the last two months the Government has been hauling cotton to the Yankees, and what do you think they have gotten for it? Fine boots and calico for the officers and their wives! But there is not a thing for the privates who have borne the burden of the war, and who have always stood to their part." A gossipy supply officer in Mouton's division who closely observed the cotton trade around Simmesport was fully convinced that high officials of the Trans-Mississippi Department were cheating the people for the officers' own benefit: "The representatives and administrators of the Confederacy, on this side of the Mississippi will have a sad accounting to render of their administration if not to their superiors at least to the Supreme Being who will not allow such injustices to go unpunished."[39]

The resentment running through the camps near Marksville erupted into near mutiny among some regiments of the Texas Division. James H. Armstrong, a private in the 14th Infantry of Randal's brigade, wrote his wife that "Randal's Regiment [the 28th Cavalry] was for 2 days in a state of insubor[di]nation. They could not be got to drill, to furnish their quota of men for guard or fatigue duty. Goulds [6th Cavalry] Battalion was but little better, our Regiment was greatly excited." In Waul's (formerly Hawes's) brigade, the 12th Infantry, the self-styled "banner regiment of the division," was particularly troublesome. They "cut up so that the officers attempted to arrest some of the men but could not get it done." Capt. Theophilus Perry of the 28th Cavalry complained to his wife that "our Regiment has been much corrupted with a spirit of Mutiny." Capt. Elijah

Petty in Scurry's brigade was as worried about the rebellious behavior as Captain Perry: "I am afraid it will ruin our army and demoralize the citizens. I am seriously alarmed about it."[40]

What skeptical soldiers did not know was that Generals Smith, Taylor, and Walker were directing the sale of huge amounts of cotton, purportedly to foreigners only and supposedly by private growers only, in exchange for gold or sterling or war materials. The funds were not destined for the pockets of the officers but for the nearly empty coffers of the Confederate Trans-Mississippi Department. The generals had to remain quiet about the trade and pretend they were not involved; otherwise, Federal gunboats and army officers would surely have confiscated the valuable bales in order to prevent money and war materials from flowing to their enemies. The necessity to pretend ignorance (in order to maintain the fiction that Confederate officials were not involved in the traffic) meant that the generals could not explain to their own soldiers and civilians that absolutely critical income was flowing into the Trans-Mississippi treasury, income that would help them to continue the war for another year and a half.[41]

The best study of this trade concluded that Trans-Mississippi officials were able to confine the traffic primarily to funds and materials that would allow them to continue the war effort, and that without this traffic, generals west of the river simply would not have been able to arm, feed, and supply their divisions in the second half of the war. Ironically, the same policy that enabled Trans-Mississippi officials to carry on the war also created resentment and harsh mutterings from the very people the policy benefited.[42]

Furloughs may have delighted the Greyhounds, and trade with the enemy may have angered them, but what occupied increasing amounts of their time that winter was digging. Under orders from Generals Smith and Taylor, Walker's regiments set about constructing elaborate defenses just west of Simmesport and just north of Marksville. Trans-Mississippi officials believed that any Federal offensive undertaken in the spring would begin in the Simmesport and Marksville areas, near the confluence of the Red, Atchafalaya, and Mississippi Rivers. The key to a successful push up the Red River valley toward Shreveport and Texas was Fort DeRussy, a strong point about three miles north of Marksville on the right bank of the river. The fort was situated to block ascent of the river by gunboats and transports, but it was vulnerable from the land side. The easiest land approach to DeRussy was from the southeast, over rich, flat farmland stretching north and west from Simmesport. Federal infantry aiming to approach DeRussy overland would most likely be landed at Simmesport and then marched the twenty miles to the fort. Thus, General Smith concluded, the formidable works at DeRussy must be strengthened further, and the western outskirts of Simmesport must become a line of trenches, gun emplacements, and rifle pits.[43]

The fort on the lower Red River, about forty miles downstream from Alexandria and fifty miles upriver from the Mississippi, was built beginning in November 1862 when General Taylor appointed Col. Lewis G. DeRussy, a graduate of the U.S. Military Academy (Class of 1814), to handle the project. DeRussy's incomplete works were abandoned, captured, and partially dismantled in May 1863 when General Banks and supporting naval vessels occupied Alexandria preparatory to the Port Hudson campaign. Determined to protect the Red River valley, trans-Mississippi Confederates salvaged what they could from the ruins left behind by the Federals and began rebuilding the fort later in 1863.[44]

When Walker's Texans finished building their winter huts just a few miles from the fort in December 1863, Confederate officials put the Greyhounds to work on the fortifications. Some regiments built up the earthen walls of the fort itself, others constructed a huge raft of felled trees to block the river about six miles below the fort, and still others dug trenches and gun emplacements near Simmesport. Units from all three of Walker's brigades cut trenches into the rich farmland a few miles west of the Atchafalaya. Capt. Theophilus Perry wrote his wife that five days before Christmas his regiment had begun digging a trench along Bayou Des Glaises, about three miles from Simmesport. "The work is heavy and on a large scale. I hear that it will take nine weeks to complete the fortification." Jonathan T. Knight of Hawes's brigade, like Captain Perry, was impressed by the scale of the undertaking: "I will tell you it is a great work. We are diging a ditch one and a half miles long, 9 foot deep and twenty foot wide and cutting the timber a mile at each end of the ditch. They detail a Regt. from this Division every day to work on it." Although his brigade had seen little action so far in the war, Knight took the earthworks near Simmesport as evidence of a willing spirit: "If we never fight the feds any we will show the rising generation that we was willing to do it if the enemy would give us an equal showing." Four regiments alternated, one per day, in building the Simmesport earthworks. "We start at 6 O'clock, march 3 miles and work until 4 O'clock and return to camp," Captain Petty informed his wife. "We work by reliefs. Work one hour and rest one hour." The harsh winter occasionally intruded. Snow and freezing rain fell on the works in the first week of the new year. "It is a miserably wet time and mud mud mud is all the go," Petty complained on January 7.[45]

A week later Petty reported that "we are still at work on our fortifications. Next Sunday will be our day again. Don't be surprised at our working on Sunday for it is the busiest day in military circles. We know no Sabbaths." The Greyhounds had begun trenches along both banks of Bayou Des Glaises, running generally east to the Atchafalaya near Simmesport, and on the west bank of Yellow Bayou, which flowed north and emptied into Des Glaises about three miles west of the town. By now, Petty wrote, the earthworks were nearly two miles long. But all the flying dirt seemed pointless to the Bastrop lawyer: the Federals could reach the Red River valley above Fort DeRussy simply by marching up from south Louisiana on a line west of the Greyhounds and their trenches or by steaming around DeRussy via a series of waterways to a point near Alexandria. The time and energy being expended on the earthworks appeared "nonsensical," he groused. "But we have no right to think. Others have been appointed to think for us and we like the automation [*sic*] must kick (or work) when the wire is pulled."[46]

While some of the Texans dug earthworks near Simmesport, others near Marksville blocked the Red River against Federal gunboats. About six miles downriver from Fort DeRussy, engineers drove long piles into the river bottom, braced them from all directions, and connected the pilings with iron plates and bolts. Farther upstream, other Greyhounds cut down hundreds of trees, dragged them to the riverbank, and pushed them into the water. The trees, branches and all, floated down to the upper crisscrossed pilings, where they snagged and jammed into an immense raft blocking the river. So many trees were lodged in the raft that they slid onto and among each other, piling the timbers to a depth of about six feet. Even Rear Adm. David D. Porter, a man who normally held rebels in the lowest contempt, admitted that the Confederates had built "a formidable obstruction." In fact, he later wrote, "when I first saw these lower obstructions I began to think that the enemy had blocked the game on us." As it turned out, the raft was more impressive in appearance than fact. Its great weakness, as General Walker observed, was that it was too far—six miles—from the guns of the fort. That would allow the enemy's steam engines to remove the snags and pilings without interference.[47]

Work on the fort itself involved more than moving dirt or cutting trees. The main stronghold was an earthen-walled square about three miles north of Marksville and seven hundred yards south of the river. A long double parapet with flanking ditches connected the fort to a water battery and its three casemated and four barbette heavy guns to command a long stretch of the river. The complex included a magazine, an underground bunker, gates, and the iron casemates and barbette mountings of the water battery, requiring the expertise of carpenters as well as the muscle of ditch diggers. In fact, in mid-January, General Walker was instructed to detail as many carpenters as possible from his various brigades and send them to work under orders of the fort's engineers. Admiral Porter, normally reluctant to praise anything relating to the rebels, later marveled at the skill of DeRussy's engineers and carpenters and gave the Confederacy high praise indeed: "Without doubt, they established a new era in military engineering which none have ever excelled, and on a scale only equaled by the works of the Titans of old."[48] Much of the credit for digging the trenches, driving the piles, cutting the trees, and constructing the fort belonged to a group of workers whose contribution was almost ignored for more than a century: slaves from surrounding parishes. Several hundred slaves, pressed into service by General Taylor, labored beside Walker's Greyhounds on every part of the defensive complex around Simmesport and Marksville. Planters, worried that the army would not look after their bondsmen's welfare, objected that they needed their workers at home, but General Taylor assured the skeptical and upset masters that their slaves were handled with care while they worked on the defenses: "Every arrangement has been made at the works . . . to secure the comfort & well being of negroes, that can be made. Temporary huts have been erected for their shelter; bountiful rations are issued to them, and a skillful Surgeon has been sent there, provided with medicines to attend them if taken sick. Last year the rations allowed to negroes at Fort De Russy were larger than the rations allowed to soldiers."[49]

Whether Taylor was simply dissembling or just did not know the real conditions in which the slaves were working is not clear, but some of Walker's Texans recognized that the black men were doing the heaviest and most dangerous part of the labor, and toiling more days and longer hours to boot. James Armstrong, a private in the 14th Infantry and a man who owned slaves back in Upshur County, mentioned to his wife that some of the slaves working on the fortifications had run away one night in early January: "I do not blame the negroes for leaving, they are worked from day break untill dark in chains and Sunday and all the time." So many slaves had run away by late January, in fact, that a company of cavalry had to be sent into nearby parishes to round them up and return them to work, and white construction workers had to be pulled off the works to unload supplies brought down from Alexandria on steamboats. In mid-February, Capt. Harvey Wallace of the 19th Infantry noted that his superiors were "pushing the work on the Fort as fast as possible." This of course affected soldiers as well as slaves, but the bondsmen got the worst of it. "Oh how I pity these poor negroes here," he wrote his wife back in Rusk County. "They work them from daybreak until dark [and] about half feed them[.] They look so bad[.] I never would let them have one of mine to treat this way[.] I would feed them in the woods [i.e., hide them] first." At least sixty-nine slaves died while working on the fortifications, paying the ultimate price for Confederate defense of the Red River valley. In February 1999, 135 years after the event, citizens of Avoyelles Parish erected an eight-foot-tall granite monument at Fort DeRussy to the sixty-nine black workers, a rare public recognition of the role slaves were forced to play in the defense of the Confederacy.[50]

The landside of Fort DeRussy and the long earthworks near Simmesport were still not complete by mid-March. But the war would not wait. The long-expected Federal offensive aimed at the Red River began rumbling forward with tens of thousands of soldiers, thousands of wagons, horses, and mules, and great expectations of victory. Ten thousand Federal veterans of the Vicksburg campaign steamed down the Mississippi from Vicksburg and into the Red River by March 12. General Banks in south Louisiana began moving his army of twenty thousand men overland toward the Red River valley on March 13. And Admiral Porter assembled the largest American war fleet ever seen on inland waters at the mouth of the Red River at the same time. Whether General Walker's Greyhounds were ready or not, the war was coming to them on a scale they had never seen before.

CHAPTER 10

# A Long Retreat

In the two months from mid-March to mid-May 1864, Walker's Texas Division did more fighting than in the entire rest of the war. They marched hundreds of miles, much of that distance under enemy pressure, fought three pitched battles, and found themselves at the center of a dispute between their highest generals, a dispute that would lead to a major reorganization of the command structure in the Confederate Trans-Mississippi Department. When those who survived the war were old men, surrounded by grandchildren and reminiscing about their days as young foot soldiers, it was the spring of 1864 that the Greyhounds recalled most vividly.

The train of events leading to that memorable spring started in Gen. Nathaniel P. Banks's Federal headquarters in New Orleans. After his first two attempts to occupy Confederate Texas failed (at Sabine Pass in September 1863 and on the Texas overland expedition), General Banks had landed seven thousand Federal soldiers on the southernmost tip of the Lone Star State, near the mouth of the Rio Grande, in early November 1863. In the following weeks, however, he had done little more than occupy a few points along the coast and on the Rio Grande. Most of his regiments were still holed up in prepared works at New Iberia, Louisiana, and his superiors were unwilling to commit more resources to the Rio Grande expedition. Still, Texas Unionists were happy now that their military governor, Andrew J. Hamilton, had been set up with an office in Brownsville. Hamilton and his followers expected to extend their control gradually, from Brownsville into the interior of the state, and thus reclaim Texas for the Union. In addition, Secretary of State William Seward and President Lincoln were apparently satisfied that the U.S. Army's new presence on the border with Mexico would be sufficient warning to the French to stay out of the American civil conflict.[1]

On the other hand, northern textile interests had gained almost no cotton at all from Banks's Rio Grande expedition. Far South Texas was not cotton country, and the stream of Confederate cotton flowing into Mexico over long roads had simply shifted farther up the Rio Grande, out of Banks's reach. Moreover, very few slaves had been freed in the Federal toeholds along the Gulf coast. And then there was General Halleck. General-in-Chief Henry Halleck was very unhappy with the Rio Grande campaign. From the beginning the professionally trained Halleck had advised the amateur soldier Banks to get at Texas via the Red River in Louisiana. The river route would provide a dependable supply line, an opportunity for the heavy artillery on Federal gunboats to cover the army, a chance to break up the Confederate Trans-Mississippi headquarters and war plants in Shreveport, and a direct route to one of the richest cotton-growing regions of the trans-Mississippi—the Red River valley and East Texas.[2]

From a strictly military point of view, Halleck was certain, an expedition up the Red River was the only legitimate operation worth consideration. He scolded Banks for flying off to the Rio Grande, lectured him about the advantages of the Red River route, and gathered the support of Gen. William T. Sherman in Mississippi and Gen. Frederick Steele in Arkansas for his own plan to take the Confederate Trans-Mississippi Department out of the war in the spring of 1864. In the end, Halleck ordered Banks to leave only a skeleton force on the lower Texas coast and concentrate his divisions in south Louisiana, preparatory to an expedition up the Red River.[3]

The Federal plan, as finally hatched by Halleck, required General Banks to march his army of twenty thousand from Berwick Bay in far south Louisiana to Alexandria in the central part of the state. Alexandria, the main port on the lower Red River, was about forty miles upstream from Fort DeRussy. Ten thousand additional Federals would be detached from General Sherman's army at Vicksburg, put on transports, and taken down the Mississippi River and into the Red River. After reducing Fort DeRussy with the help of the navy, they would steam upstream to Alexandria, where they expected to join with Banks's columns by March 17. Rear Admiral Porter would accompany the army up the Red River with the largest war fleet ever seen on inland waters: 13 heavy ironclads, 4 tinclads, 5 other gunboats, troop transports, supply ships, hospital boats—60 vessels altogether, with 210 naval guns to provide an iron umbrella for the foot soldiers.[4]

As the mighty combined forces of the U.S. Army and Navy swept up the Red River valley and approached Shreveport, General Steele's army of ten thousand would approach Shreveport from the north by marching overland from Little Rock. The forces of Banks, Steele, and Porter would join on the outskirts of Shreveport, crush the overmatched Confederates, and break up the Trans-Mississippi Department's headquarters and war plants. Confederate cotton could be seized for northern mills as the Federals advanced up the Red River valley, and the powerful force moving freely toward Texas would be a loud warning to the French to stay out of the troubled waters north of the border. General Banks would also be able to carry President Lincoln's 1863 Reconstruction plan into north Louisiana and reclaim the Pelican State for the Union. After this campaign, the Union high command would never again have to worry about enemy activity west of the Mississippi River and could concentrate on finishing off the Confederacy in Georgia and Virginia.[5]

These were the forces rumbling into place in March 1864 while Walker's Greyhounds dug trenches and gun emplacements and shored up the walls of Fort DeRussy. Neither General Taylor nor General Walker put much faith in the defensive works north of Marksville. They had dutifully carried out E. Kirby Smith's orders to build up the fort and earthworks and raft, but both realized that DeRussy could not stand up to a combined land and river assault. In early March, Taylor explained to Smith's chief of staff, William R. Boggs, that DeRussy could "make a formidable defense against gun-boats now, but the fort is in no condition to withstand an attack in the rear, and should the enemy advance in heavy force now we would inevitably lose the guns and material at De Russy. I am pushing everything to the utmost to place De Russy in as good a state as it can ever be put, but it will never stand any protracted siege." Taylor and Walker had raised objections about the defenses on the Red River as early as January, but Smith had admonished them that he and his appointees would handle the engineering and layout. In his postwar memoirs Walker wrote that no fewer than ten thousand troops would have been necessary to defend the landside of the fort, nearly three times the force he had available. Besides, Walker continued, "the [river] obstructions which should have been auxillary to the fort were placed six miles below it, thus leaving the enemy opportunity to remove them at his leisure."[6]

Taylor and Walker were not alone in realizing that the fort was vulnerable. Looking back on the U.S. Navy's experience during the war, Admiral Porter concluded that forts might stymie gunboats, but that was about all: "Indeed, I know of no instance where troops and ships properly combined have attacked a land work when the land work was not taken." The main history of Confederate engineering agreed a century later that Taylor, Walker, and Porter were correct: from Fort Henry in early 1862 to the end of the war, every time the Confederates depended on fortifications alone to turn back combined land and water operations, they failed. Their only successes, such as the defense of Fort Pemberton, Mississippi, during the Vicksburg campaign, came when the Federals cooperated by sending gunboats alone against prepared works. General Banks and Admiral Porter did not plan to make that mistake. The unfinished defenses near Simmesport were also exposed. The two ends of the long trench on Yellow Bayou were supposed to be protected by swamps, but the wetlands had dried up over the winter, leaving the earthworks hanging in mid-air, easily flanked by a resourceful adversary.[7]

If Taylor had little confidence in DeRussy, he had gained deep respect for Walker and his division over the last several months. The Texas infantry had smashed "the veterans of Vicksburg" at Bayou Bourbeau, they had provided valuable support for the artillery's war on river traffic in recent months, and they had worked like demons to prepare the defenses near Simmesport and Marksville. In mid-February, Taylor wrote Trans-Mississippi headquarters that "Major Genl Walker, whose Division is stationed near[by] has been very energetic in pushing on the work and rendered very valuable assistance. I have just made a minute inspection of Hawes and Randalls Brigades of this Division, and have never seen any troops in finer condition. No troops have ever exhibited greater improvement in all the qualities of soldiers, and their present condition reflects great credit on the Division and Brigade Commanders." If the enemy would oblige by sending no more than thirty-eight hundred soldiers against the Greyhounds (the number present for duty under General Walker in early March), General Taylor would have no worries. Unfortunately for Taylor, General Banks and Admiral Porter were planning to lead thirty thousand Federals and a monstrous river fleet to Shreveport.[8]

Confederates from Edmund Kirby Smith down to the most poorly informed foot soldier expected a Federal thrust up the Red River that spring. Reports of enemy troop movements and messages from Confederate spies all pointed in that direction. Besides, Smith could see what Halleck saw: from a strictly military point of view, the Red River was "the only true line of operation" and the most sensible route to Trans-Mississippi headquarters and mountains of Louisiana and Texas cotton. In early March, nearly two weeks before the first Federal troops arrived in the vicinity, General Walker's Texas brigades began sending their sick to the rear. Pvt. David Ray, the former schoolteacher from Grayson County, wrote his mother on March 6 that "we have had orders for several days to hold ourselves in readiness to march at a moment's warning." The Greyhounds knew the enemy was coming—they just did not understand that the Federals were coming by the tens of thousands.[9]

The first news that a large enemy force had arrived in the vicinity reached General Scurry's headquarters west of Simmesport on the Saturday afternoon of March 12. Scouts along the Mississippi and Atchafalaya Rivers reported that transports "crowded with troops" had entered the Red River and then the Atchafalaya, aiming, no doubt, for Simmesport. These were the first units of the ten thousand men General Sherman had sent down from Vicksburg, all under the command of Brig. Gen. Andrew Jackson Smith, an aggressive and gruff officer known for his no-nonsense approach to war.[10]

Not understanding at first just how many Federals were approaching his unfinished lines, the pugnacious Scurry ordered his brigade of fourteen hundred men and one field battery to hurry from the earthworks along Yellow Bayou toward Simmesport to prevent a landing. Additional scouting reports about even more transports brought him up short before he could march the three miles to Simmesport. Realizing that his lone brigade could not take on several thousand Federals, Scurry reversed field and filled the long trench west of Simmesport with his Texans. Even that was only a temporary holding action, though. Scouts indicated that gunboats had gone up the Red River, raising the possibility that the enemy might get between Scurry and the rest of the division near Marksville. Besides, the usual winter and spring rains had not come as expected, and the swamps that were supposed to protect the ends of Scurry's earthworks were dry. An imaginative foe could easily march on dry ground around the trench at Yellow Bayou, turning Scurry's whole position. The Texans near Simmesport would have to fall back toward Marksville that night or face certain capture.[11]

Scurry's dispatches to General Walker on the afternoon and night of March 12 convinced Walker that his division was in a dangerous fix. Scurry's brigade was certainly in peril, even inside the earthworks along Yellow Bayou. Even if Walker hurried his other two brigades (under Randal and Waul) the twenty road miles from Marksville to Scurry's rescue, the whole division would still be outnumbered more than two to one by the hordes of Yankees pouring off the transports at Simmesport. And then there was the problem of Fort DeRussy, unfinished on its landside and vulnerable even under perfect circumstances to an infantry assault. Walker dictated a report to General Taylor at 7 P.M. that Saturday, summarizing his dilemma. "I am embarrassed to know how to cover Fort De Russy," he confessed. The enemy's greatly superior numbers would make a defense of DeRussy "extremely hazardous."[12]

The greatest danger Walker perceived, though, was in the geography of the area. The high prairie land from the Red River and Marksville southward was like an island; it was surrounded by the river on the north, swamps on the east, more swamps on the west, and interconnected bayous (Du Lac and Des Glaises) on the south. Now heavy Federal columns were landing at Simmesport on the southeast. Walker's only practical line of retreat out of this cul-de-sac was to the southwest, via a lone bridge spanning Bayou Du Lac, about nine miles from Marksville. The road on the other side of that bridge turned northwest to safer country around Alexandria. If he kept his division "on the island" too long, Walker worried, he could be trapped.[13]

By Sunday morning the two Texas brigades that had spent the winter around Fort DeRussy (Randal's and Waul's) were rushing south with General Walker to reinforce Scurry's brigade, which had fallen back from Yellow Bayou several miles during the night. The two brigades joined Scurry's men in light entrenchments near a long bridge about five miles south of Marksville. The next morning Walker's scouts reported that the Federals were approaching from Simmesport in heavy numbers. Walker got a good look at the enemy column as it snaked its way onto the open prairie south of Marksville. The blue line—what he could see of it—was fully two and a half miles long, and the end was not in sight. Hoping to disrupt the enemy advance, Walker evacuated the works and put his three brigades into line of battle a mile west of the road to Marksville, out on the open prairie where the enemy could see the challenge. If the Federals took the bait and divided their forces—one part continuing toward DeRussy and the other part confronting the battle line on the prairie—the Texans might have a fighting chance to stymie the whole offensive.[14]

Captain Petty of the 17th Texas described the scene to his wife: "It was a grand and magnificent sight to see our troops filing into line of battle on an open prarie. It was cool, the sun shone brightly and guns & bayonets glistened. Men were cheerful and merry." A Louisiana commissary officer who happened to be with Walker's Texans that morning also noted the pageantry: "The army was making preparations to fight, the regiments lined up one behind the other, the commands were given and promptly obeyed by the various commanders, the Batteries came at a gallop dispersing here and there among the regiments, the aides-de-camp of the various generals on their beautiful horses, galloped between the lines, and transmitted the orders of their superiors."[15]

To General Walker's disappointment, the Federal infantry ignored the Confederate battle line on the prairie and pressed on toward DeRussy. Walker was forced now to face unpleasant facts: "however mortifying it might be to abandon our brave companions in arms at Fort De Russy to their fate, it became my imperative duty to do so rather than attempt assistance, which at best could delay this danger but a few hours." Accordingly, at 10 A.M. that Monday morning, Walker turned his Texans westward to slip through the back door off "the island" and join other Confederate infantry to the west. Perhaps with greater numbers and more favorable terrain, they could blunt this latest offensive somewhere up the Red River valley.[16]

Walker's retreat left about 350 men inside Fort DeRussy to face ten thousand Federals marching up from Simmesport and a large river fleet steaming up from the mouth of the Red River. About three-quarters of the DeRussy garrison were Texans, detailed from various companies in every regiment of Walker's division.

The remaining defenders were from assorted Louisiana units, mainly artillery. Commanding this miscellaneous brew of detachments was Lt. Col. William Byrd of the 14th Texas Infantry, an alumnus of the Virginia Military Institute and the law school of the University of Virginia. A member of the historically famous Byrd family of Virginia, he was a lawyer and newspaper editor in Austin before the war and served as adjutant general of Texas during the secession crisis. In the fall of 1861 he had been elected lieutenant colonel of the 14th Texas Infantry, the unit originally organized by his political colleague, former governor Edward Clark.[17]

The fort itself, still under construction on the landside, consisted of two earthworks. The main structure, set well back from the river, was a large square, about fifty yards on each side. The earthen walls of the square, about twenty feet high, were reinforced with heavy timbers and surrounded by a ditch. Seven hundred yards northeast of the main work was the river battery, a casemated, iron-reinforced structure with heavy guns that overlooked a long stretch of the river.[18]

Federal officers were impressed. "It was an extensive and beautiful structure, with a large square work . . . and heavy casemates covered with two thicknesses of railroad iron," Admiral Porter later recalled. "These portholes in the main casemate [of the river battery] were of thick iron and only large enough to admit the muzzles of the guns." The commander of one of Porter's gunboats, Thomas Selfridge of the USS *Osage,* agreed that "Fort De Russy was a formidable work, probably one of the strongest constructed by the Confederates during the war." The Federal officer assigned to dismantle the fort, Col. Thomas W. Humphrey of Illinois, marveled at its might: "The works were very formidable, being by far the most scientifically and permanently constructed works of the enemy I have seen." Nevertheless, Lieutenant Colonel Byrd had no illusions about the strength of Fort DeRussy: "The fort was planned not with the absurd expectation of defending it permanently against powerful land and naval forces combined, but to offer at least a temporary obstacle to their progress, allowing time to save our valuable stores accumulated at the Posts above, and to effect a concentration of detached bodies of our troops."[19]

After bypassing Walker's Texans on the prairie, Gen. A. J. Smith's Federal divisions tramped through Marksville and pushed on the few remaining miles to the fort by mid-afternoon. John C. Porter of the 18th Texas, recently promoted from private to sergeant, was one of those Texans left behind at the fort. Just as he and some others who had been posted to the riverbank hurried back into the main fort, an artillery exchange opened the engagement. Capt. William S. Burns of the 4th Missouri Cavalry (U.S.) was on the other side of the fort's wall and observed the artillery duel: "For two hours, shell, solid shot, shrapnel and bullets passed between the two parties. We expected every moment to hear the heavy guns from the gun-boats, but not a sound," Burns remembered. There was no sound from the gunboats because Admiral Porter's river fleet missed the fight at DeRussy. The steamboats spent the whole day pulling apart the logjam Walker's Texans had built several miles downstream from the fort. Still, General Smith had more than sufficient force to reduce the works without the aid of the navy.[20]

During the artillery exchange and scattered rifle fire, Federal regiments moved into position and lined up for a full assault against the main fort. After two hours the gunners halted their bombardment, and infantry officers finally gave the command to charge. Twice the blue line surged forward, and twice it fell back under rifle and cannon fire from the fort. The third attempt, launched near sundown, succeeded. John Ritland of the 32nd Iowa Infantry remembered that "when the summons came, we jumped to our feet and charged up the steep bluffs [i.e., the walls of the fort]. I was nearly on the top once, but became so short of breath, that I hadn't the power to hold on, and slid back a considerable distance. I grabbed hold of an exposed root and pulled myself up again. In the meantime, the bullets flew thick and fast. Tom Lein said it was so steep where he happened to be that the men had to climb on each other's backs to be able to make headway." Sergeant Porter of the 18th Texas was firing over the walls and observed the Federal assault: "When they had arranged their line, they made a general charge, and came over the works, as fast as black birds, and deeper than a man could climb out. I supposed they filled the ditch, and the others went over on their shoulders." The first men to reach the top of the embankment were particularly vulnerable to fire from the defenders. "The first man who mounted the breastworks, a color bearer, was killed. He lay that night where he fell, with the flag he bore, spread over him," Porter noted.[21]

The Federals swarmed over the walls on all sides faster than the Confederates could reload and fire, and within minutes Lieutenant Colonel Byrd mounted the wall and waved a white flag tied to a bayonet. About 50 Confederates in the water battery took advantage of the distance between them and the victorious Federals to scramble out of the works along the river and disappear into the woods, but 317 of the defenders (including 235 from Walker's division) surrendered under Byrd's white flag. Ten artillery pieces and tons of quartermaster and commissary supplies also fell into Federal hands. Sergeant Porter was just glad the ordeal was over: "My feelings at the time of the surrender, I can scarcely describe—my first impulse was a feeling of relief, for I knew that if we had not surrendered that soon, all would have been killed. I then thought of home and loved ones, and the little probability of ever returning." Federal reactions were much different, of course. Benjamin Hieronymus of the 117th Illinois Infantry, posted to the rear to keep an eye out for Walker's division, realized from the loud cheering to his front that his comrades in blue had prevailed: "For at least five minutes we did nothing but cheer and wave our hats & caps & jump around & hollow for our cause."[22]

Several miles to the southwest, Walker's Texans, marching west across the prairie, could hear the artillery fire at DeRussy. Whatever they felt about leaving their comrades behind, they crossed over Bayou Du Lac that night and burned the bridge behind them. General Walker pushed his men hard over the next few days because he feared, with good reason, that the Federals would hurry their infantry aboard river transports, steam up to Alexandria within a matter of hours, and seize the roads leading up the Red River valley before the Texans could get there. Captain Petty complained about the fast pace of the retreat after four days of extreme exertion: "The men are weary and foot sore, broke down and jaded. Even the horses have fagged under it." Volney Ellis, adjutant of the 12th Texas, was amazed that the Greyhounds could keep going. "Our men have undergone traveling 25 and 30 miles a day and sometimes all night. It is truly remarkable what man can stand!"[23]

Under such conditions, nerves sometimes frayed very easily. During a short rest on one of the night marches, soldiers of the 16th Infantry were startled by the sharp call somewhere in the darkness, "Who goes there?" A musket shot immediately after the challenge stirred the Texans into feverish activity. "The hands of every man were instantly upon his gun, and every preparation was made to resist an attack from the enemy's cavalry," Private Blessington recalled. "Presently we heard a heavy tramp coming down the road, indicating a charge from cavalry. The troops all of a sudden stampeded, some of them running down the bank of a creek alongside of the road, while others jumped a fence on the left of the road. . . . Bayonets were fixed, and triggers were cocked; but we soon discovered the cause of alarm, in beholding two Texas beeves that had escaped from the drivers, and which were followed by some of them, in order to return them to the herd." The agility of those who had jumped the fence or leaped into the creek bed must have been the subject of campfire jokes for many days afterward.[24]

Prospects turned somewhat brighter for the Texans when reinforcements—Mouton's old Louisiana brigade, now commanded by Col. Henry Gray—joined Walker's columns southeast of Alexandria on March 15. A day or so later, a new Texas brigade also joined the march. Commanded by a thirty-two-year-old French nobleman and veteran of the Crimean War, Prince Camille Armand Jules Marie de Polignac, these Texans had at first resisted orders from their exotic and diminutive European commander (whom they took to calling "General Polecat" and "a damn frog-eating Frenchman"), but recent service had warmed relations between the prince and his Texas soldiers. General Taylor ordered Walker to lead the whole force—his own division plus Gray's and Polignac's brigades—northwest through Lecompte, about twenty miles south of Alexandria. Taylor had had the foresight to establish commissary and forage depots along the route from Lecompte to Natchitoches because the sparsely settled piney woods in that region were, in his words, "utterly barren." Another series of rapid marches by the Greyhounds and their reinforcements might well put them ahead of the Federals in the race up the valley.[25]

For three weeks, from March 14 to April 4, the Texans moved northwest on a route parallel to the Red River (see Map 7). They could not afford to take the roads skirting the river itself because of the danger of enemy gunboats and troop transports. Instead, they tramped along country roads several miles south and west of the river. On March 16 they moved ahead of the Federals, who were stalled in Alexandria waiting for General Banks's army to arrive from south Louisiana. By March 17 the gray clans—Walker's division, Gray's brigade, and Polignac's brigade—began arriving at the farm of Carroll Jones, a wealthy free black man, twenty-five miles due west of Alexandria. The only experienced cavalry available to shadow the enemy, the 2nd Louisiana, trotted into camp on March 19. The Confederates halted for a few days while General Taylor gathered supplies and information about the enemy. He found the Jones farm ideal for a temporary pause: the forage depot established there earlier fed his mules and horses, and from there he could watch two main roads, receive supplies from two waterways, and keep a close eye on the Red River to detect the arrival of the Federal river fleet from Alexandria.[26]

On a cold, drizzly March 21, General Taylor assigned Capt. William Edgar's four-gun battery, the Alamo City Guards (sometimes called the Nonpareil Battery), to join with the 2nd Louisiana Cavalry as a rear guard to slow down Federal infantry now beginning to march up from Alexandria. This was the same battery, usually assigned to Scurry's brigade, that had performed so well against riverboats on the Mississippi River the previous winter. Squinting through cold rain and occasional sleet, the horsemen and gunners took an ideal position for defense, on a hill overlooking a main road and two bayous, about twenty miles west of Alexandria.[27]

This rear guard proved so troublesome to the Federals that Brig. Gen. Joseph A. Mower went to special lengths to neutralize it. Mower was the same officer whose men had chased Walker's rear guard out of Richmond and burned the little town near Milliken's Bend the previous summer. Mower had also commanded the Federals who poured over the walls at DeRussy one week earlier.

## Map 7
### The Long Retreat, March 14–April 4, 1864

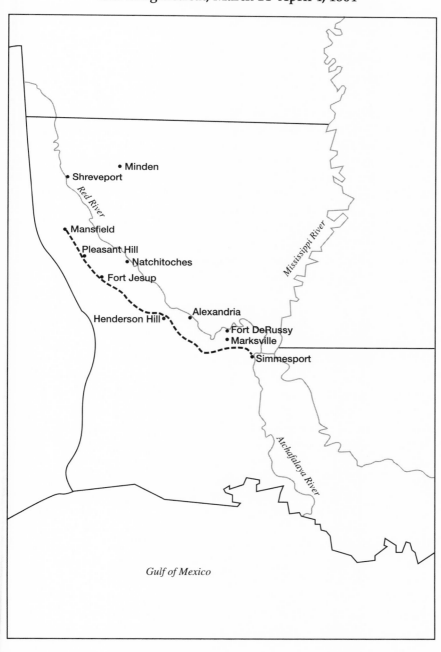

Minden

Shreveport

Red River

Mansfield

Pleasant Hill

Natchitoches

Fort Jesup

Alexandria

Henderson Hill

Fort DeRussy

Marksville

Simmesport

Mississippi River

Atchafalaya River

Gulf of Mexico

Taking an entire infantry division, a battery of field artillery, and a brigade of cavalry, Mower pressed forward late in the day to dislodge the rebels from the high ground on Henderson Hill. The weather that night was brutal—cold rain, sleet, and hail beat down on rebel and Yankee alike and apparently convinced the Louisiana cavalry pickets that the war was suspended for the evening. Far from postponing hostilities, General Mower left part of his force in front of the hill to distract the Confederates while he led the remainder through dark rain, swampy roads, and soggy fields on a roundabout path to the rear of the hill. Mower's men scooped up a few rebel couriers and pickets in the darkness, learned the countersign, ran up the rear of the hill, and surrounded the Confederate cavalry and Edgar's gunners in their camp. Although many accounts of this incident claimed that not a shot was fired, at least one was fired by Captain Edgar after a Federal color bearer struck the captain with his flagstaff. Edgar turned and fired his pistol, instantly removing the upper teeth of the Missouri standard bearer. A half-century later, the cheerful Federal veteran could describe his wounding without rancor: "I am the Boy that wounded him [Edgar] on the shoulder with the flag spear and he returned the kindness by shooting my upper teeth out. We shook hands next morning." The surprised Edgar, his men, and his four fieldpieces joined most of the Louisiana horsemen in Federal custody within a few minutes.[28]

Joseph Blessington, now a corporal on General Scurry's staff, wrote that the news of the battery's seizure "fell like a thunderbolt on our division, as each brigade exhibited considerable jealousy towards the others concerning the Nonpareil Battery; all three of the brigades claiming it as their battery." For Captain Edgar and his gunners, the high times along the Mississippi levee only a few weeks earlier were now replaced by life as Federal captives.[29]

When a Missouri cavalry officer reported the success at Henderson Hill to one of his superiors the next day, he found the Federal colonel in conversation with the wife of Louisiana's Confederate governor, Thomas O. Moore, on the front porch of the governor's plantation house near Alexandria. Mrs. Moore seemed especially interested to overhear that the Louisiana cavalry commander, William G. Vincent, had escaped capture at Henderson Hill: "As I finished, she said, 'You say the Lieut.-Col. was not captured—how did he escape?' I answered, 'As we have heard, he hid in a hen house.' Her reply came quick and sharp, 'Well, I should have supposed, that would be the first spot where your soldiers would have found anything.'" The first lady's courtesy to her front porch guest did not extend to the hen house raiders under his command.[30]

When most of the horsemen of the 2nd Louisiana Cavalry were captured on Henderson Hill, General Taylor lost the only reliable cavalry available to report on enemy movements. A division of Texas cavalry under Brig. Gen. Thomas Green was on the way to join Taylor in north Louisiana, but the various regiments were still en route through the piney woods of East Texas. Taylor looked westward daily, impatiently expecting to see the Texas horsemen, but they were still far away. Not wishing to operate blindly in the vicinity of the enemy, he resumed the retreat toward Natchitoches on March 22, now leading his men up narrow roads through the piney woods of northwest Louisiana. All told, he could muster only about fifty-six hundred infantry and artillery at this point of the campaign. Supply wagons were sent ahead to protect them from Federal cavalry, so for several days the Greyhounds and their comrades had to march long miles over rough country without tents and baggage and with only the contents of their haversacks for nourishment. Quartermaster officers had to put a guard on the corn reserved for the wagon mules each night; otherwise, the hungry soldiers would steal the forage from the animals.[31]

The retreat up the Red River valley was one of the hardest trials the Greyhounds endured in the whole war, partly because their tents and blankets and provisions were usually miles ahead of them. Dr. Edward Cade, brigade surgeon in Randal's brigade, wrote his wife that "We are living pretty rough as our train is generally from 10 to 20 miles in front of us. . . . We have done some terrible heavy marching since we have begun this retreat." Capt. Theophilus Perry of Marshall, walking along with his men, must have winced when he peeled off his boots at the end of each day: "My feet are blistered badly with great blisters as large as guinea eggs. . . . Our men have suffered very much, but marched like horses." Orange Connor of the 19th Infantry wrote his wife that "this is the hardest Soldiering I have yet seen. I have been very tired, very sleepy & very hungry & often very uneasy. . . . I have never, Suffered more fatigue & did not think [I] could stand so much. one day we marched 35 miles & stood in line-of-Battle a large portion of the time. were up all night & had not one bite to eat." Pvt. Samuel Farrow of the same regiment, never an advocate of stoicism, elaborated on March 23. "We have had nothing to eat but bread since we left Simsport and we have been without even that for two days twice. We hardly ever get more than one meal a day," he complained to his wife. "As to myself both legs of my pants are nearly torn off at the knee, and my drawers get the very mischief, though it is the best I can do."[32]

Capt. Elijah Petty of the 17th Infantry worried about maintaining morale under these conditions: "we have fared horribly having nothing but coarse cornbread and the very poorest quality of beef. . . . We have marched about 200 miles on bad fare and it takes a good patriot not to murmur under such circumstances." Petty might have worried even more if he could have read the letters and overheard the conversations about food and supplies in the Federal army not far behind him. Pvt. Edward B. Williams of the 32nd Iowa Infantry reported that "we have had plenty of everything," but he had taken to drinking tea from his division commissary because he had grown tired of the taste of coffee. Tea and coffee were luxuries the Greyhounds could barely remember.[33]

One hundred thirty years later, eight hundred Civil War reenactors "duplicated" the Confederate march up the Red River valley, covering sixty miles in eight days (a distance the Greyhounds sometimes covered in two days). The Louisiana heat felled some of the latter-day faux warriors, and others were disabled by hypothermia after a rain. Those who kept going were hobbled by sore feet and tormented by insects. They also discovered, unhappily, that "hardtack and bacon look alike after a couple of days in the haversack." Service in the Trans-Mississippi Department, as so many had learned early in the war, was not for the weak.[34]

The pine forests through which the Texans marched were only sparsely settled and provided very little in the way of good firewood, so the men were forced to burn smoky, smutty pine knots and branches when they stopped each night. Captain Perry noted the blackened, smudged faces of his men and himself: "I am as black as a pot. This lightwood smoke has painted us all." Private Farrow's comrades were filthy to boot: "We have been in the pine woods a week and have not shifted our clothes and we are as black a set of white men as you ever saw. We have nothing to cook with but Pine Knots." The remote woods of northwest Louisiana were particularly dismal for many of the Yankees coming up the same route a few days later. "The narrow winding road was rendered gloomy by the shade of a dark green canopy," Harris Beecher of the 114th New York Infantry noted. "The wind forever moaned among the tree tops. No underbrush or grass enlived the scene beneath. Nothing but tall, huge, sombre trunks rose from the white sand, like columns, to sustain the dark pall overhead. A death-like silence pervaded the dim arches." Capt. William Burns of the 4th Missouri Cavalry thought it was "a forsaken-looking country." The army was following "a rough and narrow road, winding through an almost continuous pine forest, with a few mud-thatched, miserable log houses, scattered sparsely along its length."[35]

As usual, an enemy offensive into new neighborhoods put civilians to flight. Col. Thomas R. Bonner of the 18th Texas wrote that "the inhabitants all along the route of our retreat, were hurriedly quitting their homes, and flying before the approach of the invader. Consternation and alarm everywhere prevailed among the citizens." Corporal Blessington remembered that "the whole country, far and wide, was aroused to the highest pitch of excitement by the retreat of our army. . . . Old men shouldered their muskets and came to our assistance, to help drive back the invader." These few belligerent refugees hardly frightened the Federals chasing them up the Red River. According to Harris Beecher, a New York surgeon, "the boys took great delight in witnessing the panic they had created among this ignorant people."[36]

At the end of the month, more than two weeks into the general retreat up the Red River, Taylor's haggard foot soldiers shuffled by the ruins of a former U.S. Army post, Fort Jesup, twenty-two road miles southwest of Natchitoches. Built in 1822 on the high ridge between the Red River to the east and the Sabine River on the Texas border, it had guarded the southwest frontier of the United States before the acquisition of Texas. General Taylor's thoughts must have lingered a while at the ruins. His father, Gen. Zachary Taylor, had chosen the site and supervised the construction of the fort four years before his son was born. The irony would not have escaped Richard Taylor.[37]

Such thoughts were doubtless crowded out of his mind very quickly, though, because the advancing Federal army—thirty thousand strong now that General Banks's contingent had joined A. J. Smith's veterans in Alexandria—was only a day or two behind the Confederates. General Taylor had been looking west for the arrival of Tom Green's Texas horsemen since mid-March, but still they did not appear. Taylor was especially perturbed by the delay because it meant that as he fell back every day he had to destroy Louisiana property to prevent the enemy from using it. Some of the Greyhounds, too, were tired of retreating by now. Fred Smith of the 19th Texas echoed the thoughts of many Texans: "if we keep on retreating [the Federals] will not only think we are a parcel of cowards but our own men will become still more disheartened than they now are, and give up the *whole* Red River Country to complete ruin. . . . I would rather fight them now than wait till they are stronger and nearer *my home.*" Captain Petty, the prewar lawyer from Bastrop, agreed: "We have run already unconscionably and the Country has been devast[at]ed thereby. . . . We have run until our patience has oozed out." Capt. Theophilus Perry prepared himself mentally for the moment when he and his comrades would turn on the enemy: "I shall fight like I was standing at the threshold of my door fighting against robbers and scourgers for the defense of my wife & family."[38]

The whole Red River valley was smoky from all the fires set by one army or the other. Trans-Mississippi commander Edmund Kirby Smith had ordered his officers to burn all cotton in the path of the Federals, and, according to observers, his officers were efficient in their task. The commander of one of Admiral Porter's ironclads, Thomas Selfridge, observed that "the enemy's scouts set fire to all the cotton within ten miles of the river-bank. Millions of dollars worth of it were destroyed, and so dense was the smoke that the sun was obscured, and appeared as though seen through a smoked glass." Harris Beecher of New York had a closer view: "at every plantation a black and smouldering pile showed that the rebel army in its retreat, was determined to leave nothing that could afford aid or comfort to their enemy. In some places, the wind had blown the flocculent material from the burning heaps, before they were consumed, and had covered fields, fences and brush with cotton, simulating a coating of snow." And what the retreating Confederates did not burn was taken or ruined by their enemies. Capt. Harvey Wallace of the 19th Texas, one of the captives from Fort DeRussy, witnessed the destructive talents of Federal sailors from his confinement on an enemy riverboat: "Passed gin houses burnt, houses burnt, the enemy anchoring at every farm, killing all the stock not fit for use, carrying off all provisions, fowls, and everything of value." Louisiana could not stand much more of this retreat, and neither could General Taylor.[39]

On the 1st of April, Walker's division, the two infantry brigades under Gray and Polignac (combined into a division under General Mouton), and attendant artillery batteries and wagon trains gathered at Pleasant Hill, a small village about thirty-five road miles northwest of Natchitoches and fifty straight-line miles south of Shreveport. Reunited with their knapsacks, the grimy and malodorous Confederates crowded around the supply trains and changed their clothing for the first time in three weeks. Joining them and General Taylor for the first time in this campaign was Gen. Tom Green, newly arrived from Texas with some of his "wild horsemen," and more were on the way. The Greyhounds were happy to see such fierce-looking reinforcements. A sergeant in the 19th Infantry said that Green's troopers "looked like they would saw a man to pieces if he didn't talk to suit them." Pvt. Fred Smith of the same infantry regiment took comfort at the sight of the new arrivals: "They were mounted on fine fat Texas horses, and 'all right' generally." Taylor held his newly strengthened army at Pleasant Hill for two days, waiting for more Texas horsemen to arrive. On April 4 and 5, he sent the infantry and artillery, now hidden behind a cavalry screen, twenty-two miles north to another small village, Mansfield. The Greyhounds had marched 270 miles in the three weeks since leaving Fort DeRussy and Simmesport.[40]

With more cavalry arriving from Texas and about forty-five hundred additional Arkansas and Missouri infantry approaching from Shreveport, Taylor ended the long retreat. He was ready now to make his stand. He would not retire all the way to Shreveport, and he certainly would not withdraw into Texas, two suggestions offered by his superior, General Smith. In Taylor's view, Mansfield presented the best conditions for a fight. General Banks's Federals would have to approach the village via the only road available, a narrow lane through thick pine forests, forcing him to string his army out over many miles and making the head of his column vulnerable to a sudden coup. North of Mansfield, three roads led to Shreveport, and one of those skirted the Red River, where the heavy guns of Porter's gunboats could provide impenetrable cover for Banks's infantry. No, if Taylor was going to throw back his old adversary, it would have to be on the south side of Mansfield.[41]

CHAPTER **11**

# *Mansfield and Pleasant Hill*

The regiments of the Texas Division marched north out of Pleasant Hill on Monday and Tuesday, April 4 and 5. After about twelve hours and twenty-five dusty miles, they reached Mansfield, another small farm community forty miles due south of Shreveport. The Greyhounds camped "in a swampy bottom" a few miles north of town and waited for General Taylor to make his arrangements. While Taylor planned and the foot soldiers milled around their camps, General Green's cavalrymen were busy darting back and forth in the pine forests and farm fields around Pleasant Hill, delaying the lead units of the slowly approaching Federal army. One Confederate cavalry officer, Xavier B. Debray, a former student at the French military academy of St. Cyr, boasted that "the enemy could not advance one mile without being resisted stubbornly enough to hold him three days on the march . . . between Pleasant Hill and Mansfield."[1]

In their camps north of Mansfield, the Greyhounds could hear skirmishing and occasional artillery fire in the distance, and the reality of what was about to happen began to settle over them. They had marched many hundreds of miles by now, slept in ice and snow, gasped for air in oven-like temperatures, waded through steamy swamps, slogged through mud up to their knees, choked on trail dust, gone hungry, and even fought a few times. But never had they faced an enemy this strong before. General Banks had nearly twenty thousand of his thirty thousand Federals coming up the road toward them, and they numbered fewer than nine thousand, even with Green's cavalry and Mouton's infantry division. The Arkansas and Missouri infantry that had come down from Arkansas, about forty-four hundred strong, would not be available for the coming fight. Gen. E. Kirby Smith had halted them between Shreveport and Mansfield.[2]

Surgeon William Head of the 16th Cavalry believed his fellow Confederates would handle themselves well despite the disparity in numbers. "I think they will fight like veteran soldiers," he wrote his wife. In another camp not far away, Fred Smith of the 19th Texas scribbled a letter to his father in Marshall, admitting that some of the men were nervous: "As for getting scared as some do at every report from the front and report of a few guns, which are firing very often during the day (the guards firing off their guns) I never get scared till I *see* the Feds with my own eyes and then very little as I have seen them before, and it's plenty of time then." Smith claimed to be much cooler than his comrades: "Some of our troops are continually worrying themselves into a fever about this [thing] and that, whether the Feds are going to fight soon, why we don't do so and so. For my part I let Gen'ls Scurry, Walker, Taylor and Smith do my thinking for me." In fact, he informed his father, he would welcome a scrap. "I almost wish the Feds would come up now so that we could give them a genteel whipping before they leave." That very night, the Greyhounds received orders to cook one day's rations and be prepared to move before dawn. Smith would get his wish for a fight.[3]

The civilians of Mansfield, like most caught in the path of hostile armies, were very anxious, and they regarded General Taylor's Confederates as their saviors. When the Greyhounds marched out of their camps and then south through the town early on the morning of Friday, April 8, the townspeople could not restrain themselves. The thousands of men funneling through narrow village streets, the sounds of "Dixie" from the division's bands, the regimental flags—the whole experience excited and reassured. Thomas R. Bonner found the civilian gratitude touching: "As we passed through the streets of the beautiful town, they were thronged with fair ladies—misses and matrons—who threw their bright garlands at our feet, and bade us, in God's name, drive back the Yankees, and save their cherished homes." Peter Gravis of the 17th Infantry, an itinerant Methodist preacher before the war, remembered the people of Mansfield long afterward. "The doors and windows of the houses in town were thronged. Women and children waved us on with their white handkerchiefs, as they dropped tears of gratitude for those who marched to meet the enemy." Gravis, like many other Texans, was no doubt happy to help the local people, but mainly he was determined to keep the Yankees out of Texas: "Our wives and children were there, and as Texas had never seen the blazing torch, the burning towns and homes plundered by cruel hands, we felt that we would rather die than retreat another step."[4]

South through the town and four miles farther, on the road back toward Pleasant Hill, their colonels led the Greyhound regiments to the site General Taylor had chosen to make his stand. One of the few large clearings in the dense pine wilderness, the field was about a half-mile across (north to south) and roughly three-quarters of a mile from end to end (east to west). The road from Pleasant Hill to Mansfield ran through the opening from southeast to northwest and over a rise (Honeycutt Hill) near the center of the field. A meandering east-west ravine and a few ground swells scattered here and there were the only protections from fire in the open space. When the Greyhounds reached the vicinity late in the morning, Corporal Blessington noted that Mouton's division had already formed in line of battle in the trees along the edge of the field to the left (east) of the road. The Texas Division's officers waved their regiments off to the right of the road, first Scurry's brigade, then Waul's, then Randal's. Before he was fully satisfied with the arrangements, General Taylor made a few adjustments in his line and moved Randal's brigade from the right side of the road across to the left, where it linked to the end of General Polignac's Texas brigade (see Map 8).[5]

By the time all was ready around midday, the Confederate line extended in an arc nearly three miles from end to end. On the far right, covering the flank of Walker's infantry, were two Texas cavalry regiments, one commanded by a native of Germany (Augustus Buchel) and the other by a native of France (Xavier Debray), both of whom had been educated in European military schools. Then, the Texas foot soldiers of Scurry's and Waul's brigades stretched from south to north, ending at the road to Mansfield, where the gray line bent from north-south to east-west. Unlimbered near the road were several batteries, including one that had been attached to Walker's division for most of its existence, James M. Daniel's six-gun Lamar Artillery from Paris and Lamar County, Texas. Randal's brigade lined up from the road eastward to Polignac's Texans. Gray's Louisiana infantry brigade extended from Polignac's line farther to the east, where the remainder of Green's cavalry anchored the far left of the Confederate line.[6]

Walker's Texans could hear the cavalry skirmishing to the southeast, but, like soldiers through the ages, they had hurried forward only to be ordered to wait. Standing in place for two or three hours—even on a bright, cloudless spring day—was bad enough, but soon their minds began to dwell on what might happen to them. Would they ever kiss their wives or play with their children or see their aging parents again? Would they ever return to their homes and ride their favorite horses or hunt with their favorite dogs again? Would they be torn and broken in body before nightfall? Not far south of the road, Thomas R. Bonner of the 18th Infantry found the long pause distressing: "Unsustained by the reckless excitement and wild furor of the actual strife, the strongest mind must then shudder at the fearful thought that a few short moments more may usher the soul into eternity!" The nervous dread must have been even worse in those Greyhound units that had not yet fought in a large, sustained engagement. Five regiments and one battalion—nearly half of the entire division—had not once, three years into the war, seen more than short skirmishes. They would gain all the battlefield experience they needed in the next three hours.[7]

Just as Taylor had foreseen, Banks's army approached the waiting Confederates in a long, thin column, hemmed in on the narrow road by the thick forests on either side. As they reached the opening in the woods in the early afternoon,

# Map 8
# The Battle of Mansfield, April 8, 1864

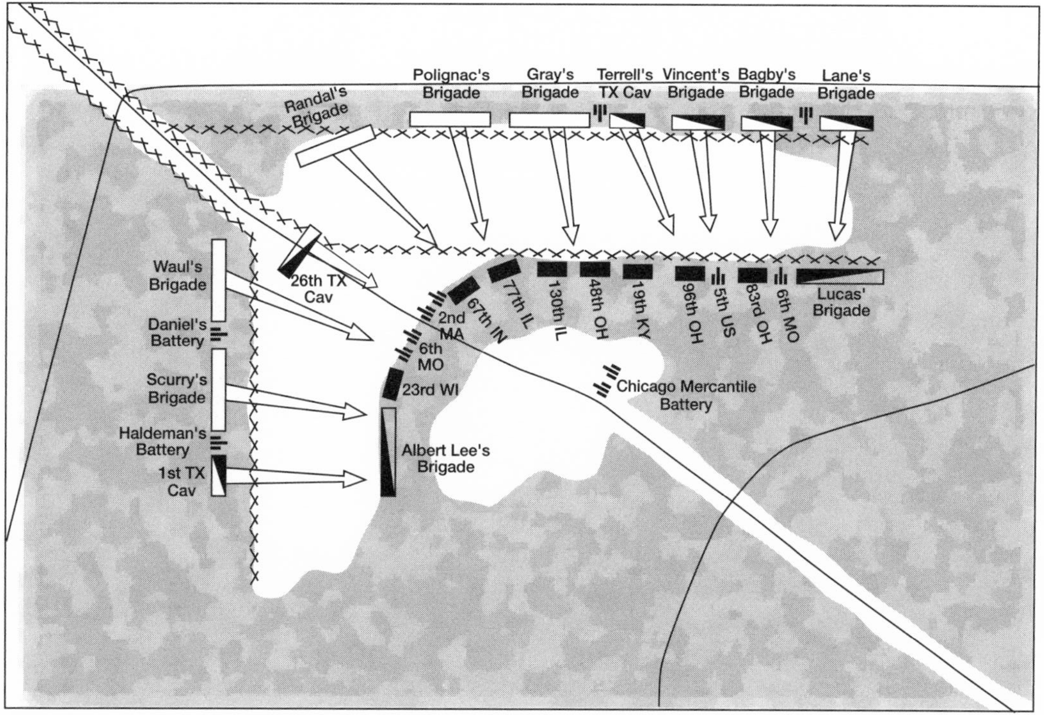

Federal cavalry and infantry officers, alerted to the presence of large numbers of rebels across the field, waved their units off the road to the left and right, creating their own long arc of regiments to face Taylor's. Directly across the open field from Walker's Texas brigades, on the Federal left, several cavalry regiments lined up on the crest of Honeycutt Hill. Their commander, Brig. Gen. Albert L. Lee, was the same officer whose horsemen had been routed by Walker's Greyhounds at Bayou Bourbeau five months earlier. Directly to the right of the cavalry were two infantry regiments that also had crossed swords with the Greyhounds at Bayou Bourbeau. The 23rd Wisconsin, the regiment whose men had been voting and receiving pay when the battle near the bayou opened, lined up just to the left of the road to Pleasant Hill. The 67th Indiana, the regiment that had formed the hollow square on the prairie and lost more than two hundred men, formed just across the road from the 23rd Wisconsin. Unlimbered on the road between these two regiments was yet another unit that had fought Walker's Texans at Bourbeau, Ormand Nims's 2nd Massachusetts Light Artillery Battery. Six more infantry regiments, five more cavalry regiments, and five more artillery batteries eventually extended the Federal line to the right, facing Mouton's infantry and Green's cavalry. Additional cavalry units and some foot regiments of the 13th Corps continued to arrive out of the woods to the rear. Altogether, Banks's army on the field before the battle numbered about five thousand.[8]

After the blue regiments lined up to face the Confederates, nothing much happened. General Taylor had expected the Yankees to push ahead in an assault on his lines to begin the battle, and General Banks had planned to do exactly that. But Lee, understanding that the enemy infantry would overmatch his Federal cavalry, was hesitant to move farther. He informed Banks that his horsemen would "be most gloriously flogged" if they followed the order to advance across the open field. Banks finally understood Lee's reluctance and ordered up more infantry from the rear. Unfortunately for Lee and Banks, the additional infantry brigades were miles to the rear, behind the cavalry wagon train, and would require three or four hours to arrive on the field. The cavalry train, bulging with luxuries and confiscated items, was undoubtedly longer than necessary. A Federal staff officer was appalled at the excess: "Crossing a ford one day, [Maj. Gen. William B.] Franklin spied a country cart drawn by a mule, containing bedding, trunks, and a negro woman. He sent the corps inspector to see to whom it belonged. It turned out to be the property of a sergeant of a cavalry regiment." A supply line with that many "extras" was a formidable obstacle on the narrow forest road.[9]

General Taylor's patience finally wore out at 4 P.M. If Banks would not attack, then he would. Taylor rode over to the left side of his line and gave General

Mouton the order to advance. The Louisiana troops were especially eager to begin the fight. They were "inflamed by many outrages on their homes, as well as by camp rumors that it was intended to abandon their State without a fight," Taylor wrote in his memoirs. When General Mouton and his two brigade commanders (Gray and Polignac) ordered the charge and moved out of the woods into the field, the response was immediate. "The ardor of Mouton's troops, especially the Louisianians, could not be restrained by their officers," Taylor observed. Gray's Louisiana regiments and Polignac's Texans, supported by Randal's Texans of the Greyhound Division on the right, swept across the farm field "under a murderous fire of artillery and musketry," as Taylor described it. This charge proved to be the last few minutes of life for many officers in Mouton's division. General Mouton himself was killed by rifle fire, and the colonels of all three regiments in his old brigade died near him. Before the day was over, Mouton's division lost one-third of its entire number in killed and wounded.[10]

When Mouton fell and the advance faltered, General Polignac stepped up to take command of the division and urged the Confederates on farther, across the field and into a belt of woods on the opposite side, all under heavy fire. General Taylor, studying the battle from the tree line on the north side of the field, was especially pleased with the performance of Horace Randal's brigade of Walker's division. Anchoring the right end of Mouton's initial attack, Randal's Greyhounds advanced en echelon across the smoky field. "In vigor, energy, and daring Randal surpassed my expectations, high as they were of him and his fine brigade," Taylor wrote in his official report. Mouton's (now Polignac's) division, Gen. Tom Green's supporting cavalry on the left, fighting dismounted, and Randal's Texans on the right pushed across the smoky field, finally cracked the Federal line, and began telescoping it from the end toward the middle.[11]

At this point, Taylor ordered General Walker to unleash the remainder of his division on the right of the road, aiming to roll up the Federal left. Walker's execution of the order was perfect, as far as Taylor was concerned: "the gallantry and vigor with which that accomplished soldier (Walker) led his fine brigades into action and pressed on the foe has never been surpassed . . . every hour . . . illustrated his capacity for command." Covered on their right by two regiments of gray cavalry, the Texans of Scurry's and Waul's brigades emerged from the tree line with a roar. The Greyhounds loped swiftly across the open space, encountering little resistance at first. A correspondent of the *Chicago Tribune*, preoccupied with the deteriorating line on the Federal right, now saw swarms of Confederates closing in from a new direction: "evidences of a much stronger and infinitely more dangerous attack were observed on our left, where the enemy in great force was charging rapidly over the field to the left of the road."[12]

The New Englanders of Nims's Massachusetts battery poured anti-personnel canister shot into the approaching Texans, charging in crowded columns of companies rather than long thin lines. A New Hampshire cavalry officer assigned to guard the battery wrote that the rebels were "yelling like crazed demons. Our guns were filled to the muzzles with grape, canister and bags of bullets, making wide gaps in the rebel ranks at every discharge." One of the gunners watched the collision of artillery and infantry: "Our guns belched forth double-shotted canister and the enemy in front, eight deep in line, suffered terribly at each discharge. Wide gaps were opened in their ranks but were immediately filled up again." Those Greyhound regiments running forward along the road were hit first. Col. Wilburn King of the 18th Texas led his men directly on the right of the 12th Texas: "The whole of Walker's Division was advancing in columns of Companies, and the second shell fired by the Yankee battery at our columns killed or mortally wounded Col. R. [James W. Raine of the 12th Texas] and eleven men behind him." Still, their officers shouted above the noise, "Close up! close up!" and the Texans filled the gaps and raced ahead.[13]

The Greyhounds' momentum could not be slowed. When they reached Honeycutt Hill, they saw the shaky Federal line through the tree line and piled into it. Some of the Texans were still armed with old smoothbores, but whether smoothbores or rifles, their weapons were within range now. Federals of all ranks began falling in numbers. A staff officer on the field immediately understood that General Walker had "completely turned our left flank, rolling our line back as he advanced." The 23rd Wisconsin, in line directly to the left of Nims's battery, suffered along with the gunners when the Texans they had first met at Bayou Bourbeau drew near. The regiment's commander, Maj. Joseph Greene, saw through the musket and cannon smoke the fractured Federal line to his right and yelling Confederates rushing forward on his right and left, "pouring hot fire" into his skirmishers: "outflanked on both sides, and in imminent danger of capture, we were compelled to retire. . . . As we retired a destructive cross-fire swept through our lines." These first few minutes were the bloodiest for the Wisconsin men, Greene reported. "Nearly all of the casualties (64 killed, wounded, and missing) were sustained by the regiment while endeavoring to hold its first position." The story was the same to the left of the Wisconsin men; the 3rd Massachusetts Cavalry lost 67 men and 121 horses in the first thirty minutes of the fight.[14]

The gray and brown wave of whooping, onrushing Texans broke up the Federal infantry and cavalry units on Honeycutt Hill and scattered them to the rear, across a second clearing behind the hill. A soldier in the 77th Illinois Infantry, stationed to the right of Nims's battery, found the whole business of running before the enemy somewhat inconvenient: "The other boys were somewhat amused at myself as we [were] retreating across that open field as I had on a pair of boots that had become badly run over at the heal and were not the best thing for fast running which we were practicing just at that time so I sat down in the middle of the field and pulled those crooked boots off and made the balance of the race barefoot."[15]

With the infantry and cavalry peeling away from them, the gunners of Nims's battery caught the brunt of the Confederate charge. Before he made his barefoot run to the rear, the Illinois soldier noticed that "the rebels consentrated their fource on Nims Battery" until the New Englanders "were driven from their guns at the point of the beyonette." Another onlooker saw that "the cannoneers lay thick about the guns. Dead and wounded Confederates lay in win-rows in front of them." Musket balls and minie balls cut down the battery's horses as well as its soldiers.[16] One member of the battery wrote that "by overwhelming numbers they succeeded in turning our left flank[.] our horses disabled we were forced to abandon our position. Leaving 3 (three) of our guns on the hill. We found ourselves utterly whipped." This soldier barely escaped by jumping onto the back of a wounded battery horse and scrambling across the field to the rear of the hill. "I succeeded in getting away with old *Bill* who had born[e] me faithfully for most three years and he was badly hurt, his jaw was shot away by a musket-Ball." The adrenaline-charged Texans swarmed over the dead men and horses and abandoned guns and then turned the cannons against the retreating Federals.[17]

The scramble to the rear across the second field was not totally disorganized. Some of the mounted regiments on the left end of the Federal line tried four times to construct a line behind Honeycutt Hill, but each time they were broken up by the enveloping Confederate advance and the artillery fire from their own recently captured cannons. John F. Wild, a Massachusetts horseman, was wounded by one of the shells. "As he reined his horse out to the rear, we could see the blood streaming to the ground from his right leg, which hung dangling by only the skin on the inside," one of his comrades noted. Similarly, a colonel on Gen. Albert Lee's staff "had his horse's head blown off, while riding across the field." Still their officers shouted orders and waved the clumps of retreating soldiers into the semblance of a line at the edge of the farm field.[18]

When the Greyhounds of the 13th Texas Cavalry worked their way through the woods atop the hill, John T. Stark looked across the second field, where the enemy was trying to rally: "the noise of the firing warned us that warm work awaited us as we came to the open ground," he wrote in his diary. "Just as we turned the crest of the hill Gen. Walker rode up in front of our line and said 'Aim low boys, and trust in God.' With a wild yell we dashed down the slope[.] here one poor wounded Texan raised on his elbow and waving his hat over his head said, 'Crowd them, boys, crowd them.' " The Federals withdrawing to the other side of the field were in no condition to resist "crowding" at that point. Many were separated from their units, the great din and clash of battle covered the shouts of frantic officers, and the thick pall of gun smoke hanging everywhere seemed to conceal dangers on all sides. Making it all worse were the cheers and shrieks of the oncoming Confederates. "Such yelling—like fiends," one Ohio soldier complained. A staff officer from Massachusetts grumbled long afterward about "that 'rebel yell' . . . [that] rang in our ears for so many days and disturbed our slumbers for so many nights."[19]

Brig. Gen. T. E. G. Ransom, immediate commander of the Federal infantry on the field, learning of the developing disaster on his left, ordered the 83rd Ohio Infantry on the right end of his line to hurry to the left. The same regiment had arrived on the battlefield at Bayou Bourbeau five months earlier only to find their comrades in a wild retreat. The Ohioans were in the middle of their own debacle near Mansfield, but they dutifully proceeded to the far left. Once again, they found Federal regiments in disarray. "Coming to the assistance of our forces on the left," one of them wrote, we saw that "their line was broken and all confusion." In fact, the far end had melted away. All the Ohio regiment could do now was try to protect the remnants of the Federal artillery near the road. General Ransom was growing more desperate now, an Ohioan remembered: "I shall never forget the look of anxious entreaty in the face of gallant General Ransom, our corps commander, as he waved his sword saying—'For God's sake boys let us try and rally here.' "[20]

With their units now mixed and disorganized at the edge of the second field, General Banks and his officers tried to build another line near the Chicago Mercantile Battery, which had escaped the disaster on Honeycutt Hill by being posted somewhat to the rear. Their efforts were partially successful, especially when a new division of the Federal 13th Corps arrived from the rear and deployed in line at the edge of the clearing. Clumps of horsemen recently chased off Honeycutt Hill rallied on the left of the new line, and on the opposite end some retreating foot soldiers were drawn like iron filings to the magnet of a new, organized position. The new stand stalled the pursuit for nearly an hour, but eventually the Confederates lapped around both ends of the new line, and the breakup resumed. Maj. Gen. William B. Franklin, the luckless commander whose rear guard had been mauled by Tom Green at Bayou Bourbeau, rode into a Greyhound volley that killed the general's horse and wounded him and two of his staff officers. The gunners of Nims's artillery, left now with only three of their six guns at the edge of the woods, tried to stand, "but the rout had become so general that the battery could not maintain its position and was almost surrounded by the enemy." When the New Englanders tried to retreat once more shortly afterward, they found their only escape route, the narrow road through the woods, clogged with wagons and panicked soldiers. Within a few more minutes, the roaring gray cloud rolled over the scene, and Captain Nims lost his entire battery—the remaining three guns, the caissons, the baggage wagons, and forges. As one of his men later put it, "We had lost our guns and everything we possessed except the clothes we had on."[21]

The Chicago Mercantile Battery struggled to hold back the hurricane sweeping across the second farm field, but the Illinois gunners too were swept up in the storm. With Confederates pouring in from left and right and their own battery horses collapsing in the hailstorm of rifle fire, the Mercantile Battery went the way of Nims's unit, washed away almost completely with the loss of all six guns. An Illinois foot soldier nearby watched the breakdown: "The lieutenant in command of the battery seeing his horses shot down and seeing that he could not save his guns refused to leave his battery and jumping onto one of his guns with a revolver in each hand fought until the rebels came up and killed him."[22]

Remarkable acts of individual courage could not stem the tide. One trooper in a Massachusetts cavalry regiment saw the beginning of the end: "Finally the whole line of battle gave way. It could not stand before such a fiery storm." A soldier in the 83rd Ohio used almost the same words: "Nothing could stand it." General Ransom realized now that he would have to abandon the field to the Confederates. Within minutes, though, his adjutant was shot off his horse before he could deliver the instructions to all units. Thus, some Federal regiments, preoccupied with the onrushing Confederates and doubtless distracted by the noise and smoke and confusion of battle, did not receive the order and stayed in place. Two of those regiments (the 48th Ohio and 130th Illinois) disappeared almost completely beneath a wave of yelling, jubilant Confederates. At about the same moment, General Ransom himself was hit in the knee and had to be carried off the field with a wound that would contribute to his death six months later. To his great distress, he found the "road filled with mounted men, flying in confusion from the field."[23]

Worse nightmares awaited in the woods behind the Federals. As they tried to funnel into the road leading back toward Pleasant Hill, fractured units broke into even smaller segments when they found the way blocked by the cavalry's wagon train. Hundreds of wagons, stretching several miles back along the narrow lane through the pines, jammed the only path to safety. Startled teamsters, panicked by the sight of frightened men running past them, cut their horses and mules from their traces, hopped on, and raced to the rear. Late reinforcements arriving from the rear, disgusted at the sight of the fleeing drivers, "pelted them with

stones, and whipped their flying animals with sticks to increase their speed."
Some drivers tried to turn their wagons and ambulances around only to create
worse roadblocks. A Maine sergeant, a veteran of the rout at the First Battle of
Manassas (Bull Run), declared that the panic at Mansfield was worse.[24]

Within minutes, what had been a severe embarrassment became a disaster. A
surgeon in the 96th Ohio Infantry witnessed the change: "In a moment the whole
train is in motion—wagons turning around; wagons turning over; wagons
slashed against trees; tongues broken; traces cut; and teamsters and mules, with
and without wagons; artillery and caissons, and artillery horses and artillery men
without artillery or caissons, mingle with horse and foot in the wild, seething
struggle through that dark forest, enshrouded in sulphur-smoke, with the shouts
of the enemy close in the rear." A member of the Chicago Mercantile Battery
and his comrades at first tried to go around the bottleneck: "Out of the track on
either side went the artillery and all else, till the woods were a moving sea of
wagons, guns, caissons, cavalry, riderless horses, ambulances with their freight of
moaning, dying humanity, bouncing over logs, ruts and underbrush." The Illinois gunners lost every remaining piece in their battery in the attempt to flee. An
officer in a Maine unit coming up from the rear could not believe his eyes: "One
little fellow who had thrown away everything belonging to Uncle Sam, and his
hat besides, was screaming and dancing up and down, imploring us 'Don't go
there!' 'It's awful!' 'You can't live a minute!' 'It's worse than Champion Hills.'
He was but one; the most of them were speechless, but were flying for dear life,
crouching to avoid the bullets. . . . Besides the infantry, there were cavalry horses
and mules with traces dangling, and artillery horses without their guns, all going
the wrong way for Texas."[25]

An Ohio chaplain caring for the wounded in a house behind the lines was
distressed to see the lines coming his way: "It was a terrible sight to see [our
men] flying before their pursuers of both cavalry and infantry, that kept up a
constant running fire. They [the Confederates] looked more like demons than
humans." One of the flying Federals, a foot soldier from Illinois, was at least as
distressed as the chaplain: "Oh! may I never see the like again. Horses, men, wagons, all going to the rear—all saying: 'Lost! lost!'" And there was nothing their
officers—those who were not fleeing themselves—could do to stop them. One
witness complained that "the effort to arrest or drive back the panic-stricken
crowd was like flinging straws back at a hurricane. Appeals, commands, threats,
curses or prayers, were alike of no avail." A Massachusetts staff officer tried:
"After riding back a little way I thought I would try to rally some of the fugitives.
As soon as I turned round my knees were knocked black and blue by the men

running against them, and by the knees of mounted fugitives, and I could do nothing."[26]

Pursuing Confederates were charged up by adrenaline and victory, and the scenes among the pine trees burned into their memories. One Texan, trying to describe the picture to his wife a few days later, asked her to imagine "thousands of men all running in thick wooded country and skared out of thar wits, one waggen run up on another with one horse or mule dead in it and one with the wheel broken with the great number of ambulances, dead men, horses and mules and wagons and all mixed and then you have just a faint idea of the sceans of the battle field." James C. Carroll of Randal's brigade exclaimed, "oh my how we scattered the blues and captured flags, killed men and now and then the Texas yell of victory rang out." A cavalryman was exhilarated: "In this pursuit no tongue, or pen can express the excitement—the joy of our men and officers. The undergrowth is all run over, without any knowledge of its being an obstacle. . . . This is hue and cry, *ne plus ultra*." A member of Debray's regiment, which charged alongside Scurry's Greyhounds, explained to his parents: "About dark we got them fairly on the run and the fun commenced. Our regiment and Buchel's being in the front just had their pick. We would run up on twenty or thirty wagons shoot or capture the drivers and then go it again, finally getting them so hard run that they abandoned the whole train and made tracks for the main army."[27]

As often happens when things go wrong, the victims blamed each other for the disaster. A New Hampshire cavalryman, cursing a foot soldier who had stolen his horse to flee to the rear, turned the air blue with explicit doubts about the value of the infantry. Nor was the forlorn New Englander much impressed by flying logistics personnel: "in some instances the drivers [were] going out of the rear of those wagons which had not been turned round, as the rebels came in at the front." But the cavalrymen came in for their own share of censure as well. One of General Franklin's staff officers considered them too soft for hard service: "After the rebels had captured their Champagne, sardines, and potted anchovies, at Sabine Cross Roads [Mansfield], they became excellent cavalry."[28]

The wild pursuit might have lasted until dark except for the arrival, about two miles behind the second farm field, of Brig. Gen. William H. Emory's division, called up from the rear by Generals Franklin and Banks hours earlier. These eastern troops, accompanied by the music of their bands, had to elbow their way through the panicky mob tumbling in the opposite direction. Emory deployed his brigades in a strong position, straddling the road to Pleasant Hill and facing a ravine and creek that the rebels would have to cross under fire. By the time the Confederates reached the ravine, their lines had become disorganized and intermingled from the chase through the woods, and men found themselves fighting beside soldiers from other units and taking orders from officers they did not recognize. The soldiers of Brig. Gen. William Dwight's Federal brigade, kneeling with loaded weapons in a peach orchard, were ready when the swarms of unwary gray and brown pursuers ran down the embankment in front of them. A New Englander remembered that Dwight's men "withheld their fire till the enemy had crossed the creek and were rising the slope, then they fired as fine a volley as was ever fired upon the drill-ground. The crash was terrific; the enemy's front line became a windrow of dead and wounded." General Emory himself, a veteran of Port Hudson and other campaigns, reported that "a more terrific wail of musketry I never heard before from one Division."[29]

Thomas R. Bonner, an officer of the 18th Texas, was in the pursuing crowd and was staggered by the fire from Emory's unexpected line: "Then came the terrible shock. Volley after volley resounded from the hill, and shower after shower of bullets came whizzing down upon us. It was utterly impossible to advance, and to retreat beneath the range of their long guns seemed equally desperate. . . . We lay down, arose again, and then involuntarily sought such shelter and protection as the ground afforded." Lt. Col. Robert S. Gould of Randal's brigade noted that "the sides of the ravine were lined with men lying down and bullets were flying around thickly, but it seemed to me that most of my men had passed on, and I followed. On emerging from the ravine, there was open ground—an old orchard, I think—and from the top of the hill the enemy were sweeping it with a tremendous fire. I hurried across and found the greater part of my command just beyond, joining others who under Colonel Clark [former governor Edward Clark] were about to charge the top of the hill. Several advances were made in that direction, but were always met with a fire so heavy as to check each effort."[30]

By then, the failing light of day and the gun smoke swirling among the pines made the virgin forest a dim and unearthly place. The surgeon of the 96th Ohio found the dusky woods almost ghostly: "The darkness every where is flecked with spectral rifle-flashes," he wrote. Still, the menacing Confederates were visible across the ravine: "their faces glimmer in the light of their musket-blaze." And from the rear came the unlikely sounds of music: "The full brass band of the Nineteenth Corps stands close by the road and pour into the darkness and the ears of the advancing rebels the exhilarating notes of 'Hail Columbia'." The Greyhounds paid much more attention to the Yankees' shoulder arms than to their cornets. A captain in the 13th Texas, running up the incline, saw "one sheet of flame from end to end of their line." On the last charge up the hill, one Texan remembered, "their rifles belched forth a bright red sheet of flame along their whole line, lighting up the expiring day with an unearthly glare." The final assault managed only to keep the Federals away from the water of the creek, a scarce and valuable resource in the pine forest.[31]

The day ended with scattered firing that gradually died away, leaving only the groans of the wounded rising into the night air. A surgeon in Emory's division could not forget those sounds: "All over the field came up the wailing cries and shrieks of the wounded and dying men, with no one to give them a drop of water or a word of comfort," he remembered. "The bewailings of the men of Louisiana, [and] Texas . . . , imploring for help, mingled and ascended with the piteous supplications of the sons of New England, New York and the West. From each and from all indiscriminately was heard the mournful and repeated cry: 'Come and get me!' 'Come and help me!' 'Oh, my dear mother, come and relieve me!' 'I am faint!' 'I am thirsty!' 'I am cold!' 'I am dying!' " Somewhere in the darkness, a corporal from Maine listened sadly to the same mournful sounds: "The cries of the wounded was dredful to hear[.] their cry was water water but they could not be helped as they were between the 2 lines."[32]

Embarrassment added to the Federals' misery, especially in the 77th Illinois, which had lost nearly two hundred men since mid-afternoon (143 of them captured), mostly at the hands of Randal's and Waul's Greyhound brigades. "No one will ever know the depth of shame our hearts experienced over this defeat," one wrote after the battle. Another survivor in the same unit contrasted the day with brighter times during the Vicksburg campaign: "We were always victorious until we came here." William Wiley, the soldier who had taken the time to sit down and tear off his boots to speed his escape, wrote that his comrades were "feeling pretty blue as it was the first time we had to retreat before the enemy." An Ohio soldier said he "never felt so exhausted or so mortified at our defeat." An officer on General Franklin's staff fairly seethed after the fighting ended: "we could hear distinctly the yells of the rebels as they found a fresh 'cache' of the good things of the cavalry. It was very aggravating. They got our head-quarters ambulance too, but there was precious little in it," he fumed. "All they got of mine was a tooth-brush. I comforted myself with the reflection that they would not know what use to put it to."[33]

If some Federal staff officers were contemptuous of their scruffy opponents, the grimy Greyhounds returned the favor, especially when they beheld the exotic and colorful uniforms of some Federal Zouave regiments. A captain in Randal's brigade laughed to his sister, "It is the most ludicrous costume, for a civilized man to wear, one could imagine." Confederates in the 18th Texas were equally scornful: "their red, uncouth, unmanly looking uniform excited much laughter among our men, and many jokes were created at the expense of these 'Joabs,' as they were called." Some of the Greyhounds swore theatrically in the presence of passing Zouave prisoners that Texans would have to stop fighting now; they "had too much honor to fight women." Some assured the Zouaves that they would be released when they reached Mansfield because the Confederacy had "scarcely provisions to feed their own troops, without providing for women prisoners." Even fellow Yankees, especially westerners, sometimes snickered at the expense of the Zouaves. A soldier in the 77th Illinois repeated a story later told around Federal campfires when the subject of Mansfield came up: "It is said that when the zouaves came to the front and then fell back, a rebel was in pursuit of a retreating zouave, and another rebel drew his gun to shoot when the first rebel said, 'Don't shoot, I want to catch the thing alive.' "[34]

For the weary Federals, the long day ended on another sour note when they were ordered to move out of their positions near the ravine late that night. General Banks was worried that fresh troops from the rear might not arrive in time to withstand another assault at daylight, and his army had no source of water now that the Confederates had occupied the ravine and creek. By midnight the blue column was backtracking toward Pleasant Hill, nearly twenty miles away. "That night we had to march eighteen miles, long weary miles they were, the intense excitement of the day making it doubly so," one Ohio soldier grumbled. "What would I not give for a rest of two hours." The surgeon of a New York regiment also noted the weariness of the men on this dark journey: "Tramp, tramp, all night long beneath the gloomy pines, on the road again to Pleasant Hill. The men were so worn with fatigue that they showed no disposition to talk, but urged forward their stiffened limbs in perfect silence. Many in the darkness fell out by the way, and were taken prisoners." A lengthy night march after such a dreadful day sealed April 8, 1864, as the worst day of the war for the Federal army west of the Mississippi.[35]

Of Taylor's eighty-eight hundred Confederates on the field at Mansfield, roughly one thousand were killed or wounded. Few, if any, were captured. Exact numbers are impossible to pin down because systematic Confederate casualty reports were lost. About twelve thousand Federals participated in the battle, either in the initial defense, behind Honeycutt Hill at the second line, or at the ravine two miles farther back. General Banks lost more than twenty-two hundred soldiers, twenty artillery pieces, at least two hundred wagons full of arms and other stores, and nearly one thousand horses and mules. Neither Taylor nor Banks had formal military training, but Taylor fought brilliantly while Banks fumbled away his advantages in numbers and resources. General Walker's Greyhounds performed at a very high level, cracking open the left side of the Federal line on Honeycutt Hill and following through rapidly and forcefully until the second line also broke and fled into the woods. Along with pursuing soldiers from Louisiana units, the Greyhounds pressed through the forest and turned the Federal retreat into a rout. At the end of the day, Walker's Texans poured across the bloody ravine, flung themselves repeatedly against Emory's strong defensive line, and took control of the only water in the area. If losses in Scurry's and Waul's brigades were comparable to those in Randal's (9 killed, 52 wounded, and 6 missing), then the Texas Division lost roughly 180 killed and wounded and about 20 missing. Though nearly half of the Greyhounds had never been in a sustained fight—and none of them in an engagement this large—their performance at Mansfield played a large part in turning back this last Federal campaign aimed at Texas.[36]

The exhausted and battered Greyhounds did not have to march all night, but they did have to mill around the dark woods and fields to find their units, answer roll call, account for missing comrades, gather up the wounded, and collect the spoils of the battlefield. Early the next morning they were put on the trail of General Banks's army. General Taylor was determined to chase Banks all the way down the Red River, apparently. The scenes along the road from Mansfield to Pleasant Hill that next morning were gruesome. A gunner in Daniel's battery described the awful sights to his wife: "for ten miles the dead Yankees were lying on the side of the road; a great many of them were stripped of their coats, pants, and boots, while others had their pockets turned wrong side out. I do not blame our men so much for so doing as they needed clothing so badly." An officer in the 18th Texas saw "dead horses, burning wagons, and broken ambulances . . . at almost every turn of the road. In one ambulance we saw an unclosed coffin, containing a dead body." One Texan described a corpse "in Yankee Uniform, over whom a hundred waggons have rolled. He is mangled until he has scarcely any resemblance of the human shape." The inhumanity and cruelty of war were on full display along the little country road to Pleasant Hill.[37]

At one rest stop on the march, some of the Greyhounds happened to halt near a home where a young girl watched with keen interest. Her description of those few minutes with the Texans reveals how near physical and emotional breakdown Walker's men were after the previous day's battle:

> They halted in front of our house, then stacked arms in the road and were told to "fall out" for a fifteen minute rest. Some had blood-stained bandages on their heads—some had an arm suspended in a bloody bandage or wore bandages on their necks or shoulders. Many of them fell prostrate on the ground, too exhausted to move. Others staggered toward the house to beg for a bite to eat. The yard and house were soon full of the tired and

haggard men—some with the most haunted look in their eyes I have ever seen. She (my mother) gave them all the leftovers from dinner (in fact we had been too excited to eat any dinner at all) but still they kept begging, "Mom, save some for me. I haven't had a bite since Thursday evening. Please, just one bite." Next Ma went out to the backyard followed by dozens of ragged, bearded men. Our big old washpot (probably a hundred years old) was full of freshly cooked lye hominy, warm and ready to eat. So she began issuing it out with a large wooden cooking spoonful to each man. Some of them took it in the crown of their dirty hats, some in their bare, dirty hands, some in cups or on pieces of boards they had picked up. All of them ate it right there like a pack of hungry wolves. . . . Soon the smokehouse as well as the washpot was empty. But the men seemed reluctant to leave, crowding around Ma to thank her again and again and to invoke the blessings of Heaven upon her. Some handed her a dollar bill, some two dollars or even five (Confederate money) and others hugged her as they left the yard. A blast of the bugle soon brought the men back to the road where they secured their rifles and quickly lined up. . . . Soon they disappeared in a cloud of dust in the direction of Pleasant Hill.[38]

General Taylor would have preferred to hold the drained Greyhound Division in reserve that Saturday. But even with forty-four hundred fresh infantrymen from Arkansas and Missouri taking the lead toward Pleasant Hill, Taylor would have only about twelve thousand men to confront Banks, now reinforced by A. J. Smith's ten thousand westerners, who had missed the debacle at Mansfield. Consequently, Taylor would ask General Walker and his Texans to cross open ground under fire and break another line of Federal veterans for the second consecutive day. Considering the losses and fatigue resulting from Friday's combat, this would be a most difficult assignment. A soldier in the 16th Cavalry recalled later that his company, normally about forty to fifty strong at that point in the war, "had only fourteen men able to go into the Pleasant Hill fight." For a division that had fought only small engagements up to now (never more than one brigade at a time), the limping Greyhounds were getting their fill of battle very quickly.[39]

By early afternoon the head of Walker's division approached Pleasant Hill via the road from Mansfield. The old stage road veered away from its usual northwest-to-southeast axis a few miles from town and turned almost due east. First settled in the mid-1840s, Pleasant Hill was only a small village of perhaps two hundred people, and the eponymous hill was mostly a gentle rise of forty feet over a distance of about two hundred yards. Some of the visitors in blue did not think the place was so pleasant: "The town boasts of a miserable one-story hut, which was dignified with the name of hotel, three stores, and an academy." Nor the hill very high: "The slightly elevated centre of the field, from which the name Pleasant Hill is taken, is nothing more than a long mound, hardly worthy the name of hill." West of the houses and dirt streets was a large "old field" (about a half-mile square) that had once been farmed by the village's founder. Soil exhaustion had overtaken the ground, and the field had been given up to scrubby pines, weeds, and dry ravines. The road from Mansfield ran across the northern edge of this field, which was surrounded on north, west, and south by an oak and pine forest.[40]

The small town and sparsely settled countryside were not capable of supporting tens of thousands of soldiers for very long. A staff officer and historian of the Federal 19th Corps wrote that Pleasant Hill "was too far from the immediate base of supplies, and there was no water to be had save from the cisterns in the village. These were merely sufficient, in ordinary times, for the storage of rain water for the daily use of the inhabitants. Now two armies had been drawing from them, and there was not enough left in them to supply the wants of Banks's men, to say nothing of the animals, for a single day." Water—or the lack of it—had helped to convince General Banks to retreat from the ravine near Mansfield, and the same water shortage would affect decisions by both Banks and Taylor at Pleasant Hill.[41]

General Taylor would have preferred to have a larger army and more fresh divisions, and he would have preferred to attack at dawn, before the Federals could prepare to receive him. But moving armies around the countryside often takes longer than expected, and it was early afternoon before he had studied his scouting reports and formulated a plan. Taylor's aggressiveness predisposed him to attack again, partly because he believed Banks was on the verge of retreating toward the Red River. A good hard shove might start another stampede. Although General Taylor was ready to resume the fight almost as soon as he encountered the enemy at Pleasant Hill, his soldiers were not. Brig. Gen. Thomas J. Churchill's Arkansas and Missouri divisions were worn out after marching forty-five miles in the last thirty-six hours. Walker's and Polignac's divisions were, of course, emotionally and physically drained after the previous day's battle, and suffering from thirst to boot. Taylor bowed to necessity and allowed a two-hour rest.[42]

Although most of the Federals waiting in line at Pleasant Hill had not fought the day before, they were nevertheless poorly organized for the looming engagement. Two brigades (Col. William T. Shaw's westerners under A. J. Smith and Col. Lewis Benedict's easterners of the 19th Corps) were placed in positions that left them "in the air"—that is, they were out in front of the rest of the army and without direct support on either side (see Map 9). On the right, Shaw's Iowa and Missouri regiments straddled the Mansfield road in a stretch of woods just west of town, between the village and the "old field." Benedict's New York and Maine regiments formed behind a dry ditch in an open field nearly a half-mile away, directly south of the streets of Pleasant Hill. The rest of the Federal army was another half-mile or even farther behind both lonely brigades. Generals Banks, A. J. Smith, and William Emory had botched the army's alignment, leaving both exposed brigades vulnerable to envelopment.[43]

By mid-afternoon General Taylor could wait no longer, and he sent Churchill's two small divisions on a two-mile march through the woods to the southeast. Churchill was to advance as far as the road from the Sabine River, which meandered into Pleasant Hill from the southwest, then turn left and roll up the left end of the enemy's line, repeating the maneuver of Walker's Texans the day before. Once Churchill engaged Banks on that end of the field, General Walker's brigades were to advance across the open field west of town and crack open the Federal right, a mirror image of their work the day before. Two brigades of General Green's cavalry, fighting dismounted north of the Mansfield road on the extreme left of the Confederate line, would take advantage of Churchill's and Walker's advances, turn the Federal right, and race around behind Banks's army to cut it off from its best line of retreat to the Red River, sixteen miles away.[44]

Churchill's column required about an hour to march through the woods to the Sabine road and another half hour to make the left turn and form a line of battle for the advance. Some in the Missouri brigades taunted the Texas cavalry covering their right flank. One horseman had to listen to it all: "they were loud-mouthed and were making all sorts of fun of us lying down in a ravine. . . . They were all armed with the best of new Enfield rifles just received from England via Mexico. These they would shake in the air and tell us in their own peculiar braggadocio way, 'We'll show you Texans how to fight. We'll show you how to do up the ——— Yankees,' and a thousand and one similar expressions." Just as the Arkansas and Missouri brigades were dressing their lines and double-checking their cartridge boxes, a mile to their left General Taylor ordered three batteries to move out of the woods into the field west of town and open fire, "to call off attention" from Churchill's pending charge. Within minutes Churchill started his line forward, aiming directly at Benedict's lone Federal brigade.[45]

The advance on the Confederate right proceeded as planned at first. An officer in the leftmost regiment of Benedict's brigade reported that the rebels "advanced at a charging pace, delivering a very heavy fire as they advanced" and even using the butts of their new Enfields on Federals at the ditch. One by one, the regiments in Benedict's brigade were overwhelmed, peeled away from the

Map 9
The Battle of Pleasant Hill, April 9, 1864

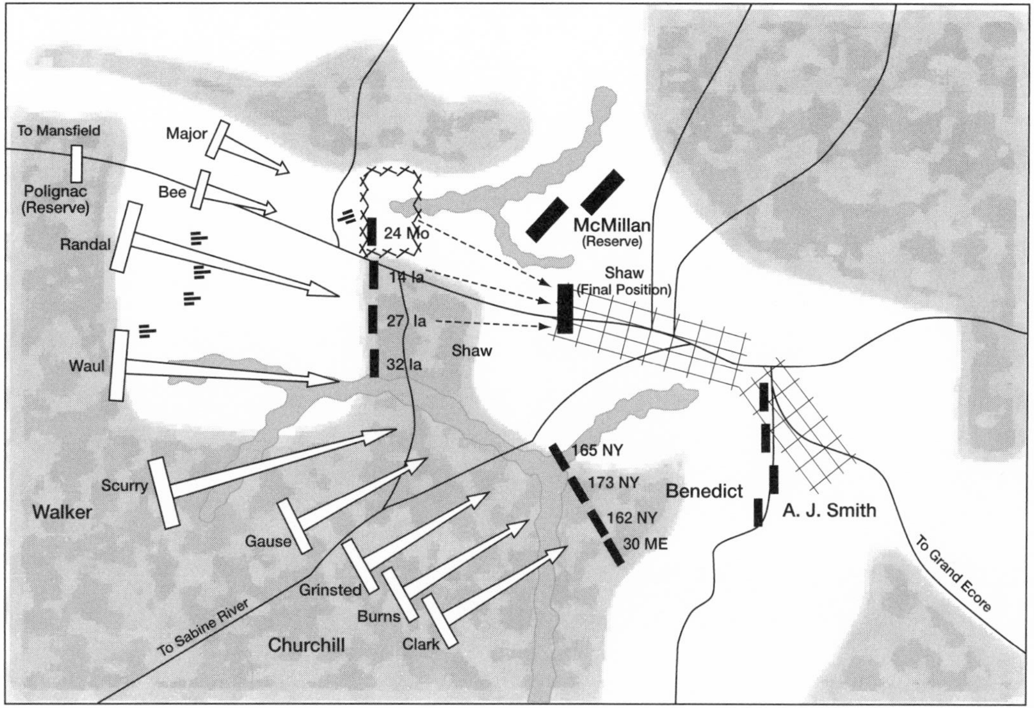

ditch, and sent scampering in disorder through the field to the rear, mostly into the streets of Pleasant Hill, with the boastful Missourians on their heels. A New Yorker watching from a distance had to admire the rebel charge: "It was a sight worth seeing that long line of butternut uniforms advancing slowly at first, and then, as if gathering momemtum [sic], faster and faster, until with a yell they charged upon, and entirely enveloping the Third Brigade, swept it along as if it were but chaff." Churchill's Arkansas and Missouri soldiers, in fact, pushed all the way through the field south of town and into the streets of the village, almost to the north-south road leading into town. Then, in a strange twist, the poorly designed Federal line that had wasted Benedict's brigade actually became an asset. The Confederates, in pursuing the fleeing easterners, were only dimly aware that other enemy units—in fact, the bulk of Banks's army—were now located in the trees on their right. In attempting to outflank the blue army, Churchill had moved into a position where his own line was outflanked on the right.[46]

An Illinois brigade—one of those that had poured over the walls of Fort De-Russy just three weeks earlier—dashed out of the woods and plowed directly into the right end of the Missouri line, driving it back across the field toward the ditch where the fighting had started. A. J. Smith and some officers of the 19th Corps, seeing the opportunity, quickly moved their brigades forward into the open, preparatory to a general counterattack. A Texas cavalryman, caught in the near ambush, had to admit that the emergence of the unseen enemy into the field was an impressive sight: "Their bayonets and burnished armors looked like a million mirrors reflecting from the hot and brightening sun, and bands that sounded as never bands had ever before sounded to us made one of the grandest battle scenes I had ever seen." The entire left side of the Federal army then rolled down the slope, across the field, and into the woods where Churchill's men had first emerged, driving the Missouri and Arkansas brigades and two Confederate batteries before them. In their effort to escape, some Missouri regiments fell back among the Arkansas troops, and they in turn retreated into the path of Walker's Greyhounds.[47]

As soon as the sounds of Churchill's advance reached his ears near the Mansfield road, General Taylor sent Walker's Greyhounds out of the woods and into the field just west of the village, *en echelon* of brigades from the right. Scurry moved first on the right, then Waul in the center, and finally Randal just south of the Mansfield road. The movement of Scurry's brigade was closely observed by Corporal Blessington, now an assistant adjutant on Scurry's staff. Hurrying along in the advance, the corporal noted that the men "stripped themselves of their blankets and knapsacks, in order that nothing might impede their work, and then swept down the hill, [and] across the field." General Scurry, true to his nature, rode to the front, shouting and encouraging his men: "Hat in hand, cheering on his men, a rifle ball glances his cheek, slightly wounding him; but without paying any attention to his wound, he continued cheering on his men." The general's task was soon complicated by the backpedaling Arkansas troops. They came reeling back through the woods on the right, under fire and without much order, stumbled backward into Scurry's path, and created an unexpected storm around the Texans. Scurry's Greyhounds, caught up in someone else's muddled retreat, hesitated in the confusion, and nearly 250 of them were swept up by the pursuing Federals. In fact, nearly 60 percent of all Confederates captured at Pleasant Hill were from Scurry's brigade. One of his regiments, the 19th Texas, lost its flag in the smoky confusion.[48]

Noting the stalled advance, Taylor hurried Waul's and Randal's brigades forward to sweep away resistance in Scurry's front. A member of the 13th Texas Cavalry, the regiment of Waul's brigade nearest Scurry's men, wrote that the Texans were ordered forward on the "double-quick" by General Walker himself, riding closely behind Waul's regiments: "The boys went at them like rabbits hiding in holes and drove them across the field to timber." In the trees across the field was Shaw's brigade of Iowa and Missouri regiments, still unsupported on either side and vulnerable to encirclement. Waul's and Randal's brigades flowed down a slight slope in the field, directly toward Shaw's westerners. A sergeant in the 32nd Iowa never forgot the sight of Walker's Texans coming across that open space: "At first they came at right shoulder shift. You could hear the command of their officers: 'Dress up on the right! Steady on the center! Steady! Steady, boys! Keep cool! Keep cool!' as with measured step they moved steadily forward." A private in the same Iowa regiment found the display somewhat disturbing: "Their bayonets were fixed ready for use and they carried their guns at a right shoulder shift. It was our time to turn pale."[49]

Skirmishers for the 32nd Iowa, about two hundred yards in front of their main line, fell back quickly once the Texas brigades bore down on them. One of the skirmishers was very relieved to reach safety in his own lines but dismayed by what happened next: "On reaching the company I dropped into a shallow and dry depression, and while regaining my wind I heard the sharp crack of a rifle, saw the smoke rise from a tree-top, heard a thud in my rear, and glancing back saw Mathias Hutchinson sink back, without a groan. His father [the captain] went to him, raised his head, but immediately laid it down, saying—'He is dead!' I think he was shot through the heart."[50]

When the Greyhounds approached within one hundred yards of Shaw's brigade, the Federals rose up from the ground and fired a withering volley into the

Texas ranks, just then topping a small rise: "At the command to fire they melted away," an Iowa sergeant wrote. "Again and again they rallied, aided by fresh troops, and came on with fierce yells to the charge." A soldier in the 13th Texas Cavalry saw the same events from the opposite angle. When his regiment approached within "a short distance" of the waiting Federals, the Yankees delivered "a deadly and continuous fire which mowed down our men like grain before the reaper." Another Iowan described the relentless enemy attack: "They crowded hard upon us, but were met with such a storm of bullets that they fell to the ground and crawled upon us like army worms. . . . While resting my elbow on the ground, taking close aim at a man, who was crawling in advance of the others, under shelter of a wash-out, my gun dropped suddenly from my grasp; my right shoulder had been pierced by a minie ball. It shattered the bone from the shoulder downward." A soldier in the 14th Iowa, positioned on the road leading into town, assured his parents that he had no fondness for such business: "I tell you it was a terrible time & the old soldiers say it was a harder fought battle than the Battle of Shiloah. But my prayer is that I may never witness another such a sight."[51]

At about the time the two sides came to grips with each other just west of town, General Walker was hit while riding back and forth along his lines. The wound was painful but not serious enough to endanger his life and was probably caused by a spent bullet or by spent shrapnel. (Taylor described it as "a contusion in the groin.") According to Corporal Blessington, "it was not until [Walker's] chief of staff . . . saw him in the act of fainting . . . that he was persuaded to dismount." General Taylor then rode over and ordered Walker to leave the field, "which he unwillingly did," according to Taylor. One of Walker's colonels, former Texas governor Edward Clark of Marshall, was out in front of his 14th Infantry when a minie ball smashed into his leg just below the knee. In the next regiment to Clark's right, one of Walker's captains, Theophilus Perry of the 28th Cavalry—the lawyer from Marshall and husband of the demanding Harriet—received a serious leg wound while leading his company. The wound was so serious that a surgeon had to amputate that night. The traumas of the wound and amputation were too great, and the captain died eight days later. Not far away across the field, Capt. Elijah Petty of the 17th Texas, the Bastrop lawyer and attentive husband and father, tumbled forward with a grapeshot wound through the chest, just below his neck. At the moment he was hit, one of his sergeants recalled, "he was in the front of the battle with only a few of his men as we were badly scattered." Petty, in severe distress, could not be moved and soon fell into enemy hands. His wound was fatal, though, and he died shortly afterward. His children later erected a monument over the spot where Petty's body was buried, and it remained the only monument on the battlefield for several decades.[52]

The Greyhounds on the field and in the woods had no time for sad reflections or grief, not in the midst of the mind-shattering roar, the shouts and groans, the gun smoke, and the general confusion of battle. Despite stout and courageous resistance by Shaw's brigade of Federals, they were gradually overwhelmed by Walker's Texans on their left and front and by Green's cavalry and Polignac's brigade (called up from reserve) on their right. Indeed, just before sunset the Confederates poured around both flanks of the enemy brigade, forcing A. J. Smith to order Shaw's regiments back from their exposed position. Some of the Federals retreated through the twilight forest, but others were already surrounded. An Iowa sergeant described the terrible predicament of those caught in the middle: "And here we were, our ammunition exhausted, and *Zip! Zip!* came the minnie balls from right, left and rear." One of those missiles struck one of his comrades in the 32nd Iowa: "A minnie ball had entered his mouth, cut off his tongue, and passed through his neck. The poor boy could not speak or eat, and at the end of about nine days died of starvation." Another Iowan was amazed that anyone survived the fight: "It was wonderful that anything could live in such a storm of iron and lead. A ball struck the ground and filled my face with dirt; another took a bit of skin from the knuckle of my right fore finger; another pulled the hair over my left; and another lodged in the rolled blanket on my shoulder." Even when he and his friends tried to retreat, the Confederates seemed to be everywhere: "[Wilbur] Hoyt was shot [and killed] after we had fallen back to a log that seemed to offer some shelter, but the balls soon struck the log from the rear, showing that we had the enemy on all sides of us."[53]

The advance by the Confederate left continued through the woods and on to the edge of the village, but the rapidly declining light made further fighting impractical. As the firing died away, some of the surrounded Federals scrambled back through the trees and underbrush to find their units. "In the hand to hand encounter which took place in the darkness, we took about fifty of their men prisoners and they captured about the same number of ours," one member of the 32nd Iowa remarked. "The question as to which man should be the prisoner depended entirely upon who got 'the drop' on the other." At about the same time, some Confederates began receiving fire from unexpected directions and concluded that their friends were mistaking them for the enemy. Recognizing the futility of continued fighting under such conditions, General Taylor called back his left wing.[54]

While Churchill's officers followed their soldiers through the woods, trying to restore order, Walker's and Polignac's officers withdrew their units from the woods, as ordered by Taylor, when failing light made further fighting unreasonable. Brig. Gen. William Dwight, commander of the Federal brigade to the right rear of Shaw's westerners, reported that "darkness put an end to the battle. The attacks of the enemy upon the position of this brigade continued to the end, and showed the enemy to be in force near my position up to the time when all firing ceased." General Taylor went to some pains in his memoirs to stress the point that his left wing had not been driven back: the disengagement west of the village "was made slowly and in perfect order, the men forming in the field as they emerged from the thicket." The reader may rightly wonder about the "perfect order"—especially after a hard struggle ending in darkness—but evidence from both sides points to a different result on the Confederate left from that on the right. When Walker's and Polignac's regiments were re-formed, Taylor left the cavalry to hold his original line and ordered his infantry divisions back up the Mansfield road seven miles to the nearest source of water.[55]

Although Taylor had hoped to rout Banks's army for a second time in two days, the Louisiana general had to settle for a tactical standoff at Pleasant Hill. Historians generally record Pleasant Hill as a tactical stalemate or a tactical Union victory. Stalemate seems the more appropriate description. The Federals certainly had the better day on their left, but the left side of the Confederate army broke Shaw's first line and was driving into the town when night ended the battle. Moreover, both armies maintained some units on the battlefield after the fighting ended. In any case, the more important point is that General Banks retreated toward the Red River that night, ending his campaign toward Shreveport and East Texas and making the battle a strategic Confederate victory.

Although the two armies may have reached an impasse on the field, their commanders continued the contest afterward with rhetorical claims of victory. In his report to General Grant, Banks alleged that "the losses were great on both sides, but that of the rebels, as we could judge from the appearance of the battlefield, more than double our own." Indeed, Banks asserted, "the rout of the enemy was complete." In this war of words, Banks was completely overmatched—Taylor had all the advantages. Referring to Banks's claims of victory, Taylor cut and slashed with dazzling style: "Here the proportion of fiction to fact surpasses that of sack to bread in Sir John's tavern bill; and it may be doubted if a mandarin from the remotest province of the Celestial Empire ever ventured to send such a report to Peking." A final flourish and the contest was over: "Homeric must have been the laughter of his troops when this report was published."[56]

The aftermath of battle—the torn human bodies, the dead and wounded horses, the ruined and abandoned equipment—seemed much worse on this Saturday night than after Mansfield on Friday, partly because more human wreckage was contained in a smaller area and partly because of the water shortage. An Illinois soldier was one of many to describe the ruins of the battlefield: "Stark and pallid lay the dead with faces upturned; gray-bearded men and beardless boys, the blue and the gray, side by side; broken wagons and disabled guns; dead animals and wounded; shattered muskets, blood stained cartridge boxes; the wounded dying, not from wounds but for want of water. There was none to be had for miles." A New Yorker could not get the sights and sounds out of his head: "The wails and cries of agony which were mingled by these hundreds of sufferers are still ringing in my ears," he wrote after the war. "Yonder comes a voice crying, 'Oh, for God's sake bring us some water.' 'Where is the Twenty-Fourth Iowa?' 'Send some one to get me.' "[57]

One of General Green's horsemen ran upon an unusually sad story on the picket line that night: "one poor fellow of a Yankee, who had got a sabre cut over the head, acted like a chicken with its head off. I made the boys wrap him up in his blanket, but could not keep him still. He would get up and wander around in a circle, fall down and kick around on the ground and do all kinds of horrible things in his insanity, and finally wound up by dying about daylight." A Louisiana quartermaster was appalled by the waste and agony. Most of the bodies he saw "were mutilated, some without heads, the faces of other[s] completely mangled, others again had their legs crushed, their feet torn away, one in particular a Confederate had had his right side torn away by a bullet, his ribs crushed and turned inside out, leaving his entrails exposed to view and one could see the flies crawling all over them. A wounded Yankee had his teeth driven in, his jaw crushed by a bullet which had lodged in his neck. With his face swollen as large as a pumpkin, unable to speak, he was a truly terrible sight." Capt. Volney Ellis of the 12th Texas Infantry found the aftermath of battle "horrible and blood-chilling." In fact, he wrote his wife, "if such sights could be vividly portrayed to those who instigate wars, methinks they would be careful indeed in inciting the minds of men to such fearful phrensies."[58]

Exact accountings of the dead, wounded, and missing were always difficult to make after a battle. Lost reports, contradictory accounts, and confusion always obscured some of the facts. Nevertheless, it appears that Banks's army, with about 12,200 men engaged that Saturday at Pleasant Hill, lost roughly 1,400 (about 1,000 killed and wounded and nearly 400 missing), most of them (937) from the two unfortunate brigades that had been deployed out in front of the rest of the army. Taylor's army, somewhat over 12,000 strong, lost roughly 1,200 men killed and wounded and 426 captured. Incomplete records make an exact calculation of losses in Walker's division impossible, but Waul's brigade lost 25 killed, 179 wounded, and 21 missing. Randal's brigade suffered similar losses (22 killed, 100 wounded, and 6 missing). Assuming that Scurry's brigade, caught up in the confused retreat on the Confederate right, was damaged at a higher level (with at least 247 captured), losses for the Greyhound Division were approximately 500 killed and wounded and 300 missing. Considering the 200 casualties from the previous day's battle, General Walker lost about 1,000 of his roughly 4,000-man division in the two days at Mansfield and Pleasant Hill.[59]

Despite their fatigue after Friday's engagement, the Greyhounds fought well again at Pleasant Hill. Once more, they crossed open ground under fire, broke open one enemy brigade firing from protected positions in the woods, and drove back Federal veterans of the Vicksburg and Port Hudson campaigns. Some of their enemies paid them the highest compliment—praise from a fellow soldier. An Illinois captain informed his wife that the Texans were formidable warriors: "The army that we have to contend with are well armed & drilled and are daring fellows to fight. they come right up, double quick in the face of our canon and musketry. . . . Noble fellows they are worthy of a better cause." An Ohio soldier, complaining about General Banks, wrote his family that the Confederates at Mansfield and Pleasant Hill had another strength: they were led by "generals who know how to fight."[60]

When the weary Greyhounds reached the creek where they were supposed to halt for the night, they collapsed into fatigued sleep. Two days of marching and fighting left them with no reserves of energy. Still, some of them must have realized, even in their exhaustion, that they had just done what they had signed up to do two years earlier: turn the enemy away from their homes and families. Meanwhile, several miles behind them, General Banks met with his generals to discuss the campaign. He thought about pushing forward the next day—visions of victory at Shreveport still swirled in his head—but by the end of the council, he decided to retreat to the Red River at Grand Ecore near Natchitoches. The divisions defeated at Mansfield needed time to reorganize, rations were short, and water was simply not available anywhere within miles, he reported to General Grant. During the night, then, about the time the Greyhounds fell to the ground to sleep, Banks's officers put their regiments on the road back toward Natchitoches. The formidable blue wave that had rushed up the Red River valley had crested and now began to recede. Taylor's army, including Walker's Texans, had won one of the last significant Confederate victories of the Civil War.[61]

# CHAPTER 12

# *Jenkins' Ferry*

Now that General Banks was backing toward the Red River, Richard Taylor was eager to follow him and strike the Federal army—and its accompanying gunboat fleet—as soon as possible. The Yankee army, though twice as large, was in retreat, many of its soldiers were fed up with Banks, and morale was dangerously low. Admiral Porter's fleet also was vulnerable. The river was unusually low, and deep-draft gunboats and transports frequently ran aground or impaled themselves on hidden snags, requiring hours of towing and backing and cursing before the procession could continue. Once he learned of Banks's withdrawal, Porter too would have to retreat from his expedition up the Red River. A harassing infantry or cavalry force might be especially effective on the banks of the narrow, winding stream, particularly when the frequent groundings and delays brought the riverboat parade to a halt.[1]

Gen. Edmund Kirby Smith, commander of the entire Confederate Trans-Mississippi Department, had other ideas for Taylor's army. Yes, Banks had been thrown back, but that very fact made him less dangerous. What if Porter's fleet pushed all the way upriver to Shreveport while Taylor was chasing Banks southward? What if Steele's Federal army from Arkansas cut its way through weak resistance all the way to department headquarters in Shreveport while Taylor strayed after a beaten army in retreat? No, Taylor's plan would not do, Smith concluded. Most of the army must be held in northwest Louisiana, to protect Shreveport and to deal with Steele's threat from the north. Taylor, never very patient with Smith's seeming timidity, argued repeatedly that Banks and Porter could be ruined and the lower Mississippi River valley therefore reclaimed for the Confederacy. He asserted more than once that Porter and Steele could not threaten department headquarters because they would be forced to retreat when they learned of Banks's defeat.[2]

Still, Smith would not budge from his determination to protect Shreveport. Taylor later sneered, in his usual polished prose, that the city was as "sacred to [Smith] and his huge staff as Benares, dwelling-place of many gods, to the Hindoo." Taylor could only contemplate the predicaments of Banks and Porter and regret the lost opportunities: "We had but to strike vigorously to capture or destroy both. But it was written that the sacrifices of my little army should be wasted, and, on the morning of the 10th, I was ordered to take all the infantry and much of the horse to Mansfield." In his postwar memoirs, General Walker blamed Banks's escape on Smith's blundering: "Gen. E. K. Smith was not the leader to comprehend the true line of action," Walker grumbled. The Greyhound general was certain that Smith's decision to divert the infantry to Arkansas wasted the golden moment to smash the Federal army: "To this fatal blunder Banks was indebted for his safety."[3]

Taylor, trying to salvage half a loaf, next offered to lead his army to Arkansas first and then, once Steele retreated or was defeated, hurry south once again to strike at Banks and Porter. That would not do, either. General Smith decided to take the bulk of Taylor's army himself—Walker's Greyhounds and Churchill's Arkansas and Missouri divisions—to confront Steele in the field. Taylor would remain in Shreveport to oversee the Trans-Mississippi Department while he (Smith) chased Steele back to Little Rock. In a concession to Taylor's feelings, Smith allowed the smoldering Louisiana general to put aside the paperwork in Shreveport and rejoin the remnants of his army (Green's cavalry and Polignac's small division) in the pursuit of Banks if he thought it advisable. Incredulous that Smith would let pass the opportunity to destroy Banks and Porter in order to go on "a wild-goose chase," the angry and disappointed Taylor indeed found it advisable to leave Trans-Mississippi headquarters and at least harass the Federals on their retreat. Still, every day or so, he looked back north, hoping to see the flags of Walker's Greyhounds approaching for a showdown with Banks.[4]

The Greyhounds were marching in the opposite direction. On the Sunday and Monday following the battle of Pleasant Hill, the Texans returned over the very familiar stage road to camps north of Mansfield, where they waited three more days for Generals Smith and Taylor to settle their differences and decide their next move. Smith having prevailed, the Greyhounds marched out of their camps near Mansfield on April 14, bound for a collision with General Steele's Federals in Arkansas. As they bounced over a pontoon bridge spanning the Red River at Shreveport the next day, they were joined by a green regiment, the 3rd Texas Infantry, added to Scurry's brigade to help compensate for his losses at Pleasant Hill. At Shreveport the division turned east and continued for two more days until they reached the vicinity of Minden, about thirty miles east of the Red River. As they tramped through the little town on April 18, "with banners flying, and keeping step to the tune of 'Dixie,'" they received the sort of welcome they had enjoyed in the early months of the war. "The streets were crowded with young ladies, waving their handkerchiefs, and cheering us most lustily," Corporal

Blessington recalled. "At every gate they stood with bouquets to present to the troops as they passed." About twelve miles past all this excitement, the Greyhounds wilted into a new camp north of Minden. "The men and animals were thoroughly fagged out," Blessington remembered. Private Farrow of the 19th Texas wrote his wife that "we are all completely worn out. I have never seen Our Boys as much fatigued before. a few days rest will set us all right again."[5]

A chronic complainer like Private Farrow would not have been surprised to learn that the reason for the halt was not to rest the men and horses. General Smith had ordered the pause because Banks's army near Natchitoches had thrown two pontoon bridges across the Red River, raising the possibility that they might advance again, this time up the east side of the river. If the Federals came north for another go at Shreveport or to join Steele, Walker's Greyhounds near Minden would be in the perfect position to blunt the offensive. Smith even tantalized Taylor with the possibility that Walker's Texans might be diverted from Arkansas and sent down to join in the pursuit of Banks. Department headquarters assigned the 8th Missouri Cavalry to scout for Walker on his contemplated trip south to join Taylor. But the possibility was snatched away two days later when Taylor learned that Walker's division would not turn south. The Federals around Natchitoches, it was now clear, were not planning another advance. Banks was still retreating and Steele was not, so the Texas Division was ordered to resume the march to Arkansas.[6]

The Greyhounds had tarried in the vicinity between Minden and the Arkansas border for six days while Smith decided what to do with them. The weather turned "dark, gloomy, and very damp," but the rest doubtless helped them regain some of their strength. Their first pay in six months probably helped restore some of their spirit as well. On the morning of April 24, they rolled up their blankets, filed back into the muddy road, and slogged north again. Later that day they crossed the state line and marched along Arkansas roads for the first time in almost exactly a year. Under gray skies, the Texans trudged through the tiny village of Calhoun on April 25 and one day later drew within twelve miles of Steele's Federal army at Camden, about ninety-five miles northeast of Shreveport.[7]

The Texans who marched into Arkansas in late April 1864 were very different from those who left Arkansas in late April 1863. In that year the previously untested division, or parts of it, had fought at Milliken's Bend, at Richmond, and at Bayou Bourbeau. The Greyhounds had disrupted shipping on the Mississippi River, shivered through the coldest winter in decades, and retreated 270 miles up the Red River valley in three weeks. Most important to them, they had performed like veterans and played central roles in two of the largest and most important battles of the war west of the Mississippi River, battles that had turned the enemy away from their families and homes in Texas. Now if they could help eliminate Steele's threat to Confederate headquarters in Shreveport, they might be able to rest assured that Texas was truly and finally safe from their enemies.

The commander of the Federal army at Camden, Maj. Gen. Frederick Steele, was a graduate of the U.S. Military Academy in the same class with Ulysses S. Grant and William B. Franklin (Class of 1843). Steele had about eleven thousand men in the earthworks at Camden. He had marched out of Little Rock on March 23, leading one of the two pincers aimed at the Confederate Trans-Mississippi headquarters in Shreveport, 175 miles to the southwest. Almost as soon as his army left the safety of Little Rock, though, things had started to go wrong. The already poor country between Steele's army and Shreveport had been badly used up during the war, and his men found little along the road to supplement the supplies in their wagon train. Indeed, Steele put his soldiers on half rations only one day out of Little Rock. Then, expected reinforcements from Fort Smith (on the border with the Indian Territory) did not show up on time, and Steele lost valuable days waiting for them. When they finally did join the main column on April 9 (the same day as the battle at Pleasant Hill), Steele was still one hundred miles north of Shreveport. He also was dismayed to learn that his reinforcements were nearly as destitute as his own soldiers. To make things worse, Confederate cavalry units constantly buzzed around his army, slowing the march and making it difficult to search for food and fodder along the route.[8]

To save his men and animals from outright starvation, Steele turned off the line toward Shreveport on April 12 and redirected his hungry army east to Camden in south-central Arkansas. He expected to hole up in Camden's well-constructed earthworks, built earlier by the Confederates, and wait for supplies to reach him from Pine Bluff and from large foraging expeditions sent deep into the countryside. One of the foraging parties—about eleven hundred men and two hundred wagons—managed to find food and other booty west of Camden in mid-April, but as the heavily loaded wagons returned on April 18, the Federal escorts were waylaid nine miles from town by Confederate cavalry three times their number. At this sharp engagement at Poison Spring, General Steele's men lost every wagon, four artillery pieces, and three hundred soldiers. Some of the Federals (especially black soldiers of the 1st Kansas [Colored] Infantry) were reportedly shot or bayoneted as they lay wounded or tried to surrender. The Federals also lost the tons of cargo that had been gathered from the farms west of Camden.[9]

One week later, as enemy infantry drew closer to Steele's earthworks, Confederate cavalry gobbled up another Federal wagon train, at Marks' Mills northeast of Camden. This left Steele's army completely isolated—and hungry—in their trenches. To complete his run of misfortune, General Steele meanwhile learned that Banks's army had been defeated and had abandoned any further attempts to move against Shreveport. The defeats at Poison Spring and Marks' Mills, the news that Banks had given up on the Red River campaign, the dangerous shortage of food and fodder, and the approaching Confederate infantry all convinced General Steele that the grand pincers movement was no more. It was time to go. As Smith's Confederate infantry swung up from the south, Steele's Federals began preparations for a fast march back toward safety at Little Rock.[10]

The retreat began on the afternoon of Tuesday, April 26, and was done hurriedly and quietly. A soldier in the 33rd Iowa Infantry wrote that "toward noon there came up word from town that preparations were making for a hasty retreat. Wagons, tents, mess-chests, cooking utensils, hard-tack and meat, were destroyed by the quantity. Box after box of crackers were burned." Civilians were kept within the lines to prevent word of the withdrawal from reaching the nearby Confederates. The escape from Camden continued all through the night across a pontoon bridge that spanned the Ouachita River. Before daylight the next morning, the last soldiers out of town dismantled the bridge, deflated the pontoons, and loaded them on wagons that would carry the bridge with the army. By taking their bridge with them, the Federals gained a day's march on the pursuing Confederates. Smith's own pontoon train was still back in Shreveport and would not reach his army in time to do any good on this campaign.[11]

While the Federals were retreating on the 26th, Gen. E. Kirby Smith was reorganizing the disparate Confederate units that had converged on Camden. Smith took command of the whole force and assigned Maj. Gen. Sterling Price, hitherto directing operations against Steele, to lead the two small divisions of Arkansas and Missouri infantry that had fought at Pleasant Hill. The Texas Division marched into Camden the next afternoon, Wednesday, April 27, to find Smith's engineers tearing down buildings in Camden and using the timbers to build a shaky, floating footbridge across the ninety-yard river. Other Confederates found a flatboat ferry that had been sunk but not destroyed by the enemy. After raising and bailing out the ferry, the Confederates used it to cross four field batteries and one wagon per regiment. The soldiers would have to carry everything else—food, bedding, and arms—with them on the chase. At sunrise on the 28th, General Price (known to his men as "Old Pap") sent his foot soldiers across the footbridge, and right behind them came the Greyhounds.[12]

The Texans stepped lightly across the wobbly bridge and began the pursuit by late morning. On the other side of the river, they began to notice the signs of a hurried retreat. A captain in the 13th Texas Cavalry wrote in his diary, "all along the road see where Feds have burned clothing, blankets beds and wagons in their haste to get away." Another Texan noted that "all along the way were wagons cut down and burning, destroying baggage and all sorts of equipment of every description." An Iowa soldier admitted that the march was messy: "Signs enough of the precipitation of our retreat appeared in the constant succession of shreds of clothing, pieces of knapsacks, and other fragments, which fatigue compelled our men to throw away," he later wrote. "Never before had we seen such haste when a whole column was moving."[13]

Steele had a day's head start, but Smith and Price were determined to run the Federals to ground before they could reach Little Rock. Price had his men on the move by 2 A.M. on the 29th and by midnight the next night, and Walker's division followed close behind each time. The Federals farther up the road were keenly aware that they were the prey in this story. A Wisconsin soldier recalled that "they pursued relentlessly and each day they gained ground on us in our flight toward Little Rock." The Confederates covered nearly thirty miles on April 29 and began to close the gap. Steele's progress that day was slowed by the necessity to bring up, deploy, and build another pontoon bridge, this time across the swollen Saline River, about forty miles south of Little Rock. The bridge was constructed at a spot known then and ever since as Jenkins' Ferry.[14]

The Greyhounds, like everyone else on the road between Camden and Little Rock, were bone weary and hungry as they marched north that Friday, three weeks after Mansfield. Then, to make the picture even gloomier, the sky darkened and rain began to fall, and it continued to pour, sometimes in torrents, all night and through the next day. The Texans may have been cheered a bit when they squished through the little town of Princeton because the citizens there hailed the Confederates as heroes and saviors. One local woman wrote excitedly in her diary, "instantly headache, heartache and fatigue took flight—and we also (went) up town—laughing and crying." To relieved civilians, the ragged and muddy Confederates must have looked much better than they felt because the same diarist wrote that "everyone looked good enough—willing enough and brave enough to save the world. All honor to the heroes of Mansfield and Shreveport." By this point in the war, emotional demonstrations by civilians probably had only minimal effect on the soldiers. They had seen all this before, and they knew that war was something much different from the visions swirling through the minds of cheering women and children. The Texas Division tramped two miles past the town and camped for the night near a creek, a bad decision under the circumstances because the relentless rain raised the creek into the campfires and blankets of the men during the night.[15]

The Greyhounds shuffled back into dark lines at 3 A.M. on Saturday and resumed the seemingly never-ending chase—wet clothes, soggy blankets, and all. A few miles ahead, an Arkansas surgeon described the eerie night march: "In the darkness one could see nothing. Then a flash of lightning would come and reveal a long line of bayonets stretching away down the road and out into the darkness." Despite the rain and the early hour, the women of the next small town, Tulip, ran out of their houses and cheered as the Texans tramped by. The early risings on successive days, the interminable marches (about 240 miles since Pleasant Hill), and the bad weather all combined to stretch the division out, with stragglers falling well behind. Corporal Blessington, traveling with General Scurry's staff, wrote that "the troops were in a wretched condition. I do not exaggerate in stating that scarcely half the effective force was in position." Indeed, Blessington's old regiment (the 16th Infantry), reduced by casualties and the extreme physical demands of the pursuit, had only about 130 men available that day. Around daylight the men heard the rumble of artillery in the distance, and by mid-morning they marched past the scene of the action: "trees cut half in two by cannon balls; limbs of trees torn off and lying in the road; fences down and scattered in endless confusion . . . houses riddled with cannon and musket balls; negro-quarters and meat-houses broken open and rifled of their contents;—in a word, a general desolation prevailing everywhere," Blessington recounted. The Confederates had caught up with Steele.[16]

The fields and woods where the two armies would fight that day would have been difficult terrain even in good weather. The ground along the right bank of the Saline River was generally low, swampy, and heavily wooded except for a few cleared farm fields bordering the right side of the road. Just to the left of the road was a parallel creek that fed into the river. The hours of pouring rain had made the land on either side of the Saline a shallow lake, and the rain and Steele's wagons had made the last few miles of road before the pontoon bridge a river of deep mud. A surgeon with the 1st Iowa Cavalry shuddered at the memory: "All night long, with the rain pouring down in torrents, the army was assisting in getting the trains and batteries over the almost bottomless road, and across a pontoon bridge which had been laid across the river. But the morning came with a portion of the train uncrossed. At this time (April 30th) all the wagons were ordered to be destroyed, except 'those for General Headquarters.'" One Federal engineer, struggling to get the army's train to safety before the Confederates attacked, reported that the "wagons settled to the axles and mules floundered about without a resting place for their feet." Finally, the soldiers and the animals "sank down in the mud and mire, wherever they were, to seek a few hours' repose" before the inevitable confrontation with the approaching enemy.[17]

The rain thus slowed Steele's army enough to allow the Confederates to close completely the steadily narrowing gap between them. In that sense, the weather benefited the pursuers. On the other hand, the swampy river bottom, now rising with rainwater, made maneuver by Smith's gray columns impossible. When Steele turned about-face to defend his pontoon bridge that morning, the right end of his line was protected by the swollen creek that meandered beside the road. His left was anchored on an impassable swamp, now about two to six feet under water. The Confederates, if they were determined to fight him, would have to approach straight on, down a funnel, through the watery woods and open farm fields directly in front of the Federals. Steele's men had made their position even stronger by hurriedly building log and fence-rail breastworks and abatis among the trees and undergrowth. From behind those defenses, they could pour sheets of fire through the rain at any approaching rebels.[18]

General Price's Arkansas and Missouri divisions were the first Confederate infantry to reach the vicinity that morning. Fully as miserable as anyone else in the rain and mud, the Arkansas foot soldiers did not like the look of things. One of them remembered the moments before the advance: "There was nothing of the romance of war or battle. No waving of banners; no martial music; no thronging of women, children and gray-haired men to the battlements of a beautiful city to witness the efforts put forth in their defense. No sentiment about this. The rain pattered down steadily. The men stood in the ranks cold, wet and hungry and gazed down into that dismal, cheerless swamp."[19]

Generals Smith and Price, more determined than imaginative, proceeded to send their soggy infantry into the funnel one brigade at a time, and, one brigade at a time, the Confederates were stopped cold. First, Churchill's Arkansas troops sloshed through the woods and into the watery farm fields, the first brigade at about 8 A.M., the next nearly an hour later, and the third not long after. One detachment crossed the creek to the left of the road and temporarily laid down damaging enfilade fire, but the Federals sent some of their own men across the creek and distracted the stillborn flanking movement. Between 8 and 10 A.M., Churchill's brigades made repeated charges through the woods and into the fields, and in some cases they succeeded in driving the Federals back a few hundred yards. But General Steele handled his forces well, shoring up his line where it bent back and assigning reinforcements efficiently. On other parts of the battlefield, his men, concealed behind their breastworks, poured a murderous fire into the exposed Confederates. After two hours of this, General Smith finally realized that the Arkansas division alone could not break Steele's line, and he called up Parsons's Missouri brigades to add force to the assault.[20]

The terrain, the river, and the rising water forced the Missouri Confederates into the same straight-on approach that had already failed for the Arkansas troops. Complicating their task was a more crowded and disorganized front now that the Arkansas brigades had been repelled and were cluttering the dripping woods and soggy farm fields. Generals Smith and Price gave Parsons contradictory orders about where to place his brigades—to the right or to the left of the Arkansas units. Parsons ended up by splitting some of his men to the right and some to the left. The results were unchanged, however. A staunch Federal defense from behind breastworks and abatis, a restricted zone of frontal assault, and the difficulty of maneuver in the mud and water kept the Confederates away from the pontoon bridge and the Federal wagon train still crossing it.[21]

Under dark skies and clouded in the smoke of the battlefield, a three-gun section of a Missouri Confederate battery pushed forward on the left to join the infantry in an attempt to break the logjam. The gunners realized too late that the supposedly friendly infantrymen were actually Federals of the 2nd Kansas (Colored) Regiment. Before the artillery could retreat, the black soldiers rushed forward and captured the three Confederate cannon. Prisoners who fell into the hands of the 2nd Kansas at Jenkins' Ferry were unfortunate indeed because the African American soldiers were still seething over reports of atrocities committed against black troops at Poison Spring and Marks' Mills. Some Confederate soldiers with hands raised in surrender were bayoneted. Some wounded men were shot, others had their throats slit, and some were mutilated when the Federals cut off ears for trophies. The Civil War in Arkansas spiraled down into a most vicious and brutal phase in the spring of 1864.[22]

By 11:30 "Old Pap" Price concluded that further frontal attacks were useless. He called off the futile assaults and ordered Churchill's Arkansas brigades and Parsons's Missouri men to withdraw from the killing zone and regroup somewhat to the rear, where the high ground began its descent to the river. Walker's Texans were arriving on the battlefield, and they would take the lead now. Smith by this time had learned of a separate approach to the Federal line, a narrow lane that branched off the main road about three miles to the rear and led down into the river bottom somewhere around the left end of the enemy position (see Map 10). Thinking that this would provide a way of coming up on the Federals from their left and rear, Smith ordered Walker to send one of his three brigades up the main road to join Price and to direct his other two brigades into the side road. While the Federals watched the enemy in their front, Walker's two brigades would "make a detour to the right, and, if possible, turn the left of the enemy and attack him in the rear," in Walker's words. And if the Greyhounds could strike unexpectedly from the left and rear, they might well start another rout.[23]

While Waul's brigade proceeded up the road to join the main body of the army, Randal's and Scurry's brigades peeled off into the little country lane lead-

# Map 10
## The Battle of Jenkins' Ferry, April 30, 1864

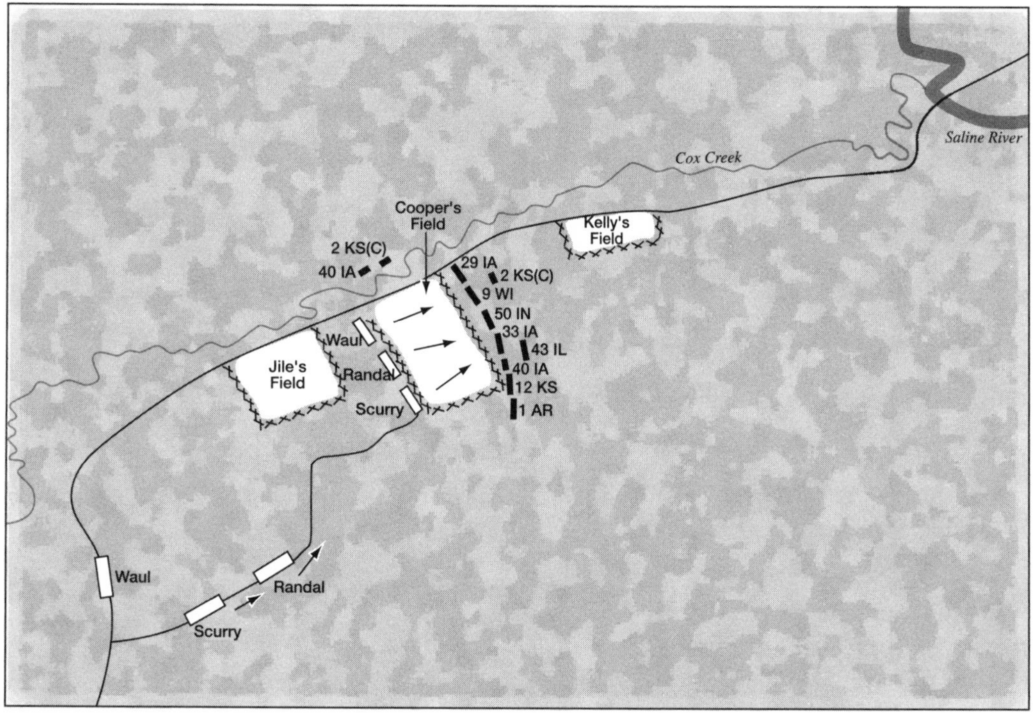

ing off to the right. At that intersection Corporal Blessington noticed "General Walker, mounted on his iron-gray war-horse, awaiting to address a few remarks of encouragement to each regiment as they passed by." Although the general was still "in a feeble state, suffering from his wound," the corporal believed Walker's presence inspired the men: "cheer after cheer was freely given him, as they passed by him." Down the path they hurried, with the sound of musketry cracking across the watery landscape. While Randal and Scurry followed the scouts down the lane and into the swamp, Waul's regiments joined Smith's main force and formed a battle line at the edge of the high ground, where Churchill's troops had formed earlier that morning.[24]

Before the other two Texas brigades reached their destination, Smith sent Waul's men down through the woods and into the farm fields where Price's infantry had fought for several hours. The Texans went right by several units that had withdrawn to reorganize and replenish their cartridge boxes. Waul drove back the first Federals he encountered, ambitious soldiers who were following Price's brigades through the woods as they withdrew to reorganize. Emerging into one of the farm fields along the road, Waul's men encountered the first real Federal battle line they had seen so far that day. Once again the advancing Greyhounds sent the enemy scampering backward, this time into their log and rail breastworks in the opposite tree line. General Waul then called a halt to the advance while he assessed the ground. He concluded that marching across the open field against veterans behind protection—and veterans arranged in a concave line that would be able to pour rifle fire into both his flanks—was not his best choice. Waul decided to wait for Randal and Scurry to uproot the left end of the enemy's line before he sent his men any farther. General Smith, meanwhile, was pointing Price's brigades into supporting positions behind Waul.[25]

Unfortunately for the Texans in Randal's and Scurry's brigades, the seldom-used road they had taken did not lead to the rear of the Federal line; instead, it fed into the same woods and farm fields where Price's men had fought all morning. Thus, rather than come up behind the enemy, Randal and Scurry led their regiments into the same watery funnel that had already proved so deadly. Nothing could be done about it now, though, so General Walker sent the two new brigades through the woods and into the farm field where Waul's brigade was waiting. In fact, the left end of Randal's line overlapped the right end of Waul's, forcing Randal to pause and re-deploy and requiring all three brigades to wait and shift around while under fire. The effort to realign the regiments was made even more difficult by the standing water. "When we got [with]in about 400 yards of the enemy," an officer in Randal's brigade wrote, "orders were given to form forward into line of battle amidst a roar of water splashing under the men's feet so that none could hear the orders except those nearest to the officers who repeated them, but the rest saw and imitated the movement." Within a few minutes, all three Greyhound brigades—what was left of them after Mansfield, Pleasant Hill, and the hard marches to Jenkins' Ferry—moved forward across the flooded landscape, and the roar of battle intensified again.[26]

On the opposite side of the field, a soldier in the 33rd Iowa Infantry noted that in the moist, heavy air, "a dense cloud of powder-smoke settled so closely down, that at a few feet distant, nothing was distinguishable. It seemed now almost impossible to fire otherwise than at random." He and his comrades "soon learned to stoop down, and look under the smoke sufficiently to discover the precise position of the rebel masses; and then a horizontal fire at the level of the breast, could not fail to hit its mark, unless a tree stood in the way." At times, the only way to detect the enemy was to watch for the flashes of their muzzles through the dense smoke. The concentrated rifle fire from behind the Federal breastworks took a severe toll on the exposed Greyhounds, especially Randal's brigade, wedged between Waul on the left and Scurry on the right. A soldier in one of Randal's regiments (the 11th Infantry) believed that "if We Had of remained in the field they Would Have killed everry one of us." Indeed, he assured his wife, "I never Want to get in as daingerous a plase as that any more for they come verry neare Killing me." Three of the regiment's ten captains and its major were killed in that farm field.[27]

Another regiment in Randal's brigade, the 14th Infantry, was cut up at about the same rate. One Texan wrote that his company "lost about half of its men, killed and wounded. After the fight we had sergeants commanding companies and captains commanding regiments." One of the regiment's wounded, J. R. Jones, still vividly remembered his misfortune nearly fifty years later. Shot in the hip, he lost consciousness for a while: "When I came to myself there was no one on the battlefield except myself and the dead and wounded. In a short time after I became rational the Yankees sent a line of skirmishers on the battlefield. They were all negroes except the officer. One of the negroes threw his gun on me to shoot, but I begged him out of it. My wound is still running. This was a hard fought battle."[28]

An officer in the 28th Cavalry, General Randal's original regiment, discovered a host of obstacles to an orderly advance. Lt. Col. Henry G. Hall noticed that his men "were exhausted to the last degree by the loss of sleep, lack of food, the heavy morning's march through the rain, and worst of all by wading and struggling through mud [m]ire and water just as they were approaching the battleground. They were discouraged by the bad condition of their guns [caused by the rain], their inability to see the enemy well and effectively assault them in their positions. They were also dismayed by the rapidity with which their comrades fell around them." Some of them stopped and huddled together behind a few dead trees in the field: "all except the one nearest to each tree were more exposed to the enemy's cross-fire than they would have been in open lines," Hall observed. The brigade surgeon noted another trauma in Randal's brigade that day. After a temporary withdrawal, the men resumed the attack, but "when they again advanced they found several of our wounded who had their throats cut from ear to ear by the Negroes."[29]

All in all, the Greyhounds had run up against an impossible task this time. Lt. Col. Robert S. Gould, commander of the 6th Texas Cavalry Battalion, fought his men alongside those of Hall and the rest of Randal's brigade, and he struggled with the same problems. In the advance, he wrote, "many men lost their shoes in the mud. Others fell, and their arms became wet and useless." Many of those who managed to keep their weapons dry fired so often that they used up their forty rounds of ammunition. Their inability to see the Federals behind the breastworks in the opposite tree line and their exposure in the open farm field, especially when they drew within the last hundred yards, made the Greyhounds pause. "It seemed to me suicidal to stand in the open ground at that distance, fighting a sheltered foe," Gould wrote. "I remember saying to Lieut. Goodwyn that the Yankees would fight us in that way all day." Minutes later, Gould's horse was hit twice, and Gould himself was shot through the leg a few inches above the knee.[30]

To the left and right of Randal's brigade, Waul's and Scurry's Texans were in similar predicaments. Corporal Blessington, slightly wounded at Pleasant Hill, suffered another injury, a minor head wound, on the Confederate right. Not far away, Sgt. John H. Thiehoff of Blessington's regiment (the 16th Infantry) was more fortunate. He boasted that he "was never wounded, but had my canteen shot off me at Jenkins' Ferry." Col. Overton Young of the 12th Infantry, in Waul's brigade on the left, was shot through his right wrist. One of Young's men, Pvt. William Elisha Stoker of Coffeeville in Upshur County—the husband who had written his wife in 1862 that "if I ever get the chance to come [home], I am a comeing like a feather in the wind"—dropped into the mud with a wound to the chest. A relative in the army had the sad task of informing Stoker's wife and daughter Priscilla: "Brother Elisha was shot just above the right nipple, the bullet coming out under his right shoulder." Everywhere—left, center, and right—Greyhounds were slumping into the water, shot down by mostly unseen foes.[31]

The division suffered its three most costly casualties of the entire war within one hour at Jenkins' Ferry. All three brigade commanders were hit by rifle fire. As usual, Generals Waul, Randal, and Scurry were in the midst of their men, waving and shouting them forward. Their physical courage had served them well in the past, and they doubtless hoped to draw their troops forward again by sharing in their peril. On the left, General Waul was hit in the arm. The ball broke the bone and caused considerable bleeding, but Waul remained in charge of his brigade until the battle ended. Then, "being much weakened from loss of blood, I withdrew from the field," he reported. He never again commanded his men. After a long convalescence on his Texas plantation, he resigned from the army.[32]

In the center brigade of Walker's line, the young general Horace Randal, West Point classmate of James E. B. Stuart (who would be mortally wounded twelve days after Randal), crumpled when a bullet hit him in the abdomen. Randal's brother Leonard helped remove him to the rear and held the wounded man's head in his lap while the ambulance carried him to a field hospital. The general's wife of less than two years, who usually accompanied him, was only a mile away when her husband was wounded, and she doubtless rushed to his side when she heard the bad news. General Randal lingered for a while but died two days later. On the right of Walker's line, General Scurry—hero of the New Mexico campaign in 1862 and the recapture of Galveston in 1863—fell with a similar wound: a minie ball pierced his lower trunk, traveling through his body from side to side. Scurry refused to be taken off the field, and he remained conscious on the battlefield for more than an hour, inquiring repeatedly about the battle. A wound into the body cavity was almost always fatal in the Civil War, and "Dirty Neck Bill" Scurry died the next day. Thus, the Greyhound Division lost three of its four generals on the same field on the same day. The state of Texas later named two counties in West Texas in honor of Randal and Scurry.[33]

The loss of their commanders introduced some confusion and hesitation into the center and right brigades. Subordinate officers had to be elevated to higher commands, and that created a domino effect of replacements, down to the regimental level. In the noise and smoke and rain, some officers were not even aware for a while that they were supposed to be heading larger units, and that left some of the men in the ranks milling around in the water, ducking Federal fire, and glancing to the rear. In the absence of strong leadership, the advance against the Federals lost coordination and momentum. Indeed, some of Randal's regimental officers could not prevent their units from withdrawing on the mere rumor of such orders. After an hour of inconclusive charges by Walker's brigades and countercharges by the Federals, General Steele took advantage of a lull in the fighting and began withdrawing his regiments across the pontoon bridge. The Federals left scores of burning wagons and hundreds of their dead and wounded on the watery battleground. A soldier in the 18th Iowa was chagrined: "The destruction of property was immense; officers and men lost all they had except what was on their backs. The loss of Government property is almost beyond calculation. Our division left [Little Rock] with 300 wagons and [returned] with three."[34]

For their part, the fatigued Confederates were glad to see their enemies leave. The last few hours had demonstrated that further fighting would be pointless. Besides, the Texans had nothing left to give. General Walker noted that "the exhaustion of the Confederates was so complete that after the retreat of the enemy the men threw themselves down for repose in the mud and water where they stood." The hard-riding 8th Missouri Cavalry did follow the Federals to the river, but the horsemen were too few to do anything but chase a few retreating skirmishers. Once the last Federal was on the other side of the Saline, a rearguard used bayonets to cut holes in the rubber pontoons and swung axes to splinter the wooden frames. General Steele no longer had enough mules or wagons to haul the pontoons, and he preferred to destroy the bridge rather than allow the Confederates to cross over it and continue the pursuit.[35]

The grisly scenes that followed any sizeable Civil War battle were different at Jenkins' Ferry only because of the swampy environment. Hospital and burial details had to slosh through water to gather wounded men and corpses, both Federal and Confederate. Some of the dead were doubtless men who had been wounded and then died of drowning or exposure in the cold water. An Arkansas soldier found the body of "a large portly" captain from Texas, lying on his back with his head in a pool of water. He was dressed in a new gray uniform and wearing new boots with a Texas star on the front. The Arkansas man raised the officer's head out of the water, laid it on a chunk of wood, and covered his face with the Texan's broad-brimmed hat. When the Good Samaritan came by the same spot somewhat later, he found the captain's body stripped of the new boots, the hat, and the uniform. A soldier in the 17th Texas saw "one of our men on his back shot through the head with an open letter before his eyes. I suppose that the letter was from his wife or some other dear one."[36]

A captain in the 13th Texas Cavalry went back onto the battlefield with some of his men to find wounded comrades. "All along the road we were constantly meeting ambulances and litters with wounded men coming to the rear showing how absolutely the field had been contested," he wrote in his diary. Along the same muddy path, the captain noted other signs of the coarsening effects of war: "Here I saw what I suppose is common to most battle-fields, hundreds of men engaged in pillaging the burning wagons[.] trunks, boxes and chests were soon broken open and their contents rifled, for 2 miles the road was lined with cast off plunder of the retreating foe." Corporal Blessington walked over the battlefield the next day and remarked on "the newly dug graves, surrounded by water."

Not all the dead had been buried, though, and Blessington gagged at the sights and smells: "The effluvium from the swollen, festering forms was too horrible for human endurance. No conception of the imagination, no power of human language, could do justice to such a horrible scene."[37]

General Steele had put about four thousand men into the fight at Jenkins' Ferry. Smith had committed about five or six thousand, but not all at once because there was too little space in the swampy bottom to fight all of them simultaneously.[38] Some Federal units crossed the river before or during the battle and saw no action. The Confederates held much of their cavalry and most of their artillery in reserve, mainly because there was no room to get them into the struggle. Steele's beleaguered army lost about six to eight hundred men, hundreds of wagons and teams, and tons of supplies in the battle, and in their haste the Federals left many of their wounded and dead behind. Smith lost at least eight hundred dead and wounded. The hard marches from Pleasant Hill to Jenkins' Ferry had left some of the Greyhounds behind, so not all of them were present at Jenkins' Ferry. Walker's division, probably numbering no more than two thousand (if that many) on the day of the battle, suffered more than the Arkansas or Missouri divisions: 84 killed, 360 wounded, and 3 missing, a casualty rate of almost 25 percent. Of the twelve thousand Texans who had first signed up for service in late 1861 and early 1862, only about 1,500 were present to huddle around smoky campfires on the night of Jenkins' Ferry.[39]

General Walker, an accomplished division commander in Robert E. Lee's eastern army before going west and a veteran of Malvern Hill and Antietam, was certainly proud of his trans-Mississippi soldiers. In his memoirs, he wrote that his division, "composed entirely of Texans, from the 13th. of March to the 30th. of April, or forty eight days, marched six hundred and twenty miles and fought three pitched battles." The retreat from Simmesport to Mansfield had been about 270 miles, according to modern highway maps, and from Pleasant Hill to Jenkins' Ferry, the Texans had walked another 286 miles at least. Because their exact route is not known for some stretches and because modern highways tend to follow straighter paths than nineteenth-century dirt roads, the actual distance may have been closer to Walker's estimate of 620 miles than to the present approximation of 556 miles. In any case, the Greyhounds had performed an extraordinary feat of endurance by marching several hundred miles and fighting three bloody engagements from mid-March to late April. Many years later, when the surviving Texans were silver-haired old men surrounded by grandchildren, the seven weeks from Simmesport to Jenkins' Ferry would remain vivid in their memories.[40]

As usual, soldiers on both sides claimed victory. Evidence from such interested parties—and parties armed with no historical perspective on the events—is perhaps not the best foundation for an evaluation of the engagement in the swamps of the Saline River. Federals boasted of a victory because they had held their ground and thrown back Smith's assaults. Confederates asserted their own success because they captured the battlefield and took possession of much of Steele's wagon train and many of his dead and wounded. Tactically, neither side could run the other off the battlefield, and the officers and men of both armies fought well under extremely difficult conditions. Considering their perilous position—backs up against the swollen river—the Federals succeeded tactically by saving themselves from disaster. The Confederates, hoping to smash Steele's army to bits or capture most of it, managed only to damage it and send it limping back to Little Rock.

Strategically, though, this was clearly a Confederate success. General Smith's purpose was to turn away a threat to Trans-Mississippi headquarters, war plants, and the rich farms of northwest Louisiana and East Texas. Steele's goal had been to join the other Federal army on the outskirts of Shreveport and break up the trans-Mississippi Confederacy. His expedition had been hounded by aggressive Confederate cavalry, which prevented easy foraging. Steele was forced to take refuge in Camden and then suffered serious losses at Poison Spring and Marks' Mills. When most of the Confederate infantry from Mansfield and Pleasant Hill converged on his earthworks at Camden, and when he learned of Banks's defeat, the Federal general gave up on his aim to capture Shreveport. The campaign ended with Steele's battered army, shorn of almost all its supplies and wagons, nowhere near his original objective. In fact, his army never got closer than one hundred road miles to Shreveport but lost about 2,800 soldiers, 635 government wagons, and 2,500 mules in the attempt. Judged on a strategic level, Steele failed and Smith succeeded. General Taylor would probably add that Smith could have had about the same success if he had only waited. In Taylor's opinion, Steele would have retreated anyway once he learned of Banks's fate. The Louisiana general believed to the end of his life that it had not been necessary to divert his infantry from the pursuit of Banks down the Red River valley. Pres. Jefferson Davis agreed with Taylor and later scolded Smith for allowing Banks's large army to escape intact and fight another day east of the Mississippi River.[41]

The soggy, worn-out Confederates remained near the battlefield for two days, burying the dead, carrying the wounded to hospitals, and resting. On May 2 the Texas Division marched back to Tulip, eight miles to the rear, to pay homage at the funeral of General Scurry, who died the night after the battle. Upon their return to camp, they learned that General Randal had died only an hour after Scurry's funeral. Randal's body was buried in Tulip with military honors the next day. On May 3 the whole army was directed back to Camden, a town better able to handle logistical and hospital duties than the villages near Jenkins' Ferry. The division crossed the Ouachita River on a ferry near Camden and placed many of its sick and wounded in hospitals and homes around the town. The women of Camden, Corporal Blessington wrote, stepped forward to help and were untiring in their efforts to relieve the suffering of the soldiers.[42]

Now that Steele's army was no longer a threat to Trans-Mississippi headquarters, General Smith finally agreed to send the infantry, including the Texas Division, down to General Taylor for his pursuit of General Banks's army, still penned up against the Red River. In fact, Banks's army and Admiral Porter's fleet were stuck fast at Alexandria because the heavy boats of the navy could not get through the low water at the falls just above the city. Thus, the Confederate infantry in Arkansas began a race of more than three hundred miles to reach Taylor before Banks and Porter could disentangle themselves from the uncooperative Red River country. The Greyhounds left Camden on May 9 and were joined that night by the Arkansas and Missouri divisions that had fought with them at Pleasant Hill and Jenkins' Ferry. Earlier on the same day, the first few ships of Porter's squadron made it past the falls at Alexandria with the help of wing dams that raised the river level slightly.[43]

Two days later the Confederate infantry column crossed the state line into Louisiana under another soaking rain. The next day, Col. Richard Waterhouse of the 19th Infantry was elevated to command Scurry's brigade, and Maj. Robert P. Maclay, a graduate of the U.S. Military Academy (Class of 1840) and chief of Walker's staff, was named to head Randal's brigade. The wounded General Waul remained the nominal commander of his brigade until a few weeks later, when Col. Wilburn King of the 18th Infantry succeeded him. King, a Georgia native who had begun the war as a private in the Missouri State Guard and later served as a drill instructor in the early days of the Texas regiments, had worked his way up through the ranks and was just recovering from a serious wound at Mansfield. Maclay, Waterhouse, and King were all respectable officers, but the division could not readily compensate for the loss of accomplished and popular leaders like Randal, Scurry, and Waul.[44]

On May 14—one day after Porter scraped his last riverboat over the falls of the Red River—the Greyhounds marched south through the little town of Mount Lebanon, 125 road miles northwest of Alexandria. A few miles farther down the road (present-day Louisiana State Highway 154), the men shuffled by a spot along the roadside that would become infamous in the history of crime in the United States. Seventy years later, almost to the day, two other Texans—Clyde Barrow and Bonnie Parker—would be ambushed at that site and shot down in a hailstorm of 167 bullets by Texas Rangers and other law officers. Two days after General Walker's infantry marched through Mount Lebanon, Smith ordered the Arkansas and Missouri troops to reverse course and return to Camden. General Banks had finally extricated his expedition from Alexandria, and Smith saw no reason now to send all his infantry to Taylor. This left the Greyhounds to proceed alone. Hoping to join Taylor before Banks could withdraw his army to complete safety across the Atchafalaya and Mississippi Rivers, General Walker pushed his men hard. They marched every day from May 8 to May 22 and averaged nearly seventeen miles per day over the last two weeks of the journey. Surgeon Ned Cade of Maclay's (formerly Randal's) brigade believed that even the Greyhounds were near the end of their endurance: "Our officials appear to think that our division is made out of iron. No rest; no rest; for two long months we have marched day and night and fought 3 severe battles. It would almost make your heart bleed could you see the haggard and worn looks of our men."[45]

While the Texans shuffled southward, General Taylor did everything he could to delay the retreat of the Federal army and navy, all the while looking north for signs of Walker's division. "Like 'Sister Ann' from her watch tower, day after day we strained our eyes to see the dust of our approaching comrades from the north bank of the Red," Taylor wrote in his memoirs.[46] "Not a camp follower among us but knew that the arrival of our men from the North would give us the great prize in sight." Confederate cavalry on both sides of the river harassed the Federal rear guard and fleet. On May 16 Taylor drew up his small army on the flat, open countryside at Mansura, between Fort DeRussy and Simmesport. For four hours the Confederate artillery and cavalry managed to hold Banks's much larger army at bay, but once the Federals poured forward en masse, Taylor withdrew to fight another day. Two days later the Louisiana planter-general made a stinging attack on the rear guard of the Federal army at Yellow Bayou, just a few miles west of Simmesport. Once again, numbers told, and Taylor, frustrated at lost opportunities, had to back off and watch the blue army march away to safety across the Atchafalaya River. The Texas Division was still five days away.[47]

Taylor vented his anger once more to Smith's adjutant: "Nothing but the withdrawal of Walker's division from me has prevented the capture of Banks' army and the destruction of Porter's fleet. I feel bitterly about this, because my army has been robbed of the just measure of its glory and the country of the most brilliant and complete success of the war." Although Taylor's frustration undoubtedly magnified the importance of the missing reinforcements in his mind, still, his comments about the Texas Division revealed his great respect for its fighting qualities. The Greyhounds, he wrote later, "held every position entrusted to them, carried every position in their front, and displayed a constancy and valor worthy of the Guards at Inkermann or Lee's veterans in the Wilderness!" High praise from a man who had marched with Stonewall Jackson in the Shenandoah Valley and knew a thing or two about good soldiering.[48]

On May 22, two days after the Federal army slipped across the Atchafalaya River, General Walker's Texans swung into Pineville across the Red River from Alexandria. Too late to pitch into the rear of Banks's army, the Greyhounds instead melted down into camps at Pineville for two weeks, drilling and recuperating from their recent ordeals. The rapid march from the Jenkins' Ferry battlefield had added another 374 miles to the Greyhound odometer, and the Texans had little strength or energy remaining by the time they reached Pineville. In seventy days they had marched, often without food or tents, about 930 miles and fought three pitched battles. This was the equivalent, roughly speaking, of a Federal army marching from Washington, D.C., to Memphis, Tennessee, and fighting along the way, all in ten weeks. It was one of the more amazing physical feats of the American Civil War.[49]

# CHAPTER 13

# The Breakup

In the most intense and eventful season of the war for the Texas Division—the spring of 1864—the Greyhounds accomplished what many of them had envisioned from the beginning as their main purpose: to defend their families and homes and communities from Yankee armies. The Texas foot soldiers played a central role in turning back General Banks's grand Red River campaign at Mansfield and Pleasant Hill, and they helped to chase General Steele's army back toward Little Rock. They paid a terrible price for their success—about 1,450 men killed, wounded, or missing at Mansfield, Pleasant Hill, and Jenkins' Ferry, or about 36 percent of the four thousand who began the campaign in March.[1]

The dead included some of the best of them. Two of their favorite brigade commanders (Scurry and Randal) and some of their ablest regimental and company officers never marched again with the long Greyhound line. Capt. Theophilus Perry, the lawyer and patient husband from Marshall, left behind a nervous wife who had trembled at his fate from the beginning. Capt. Elijah Petty of Bastrop, another lawyer, never saw his beloved wife and children—his "little rats"— again. Sgt. John Samuel Bryan of Collin County, the man who had proclaimed his intention to remarry his wife at the end of his service, never got the chance. He was laid in his grave near Mansfield in April. Pvt. William Elisha Stoker of Upshur County, who had promised to come home "like a feather in the wind," was instead lowered into a muddy grave near Jenkins' Ferry. These losses and hundreds of others weighed heavily on the men and sent a wave of lamentations across Texas when the sad news arrived.[2]

But the Greyhounds had known all along that there would be a price to pay. The high price had bought considerable benefits. A. J. Smith's ten thousand western veterans would have joined Sherman's spring campaign in Georgia, but their detour up the Red River kept them out of that operation, much to Sherman's annoyance. Thousands of other Federal soldiers would have united in an offensive against Mobile, but their fruitless journey toward Shreveport delayed the Alabama campaign for nearly a year. That freed fifteen thousand Confederates in the Deep South to buttress the army opposing Sherman in Georgia. In the end, these changes in troop dispositions north of Atlanta—ten thousand fewer Federals and fifteen thousand more Confederates—may have lengthened the war by weeks or months. For the Greyhounds, though, their success in shielding Texas from the enemy was the sweetest result of the Red River campaign. That memory remained with them for the rest of their lives.[3]

When they finally were allowed to rest for a while in Pineville in late May, some of the Texans looked back over recent events and celebrated the upward surge of Confederate fortunes. Reports from Virginia indicated that Lee's Army of Northern Virginia had defeated Grant's Federals, and every Greyhound could boast that he had helped to save the Trans-Mississippi Department from Yankee marauders. Capt. Volney Ellis of the 12th Texas Infantry assured his wife, "I think now we have greater cause of hope and confidence than ever, for up to this time the success of our armies has been almost universal." Even allowing for the usual hyperbole, morale was high among the Greyhounds in the late spring of 1864.[4]

What the Texans did not know was that they had fired their last shot of the war. They would never again scramble into line of battle and nervously survey the ground between them and the enemy. In fact, they would see no more Yankees until the war was over. While the federal government focused its attention on the war east of the Mississippi River after the spring of 1864, the Greyhounds were left on the other side, marching from one supposed threatened spot to another and building defenses against invasions that would never come.

From late May until late July, the division moved from one camp to another in the area near Alexandria—first down the Red River's left bank, then back upstream past Pineville for a few miles, always searching for a good, dry campground with plenty of water. On the morning of June 17, about fifteen miles north of Alexandria, the men learned that their beloved General Walker had been reassigned to command the District of West Louisiana. Walker replaced General Taylor, whose sharp and often intemperate criticisms of his superior, Gen. E. Kirby Smith, made his further service under Smith inconvenient, if not impossible. Taylor would soon be ordered to command the Department of East Louisiana, Mississippi, and Alabama, which would require him to cross the Mississippi River and leave his old army behind.[5]

The Greyhounds were deeply disappointed by Walker's reassignment. Halting voices and trembling lips marked the farewell ceremony at midday on the 18th. Walker had led them through every fight they had ever engaged in, had celebrated victories and lamented losses with the men in the ranks, and had shown the Greyhounds that he was one of them, leading them and sharing in their miseries rather than ordering them about from the safety and comfort of a commander's tent in the rear. Besides all that, one captain wrote, the general knew how to use his men wisely: Walker "has more *brains* than every Military Commander put together that's in the Trans Miss Dept." Considering all these qualities, Corporal Blessington was not surprised: "No wonder the men loved him and disliked to part with him."[6]

The officer who replaced Walker as division commander was Wilburn H. King, just turned twenty-five years old. The Georgia native had joined the Missouri State Guard as a private, fought at Wilson's Creek in 1861, and then later joined the 18th Texas Infantry as a private in early 1862. Because he had some little battlefield and camp experience—more than most new recruits, anyway—he had served as a drill instructor for the 18th Infantry, and the Texans elected him major of the regiment before they left for Arkansas. He rose from major to lieutenant colonel to colonel of the 18th Infantry by the summer of 1863, and he led his regiment in the Battle of Bayou Bourbeau. Wounded at Mansfield, he was promoted to brigadier general by Edmund Kirby Smith shortly afterward (although the Confederate Congress never acted on this promotion), and he led Waul's old brigade while Waul was recuperating from his Jenkins' Ferry wound in Texas. Trans-Mississippi headquarters considered King a temporary replacement as division commander, probably because of his youth and lack of formal military training. The Texas Division that King headed now numbered about thirty-three hundred men, less than one-third their original strength but about twice the number who had huddled in the cold rain after Jenkins' Ferry. Many of the sick and wounded and exhausted men who had fallen out of the ranks during the recent campaign had returned to their old campfires by mid-June, so the Greyhounds could now count enough men to fill a good-sized brigade. Unfortunately for King, he commanded them during one of their most serious crises of the war—the desertions and near mutiny of late summer 1864.[7]

The trouble started in early July when General Smith received orders from Gen. Braxton Bragg, President Davis's military adviser, to send most of the Trans-Mississippi infantry to the east side of the Mississippi River. Federal movements (and rumors of movements) toward Mobile, Atlanta, and other vulnerable cities prompted Confederate officials to demand reinforcements from the Trans-Mississippi Department, now no longer threatened by Banks or Steele. These initial orders were followed very quickly by a whole stream of directives to Smith instructing him to send all of Taylor's infantry (Walker's and Polignac's divisions at least) and "such other infantry as can be spared" to reinforce beleaguered comrades east of the Mississippi. General Taylor, now commander of the Confederate department on the other side of the river, would lead his old infantry after it crossed.[8]

Before leaving the Trans-Mississippi Department for his new command, Taylor made preliminary arrangements to transfer his former soldiers to the east side of the Mississippi. He worried over their transportation to threatened cities once they were on the other side. He demanded back pay for the men ordered eastward. He coordinated the movement of troops and pontoon boats for the passage across the Mississippi, and he tried to organize a diversion to distract enemy attention from the point of crossing (downriver from Vicksburg, upriver from Natchez, and east of Harrisonburg, near present-day Waterproof, Louisiana). While Taylor busied himself with these practical measures, his counterparts in the Federal army and navy, already aware of Confederate plans to cross the river, were scrambling to prevent any such movement. General Sherman had suspected such a ploy as early as June 6, and Federal commanders along the river were informed of the Confederate plan by July 24. Immediately they began reassigning ironclads and gunboats to take up stations at various points along the river below Vicksburg, and army patrols were ordered to search the west bank of the river for boats that might be used in the crossing.[9]

The Greyhounds were at first unaware of these moves and countermoves among the generals, although they of course had heard rumors. But few men put much stock in camp rumors by mid-1864. They were just happy to rest and recuperate for a while. In the last week of July, the Texans marched from the vicinity of Alexandria northeastward over ground they well knew to the neighborhood of Harrisonburg. Corporal Blessington noted that the river town "looked rather the worse for wear. But few houses were left standing in the place. The town was destroyed by the Federals when they took possession of the place [during the Red River campaign]." The regiments marched through Harrisonburg and then spread out in the low country just west of the Mississippi River in early August. The men did not yet realize that they were being placed there for the crossing of the river.[10]

Not until dress parade on August 16 did the men in the ranks hear about the proposed move across the Mississippi River, and many of them instantly made up their minds not to go. Their wives and children and parents would once again be vulnerable to Yankee invasions if left unprotected on the west side of the river. The Texans had signed up mainly to protect the world they knew before the war, and they now saw themselves as the only barrier between that world and chaos. They had seen the destruction and disarray in the wake of Federal armies in Louisiana and Arkansas—burned houses and barns, fallow fields without fences, dilapidated farms stripped of people and animals, slaves running free, free people running as refugees. No, it just would not do to leave Texas to the mercies of the Yankees, and many members of the Greyhound Division dug in their heels and threatened to desert rather than cross the river. They were not afraid of fighting, they said. They had fought from Milliken's Bend to Jenkins' Ferry. They were not refusing to sleep in the cold and eat inadequate rations and go unpaid for many months at a time—they were used to that, too. They were not abandoning the war at all, in fact, but they would not cross the river.[11]

W. W. Shelton of the 19th Infantry was downcast upon hearing the orders, even though he admitted he would probably go along with the majority and cross the Mississippi: "we all regret it verry much leaving our own country and homes to exchange it for a part where we cannot hear from home nor get home and leave our homes unprotected for we verry well know that our Division and Polgnac's was the main spring of keeping the feds out of our country last spring[.]" Shelton had no blame for those men threatening to desert rather than cross. "[I]f I was in some of their situations I would not cross neither and that is a helpless family at home and never been at home on furlough to see them," he assured his father. "[B]ut being as I am a single man and just from home I shall not make no great to do about it." The next day, August 18, Shelton woke to find that some of the men had already carried out their threats: "near all of my neighbor boys left last knight[.] there was 14 left the company[.] there was five went out of my mess and one of the five by reflection came back about midnight." Shelton made it plain that his absent comrades were neither cowards nor unpatriotic, and they had not given up on the war. "[T]he boys did not leave with the expectation of keeping out of the service but to report to some other command," he explained.[12]

Not all the Greyhounds were as understanding as Shelton. Capt. Virgil Rabb of the 16th Infantry, a livestock farmer back in Fayette County, was disgusted by the behavior of the fugitives. "These grand rascals that have left only wanted an excuse to leave. The last one of them ought to be *shot*," he fumed. The captain doubtless remembered that he had been ready to cross the river and fight in Virginia when his newly created regiment was waiting for orders back in 1862. What was good enough in 1862 was good enough in 1864.[13] Even a four-square patriot like Rabb preferred to stay west of the river, though: "For my part, if they want us to go over I shall go cheerfully, though I would much rather Soldier on this side." David Ray of the 16th Cavalry, the Grayson County schoolteacher, estimated that about 450 men had stolen away from camp in the week following the announcement of the crossing: "about 50 from this Brigade [Waterhouse's, formerly Scurry's], 200 from Wauls and about the same from Maclays [Randal's]. we only lost one from this regt[.] another started but was caught, but there are several in the guardhouse for talking about it from our Regt. they have a great many in the guardhouse some with irons. they have handcuffs on some and what they call stiff knee on others which is done by putting a ring around the ankle and another around the thigh with a bar of iron extending from one ring to the other." Apparently, Captain Rabb was not the only officer who took desertion, or even talk of desertion, seriously.[14]

Maj. Robert S. Gould, commander of a dismounted cavalry battalion in Maclay's (formerly Randal's) brigade, found himself caught in the middle of the Greyhound uprising. If anyone could talk this disturbance to a peaceful conclusion, Gould was the man. An accomplished attorney in Leon County before the war, he had been a member of the Texas secession convention and would later serve as chief justice of the Texas Supreme Court and as one of the first two professors of law (along with Oran M. Roberts, former colonel of the 11th Infantry) at the University of Texas. Late one night, after scores of Texans walked defiantly through camp and invited all who refused to cross the river to follow them back to Texas, General Maclay ordered Gould to take his battalion and Edward Clark's 14th Infantry, about five hundred men, to track down the fugitives and bring them back, dead or alive. Gould led his column out on the road toward Texas at about 1 A.M. and soon came upon a few of the deserters who had had second thoughts and were returning to their units. The major ordered one of the sheepish fugitives to lead him to the others, who had left the main road and were resting for a few hours about seven miles from camp. Gould and his men found their assignment disagreeable, but they pressed ahead.

> When we were getting in the vicinity I halted, and had the men to load up. Never have I seen men so silent. Scarce a whisper was heard. The men felt, and I felt, that it was a dreadful alternative ahead of us. We feared that we should be compelled to shed the blood of our fellow soldiers. For myself, I am free to confess that I thought my chances of surviving this night were not worth much. I did not doubt that some of the desperate men who had deserted would single me out as the first man to be killed. I scarcely knew how far I could depend on my own men.[15]

When the nervous pursuers approached within one hundred yards of the renegades, Gould formed a line of battle and sent a small cavalry detachment around to the rear of the fugitives to cut off their escape route. Gould's adjutant then went forward to inform the men that they were surrounded and to urge them to return to camp. The sullen Texans refused to budge, so Gould himself went forward to address them. "He gathered them around him and made them the most earnest speech of his life," a neighbor from Leon County recalled. "He presented them with all sorts of reasons why they s[h]ould return, and especially pointed out the disgrace that must follow such an act of insubordination." A long moment of silence followed the major's exhortation, and then someone in the darkness said, "Boys, let's go back." Gould's detachment and the temporary deserters, about one hundred of the latter, then backtracked through the dark, humid low-lands and reached camp about 8 A.M. "The men whom I brought back were at once placed in arrest, but I am not sure that any of them were seriously punished," Gould remembered. Looking back on these events after the war, the major could smile and feel that he had done a good thing: "That speech made in the night, in the dark, in the woods, made with so much depending on the result, was, I presume, the most earnest of my life. I have always been prouder of that night, of the conduct of the battalion that night, and of its results, than of any other single act of the war."[16]

Although the men who deserted (even temporarily) and threatened to desert attracted much attention, the great majority of the Greyhounds stayed around their campfires, continued to drill, and kept their thoughts to themselves. Most of them doubtless preferred to remain west of the river, where they could protect their families and communities—and maybe even win a furlough occasionally—but they made no trouble about the orders to cross and indeed made preparations to fight in Alabama and Georgia. One old soldier and skilled complainer grumbled that "some few are anxious to cross—such as have no connection on this side, and some few young and foolish boys." But young and foolish boys were not the only ones willing to fight on the other side. The disciplined Captain Rabb informed his mother that he would "go cheerfully." James Armstrong of the 14th Infantry adapted rather smoothly to the idea of the movement: "I feel confident & hopeful God can preserve me as well on the other side of the father of waters as on this." Volney Ellis, adjutant of the 12th Infantry, said later that he "would have regretted crossing the river, but I have no doubt but that it would have been for the best, and I wish we had gone across. I am almost willing to make any sacrifice to end this war."[17]

Approximately seven of every eight Greyhounds remained in their camps and did not desert upon hearing the orders to cross the Mississippi. About half of those who did abandon the division changed their minds within a few hours or a few days and returned to their units. Most of the other half straggled back over the next few weeks, some after taking quick unofficial furloughs home to Texas, no doubt. They were citizen soldiers, not professional warriors, and their discipline did not extend to unquestioning obedience to orders. On the other hand, they were soldiers after all, and they did consider themselves a shield for their families and communities, so most of them stuck with the division, and even most of those who did not stick did straggle back. The story of the Texas Division in August 1864 is the story of the citizen soldier in the Civil War in microcosm: the men pulled and strained against unwelcome orders, but the great majority of them did their duty because it made sense to them as citizens.[18]

Ironically, the entire, noisy uproar peaked in intensity at about the same moment that Confederate authorities abandoned the whole idea of crossing the infantry. General Taylor arrived at Harrisonburg on the night of August 16 and discovered that the cross-river movement would be even more difficult than he had anticipated. At first he decided to push on despite the obstacles, but then he learned that the Federals were aware of the plan and had been busy doing everything possible to thwart it: they "had moved their iron-clads from below, stationing them between Vicksburg and the mouth of Red River at intervals of about twelve miles, with their other gun-boats constantly patrolling between those stations, and not more than four hours ever elapsed without a gun-boat passing" every point along the river. The Confederate crossing would take days, not hours. Once again, the Greyhounds' old nemesis, the Federal river fleet, played a major role in the Texans' war.[19]

Not only did the crossing now appear impossible; the very news of it was stirring hundreds of foot soldiers to desert. Taylor knew that their determination to protect their homes was the driving force behind such rash behavior, but he identified four problems that intensified their discontent. The lack of pay for the previous twelve months for many regiments made it virtually impossible for the men to provide for their families, even if all they had was inflated Confederate currency. Moreover, many of the regular field officers in the division—the generals and colonels and majors—were on leave after the recent hard campaigning, and their usual influence with their men was therefore absent as well. The recent changes in brigade and regimental officers, necessitated by battle losses, had elevated new men, sometimes unknown to the soldiers, to positions of command before the new colonels and generals could establish trust with their units. And a problem that is too often overlooked in discussions of morale—boredom with inactivity—allowed idle minds to conjure up all sorts of mischief.[20]

General Taylor bowed to facts, abandoned the whole idea of the transfer, and sent his thoughts to Trans-Mississippi headquarters on August 18 and 19. For once Smith and Taylor agreed, and on the 22nd, Smith's chief of staff ordered Taylor to suspend the cross-river operations and send Walker's and Polignac's infantry divisions to Monroe. Headquarters also relieved Taylor of his duties west of the river and cleared him to cross the river and assume his new office on the other side. Rumors continued to circulate in division camps that the transfer would take place, and the Greyhounds remained skittish for another week or two, but the great crossing was finished before it began. The dream of using Trans-Mississippi infantry to bolster outnumbered southern armies in Alabama, Georgia, and Tennessee persisted in the minds of Confederate leaders east of the Mississippi, including Pres. Jefferson Davis, all through the autumn of 1864 and even into early 1865. Meanwhile, Federal officials and Unionist newspapers continued to worry about just such an event. But General Smith was not eager to give up the main body of his infantry, and U.S. ironclads and gunboats would not have allowed it in any case. The Greyhounds would serve out the last few months of the war crisscrossing the territory they had defended from the beginning, Louisiana and Arkansas.[21]

Unknown to the Greyhounds, while the Trans-Mississippi high command was making arrangements to put them across the river, General Smith was also settling on a successor to General Walker as commander of the Texas Division. (Wilburn H. King had been a temporary placeholder since June.) Maj. Gen. John H. Forney, a graduate of the U.S. Military Academy (Class of 1852), had fought at First Manassas, had been wounded in skirmishing in northern Virginia, had commanded the Department of Southern Alabama and West Florida in 1862–1863, and had led a division during the Vicksburg campaign. With the finest military education available to Americans and with considerable battlefield and command experience, he appeared to be a man capable of leading the Greyhounds. At age thirty-five he was also vigorous enough to handle the physical demands of war in the trans-Mississippi.[22]

On the other hand, Forney harbored a strain of waywardness that later engendered disdain among many of his subordinates—he was a relentless pursuer of women. This tendency manifested itself long before he took command of the Greyhounds. On a visit to Jefferson Barracks near St. Louis in 1856, the young army officer revealed his capacity for reckless behavior. One of Forney's West Point classmates and a future Confederate general himself, Henry Harrison Walker, arranged an unusual and risky liaison for his friend.

> Old Forney was down from Fort Snelling [Minnesota Territory]. . . . he expressed a wish to shag something. I told him I thought I could gratify him. I had been to see the widow several times and knew exactly how to get in. I told Forney how to act and how to imitate my voice. He goes over, finds a window open, jumps in and undressed himself before the widow woke up. He stayed with her all night, saying as little as possible, while she, told him every secret I had. In the morning she woke up and discovered her mistake. She immediately kicked him out and covered herself up head and ears until he had dressed and gone. This has brought her wrath down on me and she reviles me for all the rascals in the world.[23]

Forney's personal habits offended some of his men, but his personality offended virtually all of them. Indeed, he was known in the Confederate army, to superiors and subordinates alike, as an unpleasant man, and he had a reputation for harsh and unreasonable discipline. When the higher officers in the Texas Division heard rumors of Forney's assignment, they went straight to Walker (then commanding the District of West Louisiana) and asked him to do something to change Smith's mind. Walker warned headquarters that the mixture of Forney and the Greyhounds meant trouble, and Smith even considered placing Walker back in command of his old division when it crossed the Mississippi. But Walker had little hope for the cross-river operation and preferred to remain district commander in West Louisiana. Thus, Forney was appointed to lead the Texas Division on August 8 or 9 despite forecasts of turmoil. He left Shreveport to join his new command near Harrisonburg on August 12, but the uncertain status of the river crossing and the possibility that Walker might return to the Greyhounds apparently kept Forney from assuming his office until early September, after the crossing had been abandoned and while the division was marching north toward Monroe.[24]

The Texans were not at all enthusiastic when Forney and his staff joined them on the road to Monroe. Even Corporal Blessington, who seldom had a negative word for anything connected with the division, complained of Forney's new and more rigorous regulations and admitted that the general "was a strict disciplinarian." Surgeon Edwin Becton of the 22nd Infantry wrote his wife a few weeks after Forney arrived in camp that the general "has not made the most favorable impression." Even several months later, the men were still unhappy. John Simmons of the 22nd Infantry grumbled in March that "there are but few in the division that like Forney. He is a tyrant if there is any." Despite the friction between the martinet and the Greyhounds, Forney remained in command of the division until its last few days.[25]

The Texas Division along with Polignac's division left their camps in the Mississippi River lowlands near Harrisonburg on August 30, bound north for Monroe and then eighty-five miles farther north to Monticello, Arkansas, rumored to be the target of an impending Federal raid (see Map 11). Capt. John T. Stark of the 13th Cavalry noticed a marked change in attitude among townspeople along the route of march: "The difference is very plain now [compared to] the first time we were ever in these Towns. Then it was all smiles and cheers from the Ladies and huzzas from the men. Now what few citizens are left sit and look on coldly while our Army march through and not a single smile to cheer us, or a single kerchief waving good will to us and our cause." These silent civilians may simply have been war weary by September 1864. On the other hand, now that they were safe from Federal armies, the townsfolk may have looked upon the ragged, scruffy foot soldiers trudging past not as defenders, but as potential chicken thieves and corn-crib raiders. The chilly reception along their marching

# Map 11
## Winter in Arkansas and Louisiana, 1864–1865

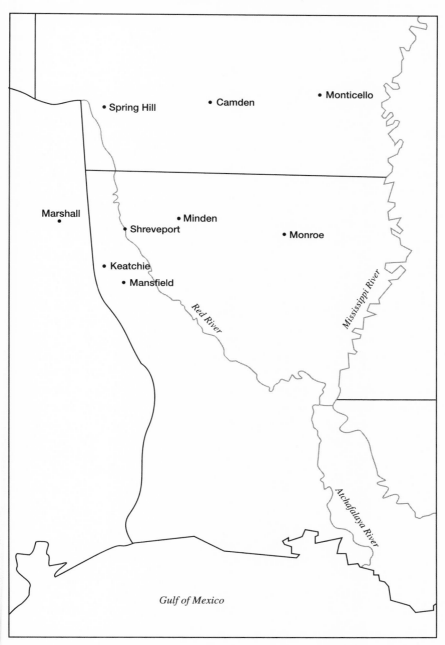

Spring Hill

Camden

Monticello

Marshall

Minden

Shreveport

Monroe

Keatchie

Mansfield

Red River

Mississippi River

Atchafalaya River

Gulf of Mexico

route was not the only unwelcome change for the Greyhounds. General Forney, unhappy with the loose configuration of the Texas marching column, ordered company officers to call roll at each rest stop in order to identify stragglers. Even Blessington considered this an imposition on men known far and wide as Greyhounds. "What his object was I am unable to say, unless it was to shorten the period of resting," Blessington groused. "No sooner was the roll called than we would be on the march again." Soldiering in the trans-Mississippi region had certainly changed since the old days when civilians celebrated every appearance of the Texas column and the men had a leader they liked.[26]

The long gray line reached Monticello in southeast Arkansas on September 20, but the supposed Federal raiders were nowhere to be found. Instead, the new commander of the District of Arkansas, the flamboyant Maj. Gen. John B. Magruder—lover of pageantry and costumes and ceremony—ordered a review of the various infantry divisions that had gathered near Monticello. For some of the veterans, these elaborate shows were a silly waste of time. John Simmons of the 22nd Texas Infantry certainly was not impressed: "They have taken a big throw a-showing off, as they have had Division Review, Brigade Inspection, and tomorrow the General Review is to come off." Forney's Texans, Polignac's Texas and Louisiana brigades, and the Arkansas and Missouri infantry that had fought at Pleasant Hill and Jenkins' Ferry—fourteen thousand men altogether—prepared to march and countermarch in a large field just north of Monticello on September 26. The men were hurried into line at mid-morning to await the arrival of General Magruder and other high officials.[27]

"Casting our eyes to the right, we perceived, at a distance, something resembling a *comet,* with a long tail, advancing toward us," Corporal Blessington wrote. "Further investigation plainly told us that what we took for a *comet* was nothing more nor less than the bunch of ostrich-feathers in General Magruder's hat." In the presence of carriages filled with ladies and accompanied by the music of "Hail to the Chief" and "Dixie," Magruder rode along the long lines of foot soldiers, nodding his approval and promising to rid the state of unwelcome Federals. General Magruder may not have been the most accomplished general in the Confederate army, but he knew how to put on a show.[28]

In early October the Greyhounds and the other infantry divisions near Monticello marched west seventy miles to Camden, the town where General Steele's Federal army had dug in before his retreat via Jenkins' Ferry to Little Rock the previous spring. The southern foot soldiers were sent to Camden mainly to build up its fortifications in the event of another enemy raid from Little Rock. The Greyhounds constructed defenses along the town's waterfront—digging trenches on the town side of the river and cutting down trees to create a clear field of fire on the opposite bank—while the three other divisions dug trenches and built gun emplacements just outside the city. The Texans were accustomed to hard physical labor, but they were surprised by the appearance of paymasters, a sight unseen in more than a year for many of them. They were probably not surprised that they received pay for only two months.[29]

Construction work was accompanied in mid-October by the public execution of one of the ringleaders of the August desertions, Capt. John Guynes of the 22nd Texas Infantry, a farmer from Polk County before the war. Guynes had apparently openly encouraged his men to desert and was therefore a natural target for army commanders who wanted to demonstrate the fate of deserters. John Porter of the 18th Infantry described Guynes as "an old man, above the conscript age, his hair tinged with gray. His going to the war was a voluntary act." All four infantry divisions near Camden (Forney's, Polignac's, Churchill's, and Parsons's) were drawn up in a large field just upriver from Camden to see the consequences of desertion.[30]

Pvt. Dunbar Affleck of Magruder's staff had a very close view of the captain's final moments:

I stood in ten steps of this Captain, and could see him well, and every thing that passed. He spoke a few words, to several friends, and then knelt in prayer. When he was through he got upon his feet and said that he was ready, a man then advanced to blind folded [sic] him, but he beged that they would not do it. The space was then cleared and we all held our breath waiting for the command to fire. I kept my eyes upon the man[;] he seamed calm and collected, but pale as death; he kept his eyes turned up toward heaven as if in prayer. The officer in command gave the order—Ready—Aim—Fire—and he was no more, he fell a corpse, with six bullets through him. The crowd rushed up to him to look at him. I had seen enough and turned away from the sad, and horrid sight.[31]

After six weeks of fortifying at Camden, Forney's division marched sixty miles west to the Red River near Spring Hill in southwest Arkansas on November 14, probably to relieve the pressure of supplying so many thousands of men, horses, and mules at Camden. One of the officers in Daniel's battery, stationed in Magnolia, Arkansas, complained that "the whole country [in southern Arkansas] is eaten out and we have to haul supplies from . . . 100 miles away." In fact, he continued, "we have five batteries and our horses are dying at the rate of three or four a day from starvation." Jonathan Knight of the 22nd Infantry noted that the trip from Camden finished off many mules already weakened by lack of forage: "The mules have been worked so much without being fed that they cant hardly get up when they are down. Our Brigade lost 17 mules on the trip from Camden."[32] After only a few days at their new camp (November 18–22), the Texans marched once again, this time eighty-five miles southeast to their winter quarters, strung along the road between Shreveport and Minden in northwest Louisiana.[33]

Upon their arrival on November 28, many of the men quickly turned to building log cabins for protection from the expected winter storms. Pvt. Samuel Farrow of the 19th Infantry, recently returned from a long-awaited furlough, deviated momentarily from his usual carping and complaining to describe his cozy cabin: "we are snugly housed in winter Quarters[.] We have log cabins 12 by 14 feet. We have comfortable fireplaces. We have no floors except the Earth, though we have Bed Scaffolds to sleep on, and stools to sit on. So we are well fixed up for Soldiers. We have chinked and daubed our houses. they are almost as tight as a jug." Farrow then remembered his station as a champion grumbler and reassured his wife that he had not changed: "please do not understand that I am as well satisfied as if I was at home."[34]

Sgt. John Porter described that winter as a busy time for the Greyhounds: "At this camp (Camp Magruder) a great many big [religious] meetings were held by the various denominations, each with some degree of success. We had made a regular camp-meeting shed. Here also, we had many big drills, reviews and sham battles." The men were not too busy to hiss at General Forney's apparent appetite for feminine charms, though. The drills, reviews, and fake battles, Porter wrote, "were attended by a great many of the fair sex, after which they would repair to Gen. Forney's headquarters, for a party at night. I have since learned from good authority, that the result was quite a number of illegitimate children in that vicinity." Stories about Forney's personal proclivities filtered through the division and usually elicited disapproval from the men. Grumbling about having to march several miles to a drill field and then putting on a sham battle for the amusement of civilians, Private Farrow blamed it all on Forney's attempt to impress his women friends: "You may guess that after walking four or five miles and drilling for an hour or two that we will not be very well pleased [at performing in a sham battle]. But I suppose Gen Forney has a pet Lady or two that he wishes [to] amuse. even if it should cost the lives of a few men, it would be the same with him." These rumors about a man who demanded strict discipline from others but could not control his own appetites were more evidence yet to the Texans that Forney was not worthy of commanding the Greyhounds. He was certainly no John G. Walker.[35]

Squeezed in among the reviews and revival meetings and sham battles was a rather bleak Christmas. Sergeant Porter made the best of the situation in the smoky camps east of Shreveport. "Here, on Christmas day, my mess made a sliced potato pie, and invited the Company officers and some other guests to dine with us," he recalled later. "They passed many compliments on our dinner. This is evidence that we made some progress in the cullinary department, as well as the military." Not far away, in another regimental camp, Private Farrow was characteristically gloomy. "Well this is a lonesome Christmas to us[.] it is dark cloudy weather and we are doing nothing. We will have nothing extra for dinner and none of the O, be joyful to kill trouble with." Farrow's dark mood was not lightened at all a day later when many of his comrades got roaring drunk. "I witnessed the most disgusting scene yesterday evening I ever saw," he wrote his wife. "One of the captains of our Regiment returned to camp Bringing with him a Barrel of Whiskey . . . the Boys pitched into it and there were more drunk men than I ever saw at one time. There was no one hurt, but of all the noise I ever heard. It took place just at dark, and they were up all night. they were making noise one way and another[.] there were two or three little fights, but no material damage except a black eye or two."[36]

The most elaborate social event of the winter took place on February 18, when citizens of the region arranged a gigantic barbecue for the troops. The division had moved on January 26–28 to camps just outside Shreveport, making such an event more convenient. Civilians in Caddo and Bossier Parishes, homes to Shreveport and Minden, as well as Harrison County, Texas, directly west of Caddo, organized the event to thank the soldiers for their successful defense of the area during the Red River campaign. The grateful citizens provided mountains of food for the Texans and a welcome distraction from drilling. The Greyhounds built a bandstand and spread sawdust around it to allow for dancing. Lt. Bruno Durst of the 13th Cavalry was impressed by the scale of it all: "Imagine 16 tables 70 yards long filled with all of the substantials, necessary to make us relish our grub[,] for instance, 140 hogs, light bread and potatoes to match, mutton, turkeys, chickens, cake, pie, etc. and etc. There were near 4000 of us present and almost as many visitors. There were preparations made also for a grand dance, but it proved a failure as the thing was too big." An officer in the 19th Infantry appreciated the hospitality but was a little embarrassed at the poor table manners of the Greyhounds: "The Barbacue like one might expect was a complete row, men rushed to the tables like hungry wolves upon their prey & the Meat & Bread was devoured in a most ravenous manner."[37]

John Simmons considered the event a success. "On the whole, it was a very good dinner. Last though not least, they issued all the soldiers a dram [of whiskey] after the drill was over. There were lots of citizens there—at least twenty-five hundred or three thousand. It was a grand affair." Lt. Orange Cicero Connor of the 19th Infantry managed to take another verbal swipe at General Forney's social behavior at the grand social: "he & a young girl seemingly about 17 opened the dance on Saw dust, but fortunately but few of the Ladies were disposed to follow the example of the young girl who so foolishly whirled herself round & round, kicking saw dust in the arms of Gen Forney & the Dance soon ended. I don't think, but, two women (I doubt their being Ladies) even entered in the dance."[38]

Not surprisingly, men in winter camps had plenty of time to ponder their futures and the progress of the great enterprise in which they were all engaged. On the heels of the fall of Atlanta, the loss of Mobile Bay, and the reelection of Abraham Lincoln, some of the Texans claimed to see the handwriting on the wall for the Confederacy. Lieutenant Connor had been an optimist for most of the war, but he claimed to see nothing but disaster ahead by the winter of 1864–1865. "I must confess that I am *low spirited* more so than I have ever been since the commencement of the War," he wrote his wife. "I now have less hope of the success of our Confederacy than I ever have had. In fact, I have no hope of our *complete* success." In relating his pessimism, Connor also revealed his understanding of what had caused secession in the first place. "I am convinced that the Institution of slavery is now virtually destroyed & with it we loose the great object for which the Confederacy was made, & without which there never would have been a Confederacy. I am now in favor of Peace on the best terms we can possibly get, for if we are to lose slavery we can not possibly make anything by a further prosecution of the War."[39]

Other men in the division were just as certain that the Confederacy would ultimately win its independence and save its way of life. Capt. Virgil Rabb of the 16th Infantry scolded his own mother for the doubts she had expressed in a recent letter: "You seemed to think that the war will never end until we are entirely subjugated or at least until we lay down our Arms, but what kind of peace would it be! It would be like that of the Panther and the Pig, and they would devour us just about as quick as the former would the latter!" Look at the positives, Rabb urged, before he had learned of the Confederate disasters at Franklin and Nashville and Sherman's march to Savannah. "We have an Army that has fought them successfully during the last 12 months at every point but one. According to their own papers Atlanta is the only place they have captured during 1864, and the taking of that did them little if any good." In fact, the captain observed, the Confederacy's prospects in the trans-Mississippi region were even better: "We hold now as much territory as we did when the war commenced with the exception of Little Rock and Pine Bluff. . . . Never, never think of despairing as long as our Armies are as large as they are now." Connor and Rabb represented the two extremes of opinion held by men in the division. The only indicator of general opinion among the Greyhounds was the fact that virtually all of them stuck to the colors during that last winter. As long as Confederate armies were in the field in the east, the west, and the trans-Mississippi, the hope of success would remain alive.[40]

Three days after the grand picnic near Shreveport, the Texas Division packed up and moved south about ten miles, making camp there on the road to Mansfield from February 21 to March 6. While at this location, the division underwent a major reorganization ordered by General Smith at Trans-Mississippi headquarters. Four cavalry regiments from Tom Green's old command and a fifth that had spent most of the war in Arkansas and the Indian Territory were dismounted and attached to the Greyhounds, and the original regiments were shuffled to create a fourth brigade, to be commanded by Wilburn H. King (see Table 7). The horse soldiers, being Texans, put up a fight about losing their mounts, but the artillery needed the animals, and the army did not need so many cavalry units.[41]

On March 7, Maj. Gen. John G. Walker, then commander of the District of Texas, New Mexico, and Arizona, with headquarters in Houston, wired General Smith in Shreveport with alarming news. Spies just arrived from New Orleans brought credible reports that Texas was once again the target of a Federal offensive. Gen. E. R. S. Canby's army of forty thousand men in New Orleans was reportedly "fitting out . . . for operations against Texas" and supposedly was to sail for the Texas coast within three days. Although the blue army at New Orleans was actually preparing for an expedition to Mobile, Alabama, neither Walker nor Smith knew this, and Trans-Mississippi headquarters began humming with preparations to fend off another thrust at the Lone Star State. Forney's Texas Division was ordered to Huntsville, Texas, about sixty-five miles north of Houston; Thomas Churchill's Arkansas infantry division was sent to Marshall in northeast Texas; Mosby Parsons's Missouri infantry division and the Missouri cavalry were relocated to Shreveport, whence they could be hurried into Texas if needed.[42]

The men of the Texas Division learned about the supposed threat to their homes and families on March 13. The next day they marched through Keatchie, thirty-five road miles southwest of Shreveport, bound for Texas. The people of Keatchie, unlike those near Monroe, were happy to see them. "The troops were hailed with enthusiasm by the citizens. Every door, window, and house-roof was crowded with eager spectators," Corporal Blessington noted. That was more like the welcome the Greyhounds expected. The division, traveling in two wings of two brigades each, crossed the state line into Texas on March 15–17, 1865. One wing entered the Lone Star State just south of Marshall, on the Harrison-Panola

TABLE 7

UNITS OF THE TEXAS DIVISION, MARCH–MAY 1865

*1st Brigade, Brig. Gen. Thomas N. Waul*
12th Texas Infantry
22nd Texas Infantry
13th Texas Cavalry (dismounted)
29th Texas Cavalry (dismounted)

*2nd Brigade, Acting Brig. Gen. Richard Waterhouse*
3rd Texas Infantry
17th Texas Infantry
19th Texas Infantry
16th Texas Cavalry (dismounted)
2nd Texas Cavalry, Partisan Rangers (dismounted)

*3rd Brigade, Maj. Robert S. Gould[?]*
11th Texas Infantry
14th Texas Infantry
5th Texas Cavalry, Partisan Rangers (dismounted)
Maj. Robert Gould's Texas Cavalry Battalion (dismounted)

*4th Brigade, Acting Brig. Gen. Wilburn H. King*
16th Texas Infantry
18th Texas Infantry
28th Texas Cavalry (dismounted)
34th Texas Cavalry (dismounted)
Col. John W. Wells's Texas Cavalry (dismounted)

Sources: *Official Records,* vol. 48, pt. 1, p. 1405–6; Blessington, *Campaigns of Walker's Texas Division,* 291–95; Sifakis, *Compendium of the Confederate Armies: Texas,* 54, 104.

County line. The other entered from Logansport, Louisiana (twenty road miles west of Mansfield), into Shelby County, Texas (see Map 12). The men thus returned to their home state for the first time in three years. Capt Virgil Rabb wrote that "our Boys were all in very fine Spirits the day we crossed the line into Texas. They were yelling and whooping nearly all day. It was one continual cheer for Texas! A great many of the Boys have never been in the State since they first left it." According to Corporal Blessington, the men "went to sleep with lighter hearts than we did since we left our beloved State" in 1862.[43]

The two wings traveled southwestward on roughly parallel lines until they converged at Crockett, Texas, about 110 miles straight north of Houston, on March 25–28. After a pause of a few days near Crockett, the various brigades resumed their march on Saturday and Sunday, April 1–2. On that same Sunday,

# Map 12
## The Return to Texas, March–April 1865

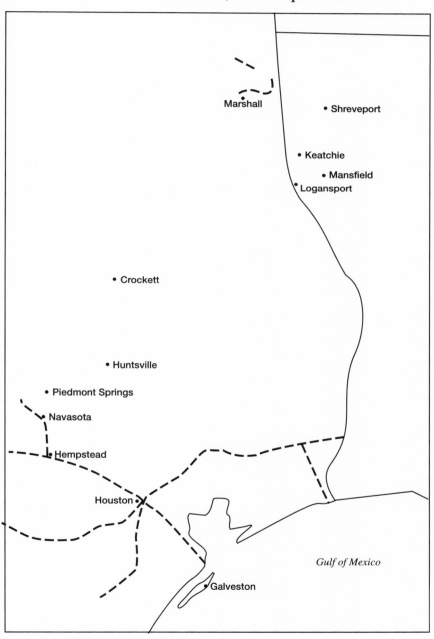

Marshall

• Shreveport

• Keatchie

• Mansfield
Logansport

• Crockett

• Huntsville

• Piedmont Springs

Navasota

Hempstead

Houston

*Gulf of Mexico*

Galveston

eleven hundred miles to the northeast, Robert E. Lee's ragged army evacuated the works around Petersburg and Richmond on its long retreat to Appomattox. The Greyhound brigades, traveling by different roads, snaked south and west, moving at a relatively leisurely pace. Some marched straight south through Huntsville, and others veered more to the southwest, all of them eventually stopping at Piedmont Springs in Grimes County on April 8 and 9. There the men were treated to several days of rest and an opportunity to "take the waters" at this popular antebellum resort and spa.[44] "The springs," the Irish-born Blessington wrote, "are situated alongside of a running creek, beautifully timbered, which sweeps closely around, shutting up the springs in a kind of a cove. The water has a very agreeable taste, resembling that of the famous Seltzer Springs, in the grand duchy of Nassau." The Texans could not have known that on their second day at this delightful retreat, far away in Virginia, Robert E. Lee surrendered his army at Appomattox. Nor could they have known that on the day they left Piedmont Springs, April 14, John Wilkes Booth shot President Lincoln in Ford's Theater in Washington.[45]

After a southward march of thirty-five miles, on April 15–16 the Greyhound regiments reached Hempstead, the place of their formation three years earlier. Numerous Texas cavalry regiments were gathering at Hempstead as well. To Blessington, the men at first "appeared to be in buoyant spirits; many of their friends came from distant parts of the State, to welcome them back once more to their beloved State." Sgt. John C. Porter observed the efforts of higher officers to carry on with the usual routines at Hempstead: "Here we encamped, went to drilling, and the non-commissioned officers [were] studying and reciting lessons in the tactics, as though the war was going on for years to come."[46]

But everything changed on April 22, when word reached Hempstead that Richmond had fallen, the Confederate government was in flight to points unknown, and Lee had surrendered his army. The news of the capitulation of Joseph E. Johnston's Confederate army in North Carolina and Richard Taylor's army in Alabama followed within the next few weeks. These reports from east of the Mississippi transformed attitudes among the soldiers camped near Hempstead. As long as the Confederacy had armies in the field, the Texans could hope that fortunes would shift and that they would win their independence. When Lee, Johnston, and Taylor surrendered, however, trans-Mississippi soldiers realized that they alone now faced the entire combined might of all U.S. forces. They had thrown back Banks and Steele, but how could they stand up also to the massive armies of Grant, Sherman, George Thomas, and Canby, now free to stamp out Confederate resistance in the trans-Mississippi?[47]

Some of the men had been expecting such bad news for some time, but the final realization that the Confederacy east of the Mississippi had crumbled to dust forced the Texans to face the inevitable. Maj. Robert Gould, commander of a dismounted battalion and the officer who had retrieved the column of deserters the previous August, noted the deep despair that settled over the men. "When the news of Lee's surrender reached us, the effect was sad, dreadful. Such depression I have never felt or seen. Hope seemed to have fled. We kept up the usual form of parades and drills, but it was without spirit. A terrible gloom overshadowed us all." Americus Nelms, a converted cavalryman from one of the regiments recently added to the Greyhound Division, admitted that most of the Texans camped around Hempstead realized now that the end had come: "They say there is [no] use in holding out any longer, and that it would be folly in us to fight on this side of the [Mississippi] river now."[48]

John Simmons of the 22nd Infantry told his wife in Smith County on April 25 that "the soldiers are getting very restless, and some talk of breaking up and going home." Four days later, after a series of fiery speeches by General Magruder and other leading figures, all urging the men to stay together and continue the war west of the Mississippi, most of the Greyhounds were still not convinced that further belligerence made any sense. "There are some very large war speeches made down here these days," Simmons wrote from Hempstead. "They attempted to make one to our division this forenoon, but there were not more than a third of the men that would listen to it. The others stood off some hundred yards and kept up a yell to break it up." By early May, Simmons could see that the men were making more sense than their leaders. "I do not believe that the soldiers will go into any more fights. There is no use of men a-going in and getting killed without any hopes of success."[49]

Not even the return of their beloved General Walker to the head of the division could change the Greyhounds' minds. On May 12 General Smith, for his own reasons, relieved General Forney from command and appointed Walker to lead his old division. Douglas French Forrest, a Confederate naval officer who found himself in Texas without a ship, had recently volunteered to serve on Walker's staff and therefore had a close view of the change in command. "Genl. Forney's Divisions [sic]," Forrest wrote, "have clamored so loudly for their old General that Forney has been relieved from the command & it has been tendered to Walker to whom they are warmly attached." Even Walker, though, had to admit that his officers and men would no longer fight, not even for him. "My observation convinces me that the troops of this district cannot be relied upon," Walker informed Smith on May 16. "They consider the contest a hopeless one, and will lay down their arms at the first appearance of the enemy. This is the unanimous opinion of the brigade and regimental commanders of Forney's [sic] division." It was clear to Walker that his men had given up on the war and would soon return to their homes, with or without the approval of Trans-Mississippi officials.[50]

General Walker was exactly right. His former followers began to drift away from their camps near Hempstead in early and mid-May, at first one or two men leaving together during the night, then small groups walking away in broad daylight, all bound for home. Sergeant Porter joined three neighbors in his regiment and made plans for their journey north to Tyler: "We cooked some rations, and at 3:00 or 4:00 o'clock, May 17th, 1865, we bid our comrades adieu, and though we were worn out with camp life, I could not keep from shedding tears, when I separated from some of my friends." As the days passed, increasing numbers of men took one last look at their camps, shook hands with friends they had marched with and fought with, and then turned away for home. The major of a cavalry regiment understood completely: "The truth was that men, who were fearless as lions—as brave as men who were ever wrapped in human hides, had grown to be timid—& fearful, in that hour—not cowards but timid & cautious. They were afraid, after boldly breasting, in battle & exposure, every danger, that they might be killed, when there was no need to die—when it would do no good to the country for them to die."[51]

Thousands of armed and hungry men—many frustrated with the loss of three years of their lives—now were loosed on southeast Texas. The more peaceful among them, like Sergeant Porter and his Smith County neighbors, were reduced to asking civilians along their route for food. Others, angry at the world they found themselves in, concluded that the Confederacy must pay for all their troubles: the wages they had never received, the meals they had never eaten, and the time they had missed with wives and children. On Saturday, May 20, what was left of the Confederate army near Hempstead went to pieces. Following the examples of some of their comrades in Galveston and Houston, the soldiers at Hempstead broke open quartermaster and commissary warehouses and snatched all the supplies and food they could carry home. Army wagons, horses, and mules were driven off by men who thought it was the least the Confederacy could provide for them.[52]

Douglas Forrest of General Walker's staff was thoroughly disgusted that Saturday:

> The Army dispersed to-day contrary to orders and in a manner most lawless & unsoldierly. By evening the *whole* country for miles around was filled with predatory bands, utterly irresponsible, recognizing no rights of property, utterly demoralized. They stood about in squads, breaking into

every depot of Q M [quartermaster], commissary & ordnance stores, robbing them of everything they cd possibly use & destroying what they could not use. Wagons & teams were stolen in every quarter & the little town of Hempstead was utterly sacked, not only public stores carried away but shops & private houses entered & robbed.[53]

General Walker now had the sad obligation to inform Trans-Mississippi headquarters that the army near Hempstead had broken up. On May 24 he confessed to General Smith: "It is my painful duty to inform you that my Corps has no longer an existence, the men having disbanded and gone to their homes. The cause leading to this sad event was the surrender successively of Lee Johnston and Taylor. The men considered our cause hopeless and no arguments or appeals could raise them from the profound discouragement these unhappy events had plunged them into. Every influence I could exact was brought to bear." Even after he visited their camps and urged them to remain in the ranks, thereby increasing the chances of a more attractive peace settlement, the soldiers would hear none of it. "I hoped by my personal influence with my old Infantry Division to save them at least from disbandment. I was mistaken." After three years of long marches across Texas, Arkansas, and Louisiana, the famed Greyhound regiments disintegrated at the very place where many of them had been formed in 1862. Walker's Texas Division no longer existed.[54]

The Texans' war thus ended without the ceremony and formality of Appomattox. The Greyhounds certainly did not want to wait in their camps for the public humiliation of such a surrender. They were long overdue at home: crops and animals needed tending, law and medical practices needed to be revived, students needed their teachers, and wives and children needed their husbands and fathers. Most of them felt no shame at simply walking away from the army—they had proved their Confederate patriotism many times over. They had marched nearly thirty-five hundred miles and steamed up and down rivers another six hundred miles—a combined distance equal to that from the Atlantic coast to the Pacific and halfway back again. Indeed, they may have walked farther than any other division on either side of this war. They had slept in snow and mud, gasped for air in hot, humid swamps, gone hungry for long stretches, and served without pay for most of the war. They had crossed bayonets with the enemy in hand-to-hand combat, dodged huge naval shells, charged across open fields, and fought desperately in water up to their knees. Except for the cause they defended, they were citizen soldiers of a high order. When their officers asked them to remain soldiers after all hope for victory had vanished, they turned almost overnight into civilians again. To resist when resistance was useless—

when, in fact, resistance would invite massive enemy armies onto their soil—made no sense to the Texans. They had seen what happened to farms and communities visited by large armies, especially enemy armies. In one sense, then, by walking away and going home to their wives and children, they saved Texas one last time from the ravages of war.

CHAPTER 14

# *Epilogue*

John G. Walker's Texas Division, the largest body of Texans to fight in the Civil War, was the only division on either side that drew all its regiments from a single state throughout the war. The Greyhound Division was the most formidable and stable infantry organization in the trans-Mississippi Confederacy. Once organized in the fall of 1862, it marched and fought as a unit until the last few weeks of the war, when additional regiments were attached to it.

The Texans fought a bloody little battle on the Mississippi River levee during the Vicksburg campaign, a battle that had no impact on Grant's operations because Trans-Mississippi headquarters sent the Greyhounds to Milliken's Bend too late to accomplish their objective. Nevertheless, the green Texas foot soldiers drove even more inexperienced Federal troops out of their earthworks and back against the river until U.S. ironclads and gunboats turned the engagement in favor of the defenders. Five months later, a detachment of Walker's infantry smashed the rear guard of a large Federal army in south Louisiana, contributing to the enemy decision to abandon an overland drive from New Orleans to Texas. The Texans spent the winter of 1863–1864 harassing Federal shipping on the Mississippi River, creating enough havoc to spread panic among Unionist merchants and civilians along the waterway.

Their greatest campaign unfolded in the spring of 1864 when they retreated nearly three hundred miles up the Red River valley before turning, along with Richard Taylor's other infantry, and shattering the leading divisions of General Banks's army at Mansfield. Another charge across open ground the following day at Pleasant Hill did not achieve the dramatic results of the previous evening, but the end result was the same: Banks's army reeled backward and ultimately retreated all the way back to New Orleans. With barely enough time to recover from these bloody clashes, the Greyhounds joined infantry from Arkansas and Missouri to chase General Steele's Federal army from southern Arkansas. When they caught up to Steele at Jenkins' Ferry, the exhausted Greyhounds fought in mud and water to a tactical stalemate but a strategic victory. Even considering all the praise they earned from their superiors for their successes during the Red

River campaign, perhaps the greatest compliment paid to them came from Lt. Gen. Richard Taylor at the end of the campaign. If only he had had Walker's Texas Division with him, Taylor insisted, he could have destroyed Banks's whole army as it retreated after Pleasant Hill. Even allowing for some hyperbole and overconfidence, Taylor's statements about the Greyhounds are solid evidence of their worth as a fighting unit. Taylor, after all, did have some idea of what good infantry looked like.

One may well wonder how the Greyhounds might have performed if they had been sent east of the Mississippi when they were first organized in 1862. Would they have been as successful and respected if they had been part of the hapless Army of Tennessee in the western theater? Could they have measured up to the Texans in Hood's Texas Brigade in Lee's Army of Northern Virginia? These are the sorts of questions that historians generally do not ask because such queries cannot be answered with any degree of certainty. Still, it is useful to remember that the Greyhounds were the brothers and cousins and school chums of the Texans who fought in Virginia and Tennessee. They were drawn from the same stock and exhibited many of the same traits as soldiers. The Confederate high command may have erred by not sending the Texas Division east of the Mississippi early in the war. Certainly, Generals Joseph E. Johnston or Braxton Bragg or Robert E. Lee would not have objected to having an additional infantry division to command, especially a division of Texans, who had such fierce reputations as warriors. On the other hand, the Greyhounds considered the protection of their families and communities and social order their highest priority. Given a choice, most of them probably would have sacrificed the fame that came with fighting for Lee for the opportunity to stand between their enemy and their homes.

Despite their success on the march and in battle, the Texans were not what a professional military man of the nineteenth century might consider a polished fighting force. They certainly did not look polished, not with their rainbow of colors and styles of clothing and their unsoldierly assortment of head coverings. And although they learned the manual of arms and drilled as much as any other Civil War infantry, most of the Texans considered drill a necessary evil, not a mark of their proficiency. When they were forced to serve with inadequate food and no pay, they kicked and grumbled. When they thought they were being sent so far away that their families and communities would be vulnerable to enemy invasion, some of them bolted and left the ranks (although most of them apparently returned within a few weeks). When their superiors asked them to stand by their colors after further resistance was useless, they refused and went home instead. They were citizen soldiers, not professionals, and their disbandment in

May 1865, from the bottom up, may well have saved their families from the consequences of war and occupation. They were disciplined when they saw good reason for discipline, which was most of the time, but blind obedience was not part of their nature.

The Greyhounds maintained close ties with their homes and communities throughout the war. Thousands of letters flowed back and forth between the men and their wives, parents, and children. Most missives from the soldiers expressed a sentimental longing for home and tender, affectionate feelings for their wives and children. The men understood that their performance as soldiers reflected on their families and communities, and this knowledge kept many of the Texans in line. On the other hand, they were far from home and wives and sweethearts, and some of them strayed into brothels and other men's beds. Similarly, some of them managed to find enough whiskey and other spirits on occasion to get howling drunk and make fools of themselves. The postwar myth of the Lost Cause, which included the idea that Confederate soldiers were invariably noble warriors of pure moral fiber, would have been a source of amusement to those who whored and drank with such abandon.

The end of the war ended the career of Walker's Texas Division, but it did not end the Greyhounds' determination to preserve the old order as much as possible. A small, almost invisible, federal government, an even smaller state government, a political system and social order controlled by traditional-minded southern whites, and a docile black laboring class—this was life as they remembered it before the war and life as they hoped to continue it. Some of them resumed public careers after the war, resisted Republican goals for the Reconstruction of the nation, and clung to the old ways as long as possible. Two of them—Col. Richard Hubbard of the 22nd Infantry and Col. Oran M. Roberts of the 14th Infantry—were elected governor of Texas in the 1870s, and both were conservative Democrats. Former brigadier general Henry McCulloch in 1874 led a company of armed volunteers to seize control of the Texas legislative chambers and protect the inauguration of the conservative Redeemer governor, Richard Coke, thereby assuring the removal from office of the Republican Reconstruction governor, Edmund J. Davis. Maj. Robert S. Gould of Gould's dismounted cavalry battalion was removed from his office as district judge by Federal military authorities in 1867. Gould was, they said, an "impediment to Reconstruction." He later served on the Texas Supreme Court and eventually became a professor of law at the University of Texas. David B. Culberson, lieutenant colonel and then colonel of the 18th Infantry, was one of numerous Greyhounds who later served in a variety of state offices and Congress. Like virtually all of them, he took a conservative line, opposing federal intervention into state affairs and helping to suppress various insurgent political movements.[1]

Most of the Greyhounds, of course, lived less public lives than these prominent political officials. The colorfully named Orange Cicero Connor, a lieutenant in the 19th Infantry and a man who saw Confederate defeat looming before most of his comrades, became a merchant and banker in Paris, Texas, after the war. He held no public office higher than justice of the peace, but he was one of the organizers of Paris's first volunteer fire company. His wife, Mary, established the Lamar County chapter of the United Daughters of the Confederacy and almost single-handedly raised a monument to Confederate soldiers at the county courthouse. When Connor, a man who loved and enjoyed his family, died in 1914, all six of his children were at his bedside. Surgeon Edward Cade of the 28th Cavalry, a native of Ohio, practiced medicine in communities near Hempstead after the war. He was shot to death under mysterious circumstances in 1869.[2]

Pvt. Samuel Farrow of the 19th Infantry, doubtless much to his surprise, survived the war and lived another four decades in Texas. He moved from his wartime home in Panola County in East Texas to Hamilton County in central Texas sometime before 1879. He served as city treasurer and justice of the peace in the small town of Hico for some years. When he applied for a state Confederate pension in 1906, he described himself as "Feeble & decrepid & almost blind." He died the same year. The division's first historian, the cheerful Irishman Joseph P. Blessington of the 16th Infantry, worked in a variety of occupations after the war. He was a salesman for a general merchandising house in Austin while he wrote his history, an employee of the State Health Office in the early 1880s, a hatter and dyer in Waco, and later a city sanitary inspector in Waco. He married a Texas woman after the war and raised four sons and a daughter. When Blessington died at the age of fifty-seven in Waco, his funeral brought out city officials, some of his old wartime comrades, and his compatriots in the Ancient Order of Hibernians.[3]

What of the wives whose husbands did not survive the war? Unfortunately, evidence on their postwar lives is far less plentiful, but the case of Harriet Perry, wife of Capt. Theophilus Perry of the 28th Cavalry, may serve as one example. Not long after receiving the devastating news of her husband's death at Pleasant Hill, Harriet had to bear up under more bad fortune. A niece and a sister-in-law died in January 1865, and her father-in-law, on whom she was often dependent, died a few days later. Fleeing the scene of so much sorrow, Harriet returned to her childhood home in North Carolina in 1865, where her own father died in 1867. She married a North Carolina man in 1872 and died at age forty-nine in late 1885. She knew little happiness after her husband left home in 1862 to go to war. The wife that Sgt. John Samuel Bryan of the 16th Cavalry promised to re-marry after the war remained with her two children in McKinney after his death during the Red River campaign. Nancy Bryan then moved back to her family's home in Indiana in 1866, eventually remarried, and had five more children. A daughter by her second husband conceded that Nancy was rarely happy after the war: "Mother was very much dejected and forlorn from the Texas experience. She wore a sunbonnet most of the time and seldom smiled." She lived nearly seven more decades in her unhappiness and died in 1931.[4]

Not all of the Greyhounds' postwar stories were so sad. The veteran who doubtless lived longer than any of his twelve thousand comrades was Cpl. Mas-ton Thomas Hickman of the 22nd Infantry. Born in August 1841 in Newton, hard by the Louisiana border in deep East Texas, Hickman was a farmer in nearby Polk County before he enlisted in future governor Richard Hubbard's regiment in March 1862. He was present for duty at every roll call throughout the war and returned to Polk County after the breakup. He celebrated his one-hundredth birthday just fourteen weeks before Pearl Harbor in 1941 by taking a ride on an airplane, a story that his Civil War messmates would never have believed. Just to prove he had done it, he posed for a photograph beside the aircraft. His own parents may well have been born as early as the administration of Thomas Jeffer-son or James Madison, but there was Corporal Hickman, several generations later, taking advantage of twentieth-century technology to mark his first century of life. He finally died in January 1945, in his 105th year, and lived almost long enough to see the dawning of the atomic age seven months later.[5]

And what of General Walker? After his division broke up near Hempstead, Walker traveled with a small party of wartime comrades to Mexico in June 1865. He moved from Monterrey to Mexico City to Vera Cruz, traversing some of the country where he had served in the U.S. Army during the Mexican War. From Vera Cruz he sailed to Havana and then to London, where he, his wife, his mother-in-law, and his sister-in-law lived from 1865 to 1868, at least part of the time with the financial aid of a Texas merchant who had made a fortune in blockade running. While in England, Walker wrote his history of the war in the Trans-Mississippi Department and worked with other Confederate expatriates in Europe to promote Confederate settlement and mining in Venezuela and various other business ventures.[6]

The Walkers returned to the United States in 1868, lived for a while in New Orleans and Texas, and in 1876 settled near Winchester, Virginia, the family home of his mother-in-law. The former general engaged in a variety of business projects in the 1870s, mainly mining and railroads. His frequent business travel and wartime reputation earned him many influential contacts, and Pres. Grover

Cleveland appointed him U.S. consul in Bogotá, Colombia, in the late 1880s. On July 20, 1893, two days before his seventy-first birthday, Walker was walking and talking with a friend in Lafayette Park across from the White House in Washington, D.C. A sudden disorientation, followed by paralysis in his extremities, seized the former general, and he died the same day. His wife, four daughters, and a son survived him and preserved his history and some of his letters. At his funeral in the Episcopal church in Winchester, an honor guard consisting of both U.S. and Confederate generals stood near his casket. The most famous Greyhound of them all was laid to rest in the family plot in Winchester, far from the roads and highways of the trans-Mississippi where his men had earned the honorific sobriquet.[7]

# APPENDIX

## *Casualties in Walker's Texas Division*

In all its confrontations with Federal forces—from Perkins Landing in May 1863 to Jenkins' Ferry in April 1864—Walker's Texas Division suffered approximately 2,175 battle casualties (i.e., roughly 1,438 killed and wounded, and 737 captured or missing). All of these casualties occurred after the division had dwindled down to about 6,000 men in the late spring of 1863, yielding a casualty rate of nearly 40 percent (2,175 of 6,000, or 36.3 percent). Most of the losses (1,447) were incurred when the division numbered about 4,000 men (i.e., in the spring of 1864). Thus, nearly two-fifths (1,447 of 4,000, or 36.2 percent) of the men serving in the division in early 1864 were battlefield casualties by late spring. Many of the wounded eventually recovered and returned to service, and some of the captured were exchanged, so the division's numbers did not decline by all 2,175 battlefield losses. Nevertheless, their frontal assaults across open ground—especially at Milliken's Bend, Mansfield, Pleasant Hill, and Jenkins' Ferry—resulted in significant and costly casualties for the Texans, more than most readers might expect from a unit that served exclusively in the Trans-Mississippi Department (see Table 8).

What sorts of soldiers were most likely to fall in battle? Did the old gripe about "a rich man's war, but a poor man's fight" reflect reality? That is, were poor men fed into the meat grinder of battle while their rich neighbors watched from safe rear areas? Were younger men more likely to die than older soldiers? Were single men more daring and foolhardy in battle than married men with families? An analysis of the sample used in this study (1,557 members of infantry and dismounted cavalry units) turned up 249 battle casualties, 16 percent of the total sample. These figures are consistent with the raw numbers of soldiers and casualties (2,175 casualties from a total of roughly 12,000 original soldiers, about 18.1 percent).

The figures in Table 9 indicate that, in most respects, those who became battlefield casualties were very much like those in the original division as a whole. In terms of age, occupation, birthplace, wealth, and slaveholding status, the two groups were nearly identical. Once again, the data do not support the idea of "a

TABLE 8

BATTLEFIELD CASUALTIES IN WALKER'S TEXAS DIVISION

| Engagement | Killed | | Wounded | Captured or Missing |
|---|---|---|---|---|
| Perkins Landing, La. | 1 | | 2 | 2 |
| Milliken's Bend, La. | 44 | | 131 | 10 |
| Richmond, La. | 10 killed and wounded (est.) | | | 10 (est.) |
| Harrisonburg, La. | 0 | | 0 | 2 |
| Bayou Bourbeau, La. | 22 | | 103 | 55 |
| Attacks on Mississippi River Boats, La. | 1 | | 0 | 0 |
| Henderson Hill, La. | 0* | 0* | 100 (est.) | |
| Fort DeRussy, La. | 0* | 0* | 235 | |
| Mansfield, La. | 180 killed and wounded | | | 20 |
| Pleasant Hill, La. | 500 killed and wounded | | | 300 |
| Jenkins' Ferry, Ark. | 84 | | 360 | 3 |
| Totals | 1,438 killed and wounded | | | 737 |

*Some of the captured soldiers may also have been wounded, and a few others may have been killed.

TABLE 9

CHARACTERISTICS OF SOLDIERS WHO WERE BATTLE CASUALTIES

| Points of Comparison | Whole Sample | Sample Casualties |
|---|---|---|
| Mean Age | 26.9 | 25.8 |
| Occupation | 78% in agriculture | 73.8% in agriculture |
| Born in Lower South | 64.5% | 59.6% |
| Mean Real Property Holdings | $1,397 | $1,590 |
| Mean Personal Property Holdings | $2,180 | $2,327 |
| Slaveholders | 27.3% | 27.3% |
| Married | 50.9% | 39% |
| Heads of Household | 50.1% | 39% |

*Note:* All figures in the table are from the sample of officers and men in the division.

rich man's war, but a poor man's fight." Wealthy men served and suffered at a rate one might expect from a group with their share of the overall population. The only significant variation among those who were battlefield casualties was in family status. Slightly more than half of all members of the division were married and heads of households, but only about two-fifths of those who were killed, wounded, or captured and missing were married and/or headed a household back in Texas. Neither the quantitative nor the qualitative data amassed for this study point to an obvious explanation for this difference, but a commonsense suggestion seems reasonable: married men and men who had households to support were probably less likely to expose themselves recklessly in battle than men without such responsibilities. This is only conjecture, however, and further research seems justified.

# NOTES

## 1. INTRODUCTION

1. *De Bow's Review of the Southern and Western States,* 43 vols. (New Orleans: J. D. B. De Bow, 1846–80), 10:642; U.S. Bureau of the Census, *Population of the United States in 1860; Compiled from the Original Returns of the Eighth Census* (Washington: Government Printing Office, 1864), 486–90, 598–9; Richard G. Lowe and Randolph B. Campbell, *Planters and Plain Folk: Agriculture in Antebellum Texas* (Dallas: Southern Methodist Univ. Press, 1987), 9–14.

2. U.S. Bureau of the Census, *Agriculture of the United States in 1860; Compiled from the Original Returns of the Eighth Census* (Washington: Government Printing Office, 1864), 140–51; Lowe and Campbell, *Planters and Plain Folk,* 19, 60–7, 70–6; Ralph A. Wooster, *Texas and Texans in the Civil War* (Austin, Tex.: Eakin Press, 1995), 2.

3. Randolph B. Campbell and Richard G. Lowe, *Wealth and Power in Antebellum Texas* (College Station: Texas A&M Univ. Press, 1977), 29–31; Randolph B. Campbell, *An Empire for Slavery: The Peculiar Institution in Texas* (Baton Rouge: Louisiana State Univ. Press, 1989), 55, 191.

4. Walter L. Buenger, *Secession and the Union in Texas* (Austin: Univ. of Texas Press, 1984), 8–10; Campbell, *Empire for Slavery,* 209–11.

5. Buenger, *Secession and the Union in Texas,* 45–6 (reaction to John Brown's raid); Donald E. Reynolds, *Editors Make War: Southern Newspapers in the Secession Crisis* (Nashville: Vanderbilt Univ. Press, 1970), 97–111 (the "Texas Troubles" of 1860).

6. Buenger, *Secession and the Union in Texas,* 147–8, 174–5. Also see Robin E. Baker and Dale Baum, "The Texas Voter and the Crisis of the Union, 1859–1861," *Journal of Southern History* 53 (August 1987): 395–420; Wooster, *Texas and Texans in the Civil War,* 209 n.–10 n.

7. The U.S. Army posts (and units) captured or abandoned are listed by date in Thomas T. Smith, *The Old Army in Texas: A Research Guide to the U.S. Army in Nineteenth-Century Texas* (Austin: Texas State Historical Assn., 2000), 103.

8. Wooster, *Texas and Texans in the Civil War,* 15–9; Thomas W. Cutrer, *Ben McCulloch and the Frontier Military Tradition* (Chapel Hill: Univ. of North Carolina Press, 1993), 177–85; Carl Newton Tyson, "Texas: Men for War; Cotton for Economy," *Journal of the West* 14 (January 1975): 133; Jeanne T. Heidler, "'Embarrassing Situation': David E. Twiggs and the Surrender of United States Forces in Texas, 1861," *Military History of the Southwest* 21 (fall 1991): 157–72.

9. Despite his stellar record as a war governor, Clark was narrowly defeated for reelection by Francis R. Lubbock a few months later. Clark then raised a new infantry regiment (the 14th Texas) around Marshall and led it through most of the war as one element of John G. Walker's Texas Infantry Division. Ralph A. Wooster, "Texas," in *The Confederate Governors,* ed. W. Buck Yearns (Athens: Univ. of Georgia Press, 1985), 195–9; Scott Dennis Parker, "'The Best Stuff Which the State Affords': A Portrait of the Fourteenth Texas Infantry in the Civil War, 1862–1865" (M.A. thesis, University of

North Texas, 1998); Tinsie Larison, "Edward Clark," in *Ten Texans in Gray,* ed. W. C. Nunn (Hillsboro, Tex.: Hill Junior College Press, 1968), 18–35.

10. For troop numbers and Clark's account of his activities, see War Department, *The War of the Rebellion: A Compilation of the Official Records of the Union and Confederate Armies,* 128 vols. (Washington: Government Printing Office, 1880–1901), series 1, vol. 3, pp. 690, 730 (hereafter cited as *Official Records*; all references to series 1 unless otherwise indicated); ibid., vol. 8, 718–9; ibid., series 4, vol. 1, pp. 630, 713–22. Also see Stephen B. Oates, *Confederate Cavalry West of the River* (Austin: Univ. of Texas Press, 1961), 28–9; Wooster, *Texas and Texans in the Civil War,* 27–31.

11. Harold B. Simpson, *Hood's Texas Brigade: Lee's Grenadier Guard* (Waco, Tex.: Texian Press, 1970); Thomas W. Cutrer, "Eighth Texas Cavalry," in *New Handbook of Texas,* ed. Ron Tyler et al., 6 vols. (Austin: Texas State Historical Assn., 1996), 2:805–6; Perry Wayne Shelton, comp., and Shelly Morrison, ed., *Personal Civil War Letters of General Lawrence Sullivan Ross, with Other Letters* (Austin, Tex.: Shelly and Richard Morrison, 1994), 97.

12. Victor M. Rose, *Ross' Texas Brigade, Being a Narrative of Events Connected with Its Service in the Late War Between the States* (Louisville, Ky.: Courier-Journal Book and Job Rooms, 1881), 16. The exact number of Texans who served in the Confederate military is virtually impossible to pin down. For two very different estimates, see Robert P. Felgar, "Texas in the War for Southern Independence, 1861–1865" (Ph.D. diss., University of Texas, 1935), 106 (as few as fifty thousand); and Stephen B. Oates, "Texas under the Secessionists," *Southwestern Historical Quarterly* 67 (October 1963): 187 (as many as eighty-eight thousand). Wooster, *Texas and Texans in the Civil War,* 32, 213 n., summarizes the various attempts to arrive at a figure.

13. James M. McPherson, *Battle Cry of Freedom: The Civil War Era* (New York: Oxford Univ. Press, 1988), 369–73 (coastal operations); Thomas Lawrence Connelly, *Army of the Heartland: The Army of Tennessee, 1861–1862* (Baton Rouge: Louisiana State Univ. Press, 1967), 97–9 (Logan's Cross Roads); Benjamin Franklin Cooling, *Forts Henry and Donelson: The Key to the Confederate Heartland* (Knoxville: Univ. of Tennessee Press, 1987); William L. Shea and Earl J. Hess, *Pea Ridge: Civil War Campaign in the West* (Chapel Hill: Univ. of North Carolina Press, 1992).

14. The eleven regiments and one battalion that would later be known as Walker's Texas Division were all formed in early 1862. This information and all other quantitative measurements not otherwise documented here are based on a statistical database (a systematic sample of twenty-two hundred soldiers) constructed from the Compiled Service Records of Confederate Soldiers Who Served in Organizations from the State of Texas, War Department Collection of Confederate Records, Record Group 109, National Archives, Washington, D.C. (Microfilm M323)—hereafter cited as Compiled Service Records, with appropriate reel number; Eighth Census of the United States, 1860, Records of the Bureau of the Census, Record Group 29, National Archives (Microfilm M653, T1134); County Real and Personal Property Tax Rolls, 1858–62, Ad Valorem Tax Division, Records of the Comptroller of Public Accounts, Record Group 304, Texas State Library and Archives Commission, Austin; and various other primary and secondary sources.

15. Biography and Diaries of R. S. Gould, p. 60, Robert Simonton Gould Papers, Center for American History, University of Texas at Austin; A. J. Coupland to O. M. Roberts, February 19, 1862, Oran Milo Roberts Papers, Center for American History; Fred F. Abbey, "Robert Simonton Gould," in *New Handbook of Texas,* ed. Tyler et al., 3:258; Randolph B. Campbell, *A Southern Community in Crisis: Harrison County, Texas, 1850–1880* (Austin: Texas State Historical Assn., 1983), 205–6. In February 1862 the Confederate secretary of war, Judah P. Benjamin, urged commanders in Texas to hurry as many Texas recruits as possible to Little Rock (*Official Records,* vol. 9, p. 700).

## 2. JOINING UP

1. For unit sizes and organization, see James M. McPherson, *Ordeal by Fire: The Civil War and Reconstruction*, 2nd ed. (New York: McGraw-Hill, 1992), 173; Marcus J. Wright, comp., *Texas in the War, 1861–1865*, ed. Harold B. Simpson (Hillsboro, Tex.: Hill Junior College Press, 1965), xviii. For typical newspaper advertisements calling for recruits, see *Houston Tri-Weekly Telegraph*, March 26, 1862; *Galveston Tri-Weekly News*, January 28, 1862, p. 1.

2. Wooster, *Texas and Texans in the Civil War*, 27–8; James C. Carroll, "Memoirs of James Craton Carroll," Civil War Times Illustrated Collection, United States Army Military History Institute (hereafter cited as USAMHI), Carlisle Barracks, Pa.; John D. Perkins, "The Titus Hunters: Company D, 11th Texas Infantry Regiment, Walker's Texas Division," *East Texas Historical Journal* 35 (spring 1997): 24; John D. Perkins, *Daniel's Battery: The 9th Texas Field Battery* (Hillsboro, Tex.: Hill College Press, 1998), 40.

3. M. Jane Johansson, *Peculiar Honor: A History of the 28th Texas Cavalry, 1862–1865* (Fayetteville: Univ. of Arkansas Press, 1998), 21. Reid Mitchell, "The Northern Soldier and His Community," in *Toward a Social History of the American Civil War*, ed. Maris A. Vinovskis (New York: Cambridge Univ. Press, 1990), 78–92, emphasizes the close connection between Federal soldiers and their hometowns. The same intimate ties bound Texas Confederates to their own home communities.

4. John T. Stark to The Dear Ones at Home, March 11, 1862, John T. Stark Letters and Diary, 13th Texas Cavalry File, Confederate Research Center, Hill College, Hillsboro, Tex.; Harvey Alexander Wallace Diary, 1829–1865, p. 4, Southwest Arkansas Regional Archives, Washington, Ark.

5. *Marshall Texas Republican*, reprinted in *Marshall News Messenger*, July 8, 1962 (from the same week one hundred years earlier). Full-color portrayals of the flags of two other companies in Walker's Texas Division are in Alan K. Sumrall, *Battle Flags of Texans in the Confederacy* (Austin, Tex.: Eakin Press, 1995), 32, 74. Descriptions and diagrams of various company and regimental flags of the division are in Howard Michael Madaus and Robert D. Needham. "Unit Colors of the Trans-Mississippi Confederacy," *Military Collector and Historian* 41 (1989): 130–2, 178–80; and Robert Maberry Jr., *Texas Flags* (College Station: Texas A&M Univ. Press, 2001), 65, 154, 156.

6. *Houston Tri-Weekly Telegraph*, April 16, 1862, p. 2.

7. Ford Dixon, "Oran Milo Roberts," in *New Handbook of Texas*, ed. Tyler et al., 5:611–2. Roberts later indicated that he received numerous such requests and that "My general rule was to appoint [to regimental office] those who in some way helped to get up the regiment" (Roberts's endorsement on G. Clark Smith to Judge Roberts, February 7, 1862, Roberts Papers).

8. Letters from S. Holland (January 9, 1862), M. W. Wheeler (January 11, 1862), O. E. Roberts (January 18, 1862), James H. Jones (January 16, 1862), Roberts Papers. See Roberts's endorsement on a letter from E. P. Nicholson (January 28, 1862), Roberts Papers. For Jones, see Thomas W. Cutrer, "James Henry Jones," in *New Handbook of Texas*, ed. Tyler et al., 3:983.

9. Roberts's endorsement on J. C. Rhea to O. M. Roberts, February 18, 1862; W. H. Shotwell to O. M. Roberts, March 29, 1862, both in Roberts Papers. Rhea's home county, Cass, was known as Davis County from 1861 to 1871.

10. The "large knives" referred to by Bolin were very popular among Texans early in the war. A veteran of the 3rd Texas Cavalry later recalled how impractical such weapons were: "Some of these knives were three feet long, and heavy enough to cleave the skull of a mailed knight through helmet and all. I think they were never used in the butchery of the Yankees, and, ere the close of the first year's service, were discarded altogether" (Rose, *Ross' Texas Brigade*, 18).

11. M. Bolin to O. M. Roberts, January 29, 1862; O. E. Roberts to Dear Uncle, January 18, 1862;

and O. M. Roberts to Samuel Boyer Davis, May 20, 1862, all in Roberts Papers. For a well-researched sketch of the raising of the 13th Cavalry, see Thomas R. Reid, "The Spartan Band: A History of Burnett's 13th Texas Cavalry Regiment, 1862–1865" (M.A. thesis, Lamar University, 2001), 1–17.

12. Eusibia Lutz, "Liendo: The Biography of a House," *Southwest Review* 16 (January 1931): 190–6.

13. Charles C. Nott, *Sketches in Prison Camps: A Continuation of Sketches of the War*, 3rd ed. (New York: Anson D. F. Randolph, 1865), 93; Joseph Palmer Blessington, *The Campaigns of Walker's Texas Division*, intro. Norman D. Brown and T. Michael Parrish (1875; reprint, Austin, Tex.: State House Press, 1994), 22 (second quotation); Brad Clampitt, "Camp Groce, Texas: A Confederate Prison," *Southwestern Historical Quarterly* 104 (January 2001): 365–84.

14. *(Marshall) Texas Republican*, February 22, 1862, p. 3, and April 26, 1862, p. 2; Ned [Edward] Cade to Dear Wife, June 24, 1862, Edward W. and Allie Cade Correspondence, John Q. Anderson Collection, Texas State Library and Archives Commission. Cade's letters were published in John Q. Anderson, ed., *A Texas Surgeon in the C.S.A.* (Tuscaloosa, Ala.: Confederate, 1957).

15. Confederate Texans were not unique in their resentment of (what seemed to them) swaggering officers. American soldiers in World War II made comments virtually identical to those found in Civil War letters: "Those officers think they are tin gods or the next thing to it." "The Army idea of class distinction between officers and men is all wrong." "Men do not like to be treated as if they were just toys and dogs for someone to play with." Samuel A. Stouffer et al., *Studies in Social Psychology in World War II*, 4 vols. (Princeton: Princeton Univ. Press, 1949–50), 1:74.

16. Mark A. Weitz, "Drill, Training, and the Combat Performance of the Civil War Soldier: Dispelling the Myth of the Poor Soldier, Great Fighter," *Journal of Military History* 62 (April 1998): 263–89.

17. Blessington, *Campaigns of Walker's Texas Division*, 21.

18. L. David Norris, ed., *With the 18th Texas Infantry: The Autobiography of Wilburn Hill King* (Hillsboro, Tex.: Hill College Press, 1996), 11–41; Arthur W. Bergeron Jr., "Wilburn Hill King," in *The Confederate General*, ed. William C. Davis, 6 vols. (Harrisburg, Pa.: National Historical Society, 1991), 6:186–7.

19. *(Galveston) Texas Christian Advocate*, May 30, 1861, p. 2 (first quotation); Simpson, *Hood's Texas Brigade*, 61 n.–62 n. (second quotation); Nicholas A. Davis, *The Campaign from Texas to Maryland with the Battle of Antietam* (1863; reprint, introduced by Donald E. Everett, under the new title, *Chaplain Davis and Hood's Texas Brigade*, San Antonio: Principia Press, 1962), 57; Thomas W. Cutrer, "Robert Thomas Pritchard Allen," in *New Handbook of Texas*, ed. Tyler et al., 1:113.

20. Blessington, *Campaigns of Walker's Texas Division*, 115.

21. *Official Records*, series 4, vol. 1, p. 977.

22. Douglas Hale, "The Third Texas Cavalry: A Socioeconomic Profile of a Confederate Regiment," *Military History of the Southwest* 19 (spring 1989): 23; Michael Robert Green, " '. . . So Illy Provided . . .': Events Leading to the Creation of the Texas Military Board," *Military History of Texas and the Southwest* 10, no. 2 (1972): 117; P. S. Heflin to P. O. Hébert, March 26, 1862, Compiled Service Records, reel 43, James T. Heflin file, Gould's Battalion.

23. *Tyler Reporter*, June 26, 1862.

24. E. W. Cade to Dear Wife, June 29, 1862, Cade Correspondence.

25. *Tyler Reporter*, July 24, 1862, p. 2.

26. Ibid., June 19, 1862, p. 3, and July 24, 1862, p. 2 (quotation).

27. Disease plagued rendezvous camps in both the North and the South. See H. H. Cunningham, *Doctors in Gray: The Confederate Medical Service* (Baton Rouge: Louisiana State Univ. Press, 1958), 165–8; Paul E. Steiner, *Disease in the Civil War: Natural Biological Warfare in 1861–1865* (Spring-

field, Ill.: Charles C. Thomas, 1968), 12–26; Alfred Jay Bollet, *Civil War Medicine: Challenges and Triumphs* (Tucson, Ariz.: Galen Press, 2002), 257–60.

28. Henry P. Howard to George R. Wilson, May 9, 1862, Trans-Mississippi Department Morning Reports, Inspection Reports, Monthly Returns, Orders, Louisiana Historical Association Collection, Howard-Tilton Memorial Library, Tulane University, New Orleans, La.; O. M. Roberts to Saml. Boyer Davis, May 20, 1862, Roberts Papers; William P. Head to Dear Wife, April 20, 1862, William P. Head Papers, Center for American History.

29. B. F. Tamplin to Dear Retincia, May 9, 1862, William H. Tamplin Letters, Louisiana and Lower Mississippi Valley Collections, Hill Memorial Library, Louisiana State University, Baton Rouge; Kenneth F. Kiple and Virginia H. Kiple, "Black Tongue and Black Men: Pellagra and Slavery in the Antebellum South," *Journal of Southern History* 43 (August 1977): 411–28.

30. J. T. Knight to Dear Wife, July 17, 1862, Jonathan Thomas Knight Letters, private collection of Gary Canada, Keller, Tex.

31. B. F. Tamplin to Dear Retincia, May 9, 1862, William H. Tamplin Letters; W. W. Malone to O. M. Roberts, [September?] 1862, Roberts Papers.

32. F. R. Tannehill to Dear Wife, June 7, 1862, in Anne Thiele Holder, *Tennessee to Texas: Francis Richardson Tannehill, 1825–1864* (Austin, Tex.: Pemberton Press, 1966), 103–4. This distrust and fear of military medicine was in marked contrast to the attitudes of U.S. soldiers in World War II. More than 80 percent of the later warriors expressed high confidence in military physicians (Stouffer et al., *Studies in Social Psychology,* 1:40).

33. Blessington, *Campaigns of Walker's Texas Division,* 20–1; E. Steele to My Dear Wife, February [?], 1862, and March 16, 1862, E. Steele Papers, private collection of Wanda Cuniff, Nacogdoches, Tex. Also see Thomas W. Cutrer, ed., " 'Bully for Flournoy's Regiment, We Are Some Punkins, You'll Bet': The Civil War Letters of Virgil Sullivan Rabb, Captain, Company 'I,' Sixteenth Texas Infantry, C.S.A.," Part One, *Military History of the Southwest* 19 (fall 1989): 166 (hereafter cited as "Letters of Virgil Sullivan Rabb").

34. S. W. Farrow to Dear Josephine, July 5, 1862 (first quotation), and August 9, 1862, Samuel Farrow Papers, Center for American History.

35. Bell Irvin Wiley, *The Life of Johnny Reb: The Common Soldier of the Confederacy* (Indianapolis: Bobbs-Merrill, 1943), 17–8.

36. Albert Burton Moore, *Conscription and Conflict in the Confederacy* (New York: Macmillan, 1924), 14.

37. Men over twenty-five years of age, married men, and fathers were less personally committed to military service in World War II as well. See Stouffer et al., *Studies in Social Psychology,* 1:106–7.

38. The birthplaces of men in the earlier and later groups do not seem to have influenced when they volunteered. Indeed, the later enlistees were slightly more likely to be from the lower South than the earlier ones. Francelle Pruitt, " 'We've Got to Fight or Die': Early Texas Reaction to the Confederate Draft, 1862," *East Texas Historical Journal* 36, no. 1 (1998): 3–17, pinpoints the date that news of the Confederate conscription law reached Texas.

39. Protection of family and community was a powerful motive for enlistment in the Confederate army. See Reid Mitchell, *Civil War Soldiers* (New York: Viking, 1988), 17; Joshua McKaughan, " 'Few Were the Hearts . . . that did not Swell with Devotion': Community and Confederate Service in Rowan County, North Carolina, 1861–1862," *North Carolina Historical Review* 73 (April 1996): 156; Martin Crawford, "Confederate Volunteering and Enlistment in Ashe County, North Carolina, 1861–1862," *Civil War History* 37 (March 1991): 29–50.

40. Governor Francis R. Lubbock's appeal for volunteers in February 1862 was designed to strike

this chord: "Your mothers, daughters, sisters, wives, and little children all appeal to you as you love them, your country, their honor, and your honor to stand as a breast-work between them and 'him who comes with lust in his eye, Poverty in his purse, and hell in his heart; who comes a robber and murderer,' seeking to destroy or subjugate us." (*Official Records,* series 4, vol. 1, p. 981).

41. These Texans certainly believed that northerners were a different sort of people—aggressive, meddling, fanatical, and savage. Randall C. Jimerson, *The Private Civil War: Popular Thought during the Sectional Conflict* (Baton Rouge: Louisiana State Univ. Press, 1988), and Mitchell, *Civil War Soldiers,* maintain that soldiers on both sides were blinded to the reality of cultural homogeneity among Americans in general by their perceptions of vast sectional differences.

42. The best treatment of this general subject is James M. McPherson's *For Cause and Comrades: Why Men Fought in the Civil War* (New York: Oxford Univ. Press, 1997).

43. W. P. Head to Dear wife, August ?, [1862], Head Papers; Ned [Cade] to [wife], February 22, 1863, Cade Correspondence; B. F. Tamplin to Dear Retincia, March 26, 1862, Tamplin Letters.

44. Soldiers in the three artillery batteries eventually attached to Walker's division (those commanded by Capts. James M. Daniel, William Edgar, and Horace Haldeman) were about two years older than the infantrymen. The mean and median ages among the foot soldiers were 26.9 and 26.0 years; among the gunners, 28.8 and 28.0.

45. The same pattern held true for slave ownership. About two-fifths (43.4 percent) of the original officers, one-third (32.0 percent) of the soldiers who rose from the enlisted ranks, and one-fifth (20.5 percent) of the enlisted men owned bondsmen.

46. Younger men replaced original officers in the 3rd Texas Cavalry as well (Hale, "Third Texas Cavalry," 24). Men promoted from the ranks to company-grade office during World War II were also wealthier than other privates and noncommissioned officers (Stouffer et al., *Studies in Social Psychology,* 1:114).

47. These Texans included more men in their thirties, 25.6 percent, than Confederates in general, about 16.7 percent (Wiley, *Life of Johnny Reb,* 331). Similarly, the Texans included fewer privates in their early twenties (27.7 percent) and more who were twenty-five or older (54.7 percent) than U.S. privates in World War II (42 percent and 40 percent). See Stouffer et al., *Studies in Social Psychology,* 1:114.

48. McPherson, *Battle Cry of Freedom,* 608; Douglas Hale, *The Third Texas Cavalry in the Civil War* (Norman: Univ. of Oklahoma Press, 1993), 44; Ralph A. Wooster and Robert Wooster, "'Rarin' for a Fight': Texans in the Confederate Army," *Southwestern Historical Quarterly* 84 (April 1981): 395. Also see Johansson, *Peculiar Honor,* 17; Perkins, *Daniel's Battery,* 33–4.

49. Wiley, *Life of Johnny Reb,* 347; James I. Robertson Jr., *Soldiers Blue and Gray* (Columbia: Univ. of South Carolina Press, 1988), 25; Earl J. Hess, "The 12th Missouri Infantry: A Socio-Military Profile of a Union Regiment," *Missouri Historical Review* 76 (October 1981): 62; Hale, "Third Texas Cavalry," 23; Stouffer et al., *Studies in Social Psychology,* 1:114.

50. For example, the men of Company H, 9th Texas Cavalry, organized in the late summer of 1861, were younger, more likely to be single, and less likely to head a household than the soldiers in Walker's Texas Division. Demographic data for this company were compiled for a study of one of its officers: Richard Lowe, ed., *A Texas Cavalry Officer's Civil War: The Diary and Letters of James C. Bates* (Baton Rouge: Louisiana State Univ. Press, 1999). See pp. xxi–xxiii for demographic patterns.

51. The same pattern has been detected in two counties of North Carolina and in the region around Augusta, Georgia. See McKaughan, "'Few Were the Hearts,'" 171–2 (for Rowan County); Crawford, "Confederate Volunteering and Enlistment," 43, 45–6 (for Ashe County); J. William Har-

ris, *Plain Folk and Gentry in a Slave Society: White Liberty and Black Slavery in Augusta's Hinterlands* (Middletown, Conn.: Wesleyan Univ. Press, 1985), 152–3.

52. Men in the three artillery batteries later attached to the division were not only older, they were more cosmopolitan in background, probably because the batteries recruited more heavily in cities like San Antonio, Houston, and Galveston, where northern and foreign-born men were more numerous. Non-southerners constituted only 4.9 percent of all soldiers in the foot units of the division, but they composed 27.2 percent of the gunners (8.4 percent from the free states; 18.8 percent from foreign countries). See Campbell and Lowe, *Wealth and Power in Antebellum Texas,* 92, for urban figures on birthplace.

53. Campbell and Lowe, *Wealth and Power in Antebellum Texas,* 29; James M. McPherson, *What They Fought For, 1861–1865* (Baton Rouge: Louisiana State Univ. Press, 1994), 16.

54. Those men in the division who operated farms had agricultural property holdings very similar to those of Texans in general. Farm operators statewide worked an average of 66.5 improved acres, and the mean cash value of their farms was $2,748.90. Farmers in the division worked 71.9 improved acres, and their farms were worth an average of $2,360.70. See Lowe and Campbell, *Planters and Plain Folk,* 63, 65, for statewide means.

55. Occupation patterns among the soldiers in the three artillery batteries assigned to the division were more complex and included more men from the skilled labor, unskilled labor, commercial, and professional categories, doubtless due to the heavier representation of men from the large towns of Galveston, Houston, and San Antonio.

56. Campbell and Lowe, *Wealth and Power in Antebellum Texas,* 58. The gunners of the three batteries later attached to the division were a shade poorer than the foot soldiers. Their mean figures for real property, personal property, and wealth were $1,335, $1,888, and $3,223.

57. Campbell, *Empire for Slavery,* 68.

58. Hale, "Third Texas Cavalry," 26. Planter families constituted 3 percent of all Texas families in 1860 but 17 percent of the 3rd Texas Cavalry (Campbell, *Empire for Slavery,* 68; Hale, *Third Texas Cavalry,* 41).

59. Campbell and Lowe, *Wealth and Power in Antebellum Texas,* 46. McPherson, *Battle Cry of Freedom,* 614–5, and Larry M. Logue, *To Appomattox and Beyond: The Civil War Soldier in War and Peace* (Chicago: Ivan R. Dee, 1996), 28, agree that wealthy southerners carried at least their share of the burden of war.

## 3. OFF TO ARKANSAS

1. Moore, *Conscription and Conflict,* 14–5; Brig. Gen. Henry E. McCulloch, General Orders no. 8, June 19, 1862, *Tyler Reporter,* June 26, 1862, p. 1; Pruitt, " 'We've Got to Fight or Die,' " 10–1, 16.

2. For an example of a regimental election, see Edward Clark to Brigadier General P. O. Hébert, July 12, 1862, Muster and Pay Rolls (14th Texas Infantry), Records Relating to Military Personnel, Records of the Adjutant and Inspector General's Department, War Department Collection of Confederate Records, Record Group 109, National Archives, Washington, D.C. Fifteen company officers were reelected, three were defeated, eight declined to run again, five were elected to other posts, and one was discharged. All three regimental officers, including the former governor and now colonel, Edward Clark, were reelected.

3. Oran M. Roberts endorsement on J. C. Rhea to O. M. Roberts, February 18, 1862, Roberts Papers; Max S. Lale, ed., "A Letter from Leonard Randal to His Son," *East Texas Historical Journal* 23, no. 2 (1985): 47–8; Compiled Service Records, reel 393 (Maples file).

4. Some men discharged because of age nevertheless later reenlisted. John D. Williams of the 13th Texas Cavalry, forty-five years old in 1862, later rejoined the regiment in another company. Duncan C. Carrington of Gould's Battalion was released because he was too old but later joined a regiment in a different division. Illinois native H. D. Pearce originally served in a Louisiana regiment, but after being released because of age he joined the 16th Texas Cavalry in Walker's division. See Compiled Service Records, reels 80 (Williams file) and 43 (Carrington file); Mamie Yeary, comp., *Reminiscences of the Boys in Gray, 1861–1865* (1912; reprint, Dayton, Ohio: Morningside Books, 1986), 595 (Pearce).

5. Report of the 14th Regiment of Texas Infantry, April 20, 1863, muster memorandum, Company A, October 31, 1862, and muster roll, Company A, February 24, 1862 (Wallace case), all in Muster and Pay Rolls (14th Texas Infantry), War Department Collection of Confederate Records; Compiled Service Records, reels 395 (Anderson file) and 396 (Hyers file).

6. Assac (Isaac?) N. Williams of the 11th Texas Infantry, thrown from a horse only one day after he enlisted, injured his left foot so severely that he was unable to walk and was therefore discharged. See Compiled Service Records, reel 350 (Williams file).

7. These figures are based on extrapolations from twelve sample companies to represent the losses of all companies in the future division. Eleven regiments and one battalion (roughly 11,500 men originally) constituted the division for most of its existence (see Table 1).

8. *Official Records,* vol. 9, pp. 707, 713 (quotation), 729–31; David P. Smith, "In Defense of Texas: The Life of Henry E. McCulloch" (M.A. thesis, Stephen F. Austin State University, 1975), 104.

9. Norman D. Brown, ed., *Journey to Pleasant Hill: The Civil War Letters of Captain Elijah P. Petty, Walker's Texas Division, C.S.A.* (San Antonio: Institute of Texan Cultures, 1982), 74; Thomas W. Cutrer, ed., "'An Experience in Soldier's Life': The Civil War Letters of Volney Ellis, Adjutant, Twelfth Texas Infantry, Walker's Texas Division, C.S.A.," *Military History of the Southwest* 22 (fall 1992): 115 (hereafter cited as "Letters of Volney Ellis").

10. Biography and Diaries of R. S. Gould, p. 62, Gould Papers; J. S. Bryan to Dear Nan, May 14, 1862, John Samuel Bryan Papers, Indiana Historical Society Library, Indianapolis; William L. Shea, "The Confederate Defeat at Cache River," *Arkansas Historical Quarterly* 52 (summer 1993): 129–55.

11. Cutrer, ed., "Letters of Volney Ellis," 115; Cutrer, ed., "Letters of Virgil Sullivan Rabb," Part One, pp. 163–5; ibid., Part Two, pp. 61–96; S. W. Farrow to Dearest Josephine, August 9, 1862, Farrow Papers; Brown, ed., *Journey to Pleasant Hill,* 74.

12. Blessington, *Campaigns of Walker's Texas Division,* 28–30 (quotations on pp. 28 and 30).

13. Ibid., 31.

14. Ibid., 32–3. Another company of the regiment, five days behind Blessington's, avoided the most extreme heat by beginning its daily treks at 3 A.M. and stopping by late morning (Cutrer, ed., "Letters of Virgil Sullivan Rabb," Part One, p. 167).

15. Blessington, *Campaigns of Walker's Texas Division,* 34, 36.

16. Ibid., 36; S. M. Farrow to My Dearest Josephine, September 10, 1862, Farrow Papers.

17. Biography and Diaries of R. S. Gould, 62; Johansson, *Peculiar Honor,* 26, 28; Oates, *Confederate Cavalry West of the River,* 47–8; Reid, "Spartan Band," 54–5. One trooper in the 16th Texas Cavalry wrote his wife that "we have been riding our horses almost day and night and had nothing to feed them untill thay war almost apast going" (J. S. Bryan to Dear Nancy, July 13, 1862, John Samuel Bryan Papers).

18. T. J. Rounsaville to Dear Niece, September 14, 1862, James B. and Thomas J. Rounsaville Letters, Civil War Miscellaneous Collection, USAMHI; John T. Stark to Dear Martha and Children, August 9, 1862, Stark Letters and Diary; E. K. Smith to Hon. F. B. Sexton, June 22, 1863, Letters Sent,

Trans-Mississippi Department, chap. II, vol. 70, Records of the Department of Texas and the Trans-Mississippi Department, Records of Military Commands, War Department Collection of Confederate Records, Record Group 109, National Archives; Johansson, *Peculiar Honor*, 28.

19. Blessington, *Campaigns of Walker's Texas Division*, 36–7. For Walker's sparkling performance at Antietam, see Stephen W. Sears, *Landscape Turned Red: The Battle of Antietam* (New Haven, Conn.: Ticknor and Fields, 1983), 214, 230–2, 248–9; Douglas Southall Freeman, *Lee's Lieutenants: A Study in Command*, 3 vols. (New York: Charles Scribner's Sons, 1942–44), 2:209–10, 214–7, 270.

20. Blessington, *Campaigns of Walker's Texas Division*, 38–9. "Hardee's Tactics" referred to W. J. Hardee's *Rifle and Light Infantry Tactics; For the Exercise and Manoeuvres of Troops When Acting As Light Infantry or Riflemen* (numerous editions, 1855).

21. Blessington, *Campaigns of Walker's Texas Division*, 39 (quotation), 40.

22. Ibid., 39–42. The rumors were false.

23. Ibid., 42–4 (quotation on pp. 42–3); Sam [Wright] to Dear Father, October 20, 1862, Samuel J. Wright Civil War Letters, Skipper Steely Collection, Texas A&M University at Commerce Library, Commerce, Tex.; John T. Stark to Dear Martha, October 9, 1862, John T. Stark Letters and Diary.

24. The journey was probably even longer. Mileage was calculated from modern highway maps, based on straighter paths than nineteenth-century roads in Texas and Arkansas.

25. Maj. Gen. William T. Sherman's famed march from Atlanta to the sea, by comparison, covered 250 miles in twenty-five days, about ten miles per day. Even armor and motorized infantry in World War II traveled only about 14.9 miles per day. See Thomas T. Smith, "Blitzkrieg: The Myth of Blitz," *Infantry* 80 (July–August 1990): 28–30.

26. Blessington, *Campaigns of Walker's Texas Division*, 44; H. A. Wallace to My Dear affectionate Wife, October 26, 1862, Harvey Alexander Wallace Papers, Southwest Arkansas Regional Archives, Washington, Ark.; Sam J. Wright to My dear Father, November 20, 1863, Wright Civil War Letters.

27. Ironically, some of the Texans' negative observations about Arkansans were almost identical to disparaging assessments of southerners in general made by Union soldiers during the war. See Mitchell, *Civil War Soldiers*, 107–17, for northern comments.

28. Brown, ed., *Journey to Pleasant Hill*, 104, 106; Ned to Darling Wife, July 29, 1862, Cade Correspondence; Theophilus Perry to Dear Harriet, [August] 5, 1862, Theophilus Perry Letters, Presley Carter Person Papers, Duke University Library, Durham, N.C. The Perry letters have been edited and published in M. Jane Johansson, ed., *Widows by the Thousand: The Civil War Letters of Theophilus and Harriet Perry, 1862–1864* (Fayetteville: Univ. of Arkansas Press, 2000).

29. Sam J. Wright to My dear Father, November 17, 1863, Wright Civil War Letters; R. Waterhouse Jr. to Dear Rose, November 26, 1862, Richard Waterhouse Letters, 1838–1872, Archives and Special Collections, University of Arkansas at Little Rock.

30. Theophilus Perry to Dear Harriet, [August] 5 and September 21, 1862, Perry Letters; H. A. Wallace to My Dear and loving wife, February 7, 1863, Harvey Alexander Wallace Papers, Southwest Arkansas Regional Archives, Washington, Ark.

31. S. C. Gordon, "Reminiscences of the Civil War from a Surgeon's Point of View," in *War Papers Read Before the Commandery of the State of Maine, Military Order of the Loyal Legion of the United States*, 4 vols. (Portland, Me.: Thurston Print, 1898), 1:141; Judith Lee Hallock, "'Lethal and Debilitating': The Southern Disease Environment as a Factor in Confederate Defeat," *Journal of Confederate History* 7, no. 1 (1991): 52–3; Alfred Jay Bollet, "Scurvy and Chronic Diarrhea in Civil War Troops: Were They Both Nutritional Deficiency Syndromes?" *Journal of the History of Medicine and Allied Sciences* 47 (January 1992): 49, 66.

32. W. P. Head to Dear Wife, June 10, 1864, Head Papers. Ipecac was a brownish powder com-

monly used to induce vomiting. See Bruce A. Evans, *A Primer of Civil War Medicine: Non-Surgical Medical Practice during the Civil War Years* ([Knoxville, Tenn.]: Bruce A. Evans, 1996), 37.

33. J. S. Bryan to Dear Nancy, August 6, 1862, Bryan Papers; H. A. Wallace to My Dear Wife, February 22, 1863, Harvey Alexander Wallace Papers, Southwest Arkansas Regional Archives, Washington, Ark. Blue mass, a dark blue concoction made of elemental mercury and various inert substances, was normally used as a laxative. When combined with opium, it served as a cathartic. See Evans, *Primer of Civil War Medicine,* 44.

34. S. P. Kirk to Mrs. E. J. Kirk, November 15, 1862, Sylvester Purl Kirk Letters, Texas Collection, Baylor University, Waco, Tex.

35. Brown, ed., *Journey to Pleasant Hill,* 98; John C. Porter, "Early Days of Pittsburg, Texas, 1859–1874; 18th Texas Infantry, Company H: Life of John C. Porter and Sketch of His Experiences in the Civil War," typescript, pp. 9–10, 18th Texas Infantry file, Confederate Research Center, Hill College; S. P. Kirk to Mrs. E. J. Kirk, November 15, 1862, Kirk Letters; D. M. Ray to Dear Sister, August 20, 1862, David M. Ray Papers, Center for American History; [Theophilus Perry] to Dear Harriet, September 4–5, 1862, Perry Letters; Robert W. Glover, ed., "The War Letters of a Texas Conscript in Arkansas," *Arkansas Historical Quarterly* 20 (winter 1961): 368; Ned [Cade] to Dear Wife, November 8, 1862, Cade Correspondence.

36. H. A. Wallace to My Dear Wife, September 16, 1862, Wallace Papers; D. M. Ray to Dear Sister, August 20, 1862, Ray Papers. Habituation to scenes of death occurred in both armies as the war dragged on. See Robertson, *Soldiers Blue and Gray,* 225–6; Logue, *To Appomattox and Beyond,* 51; Mitchell, *Civil War Soldiers,* 62–4.

37. S. P. Kirk to Mrs. E. J. Kirk, November 15, 1862, Kirk Letters; Samuel J. Wright to Dear Father, November 3, 1862, Wright Civil War Letters; H. A. Wallace to Dear and Beloved Wife, November 15, 1862, Wallace Papers; Blessington, *Campaigns of Walker's Division,* 44.

38. Blessington, *Campaigns of Walker's Texas Divi*sion, 44. The hundreds of graves at Camp Nelson remained untended until 1905, when 428 unidentified remains were moved to a nearby cemetery. The later graves too were neglected until 1980, when citizens of the area cleared away the weeds, erected a historical marker, and secured state funds for perpetual maintenance. See Field Roebuck, "The Camp Nelson Confederate Cemetery: A Tribute to Confederate Heroes," *Confederate Veteran* 40 (November–December 1992): 25–6.

39. Yeary, comp., *Reminiscences of the Boys in Gray,* 124. The division lost about 1,450 men killed and wounded during the war, so this estimate was very close to that of Blessington. For battle casualties in the division, see the appendix.

40. Exact numbers are impossible to pinpoint after 140 years, but the three brigades of the future division began with roughly 11,500 to 12,000 men. By March 1863 only 484 officers and 6,202 men were present for duty (*Official Records,* vol. 22, pt. 2, p. 810).

41. John M. Holcombe to Mandy, December 1, 1862, John and Amanda Holcombe Letters, private collection of John Wilson, Playa del Rey, Calif.; R. Waterhouse Jr. to Dear Rose, November 26, 1862, Waterhouse Letters. The new camp was near the present-day town of Lonoke, Arkansas.

42. R. Waterhouse Jr. to Dear Rose, November 26, 1862, Waterhouse Letters; Seymour V. Connor, ed., *Dear America: Some Letters of Orange Cicero and Mary America (Aikin) Connor* (Austin, Tex.: Jenkins, 1971), 65; H. A. Wallace to Achsah, November 29, 1862, Wallace Papers.

43. Ned to My dear wife, September 16, 1862, Cade Correspondence; Blessington, *Campaigns of Walker's Texas Division,* 63; D. M. Ray to Dear Sister, October 28, 1862, Ray Papers; John T. Knight to Dear Wife and Child, December 5, 1862, Knight Letters.

44. Blessington, *Campaigns of Walker's Texas Division,* 61–2; Connor, ed., *Dear America,* 69; D. M. Ray to Dear Mother, November 26, 1862, Ray Papers.

45. S. J. Wright to My dear Father, November 17, 1863, Wright Civil War Letters.

46. Ralph Masterson, ed., *Sketches from the Life of Dr. Horace Bishop* (San Angelo, Tex.: n.p., 1933), 10.

47. Blessington, *Campaigns of Walker's Texas Division,* 45.

48. Ibid., 46–59; *Official Records,* vol. 22, pt. 1, pp. 903–4.

49. Brigade commanders were natives of Tennessee (Henry McCulloch, Horace Randal, William R. Scurry, Richard Waterhouse), Kentucky (James M. Hawes), Georgia (George Flournoy, Wilburn H. King, Overton Young), South Carolina (Thomas N. Waul), and Pennsylvania (Robert P. Maclay).

50. Biographical sketches are in Tyler et al., eds., *New Handbook of Texas,* and Davis, ed., *Confederate General.*

51. Biographical sketches are in Tyler et al., eds., *New Handbook of Texas.*

52. Glover, ed., "War Letters of a Texas Conscript," 361; Porter, "Early Days," 9 (second and fourth quotations); Blessington, *Campaigns of Walker's Texas Division,* 42. About one-sixth of all ammunition produced at the Little Rock arsenal in November 1862 was for outdated flintlock muskets (William A. Albaugh, *Tyler, Texas, C.S.A.* [Harrisburg, Pa.: Stackpole Press, 1958], 34–5).

53. Brown, ed., *Journey to Pleasant Hill,* 100 (quotation), 134; [Theophilus Perry] to Dear Harriet, September 4–5, 1862, Perry Letters; Inspection Report on Walker's Division, May 27, 1863, J. L. Brent Papers, Louisiana Historical Assn. Collection, Howard-Tilton Memorial Library, Tulane University, New Orleans, La. Descriptions, specifications, and photographs of the arms used in the division are in Earl J. Coates and Dean S. Thomas, *An Introduction to Civil War Small Arms* (Gettysburg, Pa.: Thomas Publications, 1990).

54. Comparisons of military discipline to slavery were widespread among southern soldiers. See Mitchell, *Civil War Soldiers,* 58.

55. S. P. Kirk to Mrs. E. J. Kirk, November 15, 1862, Kirk Letters.

56. John T. Knight to Dear Wife and Child, December 5, 1862, Knight Letters; Jon Harrison, ed., "The Confederate Letters of John Simmons," *Chronicles of Smith County, Texas* 14 (summer 1975): 32, 33; Porter, "Early Days," 13.

57. S. W. Farrow to Dearest Josephine, April 8, 1863, Farrow Papers.

58. Executions for desertion were much more common during the Civil War than in later American wars. More than half the Union army's 267 executions (probably an undercount) were for desertion, and the Confederates may have shot or hanged even more. In all of World War II, the U.S. Army executed only one man for desertion. See Logue, *To Appomattox and Bey*ond, 50, 80; Stouffer, *Studies in Social Psychology,* 2:114.

59. D. M. Ray to Dear Sister, August 20, 1862, Ray Papers; [Edward Cade to wife, fragment], March ?, 1863, Cade Correspondence; Porter, "Early Days," 12–3.

60. S. J. Wright to My dear Father, February 10, 1863, Wright Civil War Letters. Samples for the three batteries attached to the division confirm this observation. Haldeman's unruly soldiers were several times more likely to desert than men in the other batteries.

61. J. B. Rounsaville to Dear Mother & Sisters, March 22, 1863, Rounsaville Letters; E. W. Cade to Dear Wife, March 13, 1863, Cade Correspondence.

62. Brown, *Journey to Pleasant Hill,* 148; E. W. Cade to Dear Wife, March 13, 1863, Cade Correspondence; J. T. Knight to Dear Wife & Child, March 14, 1863, Knight Letters.

63. Brown, ed., *Journey to Pleasant Hill,* 148; S. W. Farrow to My dearest Josephine, March 13, 1862, Farrow Papers; E. W. Cade to Dear Wife, March 13, 1863, Cade Correspondence.

## 4. THE FOLKS AT HOME

1. Glover, ed., "War Letters of a Texas Conscript," 356, 359–60, 364.

2. Ibid., 367, 368, 376–7.

3. Ibid., 381.

4. Ibid., 381, 385.

5. S. W. Farrow to Dear Josephine, July 28, August 9, November 26, 1862, May 13, 1863—all in Farrow Papers.

6. H. A. Wallace to My Dear Wife, September 16, 1862, Wallace Papers; J. T. Knight to Dear Wife and Child, January 3, 1863, Knight Letters; John M. Holcombe to Mandy, September 12, October 1, 1862, March 15, 1862 [1863], Holcombe Letters. For similar realizations of the importance of family, see James Marten, "Fatherhood in the Confederacy: Southern Soldiers and Their Children," *Journal of Southern History* 63 (May 1997): 292.

7. The patriarchal view of husbands is clearly expressed in Bertram Wyatt-Brown, *Southern Honor: Ethics and Behavior in the Old South* (New York: Oxford Univ. Press, 1982), 226–53; and Catherine Clinton, *The Plantation Mistress: Women's World in the Old South* (New York: Pantheon Books, 1982). The other interpretation is available in Jane Turner Censer, *North Carolina Planters and Their Children, 1800–1860* (Baton Rouge: Louisiana State Univ. Press, 1984); Jan Lewis, *The Pursuit of Happiness: Family and Values in Jefferson's Virginia* (New York: Cambridge Univ. Press, 1983); and Melinda S. Buza, " 'Pledges of Our Love': Friendship, Love, and Marriage among the Virginia Gentry, 1800–1825," in *The Edge of the South: Life in Nineteenth-Century Virginia,* ed. Edward L. Ayers and John C. Willis (Charlottesville: Univ. Press of Virginia, 1991), 9–36.

8. E. P. Becton to My Dear Mary, August 12, November 9, 1862, Edwin Pinckney Becton Papers, Center for American History.

9. H. A. Wallace to [his wife], September 6, 1862, Wallace Papers; Connor, ed., *Dear America,* 60.

10. J. S. Bryan to My Dear wife, December 10, 1862, Bryan Papers; Yeary, comp., *Reminiscences of the Boys in Gray,* 711.

11. Thomas P. Lowry, *The Story the Soldiers Wouldn't Tell: Sex in the Civil War* (Mechanicsburg, Pa.: Stackpole Books, 1994), 5–8, emphasizes the evasive and indirect references to sex by soldiers in the American Civil War.

12. H. A. Wallace to My Dear Wife, September 16, 1862, February 7, 1863, Wallace Papers; Allie [Cade] to My own Darling Husband, November 19, 1863, Cade Correspondence.

13. Glover, ed., "War Letters," 364.

14. Theophilus Perry to Dear Harriet, February 2, 1863, Perry Letters.

15. Brown, ed., *Journey to Pleasant Hill,* 145, 163.

16. H. A. Wallace to My Dear Wife, February 22, 1863, Wallace Papers; Glover, ed., "War Letters," 357.

17. Theophilus [Perry] to Dear Harriet, July 14, 1862, Perry Letters; Perry Anderson Snyder, "Shreveport, Louisiana, during the Civil War and Reconstruction" (Ph.D. diss., Florida State University, 1979), 95. For prostitution in other theaters of the war, see Robertson, *Soldiers Blue and Gray,* 117–20; Lowry, *Story the Soldiers Wouldn't Tell,* 63–9, 69–72, 77–83, 83–7.

18. Connor, ed., *Dear America,* 36.

19. John M. Holcombe to Mandy, December 1, 1862, Holcombe Letters.

20. Brown, ed., *Journey to Pleasant Hill,* 105.

21. Ibid., 104–5; E. P. Becton to My dear Mary, February 24, 1863, Becton Papers.

22. Josephine Farrow to Dear Husband, June 3, 1862, Farrow Papers; Eliza [Kirk] to S. P. Kirk, February 15, 1863[?], Kirk Letters; Cutrer, ed., "Letters of Volney Ellis," 125.

23. Harriet Perry to Theophilus Perry, September 5, 24, October 26, December 3, 13, 1862, January 18, 1863, Perry Letters.

24. Harriet Perry to Theophilus Perry, January 18, 1863, December 23, 1862, February 8, 1863, Perry Letters.

25. E. W. Cade to Dear Wife, June 29, 1862, and Allie Cade to My own loved Husband, August 5, 1862, Cade Correspondence; E. P. Becton to My dear Mary, October 10, December 14, 1862, Becton Papers.

26. Mary [Becton] to My dear Edwin, February 27, 1863, Becton Papers.

27. Mary Cheek to My Dear, February 18, 1863, T. F. Cheek, "T. F. Cheek Letters," *Confederate Reminiscences and Letters, 1861–1865,* 17 vols. to date (Atlanta, Ga.: United Daughters of the Confederacy, 1995), 2:139.

28. A convenient summary of the literature is in Marten, "Fatherhood in the Confederacy," 269–70 (quotation on p. 70). Marten's findings conflict directly with the older interpretation.

29. J. S. Bryan to Dear Nancy, July 13, 1862, Bryan Papers; E. P. Becton to My Dear Mary, August 12, 1862, Becton Papers; John T. Knight to Dear Wife, October 1, 1862, Knight Letters; Brown, ed., *Journey to Pleasant Hill,* 89; Connor, *Dear America,* 59–60; R. Waterhouse to [wife], December 23, 1862, Waterhouse Letters.

30. Pat H. Martin to Mrs. S. E. Truitt, September 22, 1862, Truitt Papers.

31. John M. Holcombe to Amandy, October 1, November 4, 1862, Holcombe Letters; D. E. Young to Dear Wife and Children, March 6, 1863, 17th Texas Infantry File, Confederate Research Center; Glover, ed., "War Letters," 65.

32. Glover, ed., "War Letters," 381; E. W. Cade to Dear Wife, March 13, 1863, Cade Correspondence.

33. J. S. Bryan to Dear Nancy, September 6, 1863, J. S. Bryan Papers; Cutrer, ed., "Letters of Volney Ellis," 139. Bertram Wyatt-Brown emphasized the heavy significance of honor among white southerners in *Southern Honor.*

34. E. Steele to My Dear Wife, February ?, March 16, 1862, E. Steele Papers, private collection of Wanda Cuniff, Nacogdoches, Tex.; E. W. Cade to Dear Wife, June 8, 18, 1862, Cade Correspondence. The dread that their children might forget them was common among Confederate soldiers (Marten, "Fatherhood in the Confederacy," 276).

35. S. W. Farrow to Dear Josephine, July 5, 1862, Farrow Papers; Glover, ed., "War Letters," 361, 383; John M. Holcombe to Mandy, September 12, 1862, Holcombe Letters.

## 5. WALKER'S GREYHOUNDS

1. Robert L. Kerby, *Kirby Smith's Confederacy: The Trans-Mississippi South, 1863–1865* (New York: Columbia Univ. Press, 1972), 34–6; McPherson, *Battle Cry of Freedom,* 577–9.

2. The Texans were proud of their nickname. "This name was given to our Division by the Yankees because they said they could hear of us one day perhaps a hundred and fifty miles off and the next day we would be fighting them," Capt. Virgil Rabb of the 16th Infantry boasted in 1863 (Cutrer, ed., "Letters of Virgil Sullivan Rabb," Part One, p. 183). At least two western Federal regiments—the 83rd Ohio Infantry and the 37th Illinois Infantry—also claimed the "greyhound" label, but the name is more generally associated with the Texans. See T. B. Marshall, *History of the Eighty-Three Ohio Volunteer Infantry: The Greyhound Regiment* (Cincinnati: Eighty-Third Ohio Volunteer Infantry

Assn., 1912); Michael A. Mullins, "The Fremont Rifles: The 37th Illinois at Pea Ridge and Prairie Grove," *Civil War Regiments* 1, no. 1 (1990): 42–68.

3. Brown, ed., *Journey to Pleasant Hill*, 106; Theophilus Perry to Dear Harriet, December 7, 1862, Perry Letters; Cutrer, ed., "Letters of Volney Ellis," 119.

4. Brown, ed., *Journey to Pleasant Hill*, 108; Theophilus Perry to Dear Harriet, December 7, 10, 1862, Perry Letters; J. S. Bryan to My Dear wife, December 10, 1862, Bryan Papers.

5. Brown, ed., *Journey to Pleasant Hill*, 111; Theophilus Perry to My dearest darling Wife, December 14, 1862, Perry Letters; Blessington, *Campaigns of Walker's Texas Division*, 63–4; John T. Knight to Dear Wife, December 14, 1862, Knight Letters; Harvey Alexander Wallace Diary, 1829–1865, p. 6, Southwest Arkansas Regional Archives, Washington, Ark.

6. Blessington, *Campaigns of Walker's Texas Division*, 64. "Blue beef" was exceptionally poor, lean beef, much despised by the soldiers (Mitford M. Mathews, ed., *A Dictionary of Americanisms on Historical Principles* [Chicago: Univ. of Chicago Press, 1956], 143).

7. Blessington, *Campaigns of Walker's Texas Division*, 65; T. H. Holmes, Special Orders No. 121, December 23, 1862, John G. Walker Papers, Southern Historical Collection, University of North Carolina, Chapel Hill.

8. Norman D. Brown, "John George Walker," in *Confederate General*, ed. Davis, 6:88–9; obituary in *Washington Post*, July 21, 1893; J. G. W[alker]. to My dear Sisters, July 1, 1853, David Walker Papers, Myron Gwinner Collection, USAMHI; Gerald M. Capers, *Stephen A. Douglas: Defender of the Union* (Boston: Little, Brown, 1959), 75–6.

9. *Official Records*, vol. 19, pt. 2, pp. 697 (quotation), 731; J. G. Walker to R. D. Minor, September 18, 1861, Minor Family Papers (Mss1M6663c2837), Virginia Historical Society, Richmond; Brown, "John George Walker," in *Confederate General*, ed. Davis, 88–9; Freeman, *Lee's Lieutenants*, 2:209–10, 214–7, 270.

10. *Charleston (S.C.) Mercury*, August 10, 1864; H. A. Wallace to My Dear Achsah, February 10, 1864, Wallace Papers; Blessington, *Campaigns of Walker's Texas Division*, 72–3; Douglas French Forrest, *Odyssey in Gray: A Diary of Confederate Service, 1863–1865*, ed. William N. Still Jr. (Richmond: Virginia State Library, 1979), 306

11. Porter, "Early Days," 10; Blessington, *Campaigns of Walker's Texas Division*, 66–7; D. M. Ray to Dear Brother, January 1, 1863, Ray Papers; Cutrer, ed., "Letters of Virgil Sullivan Rabb," Part One, p. 171.

12. Blessington, *Campaigns of Walker's Texas Division*, 67, 68; Brown, ed., *Journey to Pleasant Hill*, 124.

13. Cutrer, ed., "Letters of Virgil Sullivan Rabb," Part One, p. 172.

14. Brown, ed., *Journey to Pleasant Hill*, 126; Blessington, *Campaigns of Walker's Texas Division*, 68.

15. For the assault at Arkansas Post, see Edwin Cole Bearss, *The Campaign for Vicksburg*, 3 vols. (Dayton, Ohio: Morningside, 1985–86), 1:360–405; Richard L. Kiper, "John Alexander McClernand and the Arkansas Post Campaign," *Arkansas Historical Quarterly* 56 (spring 1997): 56–79; Shelby Foote, *The Civil War: A Narrative*, 3 vols. (New York: Random House, 1958–74), 2:134–6.

16. Brown, ed., *Journey to Pleasant Hill*, 125, 127; Blessington, *Campaigns of Walker's Texas Division*, 68–9.

17. For the advance of Walker's division, see Wallace Diary, p. 6; Blessington, *Campaigns of Walker's Texas Division*, 68–70.

18. D. M. Ray to Dear Mother, January 28, 1863, Ray Papers; E. P. Becton to My dear Mary,

January 17, 1863, Becton Papers; Cutrer, ed., "Letters of Volney Ellis," 122; Blessington, *Campaigns of Walker's Texas Division*, 70–1.

19. E. P. Becton to My dear Mary, January 17, 1863, Becton Papers; Wallace Diary, p. 7; S. J. Wright to My dear Father, January 23, 1863, Wright Civil War Letters; Blessington, *Campaigns of Walker's Texas Division*, 70–1.

20. Porter, "Early Days," 11; E. P. Becton to My dear Mary, January 17, 1863, Becton Papers; John T. Stark to Martha A. Stark, January 25, 1863, Stark Letters and Diary.

21. Wallace Diary, p. 7; E. P. Becton to My dear Mary, January 21, 1863, Becton Papers; S. J. Wright to My dear Father, January 23, 1863, Wright Civil War Letters; Harrison, ed., "Confederate Letters of John Simmons," 33; Porter, "Early Days," 12; Blessington, *Campaigns of Walker's Texas Division*, 75.

22. E. P. Becton to My dear Mary, January 21, 1863, Becton Papers; Blessington, *Campaigns of Walker's Texas Division*, 75.

23. John T. Knight to Dear Wife & Child, January 12–3, 1863, Knight Letters; T. J. Rounsaville to My dear ma & sisters, January 15, 1863, Rounsaville Letters; Theophilus Perry to Dear Harriet, January 14, 1862 [1863], Perry Letters.

24. S. J. Wright to My dear Father, January 15, 1863, Wright Civil War Letters; Cutrer, ed., "Letters of Volney Ellis," 123.

25. Blessington, *Campaigns of Walker's Texas Division*, 76. On improving health, see Edward Cade to Darling Wife, January 30, February 7, 1863, Cade Correspondence; W. S. Fowler to dear Sister, February 1, 1863, Holcombe Letters; J. J. Arberry to Dear Sallie & Relatives, February 27, 1863, John J. Arberry Letters, Gary Canada Collection.

26. Brown, ed., *Journey to Pleasant Hill*, 133–4; David M. Ray to Dear Mother, January 28, 1863, Ray Papers.

27. John T. Knight to Dear Wife & Child, January 31, 1863, Knight Letters; Glover, ed., "War Letters," 380; Cutrer, ed., "Letters of Volney Ellis," 124.

28. Carl E. Hatch, ed., *Dearest Susie: A Civil War Infantryman's Letters to His Sweetheart* (New York: Exposition Press, 1971), 37; George Hanrahan, ed., "An Iowa Private in the Civil War," *Palimpsest* 58 (November–December 1977): 186.

29. T. J. Rounsaville to My dear Ma & Sisters, February 23, 1863, Rounsaville Letters; John T. Knight to Dear Wife & Child, January 31, 1863, Knight Letters; R. Waterhouse to Dear Rose, February 18, 1863, Waterhouse Letters.

30. J. T. Knight to Dear Wife & Child, February 26, 1863, Knight Letters; Harrison, ed., "Confederate Letters of John Simmons," 32. Also see R. Waterhouse to Dear Rose, February 15, 1863, Waterhouse Letters. Several other correspondents mentioned desertions at Pine Bluff.

31. Cutrer, ed., "Letters of Volney Ellis," 128; Glover, ed., "War Letters," 382–3; Brown, ed., *Journey to Pleasant Hill*, 134.

32. Brown, ed., *Journey to Pleasant Hill*, 134; E. W. Cade to Dear Wife, March 13, 1863, Cade Correspondence. On the number of executions, see J. S. Bryan to Dear Nancy, March 29, 1863, Bryan Papers; Brown, ed., *Journey to Pleasant Hill*, 152.

33. Joseph Howard Parks, *General Edmund Kirby Smith, C.S.A.* (Baton Rouge: Louisiana State Univ. Press, 1954), 251–4; Kerby, *Kirby Smith's Confederacy*, 51–3; Anne J. Bailey, "E. Kirby Smith," in *Encyclopedia of the Confederacy*, ed. Richard N. Current, 4 vols. (New York: Simon and Schuster, 1993), 4:1472–74.

34. Brown, ed., *Journey to Pleasant Hill*, 135–6; R. Waterhouse Jr. to Dear Rose, February 18, 1863, Waterhouse Letters.

35. *Official Records*, vol. 22, pt. 2, p. 871; William R. Boggs, *Military Reminiscences of Gen. William R. Boggs, C.S.A.*, ed. William K. Boyd (Durham, N.C.: Seeman Printery, 1913), 56–7.

36. *Official Records*, vol. 24, pt. 1, pp. 46–7; Bearss, *Campaign for Vicksburg*, 2:24–25.

37. *Official Records*, vol. 15, pp. 1041, 1042–43; Parks, *General Edmund Kirby Smith*, 259–64; James G. Hollandsworth Jr., *Pretense of Glory: The Life of General Nathaniel P. Banks* (Baton Rouge: Louisiana State Univ. Press, 1998), 108–16.

38. *Official Records*, vol. 22, pt. 2, p. 828; Blessington, *Campaigns of Walker's Texas Division*, 78.

39. The 17th Infantry left one man behind. Sgt. John Holcombe, the soldier who had wept in front of his comrades upon receiving his first letter from home, was discharged on April 25 after four months of illness. He lingered on for a while and tried to return to Texas, but he was too weak. He never saw his wife Amanda again and died in Arkansas. Certificate of disability, Holcombe Letters; John Wilson to Richard Lowe, November 19, 1996, in possession of recipient.

40. W. H. Christian to O. M. Roberts, April 24, 1863, Roberts Papers; S. J. Wright to My dear Father, May 6, 1863, Wright Civil War Letters; Brown, ed., *Journey to Pleasant Hill*, 204; Theophilus Perry to My Dear Wife, April 25, 1863, Perry Letters.

41. Holder, *Tennessee to Texas*, 123; S. J. Wright to My dear Father, May 6, 1863, Wright Civil War Letters.

42. John G. Walker, "The War of Secession West of the Mississippi River During the Years 1863–4 & 5" (typescript), 26, Myron G. Gwinner Collection, USAMHI; Holder, *Tennessee to Texas*, 122–3; Blessington, *Campaigns of Walker's Texas Division*, 79–80; Brown, ed., *Journey to Pleasant Hill*, 209; S. W. Farrow to Dear Josephine, May 7, 1863, Farrow Papers.

43. Walker, "War of Secession," 26; Blessington, *Campaigns of Walker's Texas Division*, 80–1; Kerby, *Kirby Smith's Confederacy*, 106–7; Parks, *General Edmund Kirby Smith*, 260–4; Bearss, *Campaign for Vicksburg*, 3:1155–59.

44. Kerby, *Kirby Smith's Confederacy*, 106–7; Parks, *General Edmund Kirby Smith*, 260–4; Bearss, *Campaign for Vicksburg*, 3:1155–59. For the order to move south by water, see H. P. Pratt to P. O. Hébert, May 3, 1863, Letters Sent, Trans-Mississippi Department (chap. II, vol. 70), Records of the Department of Texas and the Trans-Mississippi Department, Records of Military Commands, War Department Collection of Confederate Records.

45. Theophilus Perry to Dear Harriet, May 7–8, 1863, Perry Letters.

46. Blessington, *Campaigns of Walker's Texas Division*, 81; Brown, ed., *Journey to Pleasant Hill*, 215; Arthur James Lyon Fremantle, *The Fremantle Diary: Being the Journal of Lieutenant Colonel James Arthur Lyon Fremantle, Coldstream Guards, on his Three Months in the Southern States*, ed. Walter Lord (Boston: Little, Brown, 1954), 71.

47. Porter, "Early Days," 14; Blessington, *Campaigns of Walker's Texas Division*, 81; Paul Silverstone, *Warships of the Civil War Navies* (Annapolis, Md.: Naval Institute Press, 1989), 69, 151, 161, 162. Walker's information was correct: four Federal warships were coming upstream, looking specifically for Walker's unarmed transports. "On few occasions in American military history has a naval officer been presented with such a golden opportunity for attacking unescorted troop transports" (Bearss, *Campaign for Vicksburg*, 3:700).

48. Brown, ed., *Journey to Pleasant Hill*, 215; Porter, "Early Days," 14.

49. [George William Logan], "Official Report of Colonel George William Logan," *Southern Historical Society Papers* 11 (November 1883): 497–501; Bearss, *Campaign for Vicksburg*, 3:701–5; Blessington, *Campaigns of Walker's Texas Division*, 81.

50. John Q. Anderson, ed., *Brokenburn: The Journal of Kate Stone, 1861–1868* (Baton Rouge: Louisiana State Univ. Press, 1955), 213; H. P. Pratt (Smith's adjutant) to R. Taylor, May 12, 1863, Letters

Sent, Trans-Mississippi Department (chap. II, vol. 70), Records of the Department of Texas and the Trans-Mississippi Department, Records of Military Commands, War Department Collection of Confederate Records; Blessington, *Campaigns of Walker's Texas Division*, 81–3.

51. Anderson, ed., *Brokenburn*, 212; Theophilus Perry to Dear Harriet, May 18, 1863, Perry Letters; W. H. Christian to Dear Col. [Oran Roberts], May 13, 1863, Roberts Papers; Ned [Cade] to My dear Wife, May 20, 1863, Cade Correspondence.

52. Kerby, *Kirby Smith's Confederacy*, 109–10; Blessington, *Campaigns of Walker's Texas Division*, 83; Hollandsworth, *Pretense of Glory*, 119–20.

53. Sam [Wright] to My dear Father, May 22, 1863, Wright Civil War Letters; Brown, ed., *Journey to Pleasant Hill*, 223; *Official Records*, vol. 26, pt. 1, p. 535; Kerby, *Kirby Smith's Confederacy*, 109.

54. *Official Records*, vol. 26, pt. 2, p. 11; Blessington, *Campaigns of Walker's Texas Division*, 83–4; Johansson, *Peculiar Honor*, 51.

55. Brown, ed., *Journey to Pleasant Hill*, 225. For miles traveled, see the daily ! ⸱g in Blessington, *Campaigns of Walker's Texas Division*, 79–84.

## 6. MILLIKEN'S BEND

1. *Official Records*, vol. 26, pt. 2, pp. 12–3, 15; Parks, *General Edmund Kirby Smith*, 268–9.

2. T. Michael Parrish, *Richard Taylor: Soldier Prince of Dixie* (Chapel Hill: Univ. of North Carolina Press, 1992), 17, 22 (quotations), 14–6, 33–6.

3. Ibid., 181–219 passim, 241–2.

4. Richard Taylor, *Destruction and Reconstruction: Personal Experiences of the Late War*, introduced by T. Michael Parrish (1879; reprint, New York: Da Capo Press, 1995), 115, 137–8; Parrish, *Richard Taylor*, 254–7, 281–3, 285–7; Hollandsworth, *Pretense of Glory*, 122.

5. Bearss, *Campaign for Vicksburg*, 3:1167–68. Contrary to Grant's statements in his memoirs and to many secondary accounts of the Vicksburg campaign, Grant did not "cut himself off" from his communications when he crossed to the east side of the river. His army continued to depend on the supply route in Louisiana until a new line on the opposite bank was established (ibid., 2:447, 449, 459, 461, 470, esp. 480–1, 3:791–2).

6. Walker, "War of Secession," 28.

7. Taylor, *Destruction and Reconstruction*, 138.

8. Inspection Report on Walker's Division, May 27, 1863, Brent Papers.

9. Blessington, *Campaigns of Walker's Texas Division*, 85–6; Walker's report to Smith, ibid., 119.

10. Theophilus Perry to Dear Harriet, May 29, 1863, Perry Letters; Brown, ed., *Journey to Pleasant Hill*, 229.

11. Blessington, *Campaigns of Walker's Texas Division*, 85–6; Walker's report to Smith, ibid., 119; Brown, ed., *Journey to Pleasant Hill*, 228.

12. Blessington, *Campaigns of Walker's Texas Division*, 86; Walker's report, reprinted in ibid., 119–20.

13. Edgar L. Erickson, ed., "With Grant at Vicksburg: From the Civil War Diary of Captain Charles E. Wilcox," *Journal of the Illinois State Historical Society* 30 (January 1938): 463; Leslie A. Lovett, "John Perkins Jr.," in *Encyclopedia of the Confederacy*, ed. Current, 3:1194; "John Perkins Jr.," in *Biographical Directory of the American Congress, 1774–1996* (Alexandria, Va.: CQ Staff Directories, 1997), 1650; Jeffrey Alan Owens, "The Civil War in Tensas Parish, Louisiana: Community History" (M.A. thesis, University of Texas at Tyler, 1990), 47.

14. *A Biographical History of Eminent and Self-Made Men of the State of Indiana*, 2 vols. (Cincin-

nati, Ohio: Western Biographical, 1880), 1:37–39; John Y. Simon, ed., *The Papers of Ulysses S. Grant*, 20 vols. to date (Carbondale: Southern Illinois Univ. Press, 1967), 8:551; Bearss, *Campaign for Vicksburg*, 3:1170–71.

15. Navy Department, *Official Records of the Union and Confederate Navies in the War of the Rebellion*, 31 vols. (Washington: Government Printing Office, 1894–1922), series 1, vol. 25, pp. 147–8 (hereafter cited as *Official Records, Navies*, with all references to series 1); Silverstone, *Warships of the Civil War Navies*, 151; John M. Holcombe to Wm. Fowler, November 1, 1862, Holcombe Letters (for William Edgar's field battery).

16. Blessington, *Campaigns of Walker's Texas Division*, 87–8; McCulloch's report, ibid., 89–92. Capt. Horace Haldeman's battery (formerly attached to Hawes's brigade) and half of James M. Daniel's Lamar battery (formerly attached to Randal's brigade) had been detached for service elsewhere in Louisiana and were not part of this expedition (Perkins, *Daniel's Battery*, 13; Edgar E. Lackner, ed., "Civil War Diaries of Edwin F. Stanton, U.S.A., and William Quensell, C.S.A.: 'Yank and Reb' under One Cover," *East Texas Historical Journal* 18, no. 2 [1980]: 33).

17. Blessington, *Campaigns of Walker's Texas Division*, 88 (quotation), 90–1 (McCulloch's report); Brown, ed., *Journey to Pleasant Hill*, 231–2; Simon, ed., *Papers of Ulysses S. Grant*, 8:551. "Shot" was a nonexploding solid sphere or oblong artillery projectile; "shell" could be either shape, but it contained a charge of powder to burst it over the heads of the enemy.

18. Brown, ed., *Journey to Pleasant Hill*, 233; Blessington, *Campaigns of Walker's Texas Division*, 88; McCulloch's report, ibid., 90–2.

19. *Official Records, Navies*, vol. 25, pp. 63–4; Theophilus Perry to Dear Harriet, June 1, 1863, Perry Letters; McCulloch's report in Blessington, *Campaigns of Walker's Texas Division*, 91.

20. Brown, ed., *Journey to Pleasant Hill*, 232; Theophilus Perry to Dear Harriet, June 1, 1863, Perry Letters.

21. Blessington, *Campaigns of Walker's Texas Division*, 93; Theophilus Perry to Dear Harriet, June 1, 1863, Perry Letters; [E. W. Cade] to wife, June ?, 1863, Cade Correspondence.

22. *Official Records*, vol. 24, pt. 2, pp. 457–8; Bearss, *Campaign for Vicks*burg, 3:1174–75.

23. Ibid.

24. Report of Colonel Hermann Lieb, June 8, 1863, reprinted in David Cornwell, "Dan Caverno: A True Tale of American Life on the Farm, in a Country Store, and in the Volunteer Army," 136, David Cornwell Papers, Civil War Miscellaneous Collection, USAMHI; *Official Records, Navies*, vol. 25, p. 163; Bearss, *Campaign for Vicks*burg, 3:1175.

25. Cornwell, "Dan Caverno," 132; Cyrus Sears, *Paper of Cyrus Sears, Read Before the Ohio Commandery of the Loyal Legion, October 7th 1908* (Columbus, Ohio: F. J. Heer Printing Co., 1909), 13; Frank Moore, ed., *The Rebellion Record: A Diary of American Events . . .* , 12 vols. (New York: G. P. Putnam, 1861–63, vols. 1–6; New York: D. Van Nostrand, 1864–68, vols. 7–12), 7:12–13 (document 8); Capt. W. M. Little to his wife, June 9, 1863, in *Washington National Tribune*, January 13, 1916. Estimates of Federal strength during the fight range from eleven to fourteen hundred. The estimate (1,328) of Lt. David Cornwell, an officer in one of the black regiments, because it is more detailed and precise than any others, seems most reliable.

26. Blessington, *Campaigns of Walker's Texas Division*, 94; *Official Records*, vol. 24, pt. 2, p. 458.

27. *Official Records*, vol. 24, pt. 2, pp. 458–9. Also see Noah Andre Trudeau, *Like Men of War: Black Troops in the Civil War, 1862–1865* (Boston: Little, Brown, 1998), 46–59; and Terrence J. Winschel, "To Rescue Gibraltar: John Walker's Texas Division and Its Expedition to Relieve Fortress Vicksburg," *Civil War Regiments* 3, no. 3 (1993): 33–58.

28. Peter W. Gravis, *Twenty-Five Years on the Outside Row of the Northwest Conference: Autobiography of Rev. Peter W. Gravis* (1892; reprint, Brownwood, Tex.: Cross Timbers Press, 1966), 28.

29. Blessington, *Campaigns of Walker's Texas Division*, 95; *Official Records*, vol. 24, pt. 2, p. 467.

30. Cornwell, "Dan Caverno," 132; William Eliot Furness, "The Negro As a Soldier," in *Military Essays and Recollections: Papers Read before the Commandery of the State of Illinois, Military Order of the Loyal Legion of the United States* (Chicago: A.C. McClurg, 1894), 476; *Official Records*, vol. 24, pt. 2, p. 467; Blessington, *Campaigns of Walker's Texas Division*, 96.

31. Yeary, comp., *Reminiscences of the Boys in Gray*, 665–6; Moore, ed., *Rebellion Record*, 7:12 (document 8); *Official Records*, vol. 24, pt. 2, p. 469; Cornwell, "Dan Caverno," 132.

32. D. E. Young to Dear Wife and Children, June 7, 1863, 17th Texas Infantry file, Confederate Research Center, Hill College; Gravis, *Twenty-Five Years*, 28; Brown, ed., *Journey to Pleasant Hill*, 236, 245; Yeary, comp., *Reminiscences of the Boys in Gray*, 609–10.

33. Capt. W. M. Little to his wife, June 9, 1863, in *Washington National Tribune*, January 13, 1916; Robert Henry to Dear Wife, June 12, 1863, Robert W. Henry Letters, State Historical Society of Iowa, Des Moines; A. A. Stuart, *Iowa Colonels and Regiments: Being a History of Iowa Regiments in the War of the Rebellion* (Des Moines: Mills, 1865), 392; Furness, "Negro As a Soldier," 475–6; Leonard Brown, *American Patriotism; or, Memoirs of "common men"* (Des Moines: Redhead and Wellslager, 1869), 269, 282.

34. Cornwell, "Dan Caverno," 131, 133 (quotation).

35. Ibid., 133; account of Capt. Matthew M. Miller in Furness, "Negro As a Soldier," 475; account of Corwin Frederick in Brown, *American Patriotism*, 305. Also see Benjamin Quarles, *The Negro in the Civil War*, 2nd ed. (Boston: Little, Brown, 1969), 220–5.

36. *Official Records*, vol. 24, pt. 2, pp. 468, 470; Blessington, *Campaigns of Walker's Texas Division*, 98–9.

37. *Official Records*, vol. 24, pt. 2, pp. 468–9; *Austin Tri-Weekly Gazette*, August 20, 1863, p. 2 (Walker's special order commending Schultz).

38. Lieb's report, in Cornwell, "Dan Caverno," 137; Capt. W. M. Little to his wife, June 9, 1863, in *Washington National Tribune*, January 13, 1916; account of Corwin Frederick in Brown, *American Patriotism*, 305.

39. Your Husband (Theophilus Perry) to Dear Harriet, June 11, 1863, Perry Letters; Lieb's report, in Cornwell, "Dan Caverno," 137; Capt. W. M. Little to his wife, June 9, 1863, in *Washington National Tribune*, January 13, 1916; Robert Henry to Dear Wife, June 12, 1863, Henry Letters; Gravis, *Twenty-Five Years*, 28; G. G. Edwards, "Fight at Milliken's Bend, Miss. [*sic*]," *Rebellion Record* 7 (1869): 12–3; Sears, *Paper of Cyrus Sears*, 6; "Battle of Milliken's Bend," *Confederate Veteran* 8 (February 1900): 67; Walker, "War of Secession," 29; Blessington, *Campaigns of Walker's Texas Division*, 100, 121–2.

40. *Official Records, Navies*, vol. 25, p. 163; Silverstone, *Warships of the Civil War Navies*, 157.

41. Sears, *Paper of Cyrus Sears*, 15–6; James Russell Soley, "Naval Operations in the Vicksburg Campaign," in *Battles and Leaders of the Civil War*, ed. Robert Underwood Johnson and Clarence Clough Buel, 4 vols. (New York: Century, 1887–88), 3:570; *Official Records, Navies*, vol. 25, p. 163.

42. *Official Records*, vol. 24, pt. 2, pp. 447–8, 453–4, 459, 464, 469; Lieb's report, in Cornwell, "Dan Caverno," 137; Walker, "War of Secession," 29; Blessington, *Campaigns of Walker's Texas Division*, 100; Yeary, comp., *Reminiscences of the Boys in Gray*, 609–10; Furness, "Negro As a Soldier," 477; Edwards, "Fight at Milliken's Bend," 12; Wallace Diary, June 7, 1863. Talk among Federal soldiers in the vicinity was that the gunboats had been the decisive turning point. An Illinois soldier wrote his father that the "timely assistance [of the gunboats] checked the enemy and prevented the entire rout

of our men. . . . The rebels were driven back by the gunboats" (Chas. Otto Henthorn to Dear Father, June 10, 1863, Charles Otto Henthorn Papers, Clements Library, University of Michigan, Ann Arbor).

43. Blessington, *Campaigns of Walker's Texas Division*, 101–2.

44. Ibid., 102; Gravis, *Twenty-Five Years*, 28; Cornwell, "Dan Caverno," 149. Surgeons in both armies amputated limbs from about sixty thousand soldiers, more than in any other American war, and about three of every four of the victims survived the ordeal (Laurann Figg and Jane Farrell-Beck, "Amputation in the Civil War: Physical and Social Dimensions," *Journal of the History of Medicine and Allied Sciences* 48 [October 1993]: 454).

45. *Official Records*, vol. 24, pt. 2, pp. 447–8, 470; William F. Fox, *Regimental Losses in the American Civil War, 1861–1865* (Albany, N.Y.: Albany, 1889), 54; Cornwell, "Dan Caverno," 132; Joseph T. Glatthaar, *Forged in Battle: The Civil War Alliance of Black Soldiers and White Officers* (New York: Free Press, 1990), 134. The name and description of the wound for each Confederate casualty are available in "Confederate States Army Casualties: Lists and Narrative Reports, 1861–1865," War Department Collection of Confederate Records (Microfilm M836, roll 2).

46. See Fox, *Regimental Losses*, 54 (for deaths); Cornwell, "Dan Caverno," 132 (for numbers engaged); John Cimprich and Robert C. Mainfort Jr., "The Fort Pillow Massacre: A Statistical Note," *Journal of American History* 76 (December 1989): 836.

47. Sears, *Paper of Cyrus Sears*, 15; Cornwell, "Dan Caverno," 136–7, 138–40; *Official Records*, ser. 3, vol. 3, p. 454.

48. *Official Records*, ser. 1, vol. 24, pt. 2, pp. 468–9; "Battle of Milliken Bend," *Confederate Veteran* 8 (February 1900): 67.

49. *Official Records*, vol. 24, pt. 2, p. 459; Parrish, *Richard Taylor*, 292–3.

50. For Confederate statements about the capture of black prisoners, see Blessington, *Campaigns of Walker's Texas Division*, 99–100; Taylor, *Destruction and Reconstruction*, 139; Ned [Cade] to Dear Wife, June 8[?], 1863, Cade Correspondence; McCulloch's report, *Official Records*, vol. 24, pt. 2, p. 468; Walker's special order, June 20, 1863, reprinted in *Austin (Tex.) Tri-Weekly State Gazette*, August 20, 1863. The *Shreveport (La.) News* reported on June 13 that sixty black prisoners from Milliken's Bend had been escorted to Monroe on June 11.

51. For evidence that other black soldiers captured by Texas troops were turned over to rear-area officials, see *Official Records*, ser. 2, vol. 8, pp. 646, 652, 703.

52. Sears, *Paper of Cyrus Sears*, 15. For later allegations about black flags and the killing of prisoners, all repeated by men who had not been in the fight and nearly all including erroneous information, see, for example, *Washington National Tribune*, December 7, 1905; *Burlington (Iowa) Weekly Hawk-Eye*, June 27, 1863; *Keokuk (Iowa) Daily Gate City*, June 12, 1863; *New Orleans Times Picayune*, June 23, 1863; Furness, "Negro As a Soldier," 475; *Harper's Weekly* 7 (July 4, 1863): 427, and 8 (May 21, 1864): 334.

53. *Official Records*, vol. 24, pt. 3, pp. 425–6, 443–4, 469 (Grant-Taylor correspondence); James G. Hollandsworth Jr., "The Execution of White Officers from Black Units by Confederate Forces During the Civil War," *Louisiana History* 35 (fall 1994): 479, 489.

54. Yeary, comp., *Reminiscences of the Boys in Gray*, 609–10 (quotation). For other Confederate opinions, see ibid., 759–60; Gravis, *Twenty-Five Years*, 28; "Battle of Milliken Bend," *Confederate Veteran* 8 (February 1900): 67; Blessington, *Campaigns of Walker's Texas Division*, 96–7. Taylor's assessment is in his *Destruction and Reconstruction*, 136. Federal judgments are in Lieb's report, in Cornwell, "Dan Caverno," 134, 137; Sears, *Paper of Cyrus Sears*, 15–6; Soley, "Naval Operations in the Vicksburg Campaign," 570; *Official Records*, vol. 24, pt. 1, p. 95, and pt. 2, pp. 453–4; Ulysses S. Grant, "The

Vicksburg Campaign," *Battles and Leaders*, 3:524–5; Henry Burrell to Dear Bro., June 17, 1863, Henry Burrell Papers, USAMHI; Furness, "Negro As a Soldier," 477.

55. Walker, "War of Secession," 33.

56. *Official Records*, vol. 24, pt. 1, p. 106; Walker, "War of Secession," 29. One Texan who had missed the fight at the Bend learned from those who had been there that the black soldiers had fought well. In fact, "they say the negroes fought braver than the Feds." John T. Stark to Dear Martha, June 14, 1863, J. T. Stark Letters and Diary.

57. *Official Records*, vol. 24, pt. 2, pp. 471–2; *Official Records, Navies*, vol. 25, pp. 161–2; Bearss, *Campaign for Vicksburg*, 3:1183–85.

58. Porter, "Early Days," 15. Porter regretfully recorded that "owing to Col. Culberson's mistakes, we were pronounced badly drilled, and ordered to drill four hours per day" (16).

59. *Official Records*, vol. 24, pt. 2, pp. 471–2. The gunboats launched at least twenty-eight 24-pound shells at the Texans (*Official Records, Navies*, vol. 25, pp. 161–2).

60. Porter, "Early Days," 15; *Official Records*, vol. 24, pt. 2, p. 472; Bearss, *Campaign for Vicksburg*, 3:1185.

61. *Official Records*, vol. 24, pt. 2, pp. 448–50; ibid., pt. 3, pp. 405–6; John T. Stark to Dear Martha, June 14, 1863, J. T. Stark Letters and Diary; Theodore Calhoun, *The Life Story of Theodore Calhoun: A Native Texan, Born in 1837 at Fort Crockett, Houston County, Texas* (Austin, Tex.: self-published, 1930), n.p.; Reid, "Spartan Band," 103–14; Bearss, *Campaign for Vicksburg*, 3:1186–87.

62. Blessington, *Campaigns of Walker's Texas Division*, 76.

## 7. THE DISMAL SUMMER OF 1863

1. *Official Records*, vol. 24, pt. 2, pp. 459, 460.

2. Lee and Davis quoted in Kurt Hackemer, "The Other Union Ironclad: The USS *Galena* and the Critical Summer of 1862," *Civil War History* 40 (September 1994): 244.

3. Walker's report, reprinted in Blessington, *Campaigns of Walker's Texas Division*, 121; Walker, "War of Secession," 29; *Official Records*, vol. 24, pt. 2, p. 464.

4. *Official Records*, vol. 24, pt. 2, p. 462.

5. Ibid., pp. 460, 464–5, 471 (quotation); R. Taylor to William R. Boggs, February 16, 1864, Letters Sent, District of West Louisiana (Ch. II, vol. 75), Records of the Department of Texas and the Trans-Mississippi Department, Records of Military Commands, War Department Collection of Confederate Records; Thomas W. Cutrer, "James Morrison Hawes," in *New Handbook of Texas*, ed. Tyler et al., 3:509.

6. Blessington, *Campaigns of Walker's Texas Division*, 110; Walker's report, ibid., 123–4 (quotations, p. 124); *Official Records*, vol. 24, pt. 2, pp. 460–1; Taylor, *Destruction and Reconstruction*, 139; Johansson, *Peculiar Honor*, 55–6.

7. Simon, ed., *Papers of Ulysses S. Grant*, 8:326, 354 (quotation); *Official Records, Navies*, vol. 25, pp. 65, 164; Bearss, *Campaign for Vicksburg*, 3:1191.

8. Blessington, *Campaigns of Walker's Texas Division*, 110–2, 124; Bearss, *Campaign for Vicksburg*, 3:1192–93.

9. *Official Records*, vol. 24, pt. 2, pp. 451–3; *Official Records, Navies*, vol. 25, pp. 175–6; Walker's report, reprinted in Blessington, *Campaigns of Walker's Texas Division*, 124; ibid., 110–1; Porter, "Early Days," 16; Cloyd Bryner, *Bugle Echoes: The Story of the Illinois 47th* (Springfield, Ill.: Phillips Bros., 1905), 88; Anne W. Hooker, "David Browning Culberson," in *New Handbook of Texas*, ed. Tyler et al., 2:436. A hand-drawn map of the Richmond battlefield is in the Hiram C. Crandall Diary, Illinois State Historical Library, Springfield.

10. *Official Records*, vol. 24, pt. 2, pp. 451–3; *Official Records, Navies*, vol. 25, pp. 175–6; Walker's report, reprinted in Blessington, *Campaigns of Walker's Texas Division*, 124, 110–1; Porter, "Early Days," 16; Bryner, *Bugle Echoes*, 88; Anne W. Hooker, "David Browning Culberson," in *New Handbook of Texas*, ed. Tyler et al., 2:436. The burned town was never restored. The present town of Richmond is several miles east of the original (Terrence J. Winschel, "Walker's Texas Division: Milliken's Bend," *Civil War Regiments* 3, no. 3 [1993]: 90).

11. Walker's report, reprinted in Blessington, *Campaigns of Walker's Texas Division*, 124.

12. Porter, "Early Days," 16.

13. Gravis, *Twenty-Five Years*, 28–9; Porter, "Early Days," 17; Blessington, *Campaigns of Walker's Texas Division*, 112.

14. Charles Elgee to Jno. G. Walker, June 22, 1863, Walker Papers; *Official Records*, vol. 24, pt. 2, p. 466; *Official Records, Navies*, vol. 25, p. 216; Blessington, *Campaigns of Walker's Texas Division*, 113–6; Anne J. Bailey, "A Texas Cavalry Raid: Reaction to Black Soldiers and Contrabands," *Civil War History* 35 (June 1989): 140–1; Anne J. Bailey, *Between the Enemy and Texas: Parsons's Texas Cavalry in the Civil War* (Fort Worth: Texas Christian Univ. Press, 1989), 133–44.

15. Junius Newport Bragg, *Letters of a Confederate Surgeon, 1861–1865*, ed. Mrs. T. J. Gaughan (Camden, Ark.: Hurley, 1960), 143; Harrison, ed., "Confederate Letters of John Simmons," 34; John T. Stark to Dear Martha, June 14, 1863, Stark Letters and Diary.

16. Bragg, *Letters of a Confederate Surgeon*, 144; *Official Records*, vol. 30, pt. 4, p. 376; Thomas W. Knox, *Camp-Fire and Cotton-Field: Southern Adventure in Time of War* (New York: Blelock, 1865), 315–6. Walker estimated that his command captured two thousand black workers (*Official Records*, vol. 24, pt. 2, p. 466).

17. *Official Records, Navies*, vol. 25, pp. 213–4.

18. Theophilus Perry to Dear Harriet, June 20, 1863, Perry Letters; Samuel W. Farrow to Dearest Josephine, July 17, 1863, Farrow Papers; Blessington, *Campaigns of Walker's Texas Division*, 115, 116.

19. John T. Stark to Dear Martha, June 14, 1863, Stark Letters and Diary; *Official Records*, vol. 24, pt. 2, pp. 454–5; report of Joseph A. Mower, February 14, 1864, U.S. Army Generals' Reports of Civil War Service, 1864–1887, Records of the Adjutant General's Office, 1780s–1917, Record Group 94, National Archives (Microfilm M1098, roll 1, vol. 2, p. 103).

20. *Official Records*, vol. 22, pt. 2, p. 916; S. W. Farrow to Dearest Josephine, July 4, 1863, Farrow Papers. A brief and authoritative synthesis of the Vicksburg campaign is Terry J. Winschel's *Vicksburg: Fall of the Confederate Gibraltar* (Abilene, Tex.: McWhiney Foundation Press, 1999).

21. *Official Records*, vol. 24, pt. 2, pp. 466; ibid., vol. 26, pt. 1, p. 211.

22. J. T. Knight to Dear Wife and Child, July 11, 1863, Knight Letters; S. W. Farrow to My Dear Josephine, July 11, 1863, Farrow Papers; J. B. Rounsaville to Dear Family, July 9, 1863, Rounsaville Letters; Cutrer, ed., "Letters of Volney Ellis," 133.

23. J. S. Bryan to Dear Nancy, July 9, 1863, Bryan Papers; Theophilus Perry to Dear Harriet, July 9, 1863, Perry Letters; Ned [Cade] to Dear Wife, July 9, 1863, Cade Correspondence; Blessington, *Campaigns of Walker's Texas Division*, 117.

24. *Official Records*, vol. 24, pt. 2, p. 466; summary report for July 1863, William S. Fowler Medical Register, 1863–1865, p. 8, Center for American History; H. A. Wallace to My Beloved Wife, July 17, 1863, Wallace Papers.

25. Ned [Cade] to Dear Wife, July 9, 1863, Cade Correspondence.

26. Taylor, *Destruction and Reconstruction*, 139–45 (quotation on p. 145); *Official Records*, vol. 26, pt. 1, pp. 211–4; Parrish, *Richard Taylor*, 296–303.

27. *Official Records*, vol. 26, pt. 2, pp. 110–1; Taylor, *Destruction and Reconstruction*, 139; Frank M.

Flinn, *Campaigning With Banks in Louisiana, '63 and '64, and With Sheridan in the Shenandoah Valley in '64 and '65* (Lynn, Mass.: Thos. P. Nichols, 1887), 90. Also see George Haven Putnam, *Memories of My Youth, 1844–1865* (New York: G. P. Putnam's Sons, 1914), 271; Rowena Reed, *Combined Operations in the Civil War* (Annapolis, Md.: Naval Institute Press, 1978), 259; Stephen S. Michot, "In Relief of Port Hudson: Richard Taylor's 1863 Lafourche Offensive," *Military History of the West* 23 (fall 1993): 134.

28. J. G. Walker to O. M. Roberts, July 13, 1863, Roberts Papers; Ned [Cade] to Dear Wife, July 16, 1863, Cade Correspondence; H. A. Wallace to My Beloved Wife, July 17, 1863, Wallace Letters; Cutrer, ed., "Letters of Volney Ellis," 133; Blessington, *Campaigns of Walker's Texas Division,* 118, 127.

29. Walker, "War of Secession," 31–2; S. W. Farrow to Dearest Josephine, July 21, 1863, Farrow Papers; Cutrer, ed., "Letters of Volney Ellis," 135.

30. Blessington, *Campaigns of Walker's Texas Division,* 127–8; David Paul Smith, *Frontier Defense in the Civil War: Texas' Rangers and Rebels* (College Station: Texas A&M Univ. Press, 1992), 70–1.

31. Porter, "Early Days," 18–9; Ned [Cade] to Dear Wife, July 30, 1863, Cade Correspondence; Cutrer, ed., "Letters of Volney Ellis," 137; Blessington, *Campaigns of Walker's Texas Division,* 128–9.

32. Porter, "Early Days," 19; G. P. Whittington, "Rapides Parish, Louisiana—A History," 10th installment, *Louisiana Historical Quarterly* 18 (January 1935): 9–10; Blessington, *Campaigns of Walker's Texas Division,* 130; J. T. Knight to Affectionate Wife & Child, August 15, 1863, Knight Letters.

33. Blessington, *Campaigns of Walker's Texas Division,* 131–2 (quotation on p. 132); Porter, "Early Days," 19–20.

34. Harrison, ed., "Confederate Letters of John Simmons," 35; Harry N. Scheiber, "The Pay of Troops and Confederate Morale in the Trans-Mississippi West," *Arkansas Historical Quarterly* 18 (winter 1959): 357–60; Gary M. Pecquet, "Money in the Trans-Mississippi Confederacy and the Currency Reform Act of 1864," *Explorations in Economic History* 24 (April 1987): 219; James L. Nichols, *The Confederate Quartermaster in the Trans-Mississippi* (Austin: Univ. of Texas Press, 1964), 98–9.

35. J. T. Knight to Affectionate Wife & Child, August 15, 1863, Knight Letters.

36. J. R. K. Brooks to Capt [Harvey A.] Wallace, September 4, 1863, Wallace Papers; D. M. Ray to Dear Mother, September 11, 1863, Ray Papers; Brown, ed., *Journey to Pleasant Hill,* 256.

37. Brown, ed., *Journey to Pleasant Hill,* 247; Samuel W. Farrow to Dearest Josephine, February 21, 1864, Farrow Papers; J. S. Bryan to Dear Nancy, August 9, 1863, Bryan Papers; Compiled Service Records, roll 397 (Lakey brothers). For references to Spanish furloughs and temporary absences, see S. W. Farrow to Dearest Josephine, August 6, 1863, Farrow Papers; J. T. Knight to Affectionate Wife & Child, August 15, 1863, Knight Letters; J. R. K. Brooks to Capt [Harvey A.] Wallace, September 4, 1863, Wallace Papers.

38. Blessington, *Campaigns of Walker's Texas Division,* 132.

39. R. Waterhouse to Dear Rose, September 11, 1863, Waterhouse Letters; Brown, ed., *Journey to Pleasant Hill,* 256–7 (quotation on p. 256); *Official Records,* vol. 22, pt. 2, p. 980; ibid., vol. 26, pt. 2, p. 241.

40. D. M. Ray to Dear Martha, October 7 and September 12, 1863, Ray Papers; Ned [Cade] to My dear Wife, November 22, 1863, Cade Correspondence. Also see Theophilus Perry to Dear Harriet, December 8, 1863, Perry Letters, for similar statements about the new emphasis on religion.

41. D. M. Ray to Dear Mother, October 11, 1863, Ray Papers; Martin [Smith] to My dear little Sister, November 3, 1863, and Ned [Cade] to My [dear] Wife, October 6, 1863, both in Cade Correspondence.

42. The best general treatment of religion among the soldiers is Gardiner H. Shattuck Jr., *A Shield and Hiding Place: The Religious Life of the Civil War Armies* (Macon, Ga.: Mercer Univ. Press,

1987). Also see Johansson, *Peculiar Honor*, 76–8; Samuel J. Watson, "Religion and Combat Motivation in the Confederate Armies," *Journal of Military History* 58 (January 1994): 34–5; and Reid Mitchell, "Christian Soldiers? Perfecting the Confederacy," in *Religion and the American Civil War*, ed. Randall M. Miller, Harry S. Stout, and Charles Reagan Wilson (New York: Oxford Univ. Press, 1998), 297–309.

43. Brown, ed., *Journey to Pleasant Hill*, 249; Blessington, *Campaigns of Walker's Texas Division*, 131; Edwin C. Bearss, "The Story of Fort Beauregard, Part I," *Louisiana Studies* 3 (winter 1964): 354–5. A good description of Harrisonburg and Fort Beauregard is in Fremantle, *Fremantle Diary*, 71, 74–5.

44. F. M. Oden to Dear wife, September 7, 1863, William Oden Papers, Center for American History; *Official Records*, vol. 26, pt. 1, pp. 273–82; Johansson, *Peculiar Honor*, 78–9; Bearss, "Story of Fort Beauregard, Part I," 364–77. For Randal, see Norman D. Brown, "Horace Randal," in *Confederate General*, ed. Davis, 6:192–3.

45. Porter, "Early Days," 20; J. S. Bryan to Dear Nancy, September 6, 1863, Bryan Papers; Blessington, *Campaigns of Walker's Texas Division*, 131–2.

8. BAYOU BOURBEAU

1. Ludwell Johnson, *Red River Campaign: Politics and Cotton in the Civil War* (1958; reprint, Kent, Ohio: Kent State Univ. Press, 1993), 7–17, 33; Hollandsworth, *Pretense of Glory*, 134–5.

2. Eugene H. Berwanger, "Union and Confederate Reaction to French Threats Against Texas," *Journal of Confederate History* 7, no. 1 (1991): 97–111; Kurt Henry Hackemer, "Strategic Dilemma: Civil-Military Friction and the Texas Coastal Campaign of 1863," *Military History of the West* 26 (fall 1996): 187–214; McPherson, *Battle Cry of Freedom*, 683; Foote, *Civil War*, 2:771–2.

3. Andrew Forest Muir, "Dick Dowling and Sabine Pass," *Civil War History* 4 (December 1958): 399–428; Alwyn Barr, "Sabine Pass, September 1863," *Texas Military History* 2, no. 1 (1962): 17–22.

4. *Official Records*, vol. 26, pt. 1, pp. 673, 682–3, 767–8; Waldo W. Moore, "The Defense of Shreveport—The Confederacy's Last Redoubt," *Military Affairs* 17 (summer 1953): 74. Niblett's Bluff, Louisiana, was a small river port located near the intersection of present-day Interstate Highway 10 and the Sabine River (Madeline Martin, "Niblett's Bluff," in *New Handbook of Texas*, ed. Tyler et al., 4:1010). A brief examination of the entire campaign is Richard Lowe, *The Texas Overland Expedition of 1863* (1996; reprint, Abilene, Tex.: McWhiney Foundation Press, 1998).

5. Walker, "War of Secession," 35–8; *Official Records*, vol. 26, pt. 1, p. 783; Blessington, *Campaigns of Walker's Texas Division*, 132. Division records for November 1863 show 364 officers and 3,878 enlisted men present for duty (Post, Department and Army Returns [Box 9, Entry 65, Folder 43], Rosters and Lists, Records of Military Commands, War Department Collection of Confederate Records). Also see David C. Edmonds, *Yankee Autumn in Acadiana: A Narrative of the Great Texas Overland Expedition through Southwestern Louisiana, October–December, 1863* (Lafayette, La.: Acadiana Press, 1979), 1, 16, 23, 236.

6. S. W. Farrow to My Dearest Josephine, October 28, 1863, Farrow Papers; W. B. Hunter to Dear Sister Mary, October 11, 1863, Mary J. Minor Civil War Letters, Center for American History; J. T. Knight to Affectionate wife & Child, October 15, 1863, Knight Letters; Taylor, *Destruction and Reconstruction*, 150; Camille Polignac, "Diary of the War between the States," p. 143, Civil War Times Miscellaneous Collection, USAMHI; Brown, ed., *Journey to Pleasant Hill*, 258; Blessington, *Campaigns of Walker's Texas Division*, 132–4.

7. Blessington, *Campaigns of Walker's Texas Division*, 134; Wm. M. Levy to J. G. Walker, October 11, 1863, Walker Papers; Brown, ed., *Journey to Pleasant Hill*, 268.

8. Cutrer, ed., "Letters of Virgil Sullivan Rabb," Part One, p. 184; J. S. Bryan to Dear Nancy, October 4, 1863, John Samuel Bryan Papers; Brown, ed., *Journey to Pleasant Hill*, 267–8.

9. Brown, ed., *Journey to Pleasant Hill*, 260; Cutrer, ed., "Letters of Virgil Sullivan Rabb," Part One, p. 184.

10. D. M. Ray to Dear Mother, October 28, 1863, Ray Papers; Cutrer, ed., "Letters of Virgil Sullivan Rabb," Part One, p. 188.

11. Blessington, *Campaigns of Walker's Texas Division*, 135; Brown, ed., *Journey to Pleasant Hill*, 271, 278 (quotation); *Official Records*, vol. 26, pt. 1, p. 390.

12. Brown, ed., *Journey to Pleasant Hill*, 271; Blessington, *Campaigns of Walker's Texas Division*, 136–7; Cutrer, ed., "William Read Scurry," in *New Handbook of Texas*, ed. Tyler et al., 5:946; Lawrence L. Hewitt, "William Read Scurry," in *Confederate General*, ed. Davis, 5:133–5; Charles G. Anderson, *Confederate General William Read "Dirty Neck Bill" Scurry (1821–1864)* (Snyder, Tex.: Charles G. Anderson, 1999), xi.

13. *Official Records*, vol. 26, pt. 1, pp. 340, 355.

14. Although Franklin's army showed a paper strength of 37,500 in late October, it had shaken down to 24,500 men present for duty. Detachments of various units for other duties, detachments to protect the route from Brashear City to Opelousas, illness, arrests for various causes, and other factors explain the difference. For exact numbers, see ibid., p. 783.

15. Ibid., 335, 340–1, 354; W. H. H. Terrell, comp., *Indiana in the War of the Rebellion: Report of the Adjutant General* (1869; reprint, Indianapolis: Indiana Historical Society, 1960), 565, 572–3; Frederick H. Dyer, *A Compendium of the War of the Rebellion*, 2 vols. (1908; reprint, Dayton, Ohio: Broadfoot Publishing Co. and Morningside Press, 1994), 2:1142, 1143–44, 1535, 1539, 1683. Owen's brigade included the 60th and 67th Indiana, the 83rd and 96th Ohio, and the 23rd Wisconsin Infantry Regiments.

16. *New York Herald*, October 25, 1863, p. 5; *Official Records*, vol. 26, pt. 1, pp. 338, 339; ibid., pt. 2, p. 380; Blessington, *Campaigns of Walker's Texas Division*, 134–6; O. M. Roberts's later endorsement on E. R. Wells to Officer Comdg Infantry at Washington Bridge, November 2, 1863, Roberts Papers; James A. Hamilton Diary, October 30, November 2, 3, 1863, Center for American History; Edmonds, *Yankee Autumn in Acadiana*, 273–4.

17. Blessington, *Campaigns of Walker's Texas Division*, 138–9; O. M. Roberts's later endorsement of E. R. Wells to Officer Comdg Infantry at Washington Bridge, November 2, 1863, Roberts Papers; Alwyn Barr, ed., "The Battle of Bayou Bourbeau, November 3, 1863: Colonel Oran M. Roberts' Report," *Louisiana History* 6 (winter 1965): 85–6 (hereafter cited as "Roberts' Report"); Blake Richard Hamaker, "Making a Good Soldier: A Historical and Quantitative Study of the 15th Texas Infantry, C.S.A." (M.A. thesis, University of North Texas, 1998), 30–1, 34–6.

18. Perkins, *Daniel's Battery*, 16–7; Moore, ed., *Rebellion Record*, 8:151–3 (document 7); *Official Records*, vol. 26, pt. 1, pp. 357, 364–5, 366; Reuben B. Scott, *The History of the 67th Regiment Indiana Infantry Volunteers* (Bedford, Ind.: Herald Book and Job Print, 1892), 51.

19. Porter, "Early Days," 22; *Official Records*, vol. 26, pt. 1, pp. 393–4; Barr, ed., "Roberts' Report," 85–7.

20. *Official Records*, vol. 26, pt. 1, pp. 363–4; Moore, ed., *Rebellion Record*, 8:151–2 (document 7); T. J. Woods, *Services of the Ninety-Sixth Ohio Volunteers* (Toledo, Ohio: Blade Printing and Paper Co., 1874), 39–42.

21. Barr, ed., "Roberts' Report," 85–7 (quotation on p. 87); Porter, "Early Days," 22.

22. Porter, "Early Days," 22.

23. Barr, ed., "Roberts' Report," 88; Porter, "Early Days," 22.

24. Porter, "Early Days," 22; Barr, ed., "Roberts' Report," 88.

25. Moore, ed., *Rebellion Record*, 8:151–3 (document 7); *Official Records*, vol. 26, pt. 1, pp. 357, 365 (quotation); Scott, *History of the 67th Regiment*, 51.

26. Porter, "Early Days," 22–3; *Official Records*, vol. 26, pt. 1, pp. 364–5; James E. Harrison to Dear Ballinger, November 9, 1863, William Pitt Ballinger Collection, Center for American History.

27. *Houston Tri-Weekly Telegraph*, November 14, 1863, p. 1; *Official Records*, vol. 26, pt. 1, p. 365; *Galveston Weekly News*, November 25, 1863 (list of casualties by name).

28. *Galveston Weekly News*, November 25, 1863; Porter, "Early Days," 22; Norris, ed., *With the 18th Texas Infantry*, 63–4, 74; Blessington, *Campaigns of Walker's Texas Division*, 142.

29. *Official Records*, vol. 26, pt. 1, p. 365–6; Edmonds, *Yankee Autumn in Acadiana*, 283.

30. *Official Records*, vol. 26, pt. 1, p. 394; Woods, *Services of the Ninety-Sixth Ohio*, 42–3.

31. George Chittenden to My Dear Wife, November 5, 1863, Chittenden Collection, Indiana State Library, Indianapolis; Frank [McGregor] to Dear Folks at Home, November 6, 1863, McGregor Papers, USAMHI.

32. Joseph Orville Jackson, ed., *"Some of the Boys . . .": The Civil War Letters of Isaac Jackson, 1862–1865* (Carbondale: Southern Illinois Univ. Press, 1960), 146, 147; *New York Times*, November 22, 1863, p. 8; Ruth Peebles, *There Never Were Such Men Before: The Civil War Soldiers and Veterans of Polk County, Texas, 1861–1865* (Livingston, Tex.: Polk County Historical Commission, 1987), 309; Frank [McGregor] to My dear Susie, November 12, 1863, McGregor Papers.

33. James E. Harrison to Dear Ballinger, November 9, 1863, Ballinger Collection; Porter, "Early Days," 23; Barr, ed., "Roberts' Report," 88–9; *Official Records*, vol. 26, pt. 1, pp. 372–3.

34. Porter, "Early Days," 23–4; Barr, ed., "Roberts' Report," 89; Norris, ed., *With the 18th Texas Infantry*, 63–5; Blessington, *Campaigns of Walker's Texas Division*, 143.

35. Woods, *Services of the Ninety-Sixth Ohio*, 44; Moore, ed., *Rebellion Record*, 8:152 (document 7).

36. Harry Watts Diary, 109, Harry Watts Collection, Indiana State Library, Indianapolis; James R. Slack to My Dear Ann, November 6, 1863, James R. Slack Correspondence, Indiana State Library.

37. Barr, ed., "Roberts' Report," 89–90; *Official Records*, vol. 26, pt. 1, pp. 357–8, 394; James R. Slack to My Dear Ann, November 6, 1863, Slack Correspondence; Marshall, *History of the Eighty-Third Ohio*, 114; J. L. Brent to J. A. Galt, November 9, 1863, bound vol. 2, pp. 137–9, Brent Papers.

38. Porter, "Early Life," 24.

39. *Official Records*, vol. 26, pt. 1, pp. 344 (quotation), 359 (casualties); U.S. Army Generals' Reports of Civil War Service, roll 1, vol. 2, p. 523 (second quotation); David C. Edmonds, "Surrender on the Bourbeux: Honorable Defeat or Incompetency under Fire," *Louisiana History* 18 (winter 1977): 63–86.

40. Joshua L. Halbert to My Dear Wife, November 13, 1863, Joshua L. Halbert Letters, 15th Texas Infantry File, Confederate Research Center, Hill College; Walker, "War of Secession," 39; *Official Records*, vol. 26, pt. 1, p. 395.

41. *Official Reports*, vol. 26, pt. 1, p. 354; U. S. Army Generals' Reports of Civil War Service, roll 1, vol. 2, p. 523; Hollandsworth, *Pretense of Glory*, 141–3; Edmonds, *Yankee Autumn in Acadiana*, 309–57.

42. Jackson, *Some of the Boys*, 147; Frank [McGregor] to Dear Folks at Home, November 6, 1863, McGregor Papers; Scott, *History of the 67th Regiment*, 65; Frank [McGregor] to My dear Susie, November 12, 1863, McGregor Papers; Harry Watts Diary, 111.

43. *Houston Tri-Weekly Telegraph*, November 14, 1863; *Galveston Weekly News*, December 2, 1863.

44. Walker, "War of Secession," 40; Geo. McKnight to Col. Roberts, November 4, 1863, Roberts Papers; *Houston Tri-Weekly Telegraph*, November 11, 1863.

45. Blessington, *Campaigns of Walker's Texas Division*, 145; Joshua L. Halbert to My Dear Wife, November 13, 1863, Halbert Letters.

46. Taylor's congratulations, reprinted in Blessington, *Campaigns of Walker's Texas Division*, 145; *Official Records*, vol. 26, pt. 1, p. 854; Edmonds, *Yankee Autumn in Acadiana*, 309–57; Alwyn Barr, *Polignac's Texas Brigade* (1964; reprint, College Station: Texas A&M Univ. Press, 1998), 32.

## 9. WINTER ON THE RIVER

1. Blessington, *Campaigns of Walker's Texas Division*, 150–1; Kerby, *Kirby Smith's Confederacy*, 240–1, 248–9, 283–6.

2. Blessington, *Campaigns of Walker's Texas Division*, 150–2; "Destruction of Simmsport," *Rebellion Record*, Doc. 53, 7 (1869): 276; Polignac, "Diary of the War," p. 153.

3. Porter, "Early Days," 25; Wallace Diary, November 4–9, 1863; N. S. Allen Diary, November 8–14, 1863, Louisiana State University Library, Shreveport; Arthur Hyatt Diary, November 15, 1863, Arthur W. Hyatt Papers, Louisiana and Lower Mississippi Valley Collections, Hill Memorial Library, Louisiana State University, Baton Rouge.

4. J. S. Bryan to Dear Nancy, November 16, 1863, Bryan Papers; Brown, ed., *Journey to Pleasant Hill*, 282; *Official Records, Navies*, vol. 25, pp. 563, 572.

5. *Official Records, Navies*, vol. 25, pp. 572 (first quotation), 571 (second quotation); Silverstone, *Warships of the Civil War Navies*, 178.

6. *Official Records, Navies*, vol. 25, pp. 570–1; *Official Records*, vol. 26, pt. 1, pp. 454–5.

7. George C. Harding, *The Miscellaneous Writings of George C. Harding* (Indianapolis: Carlon and Hollenbeck, 1882), 330; Janet B. Hewett, Noah Andre Trudeau, and Bryce A. Suderow, eds., *Supplement to the Official Records of the Union and Confederate Armies*, 95 vols. to date (Wilmington, N.C.: Broadfoot Publishing Co., 1994), 4:839–40 (hereafter cited as *Supplement to the Official Records*).

8. *Official Records, Navies*, vol. 25, p. 573. Foster's information was nearly exact. Walker's division counted nearly five thousand effectives, and some of Mouton's regiments occasionally joined them on the riverbank. At least five batteries (William Edgar's, James Daniel's, and Horace Haldeman's Texas units and Oliver J. Semmes's and John A. A. West's Louisiana units) with four to six guns each, were scattered along the Mississippi's right bank. For units and strengths, see J. L. Brent to Maj. Gen. Taylor, November 8, 1863, bound vol. 2, p. 136, Brent Papers; Blessington, *Campaigns of Walker's Texas Division*, 150–1; Kerby, *Kirby Smith's Confederacy*, 248–9.

9. *Supplement to the Official Records*, 4:841–2. Edgar's report and Federal damage assessments indicated that twenty of Edgar's twenty-five shells struck the *Black Hawk* (ibid.; *Official Records, Navies*, vol. 25, p. 574).

10. William Edgar's report, November 21, 1863, J. L. Brent Papers; A. P. Page to Dear Mother & Sister, November 29, 1863, Page Family Letters, Mansfield State Historic Site, Mansfield, La.; Calhoun, *Life Story*, n.p.; Blessington, *Campaigns of Walker's Texas Division*, 152; *Official Records, Navies*, vol. 25, p. 574.

11. *New York Herald*, December 7, 1863.

12. Ibid.; Ned to My dear Wife, November 22, 1863, Cade Correspondence; S. W. Farrow to Dearest Josephine, November 23, 1863, Farrow Papers; Cutrer, ed., "Letters of Volney Ellis," 141; Polignac, "Diary of the War," p. 156. Federal soldiers and civilians often, and mistakenly, used the term "guerrillas" to refer to standard Confederate army forces. For the state of historical writing on guerrilla warfare during the 1860s, see Daniel E. Sutherland, "Sideshow No Longer: A Historiographical Review of the Guerrilla War," *Civil War History* 46 (March 2000): 5–23.

13. James Marten, ed., "On the Road with Thomas H. Duval: A Texas Unionist's Travel Diary, 1863," *Journal of Confederate History* 6, no. 1 (1990): 91; *Official Records, Navies*, vol. 25, p. 636.

14. E. Cort Williams, "Recollections of the Red River Expedition," in *Sketches of War History, 1861–1865: Papers Read before the Ohio Commandery of the Military Order of the Loyal Legion of the United States, 1886–1888*, 8 vols. (Cincinnati, Ohio: Robert Clarke, 1888–1908), 2:97.

15. Brown, ed., *Journey to Pleasant Hill*, 283–4; Blessington, *Campaigns of Walker's Texas Division*, 152–3.

16. Blessington, *Campaigns of Walker's Texas Division*, 153, 155–6 (Walker's report); Polignac, "Diary of the War," p. 156; Brown, ed., *Journey to Pleasant Hill*, 286.

17. Blessington, *Campaigns of Walker's Texas Division*, 153; H. A. Wallace to My Dear Achsah, December 6, 1863, Wallace Letters; Polignac, "Diary of the War," p. 156.

18. *New York Herald*, December 21, 1863; Perkins, *Daniel's Battery*, 5.

19. Knox, *Camp-Fire and Cotton-Field*, 472, 473, 475; Blessington, *Campaigns of Walker's Texas Division*, 153–4; Silverstone, *Warships of the Civil War Navies*, 149.

20. *Official Records, Navies*, vol. 25, pp. 625–6; Knox, *Camp-Fire and Cotton-Field*, 475, 477. For reports by Confederate artillery commanders, see "Report of an engagement between the Howitzer section of Edgar's Battery and the Transport Von Phul," box 9, folder 15, Group 55-B, Civil War Papers, Louisiana Historical Association Collection; Lieut. J. D. Girtman to Major T. B. French, December 8, 1863, ibid.; Capt. J. M. Daniel to Major T. B. French, Dec. 9, 1863, ibid.

21. Blessington, *Campaigns of Walker's Texas Division*, 154.

22. S. W. Farrow to Dearest Josephine, November 23, 1863, Farrow Papers. Gary W. Gallagher's *Confederate War* (Cambridge, Mass.: Harvard Univ. Press, 1997) and William Blair's *Virginia's Private War: Feeding Body and Soul in the Confederacy, 1861–1865* (New York: Oxford Univ. Press, 1998) stress the endurance of Confederate soldiers' commitment to the war effort even after the defeats at Gettysburg, Vicksburg, and Chattanooga. Mark Grimsley's *The Hard Hand of War: Union Military Policy Toward Southern Civilians, 1861–1865* (New York: Cambridge Univ. Press, 1995) traces the evolution of Federal "hard war" policy toward southern white civilians.

23. Edwin C. Bearss, ed., *A Louisiana Confederate: Diary of Felix Pierre Poché*, trans. Eugenie Watson Somdal (Natchitoches: Louisiana Studies Institute, Northwestern State University, 1972), 62 (hereafter cited as *Diary of Felix Pierre Poché*); *Official Records, Navies*, vol. 25, p. 637; Brown, ed., *Journey to Pleasant Hill*, 291.

24. Blessington, *Campaigns of Walker's Texas Division*, 157–8; Brown, ed., *Journey to Pleasant Hill*, 291.

25. Theophilus Perry to Dear Harriet, January 29, 1864, Perry Letters; Porter, "Early Days," 26; Cutrer, ed., "Letters of Volney Ellis," 146.

26. *Official Records*, vol. 34, pt. 2, p. 898; H. A. Wallace to My Dear Achsah, December 6, 1863, Wallace Letters; Lackner, ed., "Civil War Diaries," 45; E. P. Becton to My dear Mary, January 2, 1864, Becton Papers.

27. Blessington, *Campaigns of Walker's Texas Division*, 162; Hyatt Diary, January 1, 1864, Hyatt Papers.

28. Harris H. Beecher, *Record of the 114th Regiment, N.Y.S.V.: Where it Went, What it Saw, and What it Did* (Norwich, N.Y.: J. F. Hubbard, Jr., 1866), 277; Knox, *Camp-Fire and Cotton-Field*, 331–2.

29. Allie [Cade] to My own dear one, December 24, 1863, Cade Correspondence; Blessington, *Campaigns of Walker's Texas Division*, 159; Porter, "Early Days," 26.

30. Porter, "Early Days," 26; Cutrer, "Letters of Volney Ellis," 148; Theophilus Perry to Dear Harriet, January 29, 1864, Perry Letters; Johansson, *Peculiar Honor*, 87.

31. *Official Records,* vol. 34, pt. 2, p. 971; Blessington, *Campaigns of Walker's Texas Division,* 165; E. Cunningham to R. Taylor, February 23, 1864, Letters Sent, Trans-Mississippi Department (chap. II, vol. 73½).

32. Anne Bailey, "Thomas Neville Waul," in *Confederate General,* ed. Davis, 6:113–5; Buenger, *Secession and the Union in Texas,* 38; Thomas W. Cutrer, "Waul's Texas Legion," in *New Handbook of Texas,* ed. Tyler et al., 6:852.

33. Blessington, *Campaigns of Walker's Texas Division,* 164; Samuel W. Farrow to Dearest Josephine, December 31, 1863, Farrow Papers; Harrison, ed., "Confederate Letters of John Simmons," 38–9; Theophilus Perry to Dear Harriet, January 18, 1864, Perry Letters; Johansson, *Peculiar Honor,* 86–7.

34. Frank Lawrence Owsley, *King Cotton Diplomacy: Foreign Relations of the Confederate States of America* (Chicago: Univ. of Chicago Press, 1931), 151–3, measures the wartime increase in cotton prices in England.

35. R. Taylor to J. G. Walker, January 15, 1864, pp. 15–6, Letters Sent, District of West Louisiana (Ch. II, vol. 76), Records of the Department of Texas and the Trans-Mississippi Department, Records of Military Commands, War Department Collection of Confederate Records; Will M. Levy to J. G. Walker, January 16, 1864, pp. 27–8, ibid.; P. E. Buford to J. G. Walker, n.d., pp. 39–40, ibid.; R. Taylor to J. G. Walker, January 15, 1864, p. 16, Letters Sent, District of West Louisiana (Ch. II, vol. 75), ibid.; R. Taylor to E. K. Smith, January 6, 1864, Letters and Telegrams Received, box 52, Records of the Department of Texas and the Trans-Mississippi Department; Boggs, *Military Reminiscences,* 63.

36. Lackner, ed., "Civil War Diaries," 48, 49; Samuel W. Farrow to Dearest Josephine, January 18, 1864, Farrow Papers; *Official Records, Navies,* vol. 25, p. 771.

37. Brown, ed., *Journey to Pleasant Hill,* 324.

38. Ibid.

39. Harrison, ed., "Confederate Letters of John Simmons," 39; Bearss, ed., *Diary of Felix Pierre Poché,* 89.

40. J. H. Armstrong to My Dear Martha, March 9, 1864, James Harvey Armstrong Letters, 14th Texas Infantry file, Confederate Research Center, Hill College; Theophilus Perry to Dear Wife, March 9, 1864, Perry Letters; Brown, ed., *Journey to Pleasant Hill,* 376–7; Johansson, *Peculiar Honor,* 88–9.

41. Judith F. Gentry, "White Gold: The Confederate Government and Cotton in Louisiana," *Louisiana History* 33 (spring 1992): 229–40.

42. Ibid. In early February, Trans-Mississippi officials revoked all permits to pass cotton through the lines (E. Surget to J. G. Walker, February 10, 1864, pp. 226–8, Letters Sent, District of West Louisiana [Ch. II, vol. 75]).

43. John D. Winters, *The Civil War in Louisiana* (Baton Rouge: Louisiana State Univ. Press, 1963), 324–5, 327–8; Kerby, *Kirby Smith's Confederacy,* 284–5, 288.

44. *Official Records,* vol. 15, pp. 876–7; Mark Mayo Boatner, *The Civil War Dictionary,* rev. ed. (New York: David McKay, 1988), 237; Winters, *Civil War in Louisiana,* 196–7; James L. Nichols, *Confederate Engineers,* Confederate Centennial Studies (Tuscaloosa, Ala.: Confederate, 1957), 58–60; Kerby, *Kirby Smith's Confederacy,* 109–10.

45. Theophilus Perry to Dear Harriet, December 20, 1863, Perry Letters; J. T. Knight to Dear Wife & Child, December 28, 1863, Knight Letters; Brown, ed., *Journey to Pleasant Hill,* 301–2.

46. Brown, ed., *Journey to Pleasant Hill,* 304.

47. David Dixon Porter, *Incidents and Anecdotes of the Civil War* (New York: D. Appleton, 1885), 214; Thomas O. Selfridge, "The Navy in the Red River," in *Battles and Leaders,* ed. Johnson and Buel, 4:362–6; Walker, "War of Secession," 42–3.

48. Porter, *Incidents and Anecdotes*, 217; *Official Records*, vol. 34, pt. 1, p. 224; ibid., pt. 2, p. 864. For a map of the fort, see *Official Records*, vol. 34, pt. 1, p. 224.

49. A. H. May to G. Mason Graham, February 2, 1864, pp. 167–70, Letters Sent, District of West Louisiana (Ch. II, vol. 75); A. H. May to D. F. Boyd, January 28, 1864, pp. 133–4, ibid.; A. H. May to W. L. Sandford, January 19, 1864, p. 50 (Ch. II, vol. 76), ibid.; Theophilus Perry to Dear Harriet, December 29, 1863, Perry Letters.

50. J. H. Armstrong to My Dear Martha, January 5, 1864, Armstrong Letters; H. A. Wallace to My Dear Achsah, February 10, 1864, Wallace Letters; A. H. May to D. F. Boyd, January 28, 1864, pp. 133–4, Letters Sent, District of West Louisiana (Ch. II, vol. 75); "Slave Monument Installed and Dedicated," *Fort DeRussy News* (July 1999), 3.

## 10. A LONG RETREAT

1. Johnson, *Red River Campaign*, 39–44; Wooster, *Texas and Texans in the Civil War*, 94, 135.

2. Hackemer, "Strategic Dilemma," 209–10; Wooster, *Texas and Texans in the Civil War*, 119–20. For the wartime cotton trade in Texas, see Ronnie C. Tyler, "Cotton on the Border, 1861–1865," *Southwestern Historical Quarterly* 73 (April 1970): 456–77; and James W. Daddysman, *The Matamoros Trade: Confederate Commerce, Diplomacy, and Intrigue* (Newark, Del.: Univ. of Delaware Press, 1984).

3. Hackemer, "Strategic Dilemma," 209–12; Johnson, *Red River Campaign*, 40–5; Wooster, *Texas and Texans in the Civil War*, 135. General Grant was puzzled by Halleck's unbending determination to send a large expedition up the Red River: "The possession of the trans-Mississippi by the Union forces seemed to possess more importance in his mind than almost any campaign east of the Mississippi" (Ulysses S. Grant, *Personal Memoirs of U.S. Grant*, ed. E. B. Long, intro. William S. McFeely [1885; reprint, New York: Da Capo Press, 1982], 303). Also see Brooks D. Simpson, *Ulysses S. Grant: Triumph over Adversity, 1822–1865* (Boston: Houghton Mifflin, 2000), 275–6.

4. Thomas O. Selfridge, "The Navy in the Red River," in *Battles and Leaders*, ed. Johnson and Buel, 4:362–6; "The Mississippi Flotilla in the Red River Expedition," ibid., 366; Johnson, *Red River Campaign*, 81–6; Ludwell Johnson, "The Red River Campaign, 11 March–20 May 1864," in Frances H. Kennedy, ed., *The Civil War Battlefield Guide* (Boston: Houghton Mifflin, 1990), 163–4; Gary D. Joiner and Charles E. Vetter, "The Union Naval Expedition on the Red River, March 12–May 22, 1864," *Civil War Regiments* 4, no. 2 (1994): 36, 47.

5. Johnson, *Red River Campaign*, 80, 85; Johnson, "Red River Campaign," 163; A. Lincoln to Maj. Gen. Banks, November 5, 1863 (microfilm roll 62, no. 27837), Robert Todd Lincoln Collection of Abraham Lincoln Papers, 1833–1916, Manuscripts Division, Library of Congress, Washington, D.C. For Shreveport's role as Trans-Mississippi headquarters, see Snyder, "Shreveport, Louisiana, during the Civil War and Reconstruction."

6. *Official Records*, vol. 34, pt. 2, p. 1024; Walker, "War of Secession," 42–3; E. Buford to J. G. Walker, January 20, 1864, p. 63, Letters Sent, District of West Louisiana (Ch. II, vol. 75).

7. *Official Records, Navies*, vol. 11, p. 727; Nichols, *Confederate Engineers*, 62–3; *Official Records*, vol. 34, pt. 1, p. 598.

8. *Official Records*, vol. 34, pt. 2, p. 971; Walker, "War of Secession," 43. Taylor's praise of the division may have been intended partly to counter a recent critical inspection report, which pointed out deficient discipline, inadequate clothing and equipment, and messy campsites (W. M. Levy's inspection, January 19, 1864, Inspection Reports and Related Records Received by the Inspection Branch in the Confederate Adjutant and Inspector General's Office, War Department Collection of Confederate Records [Microfilm M935, 18 rolls], roll 8, frame 476).

9. Smith, quoted in Parks, *General Edmund Kirby Smith*, 366; [D. M. Ray] to Very Dear Mother, March 6, 1864, Ray Papers; W. R. Boggs to [Richard] Taylor, January 26, 1864, Letters Sent, Trans-Mississippi Department (chap. II, vol. 70), Records of the Department of Texas and the Trans-Mississippi Department; E. Cunningham to My Dear Uncle, June 27, 1864, Letters and Telegrams Received, Box 52, ibid.

10. Blessington, *Campaigns of Walker's Texas Division*, 169–71; Ezra J. Warner, *Generals in Blue: Lives of the Union Commanders* (Baton Rouge: Louisiana State Univ. Press, 1964), 454–5. At one point early in this campaign, General Smith referred to one of his own officers as a "Miss Nancy kind of a fellow" because the officer used a tent while his men were sleeping in the open (Porter, *Incidents and Anecdotes*, 217).

11. Blessington, *Campaigns of Walker's Texas Division*, 169–71; Burns Scrapbook, 36, William S. Burns Papers and Scrapbook, Clements Library, University of Michigan, Ann Arbor; John Scott, *Story of the Thirty Second Iowa Infantry Volunteers* (Nevada, Iowa: self-published, 1896), 130.

12. *Official Records*, vol. 34, pt. 1, p. 597; Walker, "War of Secession," 43–5.

13. *Official Records*, vol. 34, pt. 1, pp. 597–9; Walker, "War of Secession," 43–5.

14. *Official Records*, vol. 34, pt. 1, pp. 597–9; Brown, ed., *Journey to Pleasant Hill*, 378.

15. Brown, ed., *Journey to Pleasant Hill*, 378; Bearss, ed., *Diary of Felix Pierre Poché*, 94.

16. *Official Records*, vol. 34, pt. 1, p. 599; Walker, "War of Secession," 43–5. The Louisiana brigade formerly commanded by Alfred Mouton and Camille de Polignac's Texas brigade were marching to join Walker's division west of the Bayou Du Lac bridge (*Official Records*, vol. 34, pt. 1, p. 492).

17. "Rebels: List of Prisoners Captured at Fort De Russy, La.," pp. 1–12, Baton Rouge List #1, Louisiana Station Rolls, War Department Collection of Confederate Records. Colonel Byrd was the grandfather of the world-famous polar explorer Richard Byrd and Virginia governor and U.S. senator Harry Byrd (Thomas W. Cutrer, "William Byrd," in *New Handbook of Texas*, ed. Tyler et al., 1:875).

18. *Official Records*, vol. 34, pt. 1, p. 387; *Official Records, Navies*, vol. 11, p. 732. For a map of the fort, see *Official Records*, vol. 34, pt. 1, p. 224.

19. *Official Records, Navies*, vol. 11, p. 732; Thomas O. Selfridge Jr., *What Finer Tradition: The Memoirs of Thomas O. Selfridge, Jr., Rear Admiral, U.S.N.* (Columbia: Univ. of South Carolina Press, 1987), 95; *Official Records*, vol. 34, pt. 1, p. 387; William Byrd, "The Capture of Fort De Russy, La.," *The Land We Love* 6 (January 1869): 187.

20. Burns Scrapbook, 37; Porter, "Early Days," 27–8; Porter, *Incidents*, 214–5; *Official Records, Navies*, vol. 26, pp. 28, 30–1.

21. John Ritland, "The Civil War History of John Ritland," chap. 3 (reprinted from *Story City (Iowa) Herald*, March 9–April 6, 1922, at http://www.iowa-counties.com/civilwar/ritland/rcw.3.html on the World Wide Web, 28 July 2003; Porter, "Early Days," 27–8; Wallace Diary, 11.

22. Porter, "Early Days," 28; Benjamin R. Hieronymus Diary, March 14, 1864, Illinois State Historical Library, Springfield; Byrd, "Capture of Fort De Russy," 186; *Official Records*, vol. 34, pt. 1, pp. 578, 600–1; "Rebels: List of Prisoners," pp. 1–12; Walter George Smith, *Life and Letters of Thomas Kilby Smith, Brevet Major-General, United States Volunteers, 1820–1887* (New York: G. P. Putnam's Sons, 1898), 91; *New York Tribune*, quoted in *Charleston (S.C.) Mercury*, April 21, 1864.

23. Brown, ed., *Journey to Pleasant Hill*, 378–9 (quotation on p. 379); Cutrer, ed., "Letters of Volney Ellis," 150–1; *Official Records*, vol. 34, pt. 1, pp. 599–600; *Official Records, Navies*, vol. 26, p. 26; Blessington, *Campaigns of Walker's Texas Division*, 173–4.

24. Blessington, *Campaigns of Walker's Texas Division*, 175.

25. *Official Records*, vol. 34, pt. 1, pp. 578, 600; Taylor, *Destruction and Reconstruction*, 149, 153–4;

Jeff Kinard, *Lafayette of the South: Prince Camille de Polignac and the American Civil War* (College Station: Texas A&M Univ. Press, 2001), 113, 131.

26. *Official Records*, vol. 34, pt. 1, p. 561; H. F. Gregory, et al., *A Civil War Military Site Survey: Natchitoches Parish and Environs* (Baton Rouge: Division of Archaeology, Office of Cultural Development, State of Louisiana, 1984), 60; Patsy K. Barber, *Historic Cotile* ([Alexandria, La.]: Baptist Message Press, 1967), 21; Johnson, *Red River Campaign*, 96.

27. *Official Records*, vol. 34, pt. 1, p. 506; Bearss, ed., *Diary of Felix Pierre Poché*, 98; Winters, *Civil War in Louisiana*, 330.

28. *Official Records*, vol. 34, pt. 1, pp. 306–7, 315–6, 332, 506, 561–2; James McSorly file, Confederate Pension Applications, Records of the Comptroller of Public Accounts, Record Group 304, Texas State Library and Archives Commission; James K. Ewer, *The Third Massachusetts Cavalry in the War for the Union* (Maplewood, Mass.: Historical Committee of the Regimental Assn., 1903), 137–9; James McSorly file, Confederate Pension Applications.

29. Blessington, *Campaigns of Walker's Texas Division*, 177. Captain Edgar and his gunners were exchanged in late July and returned to service (Lester N. Fitzhugh, "Texas Forces in the Red River Campaign, March–May, 1864," *Texas Military History* 3 [spring 1963]: 18 n.).

30. Burns Scrapbook, 39. Only three days earlier, men from an Illinois regiment had raided Governor Moore's plantation and hauled away "about 10 thousand lbs. cured meat—two wagon loads sweet potatoes—a lot of sugar & salt, etc. And the boys brought away from 3 to 8 chickens each—geese—lettuce, onions, & so on" (Hieronymus Diary, March 19, 1864).

31. *Official Records*, vol. 34, pt. 2, p. 1027; Taylor, *Destruction and Reconstruction*, 156; Arthur W. Bergeron Jr., *The Civil War Reminiscences of Major Silas T. Grisamore, C.S.A.* (Baton Rouge: Louisiana State Univ. Press, 1993), 142; Blessington, *Campaigns of Walker's Texas Division*, 175–6.

32. Ned [Cade] to My dear Wife, March 22, 1864, Cade Correspondence; Theophilus Perry to Dear Harriet, March 17/19, 1864, Perry Letters; Connor, ed., *Dear America*, 94–5; [S. W. Farrow] to Dearest Josephine, March 23, 1864, Farrow Papers.

33. Brown, ed., *Journey to Pleasant Hill*, 383; [Edward B. Williams] to My Dear Kate, March 31, 1864, Edward B. Williams Civil War Letters, University of Oregon Library, Eugene.

34. *Fort Worth (Texas) Star-Telegram*, April 30, 1994, section D, pp. 1, 3 (quotation on p. 3).

35. Theophilus Perry to Dear Harriet, March 23, 1864, Perry Letters; [S. W. Farrow] to Dearest Josephine, March 23, 1864, Farrow Papers; Beecher, *Record of the 114th Regiment*, 303; Burns Scrapbook, 40.

36. T. R. Bonner, "Sketches of the Campaign of 1864," *The Land We Love* 5 (October 1868): 462; Blessington, *Campaigns of Walker's Texas Division*, 179; Beecher, *Record of the 114th Regiment*, 305.

37. K. Jack Bauer, *Zachary Taylor: Soldier, Planter, Statesman of the Old Southwest* (Baton Rouge: Louisiana State Univ. Press, 1985), 40–1; Bergeron, ed., *Reminiscences of Major Silas T. Grisamore*, 143; Max S. Lale, ed., "For Lack of a Nail," *East Texas Historical Journal* 30, no. 1 (1992): 38.

38. Fred Smith to My dear father, April 1, 1864, Fred Smith Correspondence, Civil War Times Illustrated Collection, USAMHI; Brown, ed., *Journey to Pleasant Hill*, 386, 387; Theophilus Perry to Dear Harriet, March 23, 1864, Perry Letters; Parrish, *Richard Taylor*, 331–3.

39. Selfridge, "Navy in the Red River," 363; Beecher, *Record of the 114th Regiment*, 304–5; Wallace Diary, 13; E. Kirby Smith, "The Defense of the Red River," in *Battles and Leaders*, ed. Johnson and Buel, 4:374.

40. Fred Smith to My dear father, April 1, 1864, Fred Smith Correspondence; Taylor, *Destruction and Reconstruction*, 157–8, 160; Bergeron, ed., *Reminiscences of Major Silas T. Grisamore*, 144. The mileage estimate is based on distances marked on modern highway maps for the closest present-day

approximation of the route of the retreat. Walker's retreat (270 miles in 23 days) was slightly longer and faster than General Sherman's "March to the Sea" (250 miles in 25 days). See Smith, "Blitzkrieg," 28–30.

41. Taylor, *Destruction and Reconstruction*, 158–60; Smith, "Defense of the Red River," 371.

## 11. MANSFIELD AND PLEASANT HILL

1. Blessington, *Campaigns of Walker's Texas Division*, 180; [Xavier B. Debray], *A Sketch of the History of DeBray's 26th Regiment of Texas Cavalry* (Austin, Tex.: E. von Boeckman, 1884), 16; Allen diary, April 4, 1864.

2. Boggs, *Military Reminiscences*, 76; Taylor, *Destruction and Reconstruction*, 159–60, 162; Lale, ed. "For Lack of a Nail," 39.

3. W. P. Head to Dear Wife, April 7, 1864, Head Papers; Fred Smith to My dear father, April 7, 1864, Fred Smith Correspondence; Blessington, *Campaigns of Walker's Texas Division*, 181.

4. Bonner, "Sketches of the Campaign," 5:462: Gravis, *Twenty-Five Years*, 29, 30; Blessington, *Campaigns of Walker's Texas Division*, 183. Some Texans, of course, had seen enemy troops on their soil. Several thousand Federals under General Banks had occupied the lower Rio Grande valley and the lower Gulf coast five months earlier. See Stephen Andrew Townsend, "The Rio Grande Expedition, 1863–1865" (Ph.D. diss., University of North Texas, 2001), for a recent and detailed account of that campaign.

5. For descriptions of the field, see Richard B. Irwin, "The Red River Campaign," in *Battles and Leaders*, ed. Johnson and Buel, 4:352; Charles B. Hall, "Notes of the Red River Campaign of 1864," in *War Papers: Read Before the Commandery of the State of Maine, Military Order of the Loyal Legion of the United States*, 4 vols. (1898–1915; reprint, Wilmington, N.C.: Broadfoot, 1992), 4:269; *History of the Forty-Sixth Regiment Indiana Volunteer Infantry, September, 1861–September, 1865* ([Logansport, Ind.]: Wilson, Humphreys, 1888), 88; and Walker, "War of Secession," 50. For troop dispositions, see Taylor, *Destruction and Reconstruction*, 163; Blessington, *Campaigns of Walker's Texas Division*, 185; and *Official Records*, vol. 34, pt. 1, p. 564.

6. Taylor, *Destruction and Reconstruction*, 162–3; Walker, "War of Secession," 50; Stanley S. Mc-Gowen, *Horse Sweat and Power Smoke: The First Texas Cavalry in the Civil War* (College Station: Texas A&M Univ. Press, 1999), 131. For biographical sketches of Debray and Buchel, see entries by Anne J. Bailey and Robert W. Stephens in *New Handbook of Texas*, ed. Tyler et al., 2:554 and 1:799–800, respectively.

7. Bonner, "Sketches of the Campaign," 5:463. The untested regiments were the 14th Infantry, 28th Cavalry, and 6th Texas Cavalry Battalion in Randal's brigade, and the 12th Infantry, 22nd Infantry, and 13th Cavalry in Waul's brigade. For comments on the weather, see Bonner, "Sketches of the Campaign," 5:462; and *History of the Forty-Sixth*, 87.

8. Troop dispositions are outlined in *Official Records*, vol. 34, pt. 1, pp. 265–6; Johnson, *Red River Campaign*, 130, 133; and in maps displayed at the Mansfield State Historic Site.

9. Johnson, *Red River Campaign*, 134; Wickham Hoffman, *Camp, Court and Siege: A Narrative of Personal Adventure and Observation during Two Wars* (New York: Harper and Brothers, 1877), 84; Taylor, *Destruction and Reconstruction*, 162–3; Parrish, *Richard Taylor*, 342–3.

10. Taylor, *Destruction and Reconstruction*, 162, 163; *Official Records*, vol. 34, pt. 1, p. 564; ibid., pp. 266–7; Johnson, *Red River Campaign*, 134–5; William Arceneaux, *Acadian General: Alfred Mouton and the Civil War*, 2nd ed. (Lafayette: Center for Louisiana Studies, University of Southwestern Louisiana, 1981), 132.

11. *Official Records*, vol. 34, pt. 1, p. 564; Taylor, *Destruction and Reconstruction*, 163; Johnson, *Red River Campaign*, 134–5; Kinard, *Lafayette of the South*, 142–3.

12. *Official Records*, vol. 34, pt. 1, pp. 565–6; Bonner, "Sketches of the Campaign," 5:463–4; "Red River Expedition," *Rebellion Record* 8 (1867): 558; Stark Diary, April 8–9, 1864, Stark Letters and Diary. Taylor's respect for General Walker was shared by the Greyhounds. Thomas R. Bonner, an officer in the 18th Texas, called Walker "the idol of his division" (Bonner, "Sketches of the Campaign," 5:464).

13. John M. Stanyan, *A History of the Eighth Regiment of New Hampshire Volunteers* (Concord, N.H.: Ira C. Evans, Printer, 1892), 403; Caroline E. Whitcomb, *History of the Second Massachusetts Battery (Nims' Battery) of Light Artillery, 1861–1865* (Concord, N.H.: Rumford Press, 1912), 69; Norris, ed., *With the 18th Texas Infantry*, 65; Bonner, "Sketches of the Campaign," 5:464.

14. Bonner, "Sketches of the Campaign," 5:464, 6:12; G. H. Hill to Thos. G. Rhett, April 5, 1864, Letters Sent by Lt. Col. G[abriel]. H. Hill, Commander of the Confederate Ordnance Works at Tyler, Texas, 1864–1865, Ordnance Records, War Department Collection of Confederate Records; Hall, "Notes of the Red River Campaign," 270–1; *Official Records*, vol. 34, pt. 1, p. 298. Shocked by the destructive musketry near the road, an Illinois captain who had been with Grant in Mississippi wrote that "nothing at Vicksburg ever equaled it" (W. H. Bentley, *History of the 77th Illinois Volunteer Infantry, Sept. 2, 1862–July 10, 1865* [Peoria, Ill.: Edward Hine, Printer, 1883], 258).

15. Terrence J. Winschel, ed., *The Civil War Diary of a Common Soldier: William Wiley of the 77th Illinois Infantry* (Baton Rouge: Louisiana State Univ. Press, 2001), 103.

16. Some accounts by Louisiana Confederates claimed that *their* units had captured Nims's battery, but either they were mistaken about the identity of the battery they captured or they referred to a later phase of the engagement when Louisiana and Texas troops converged on the remnants of the battery to the rear of Honeycutt Hill. For examples, see "The Battle of Mansfield," *Southern Bivouac* 3 (April 1885): 413; John G. Belisle, *History of Sabine Parish, Louisiana* ([Many, La.]: Sabine Banner Press, 1912), 162.

17. Winschel, ed., *Civil War Diary*, 103; Sally P. Power, ed., "A Vermonter's Account of the Red River Campaign," *Louisiana History* 40 (summer 1999): 363, 364; Ewer, *Third Massachusetts Cavalry*, 148; *Official Records*, vol. 34, pt. 1, p. 266.

18. Ewer, *Third Massachusetts Cavalry*, 155, 156 (first quotation); *New Orleans Times Picayune*, April 16, 1864. Only ten days after the rout of their units, Brig. Gen. Albert Lee and Col. N. A. M. Dudley, brigade commander of the Union cavalry on the Federal left, were relieved of field command and assigned to administrative posts in New Orleans (*Official Records*, vol. 34, pt. 3, p. 211).

19. Stark Diary, April 8–9, 1864, Stark Letters and Diary; Frank McGregor to [Susie], April 12, 1864, McGregor Papers; Ewer, *Third Massachusetts Cavalry*, 154.

20. Frank McGregor to [Susie], April 12, 1864, McGregor Papers; *Official Records*, vol. 34, pt. 1, pp. 266, 301.

21. Whitcomb, *History of the Second Massachusetts Battery*, 67, 69; *Official Records*, vol. 34, pt. 1, p. 273; Ewer, *Third Massachusetts Cavalry*, 149–50; Winschel, ed., *Civil War Diary*, 104.

22. Winschel, ed., *Civil War Diary*, 103–4.

23. Ewer, *Third Massachusetts Cavalry*, 148; Frank McGregor to [Susie], April 12, 1864, McGregor Papers; *Official Records*, vol. 34, pt. 1, p. 267; Johnson, *Red River Campaign*, 136; Warner, *Generals in Blue*, 590.

24. Henry N. Fairbanks, "The Red River Expedition of 1864," in *War Papers: Read Before the Commandery of the State of Maine, Military Order of the Loyal Legion of the United States*, 4 vols.

(1898–1915; reprint, Wilmington, N.C.: Broadfoot, 1992), 1:182; "Red River Expedition," in *Rebellion Record* 8 (1867): 548; Winschel, ed., *Civil War Diary*, 104.

25. Woods, *Services of the Ninety-Sixth Ohio*, 65; Jim Huffstodt, *Hard Dying Men: The Story of General W. H. L. Wallace, General T. E. G. Ransom, and Their "Old Eleventh" Illinois Infantry in the American Civil War (1861–1865)* (Bowie, Md.: Heritage Books, 1991), 179–80; John M. Gould, *History of the First-Tenth-Twenty-ninth Maine Regiment* (Portland, Me.: Stephen Berry, 1871), 413.

26. Gregg Potts and Kevin Hardy Jr., eds., "Letters of a Union Chaplain at Mansfield, 1864," *North Louisiana Historical Association Journal* 16 (spring and summer 1985): 71; "Red River Expedition," *Rebellion Record*, 8 (1867): 553, 559; John Homans, "The Red River Expedition," in *Papers of the Military Historical Society of Massachusetts*, 13 vols. (Boston: Military Historical Society of Massachusetts, 1895–1913), 8:80.

27. Peebles, *There Never Were Such Men*, 313; Carroll, "Memoirs," 5; Rebecca W. Smith and Marion Mullins, eds., "The Diary of H. C. Medford, Confederate Soldier, 1864," *Southwestern Historical Quarterly* 34 (January 1931): 218; L. C. Taylor to Dear Father and Mother, April 19, 1864, in *Galveston Weekly News*, June 8, 1864.

28. Stanyan, *History of the Eighth Regiment*, 404, 419; Hoffman, *Camp, Court and Siege*, 84.

29. Edwin B. Lufkin, *History of the Thirteenth Maine Regiment from Its Organization in 1861 to Its Muster-Out in 1865* (Bridgton, Me.: H. A. Shorey and Son, 1898), 78; W. H. Emory report, undated but late 1864 or early 1865, U.S. Army Generals' Reports, roll 4, vol. 6, p. 337; *Official Records*, vol. 34, pt. 1, p. 392; Orton S. Clark, *The One Hundred and Sixteenth Regiment of New York State Volunteers* (Buffalo, N.Y.: Matthews and Warren, 1868), 155–6; Elias P. Pellet, *History of the 114th Regiment, New York State Volunteers* (Norwich, N.Y.: Telegraph and Chronicle Power Press Print, 1866), 197.

30. Bonner, "Sketches of the Campaign," 5:465; Gould Papers, 64–5.

31. Woods, *Services of the Ninety-Sixth Ohio*, 66, 67; Stark Diary, April 8–9, 1864, Stark Letters and Diary; Bonner, "Sketches of the Campaign," 5:465.

32. Beecher, *Record of the 114th Regiment*, 314–5; Beverly Hayes Kallgren and James L. Crouthamel, eds., *"Dear Friend Anna": The Civil War Letters of a Common Soldier from Maine* (Orono: Univ. of Maine Press, 1992), 86.

33. Bentley, *History of the 77th Illinois*, 253, 254; "Red River Expedition," *Rebellion Record*, 8 (1867): 554; Winschel, ed., *Civil War Diary*, 105; Frank McGregor to [Susie], April 12, 1864, p. 182, McGregor Papers; Hoffman, *Camp, Court and Siege*, 91–2.

34. *Galveston Weekly News*, May 4, 1864; Bonner, "Sketches of the Campaign," 6:8; Blessington, *Campaigns of Walker's Texas Division*, 193, 194; Bentley, *History of the 77th Illinois*, 254.

35. Frank McGregor to [Susie], April 12, 1864, p. 184, McGregor Papers; Beecher, *Record of the 114th Regiment*, 319; *Official Records*, vol. 34, pt. 1, p. 183; Johnson, *Red River Campaign*, 146–7.

36. Johnson, *Red River Campaign*, 140–1; Stark Diary, April 8–9, 1864, Stark Letters and Diary; Gould Papers, 64–5; Jane Harris Johansson and David H. Johansson, eds., "Two 'Lost' Battle Reports: Horace Randal's and Joseph L. Brent's Reports of the Battles of Mansfield and Pleasant Hill, 8 and 9 April 1864," *Military History of the West* 23 (fall 1993): 174. Generals Walker and Taylor counted 250 captured wagons and ambulances (Walker, "War of Secession," 51–2; Taylor, *Destruction and Reconstruction*, 161).

37. Josh Wilson to Dear Mag, April 12, 1864, Samuel J. Wright Civil War Letters; Bonner, "Sketches of the Campaign," 6:8, 5:465; Smith and Mullins, eds., "Diary of H. C. Medford," 221; Walker, "War of Secession," 51; Lale, "For Lack of a Nail," 39; Carroll, "Memoirs of James Craton Carroll," 5–6; Stark Diary, April 8–9, 1864, Stark Letters and Diary; Hoffman, *Camp, Court and Siege*, 91.

38. Clarence Poe, ed., *True Tales of the South at War: How Soldiers Fought and Families Lived, 1861–1865* (Chapel Hill: Univ. of North Carolina Press, 1961), 91–2.

39. R. Taylor to General [Walker], April 9, 1864, Walker Papers; Yeary, ed., *Reminiscences of the Boys in Gray*, 453; Taylor, *Destruction and Reconstruction*, 165; Johnson, *Red River Campaign*, 147.

40. "Red River Expedition," *Rebellion Record* 8 (1867): 535, 556; S. F. Benson, "The Battle of Pleasant Hill, Louisiana," *Annals of Iowa*, 3rd series, 7 (October 1906): 503; Taylor, *Destruction and Reconstruction*, 166; Henry H. Childers, "Reminiscences of the Battle of Pleasant Hill," *Annals of Iowa*, 3rd series, 7 (October 1906): 515; Lufkin, *History of the Thirteenth Maine*, 83; Walker, "War of Secession," 53–4.

41. Richard B. Irwin, *History of the Nineteenth Army Corps* (New York: G. P. Putnam's Sons, 1892), 314; Hall, "Notes of the Red River Campaign," 273–4.

42. R. Taylor to General [Walker], April 9, 1864, Walker Papers; Taylor, *Destruction and Reconstruction*, 165–6; *Official Records*, vol. 34, pt. 1, p. 605.

43. *Official Records*, vol. 34, pt. 1, pp. 354–5, 423, 430; Johnson, *Red River Campaign*, 147–50. A thoroughly researched map ("Battle of Pleasant Hill, La.") prepared by Tom J., Terry G., and H. G. Waxham, on display at the Mansfield State Historic Site, provides unusually rich detail on troop placements and movements at Pleasant Hill.

44. *Official Records*, vol. 34, pt. 1, pp. 566–7; Taylor, *Destruction and Reconstruction*, 166–7.

45. Theophilus Noel, *Autobiography and Reminiscences of Theophilus Noel* (Chicago: Theo. Noel Co., 1904), 139; Taylor, *Destruction and Reconstruction*, 167.

46. Clark, *One Hundred and Sixteenth Regiment*, 162; *Official Records*, vol. 34, pt. 1, p. 431; Taylor, *Destruction and Reconstruction*, 167–8; Johnson, *Red River Campaign*, 155.

47. Noel, *Autobiography*, 140; *Official Records*, vol. 34, pt. 1, pp. 317–8, 328–9, 340, 346, 350, 605; Perkins, *Daniel's Battery*, 22–3; Johnson, *Red River Campaign*, 160–1.

48. Blessington, *Campaigns of Walker's Texas Division*, 196; Taylor, *Destruction and Reconstruction*, 167–8, 171; Alwyn Barr, "Texan Losses in the Red River Campaign, 1864," *Texas Military History* 3 (summer 1963): 104–5.

49. Calhoun, *Life Story*, 5; Scott, *Story of the Thirty Second Iowa*, 140, 158; Taylor, *Destruction and Reconstruction*, 169.

50. Scott, *Story of the Thirty Second Iowa*, 144–5.

51. Ibid., 154–5; Starks Diary, April 8–9, 1864, Stark Letters and Diary; A. J. Barkley, "The Battle of Pleasant Hill, Louisiana: Recollections of a Private Soldier," *Annals of Iowa*, 3rd series, 3 (April 1897): 26; W. C. Littlefield to Dear Father and Mother, April 13, 1864, W. C. Littlefield Letters, Illinois State Historical Library, Springfield.

52. Taylor, *Destruction and Reconstruction*, 169; Blessington, *Campaigns of Walker's Texas Division*, 197; Larison, "Edward Clark," in *Ten Texans in Gray*, ed. Nunn, 31–2; Johansson, ed., *Widows by the Thousand*, 241; Brown, ed., *Journey to Pleasant Hill*, 412–20 (quotation on p. 420).

53. Scott, *Thirty Second*, 139, 147–8; William T. Shaw, "The Battle of Pleasant Hill," *Annals of Iowa*, 3rd series, 3 (April–July 1898): 405–9; *Official Records*, vol. 34, pt. 1, pp. 355–6, 360–1, 363, 423–4; Walker, "War of Secession," 54–5.

54. Barkley, "Battle of Pleasant Hill," 27; Taylor, *Destruction and Reconstruction*, 170.

55. *Official Records*, vol. 34, pt. 1, pp. 424, 568; Taylor, *Destruction and Reconstruction*, 170; Hamilton P. Bee, "Battle of Pleasant Hill—An Error Corrected," *Southern Historical Society Papers* 8 (April 1880): 184–6.

56. *Official Records*, vol. 34, pt. 1, p. 184; Taylor, *Destruction and Reconstruction*, 175.

57. Bryner, *Bugle Echoes*, 106; Pellet, *History of the 114th Regiment*, 212.

58. L. C. Taylor to Dear Father and Mother, April 19, 1864, *Galveston Weekly News*, June 8, 1864; Bearss, ed., *Diary of Felix Pierre Poché*, 111; Cutrer, ed., "Letters of Volney Ellis," 156.

59. Taylor, *Destruction and Reconstruction*, 171; Blessington, *Campaigns of Walker's Texas Division*, 199; Johnson, *Red River Campaign*, 169; Barr, "Texan Losses," 104–5; *Galveston Tri-Weekly News*, supplement, May 8, 1864; Johansson and Johansson, eds., "Two 'Lost' Battle Reports," 175.

60. D. McFarland to Dear Wife, April 18, 1864, David McFarland Papers, Illinois State Historical Library; Frank McGregor to Dear Folks at Home, April 20, 1864, McGregor Papers.

61. Blessington, *Campaigns of Walker's Texas Division*, 200; *Official Records*, vol. 34, pt. 1, pp. 184–5, 432; Johnson, *Red River Campaign*, 162–4.

## 12. JENKINS' FERRY

1. Selfridge, "Navy in the Red River," 363; *Official Records, Navies*, vol. 26, pp. 49, 778, 781, 789.

2. Taylor, *Destruction and Reconstruction*, 189; *Official Records*, vol. 34, pt. 1, pp. 479–81, 541, 545; Smith, "Defense of the Red River," 372–3; Parrish, *Richard Taylor*, 369–73; Parks, *General Edmund Kirby Smith*, 393–6.

3. Taylor, *Destruction and Reconstruction*, 176, 186; Walker, "War of Secession," 56. Corporal Blessington implied that the men in the ranks also blamed Smith for the decision to send the Greyhounds to Arkansas (Blessington, *Campaigns of Walker's Texas Division*, 265).

4. Taylor, *Destruction and Reconstruction*, 178–80, 188–90 (quotation on p. 178); *Official Records*, vol. 34, pt. 1, pp. 476–7, 572; *Official Records, Navies*, vol. 26, pp. 173–4.

5. Blessington, *Campaigns of Walker's Texas Division*, 241–3 (quotations on p. 243); Samuel W. Farrow to Dearest Josephine, April 19, 1864, Farrow Papers; James Fancher Diary, April 14–20, 1864, Kevin Anderson Collection, Shreveport, La.; W. R. Boggs to Lt. Col. [Edward F.] Gray, April 15, 1864, Letters Sent, Trans-Mississippi Dept. (chap. II, vol 73¹/₂); Stewart Sifakis, *Compendium of the Confederate Armies: Texas* (New York: Facts on File, 1995), 110–1.

6. *Official Records*, vol. 34, pt. 1, pp. 481, 534, 555, 582; ibid., pt. 3, p. 786.

7. Blessington, *Campaigns of Walker's Texas Division*, 246; Stark Diary, April 21, 1864, Stark Letters and Diary; Fancher Diary, April 24–6, 1864.

8. *Official Records*, vol. 34, pt. 1, pp. 657, 692; ibid., pt. 2, p. 704; Warner, *Generals in Blue*, 474; Lonnie J. White, ed., "A Bluecoat's Account of the Camden Expedition," *Arkansas Historical Quarterly* 24 (spring 1965): 82–9; Johnson, *Red River Campaign*, 170–6.

9. *Official Records*, vol. 34, pt. 1, pp. 675–6, 661, 744–6, 791–2, 842, 848–9; Johnson, *Red River Campaign*, 178–9; Edwin C. Bearss, *Steele's Retreat from Camden and the Battle of Jenkins' Ferry* (Little Rock: Arkansas Civil War Centennial Commission, 1967), 15–37; Anne J. Bailey, "Was There a Massacre at Poison Spring?" *Military History of the Southwest* 20 (fall 1990): 157–68.

10. *Official Records*, vol. 34, pt. 1, pp. 668, 692, 714, 788–9, 794–5, 798, 835–6; Johnson, *Red River Campaign*, 188–94; Bearss, *Steele's Retreat*, 62–76; Kerby, *Kirby Smith's Confederacy*, 312–3.

11. A. F. Sperry, *History of the 33d Iowa Infantry Volunteer Regiment, 1863–6*, ed. Gregory J. W. Urwin and Cathy Kunzinger Urwin (1866; reprint, Fayetteville: Univ. of Arkansas Press, 1999), 95; Walker, "War of Secession," 61–2; S. S. Anderson to Genl. Boggs, April 25, 1864, and S. S. Anderson to E. Kirby Smith, May 6, 1864, both in Letters Sent, Trans-Mississippi Department (Chapter II, vol. 73¹/₂); Ira Don Richards, "The Battle of Jenkins' Ferry," *Arkansas Historical Quarterly* 20 (spring 1961): 3–4; Bearss, *Steele's Retreat*, 91.

12. Walker, "War of Secession," 61–2; H. T. Douglas, "The Trans-Mississippi Department," *Confederate Veteran* 25 (April 1917): 153; Blessington, *Campaigns of Walker's Texas Division*, 247; *Official Records*, vol. 34, pt. 1, pp. 556, 782.

13. Stark Diary, April 28, 1864, Stark Letters and Diary; *Confederate Veteran* 18 (October 1910): 468; Sperry, *History of the 33d Iowa*, 96, 97.

14. Louis F. Kakuse, *A Civil War Drama: The Adventures of a Union Soldier in Southern Imprisonment*, trans. Herbert P. Kakuske (New York: Carlton Press, 1970), 28; *Official Records*, vol. 34, pt. 1, p. 782; Blessington, *Campaigns of Walker's Texas Division*, 248.

15. Carl H. Moneyhon, ed., "Life in Confederate Arkansas: The Diary of Virginia Davis Gray, 1863–1865, Part I," *Arkansas Historical Quarterly* 42 (spring 1983): 83; *Official Records*, vol. 34, pt. 1, p. 677; Blessington, *Campaigns of Walker's Texas Division*, 248.

16. Bragg, *Letters of a Confederate Surgeon*, 225; Blessington, *Campaigns of Walker's Texas Division*, 248; Ben T. Harris to Editor, *Galveston Weekly News*, June 8, 1864.

17. Charles H. Lothrop, *A History of the First Regiment Iowa Cavalry Veteran Volunteers, from Its Organization in 1861 to Its Muster Out of the United States Service in 1866* (Lyons, Iowa: Beers and Eaton, 1890), 166; *Official Records*, vol. 34, pt. 1, p. 677; Johnson, *Red River Campaign*, 196–7.

18. O. E. Roberts to Dear Uncle [Oran M. Roberts], April 5 [*sic*], 1864 [actually May 5], Roberts Papers; Walker, "War of Secession," 64; *Official Records*, vol. 34, pt. 1, p. 556.

19. Bragg, *Letters of a Confederate Surgeon*, 227.

20. *Official Records*, vol. 34, pt. 1, pp. 697–8, 724–6, 799–800, 801–2, 808; Johnson, *Red River Campaign*, 198–9; Bearss, *Steele's Retreat*, 122–30.

21. *Official Records*, vol. 34, pt. 1, pp. 811–2; Ralph R. Rea, ed., "Diary of Private John P. Wright, U.S.A, 1864–1865," *Arkansas Historical Quarterly* 16 (autumn 1957): 316; Johnson, *Red River Campaign*, 199; Bearss, *Steele's Retreat*, 135–45.

22. *Official Records*, vol. 34, pt. 1, pp. 757–8, 812–3; Gregory J. W. Urwin, ed., "'We Cannot Treat Negroes . . . as Prisoners of War': Racial Atrocities and Reprisals in Civil War Arkansas," *Civil War History* 42 (September 1996): 207–8; White, ed., "Bluecoat's Account," 87–8; Bearss, *Steele's Retreat*, 142–4.

23. Walker, "War of Secession," 64; *Official Records*, vol. 34, pt. 1, pp. 556, 802, 806–7, 810, 816; Johnson, *Red River Campaign*, 199–200; Bearss, *Steele's Retreat*, 148–9.

24. Blessington, *Campaigns of Walker's Texas Division*, 73, 249, 250; Henry [Hall] to Dear Mother, May 8, 1864, reprinted in [Mrs. Walter Gray Davis], "Hall, Henry Gerard: Lieut. Colonel, 1833–1873," in *Who's Who of the Confederacy: A Symposium by the Members of the Albert Sidney Johnston Chapter No. 2060, United Daughters of the Confederacy*, composited by Susan Merle Dotson (San Antonio: Naylor, 1966), 84; *Official Records*, vol. 34, pt. 1, p. 817.

25. *Official Records*, vol. 34, pt. 1, pp. 800–17 passim.

26. Henry [Hall] to Dear Mother, May 8, 1864, reprinted in [Mrs. Walter Gray Davis], "Hall, Henry Gerard: Lieut. Colonel, 1833–1873," in *Who's Who of the Confederacy*, composited by Susan Merle Dotson, 84; *Official Records*, vol. 34, pt. 1, pp. 557, 817; Walker, "War of Secession," 64; Bearss, *Steele's Retreat*, 151–2.

27. Sperry, *History of the 33d Iowa*, 100; Wm. H. Tamplin to Mrs. R. A. Tamplin, May 7, 1864, Tamplin Letters; W. H. Tamplin to Dear Retincia, May 15, 1864, ibid.; Yeary, comp., *Reminiscences of the Boys in Gray*, 371; Blessington, *Campaigns of Walker's Texas Division*, 250.

28. *Confederate Veteran* 18 (October 1910): 468; Yeary, comp., *Reminiscences of the Boys in Gray*, 390.

29. Henry [Hall] to Dear Mother, May 8, 1864, reprinted in [Mrs. Walter Gray Davis], "Hall, Henry Gerard: Lieut. Colonel, 1833–1873," in *Who's Who of the Confederacy*, composited by Susan Merle Dotson, 85; Ned [Cade] to My dear Wife, May 6, 1864, Cade Correspondence.

30. Biography and Diaries of R. S. Gould, Gould Papers, 71–2; Walker, "War of Secession," 65; D. M. Ray to Dear Mother, May 7, 1864, Ray Papers; Johansson, *Peculiar Honor,* 117–21.

31. Yeary, comp., *Reminiscences of the Boys in Gray,* 744; Glover, ed., "War Letters," 387; *Galveston Weekly News,* May 18 and 25, 1864.

32. *Official Records,* vol. 34, pt. 1, p. 818; Anne Bailey, "Thomas Neville Waul," in *The Confederate General,* ed. Davis, 6:113–5. Confederate generals were more than twice as likely to die in battle as Union generals. Indeed, almost one-fifth of all Confederate generals (77 of 425) were killed in action or mortally wounded (E. B. Long, *The Civil War Day by Day: An Almanac, 1861–1865* [Garden City, N.Y.: Doubleday, 1971], 713).

33. Horace Randal vertical file, p. 13, Harrison County Historical Museum, Marshall, Tex.; Yeary, comp., *Reminiscences of the Boys in Gray,* 371; Anderson, *Confederate General William Read "Dirty Neck Bill" Scurry,* 205; Tom Jones, "Horace Randal," in *New Handbook of Texas,* ed. Tyler et al., 5:436; Thomas W. Cutrer, "William Read Scurry," ibid., 946.

34. *Burlington Weekly Hawk-Eye,* June 11, 1864, p. 6; Henry [Hall] to Dear Mother, May 8, 1864, reprinted in [Mrs. Walter Gray Davis], "Hall, Henry Gerard: Lieut. Colonel, 1833–1873," in *Who's Who of the Confederacy,* composited by Susan Merle Dotson, 85–6; *Official Records,* vol. 34, pt. 1, pp. 557, 690; Lothrop, *History of the First Regiment Iowa Cavalry,* 166.

35. Walker, "War of Secession," 65; *Official Records,* vol. 34, pt. 1, pp. 677, 830.

36. Silas Claborn Turnbo, *History of the Twenty-Seventh Arkansas Confederate Infantry,* ed. Desmond Walls Allen (Conway, Ark.: Arkansas Research, 1988), 194–5; Yeary, comp., *Reminiscences of the Boys in Gray,* 206, 583–4 (second quotation).

37. Stark Diary, April 30, 1864, Stark Letters and Diary; Blessington, *Campaigns of Walker's Texas Division,* 254, 255.

38. Johnson, *Red River Campaign,* and Bearss, *Steele's Retreat,* estimate a total of about six thousand Confederates engaged at Jenkins' Ferry, but their figures assume that Churchill's small Arkansas division was equal in size to Walker's division. For that reason, I estimate the number engaged at a lower level, somewhere between five and six thousand. See Johnson, *Red River Campaign,* 202 n. 107; and Bearss, *Steele's Retreat,* 166 n. 123.

39. Barr, "Texan Losses in the Red River Campaign," 106–7; Henry [Hall] to Dear Mother, May 8, 1864, reprinted in [Mrs. Walter Gray Davis], "Hall, Henry Gerard: Lieut. Colonel, 1833–1873," in *Who's Who of the Confederacy,* composited by Susan Merle Dotson, 86; Johnson, *Red River Campaign,* 202; Bearss, *Steele's Retreat,* 161.

40. Walker, "War of Secession," 67–8.

41. *Official Records,* vol. 34, pt. 1, p. 684; ibid., vol. 41, pt. 1, pp. 102, 123; Bearss, *Steele's Retreat,* 178.

42. Walker, "War of Secession," 67; Blessington, *Campaigns of Walker's Division,* 256, 259.

43. *Official Records,* vol. 34, pt. 1, p. 482; Blessington, *Campaigns of Walker's Texas Division,* 261; Irwin, "Red River Campaign," in *Battles and Leaders,* ed. Johnson and Buel, 4:358–60; Chester G. Hearn, *Admiral David Dixon Porter: The Civil War Years* (Annapolis, Md.: Naval Institute Press, 1996), 257–61.

44. Ned [Cade] to My dear Wife, May 14, 1864, Cade Correspondence; Norris, ed., *With the 18th Texas Infantry,* 7, 9, 21, 41, 61, 74; Blessington, *Campaigns of Walker's Texas Division,* 261; Arthur W. Bergeron Jr., "Wilburn Hill King," and "Robert Plunket Maclay," both in *Confederate General,* ed. Davis, 6:186–7, 190–1; Anne Bailey, "Richard Waterhouse," ibid., 6:108–9.

45. Ned [Cade] to My dear Wife, May 14, 1864, Cade Correspondence; Blessington, *Campaigns of Walker's Texas Division,* 261–2; *Official Records,* vol. 34, pt. 3, pp. 826–7; Hearn, *Admiral David*

*Dixon Porter,* 261–3; Kristi Strickland, "Bonnie Parker," in *New Handbook of Texas,* ed. Tyler et al., 5:56–7.

46. The reference to Sister Ann was from the children's tale of Bluebeard, the wife murderer. Ann, sister of the last wife, watched for rescuers from a tower in Bluebeard's castle. Thanks to Vicki Betts, University of Texas at Tyler, for identifying the quotation.

47. Taylor, *Destruction and Reconstruction,* 188; Winters, *Civil War in Louisiana,* 374–7. The Greyhounds reached Pineville on May 22. Allowing for one day to cross the Red River by ferry and two more days to march the fifty miles to Yellow Bayou, the Texans were five days too late.

48. *Official Records, Navies,* vol. 26, pp. 173–4; Taylor, *Destruction and Reconstruction,* 188. At the Battle of Inkerman (1854) in the Crimean War, British troops stood fast against a powerful Russian offensive.

49. Mileage figures were derived from daily accounts by Blessington and other members of the division who recorded such information. Using modern highway maps and closely approximating the route followed by Walker's division, the total mileage amounts to 828. The difference between the two figures (930 and 828) is doubtless due to rougher approximations in the 1860s on the one hand, and straighter highways today on the other hand. Today's highway mileage from Washington to Memphis is 872.

## 13. THE BREAKUP

1. For an analysis of battlefield casualties in the division, see the appendix.

2. Brown, ed., *Journey to Pleasant Hill,* 456–7.

3. Johnson, "Red River Campaign," 166.

4. Cutrer, ed., "Letters of Volney Ellis," 163–4. Gallagher, *Confederate War,* and Blair, *Virginia's Private War,* have noted continuing high levels of morale and commitment to the cause in the spring and summer of 1864 in the eastern theater of the Confederacy as well.

5. Blessington, *Campaigns of Walker's Texas Division,* 269–70; *Official Records,* vol. 34, pt. 4, p. 664; Parrish, *Richard Taylor,* 406.

6. Cutrer, ed., "Letters of Virgil Sullivan Rabb," Part Two, p. 77; Blessington, *Campaigns of Walker's Texas Division,* 270.

7. Norris, ed., *With the 18th Texas Infantry,* 7, 9, 21, 41, 61, 62, 63, 75; Arthur W. Bergeron Jr., "Wilburn Hill King," in *Confederate General,* ed. Davis, 6:186–7; Bruce S. Allardice, *More Generals in Gray* (Baton Rouge: Louisiana State Univ. Press, 1995), 141–2; Report of Ordnance and Ordnance Stores for Walker's Division, June 15, 1864, in Trans-Mississippi Department Morning Reports, Inspection Reports, Monthly Returns, Orders, June 18, 1864, in Civil War Papers (Collection 55-B), vol. 41, item 103, Louisiana Historical Association Collection, Howard-Tilton Memorial Library, Tulane University.

8. *Official Records,* vol. 41, pt. 1, pp. 89–94 (quotation on p. 90); Kerby, *Kirby Smith's Confederacy,* 324–5; Parrish, *Richard Taylor,* 406–7; Parks, *General Edmund Kirby Smith,* 420–4.

9. *Official Records,* vol. 38, pt. 4, p. 426; ibid., vol. 41, pt. 1, p. 101, 105, 107, 110, 112; ibid., pt. 2, pp. 555–6, 605; *Official Records, Navies,* vol. 21, p. 530; Taylor, *Destruction and Reconstruction,* 195.

10. Blessington, *Campaigns of Walker's Texas Division,* 273; W. W. Shelton to Dear Father, August 17–8, 1864, W. W. Shelton Letters, Gary Canada Collection; David M. Ray to Dear Mother, July 30, 1864, Ray Papers; Cutrer, ed., "Letters of Virgil Sullivan Rabb," Part Two, p. 73; M. W. Barber and C. S. Durning Diary, entries for first half of August, Center for American History.

11. For timing of the announcement, see W. W. Shelton to Dear Father, August 17–8, 1864, Shelton Letters; Barber-Durning Diary, August 17, 1864.

12. W. W. Shelton to Dear Father, August 17–8, 1864, Shelton Letters.

13. Cutrer, ed., "Letters of Virgil Sullivan Rabb," Part Two, pp. 74–5. When rumors of crossing the Mississippi River had run through the division in 1862, the Texans in general had accepted the idea without quibbling. For examples, see ibid., Part One, p. 167; Brown, ed., *Journey to Pleasant Hill,* 108; J. S. Bryan to My Dear wife, December 10, 1862, Bryan Papers; Cutrer, ed., "Letters of Volney Ellis," 119.

14. David M. Ray to Dear Mother, August 24, 1864, Ray Papers. A disdainful supply officer in Polignac's division estimated that four hundred men in Walker's division had deserted, though he admitted that half had returned within a few days (Bearss, ed., *Diary of Felix Pierre Poché,* 156).

15. Biography and Diaries of R. S. Gould, p. 75, Gould Papers; Fred F. Abbey, "Robert Simonton Gould," in *New Handbook of Texas,* ed. Tyler et al., 3:258.

16. Biography and Diaries of R. S. Gould, pp. 76–9 (quotations on pp. 77, 78, and 79).

17. Harrison, ed., "Confederate Letters of John Simmons," 42; Cutrer, ed., "Letters of Virgil Sullivan Rabb," Part Two, p. 75; J. H. Armstrong to My Dear Martha, August 17, 1864, Armstrong Letters; Cutrer, ed., "Letters of Volney Ellis," 166.

18. Several Greyhounds remarked on the voluntary return of deserters. James B. Rounsaville of the 13th Cavalry wrote that "nearly all" the men who had deserted because of orders to cross the Mississippi had returned to the division by late September (J. B. Rounsaville to Dear Mattie, September 25, 1864, Rounsaville Letters).

19. *Official Records,* vol. 41, pt. 1, pp. 110–1, 112.

20. Ibid., 112.

21. Ibid., 110–1, 112, 117, 123, 124; *Official Records, Navies,* vol. 26, pp. 695–9; *New York Herald,* October 22, 1864; David M. Ray to Dear Mother, August 24, 1864, Ray Papers; Barber-Durning Diary, August 27, 1864; Harrison, ed., "Confederate Letters of John Simmons," 41–2.

22. Bergeron, "John Henry Forney," in *Confederate General,* ed. Davis, 2:134–5; Ezra J. Warner, *Generals in Gray: Lives of the Confederate Commanders* (Baton Rouge: Louisiana State Univ. Press, 1959), 90–1; Boatner, *Civil War Dictionary,* 288.

23. Lowry, *Story the Soldiers Wouldn't Tell,* 139.

24. *Official Records,* vol. 41, pt. 1, pp. 91, 95, 120; ibid., pt. 2, p. 1063; Blessington, *Campaigns of Walker's Texas Division,* 276; Kerby, *Kirby Smith's Confederacy,* 327.

25. Blessington, *Campaigns of Walker's Texas Division,* 276, 277; E. P. Becton to My dear Mary, September 20, 1864, Becton Papers; Harrison, ed., "Confederate Letters of John Simmons," 48. Also see J. B. Rounsaville to Dear Mattie, September 25, 1864, Rounsaville Letters.

26. Stark Diary, September 14, 1864, Stark Letters and Diary; Blessington, *Campaigns of Walker's Texas Division,* 275.

27. Harrison, ed., "Confederate Letters of John Simmons," 43; Blessington, *Campaigns of Walker's Texas Division,* 277; Kerby, *Kirby Smith's Confederacy,* 333.

28. Blessington, *Campaigns of Walker's Texas Division,* 278.

29. Blessington, *Campaigns of Walker's Texas Division,* 279; J. H. Armstrong to My Dear Martha, October 19, 1864, Armstrong Letters; Sam Wright to My dear Father, November 16, 1864, Wright Civil War Letters. According to Wright, the entire army near Camden was paid in mid-November, the first compensation for most of them since August 1863.

30. Porter, "Early Days," 34; Blessington, *Campaigns of Walker's Texas Division,* 279–80; Peebles, *There Never Were Such Men Before,* 185; Bergeron, ed., *Reminiscences of Major Silas T. Grisamore,* 173.

31. Ralph A. Wooster, ed., "With the Confederate Cavalry in the West: The Civil War Experiences of Isaac Dunbar Affleck," *Southwestern Historical Quarterly* 83 (July 1979): 20.

32. S. J. Wright to My dear Mother, November 8, 1864, Wright Civil War Letters; J. T. Knight to Affectionate Wife & Child, November 30, 1864, Knight Letters.

33. Harrison, ed., "Confederate Letters of John Simmons," 46; Blessington, *Campaigns of Walker's Texas Division*, 280–1; Samuel J. Touchstone, "Camp Magruder and General Thomas J. Churchill's Civil War Camp," *North Louisiana Historical Association Journal* 24 (winter 1993): 40.

34. Sam W. Farrow to Dearest Josephine, December 16, 1864, Farrow Papers; Blessington, *Campaigns of Walker's Texas Division*, 281, 282.

35. Porter, "Early Days," 34; S. W. Farrow to Dearest Josephine, January 7, 1865, Farrow Papers; Blessington, *Campaigns of Walker's Texas Division*, 281–2.

36. Porter, "Early Days," 34; S. W. Farrow to Dearest Josephine, December 25 and 27, 1864, Farrow Papers.

37. Leon Durst, ed., "A Confederate Texas Letter: Bruno Durst to Jet Black," *Southwestern Historical Quarterly* 57 (July 1953): 95–6; Connor, ed., *Dear America*, 108; W. H. Tamplin to Mrs. R. A. Tamplin, February 11, 1865, Tamplin Letters; Blessington, *Campaigns of Walker's Texas Division*, 285–6, 288–90.

38. Harrison, ed., "Confederate Letters of John Simmons," 48; Connor, ed., *Dear America*, 107–8.

39. Connor, ed., *Dear America*, 105–6.

40. Cutrer, ed., "Letters of Virgil Sullivan Rabb," Part Two, p. 84.

41. *Official Records*, vol. 48, pt. 1, pp. 1405–6; Blessington, *Campaigns of Walker's Texas Division*, 291–2; Robert S. Weddle, *Plow-Horse Cavalry: The Caney Creek Boys of the Thirty-Fourth Texas* (Austin, Tex.: Madrona Press, 1974), 153; W[illiam] W. Heartsill, *Fourteen Hundred and 91 Days in the Confederate Army*, ed. Bell Irvin Wiley (1867; reprint, Wilmington, N.C.: Broadfoot, 1992), 236–7.

42. *Official Records*, vol. 48, pt. 1, pp. 1412, 1416–19; Kerby, *Kirby Smith's Confederacy*, 406–7.

43. Blessington, *Campaigns of Walker's Texas Division*, 299; Cutrer, ed., "Letters of Virgil Sullivan Rabb," Part Two, p. 89; Porter, "Early Days," 35; Fancher Diary, March 17, 1865.

44. "Piedmont Springs," in *New Handbook of Texas*, ed. Tyler et al., 5:192–3.

45. Blessington, *Campaigns of Walker's Texas Division*, 299–302 (quotation on p. 302); Porter, "Early Days," 35; Harrison, ed., "Confederate Letters of John Simmons," 49–50. Apparently, Forney's destination had been shifted to Hempstead, sixty-five road miles southwest of Huntsville, probably because the training camps outside Hempstead could accommodate more soldiers than Huntsville. The division often required two or more days to arrive at any one location and one or two days to leave it completely behind.

46. Blessington, *Campaigns of Walker's Texas Division*, 303; Porter, "Early Days," 37.

47. Harrison, ed., "Confederate Letters of John Simmons," 51; Heartsill, *Fourteen Hundred and 91 Days*, 240; *Official Records*, vol. 48, pt. 1, pp. 186–7.

48. Biography and Diaries of R. S. Gould, p. 80; Weddle, *Plow-Horse Cavalry*, 158.

49. Harrison, ed., "Confederate Letters of John Simmons," 52, 53.

50. Forrest, *Odyssey in Gray*, 306–7; *Official Records*, vol. 48, pt. 2, pp. 1300, 1308–9 (quotation on pp. 1308–9).

51. Porter, "Early Days," 37; [William Martin Walton], *An Epitome of My Life: Civil War Reminiscences of Major Buck Walton* (Austin, Tex.: Waterloo Press, 1965), 92.

52. Porter, "Early Days," 37–8; G. W. Baylor, " 'Mister, Here's Your Mule,' " *Confederate Veteran* 14 (October 1906): 463; Bradley Ray Clampitt, "The Break-Up of the Confederate Trans-Mississippi Army, 1865" (M.A. thesis, University of North Texas, 2001). Confederate troops in Louisiana ended their war in much the same way. See Bergeron, ed., *Civil War Reminiscences of Major Silas T. Grisa-*

*more*, 180–3; John Kelly Damico, "Confederate Soldiers Take Matters into Their Own Hands: The End of the Civil War in North Louisiana," *Louisiana History* 39 (spring 1998): 189–205.

53. Forrest, *Odyssey in Gray*, 309.

54. J. G. Walker to [Assistant Adjutant General] S. S. Anderson, May 24, 1865, Edmund Kirby Smith Family Papers, Southern Historical Collection, University of North Carolina, Chapel Hill. General Smith's chief of staff, Lt. Gen. Simon B. Buckner, formally surrendered the Trans-Mississippi Department on May 26 in New Orleans, and Smith himself ratified the agreement in Galveston on June 2 (*Official Records*, vol. 48, pt. 2, pp. 581, 591, 600–1).

## 14. EPILOGUE

1. Kenneth E. Hendrickson Jr., *The Chief Executives of Texas: From Stephen F. Austin to John B. Connally, Jr.* (College Station: Texas A&M Univ. Press, 1995), 101–9; Harold J. Weiss, Jr., "Henry Eustace McCulloch," in *New Handbook of Texas*, ed. Tyler et al., 4:386; Curtis Bishop, "The Coke-Davis Controversy," ibid., 2:195; Abbey, "Robert Simonton Gould," in *New Handbook of Texas*, ed. Tyler et al., 258.

2. Connor, ed., *Dear America*, xi–xv, 117–25; Anderson, ed., *Texas Surgeon in the C.S.A.*, 15–8.

3. Samuel W. Farrow file, Confederate Pension Applications, Texas State Library and Archives Commission; T. Michael Parrish, "Joseph P. Blessington and His Book," in Blessington, *Campaigns of Walker's Texas Division*, xxv–xxvi.

4. Johansson, ed., *Widows by the Thousand*, 244–5; genealogical sketch of Nancy Bryan, Bryan Papers.

5. Peebles, *There Never Were Such Men Before*, 205.

6. Forrest, *Odyssey in Gray*, 317–21; John G. Walker to [Edward C. Wharton], no date, but probably 1865, Edward Clifton Wharton and Family Papers, Louisiana and Lower Mississippi Valley Collections, Hill Memorial Library, Louisiana State University; Thomas W. Cutrer, "John George Walker," in *New Handbook of Texas*, ed. Tyler et al., 6:795–6; Frances A. Walker to Major Freehoff, October 11, 1933, Gwinner Collection.

7. Cutrer, "John George Walker," 795; *Washington (D.C.) Post*, July 21, 1893 (obituary).

# BIBLIOGRAPHY

PRIMARY SOURCES

MANUSCRIPTS

*Arkansas, University of, at Little Rock*
Waterhouse, Richard. Letters, 1838–1872.

*Baylor University, Waco, Texas*
Kirk, Sylvester Purl, and Eliza Jane White. Letters (Texas Collection).

*Center for American History, University of Texas at Austin*
Ballinger, William Pitt. Collection.
Barber, M. W., and C. S. Durning. Diary.
Becton, Edwin Pinckney. Papers.
Farrow, Samuel. Papers.
Fowler, William S. Medical Register.
Gould, Robert Simonton. Papers (Biography and Diaries).
Hamilton, James A. Diary.
Head, William P. Papers.
Minor, Mary. Papers.
Oden, William. Papers.
Ray, David M. Papers.
Roberts, Oran Milo. Papers.
Truitt, James W. Papers.

*Clements Library, University of Michigan, Ann Arbor*
Burns, William S. Papers and Scrapbook (Schoff Civil War Collections).
Henthorn, Charles Otto. Papers (Schoff Civil War Collections).

*Confederate Research Center, Hill College, Hillsboro, Texas*
Armstrong, James Harvey. Letters (14th Texas Infantry file).
Halbert, Joshua L. Letters (15th Texas Infantry file).

Porter, John C. "Early Days of Pittsburg, Texas, 1859–1874; 18th Texas Infantry, Company H: Life of John C. Porter and Sketch of His Experiences in the Civil War" (18th Texas Infantry file).
Regimental files.
Stark, John T. Letters and Diary (13th Texas Cavalry file).

*Duke University, Durham, North Carolina*
Perry, Theophilus. Letters (Presley Carter Person Papers).

*Harrison County Historical Museum, Marshall, Texas*
Randal, Horace. Vertical file.

*Howard-Tilton Memorial Library, Tulane University, New Orleans*
Brent, J. L. Papers (Collection 55-L, Louisiana Historical Association Collection).
Civil War Papers (Collection 55-B, Louisiana Historical Association Collection).
Trans-Mississippi Department Morning Reports, Inspection Reports, Monthly Returns, Orders (Louisiana Historical Association Collection).

*Illinois State Historical Library, Springfield*
Crandall, Hiram C. Diary.
Hieronymus, Benjamin R. Diary.
Littlefield, W. C. Letters.
McFarland, David. Papers.

*Indiana Historical Society Library, Indianapolis*
Bryan, John Samuel. Papers.

*Indiana State Library, Indianapolis*
Chittenden, George. Collection.
Slack, James R. Correspondence.
Watts, Harry. Diary (Harry Watts Collection).

*Iowa, State Historical Society of, Des Moines*
Henry, Robert W. Letters.

*Library of Congress (Manuscripts Division), Washington, D.C.*
Lincoln, Abraham. Papers, 1833–1916.

*Louisiana and Lower Mississippi Valley Collections, Hill Memorial Library, Louisiana State University, Baton Rouge*
Hyatt, Arthur W. Diary.
Tamplin, William H. Letters.
Wharton, Edward Clifton. Papers.

*Louisiana State University, Shreveport*
Allen, N. S. Diary.

*Mansfield State Historic Site, Mansfield, Louisiana*
Page Family. Letters.

*Oregon, University of, Eugene*
Williams, Edward B. Civil War Letters.

*Southern Historical Collection, University of North Carolina, Chapel Hill*
Smith, Edmund Kirby. Family Papers.
Walker, John G. Papers.

*Southwest Arkansas Regional Archives, Washington*
Wallace, Harvey Alexander. Diary.
Wallace, Harvey Alexander. Papers.

*Texas A&M University at Commerce*
Wright, Samuel J. Civil War Letters (Skipper Steely Collection).

*Texas State Library and Archives Commission, Austin*
Cade, Edward W. and Allie. Correspondence (John Q. Anderson Collection).

*United States Army Military History Institute, Carlisle Barracks, Pennsylvania*
Burrell, Henry. Papers.
Carroll, James C. "Memoirs of James Craton Carroll" (Civil War Times Illustrated Collection).
Cornwell, David. Papers. "Dan Caverno: A True Tale of American Life on the Farm, in a Country Store, and in the Volunteer Army" (Civil War Miscellaneous Collection).
McGregor, Frank. Papers.
Polignac, Camille. "Diary of the War between the States" (Civil War Times Miscellaneous Collection).
Rounsaville, James B[rown], and Thomas J. Letters (Civil War Times Miscellaneous Collection).
Smith, Fred. Correspondence (Civil War Times Illustrated Collection).
Walker, David. Correspondence (Myron G. Gwinner Collection).
Walker, John G. "The War of Secession West of the Mississippi River During the Years 1863–4–& 5" (Myron G. Gwinner Collection).

*Virginia Historical Society, Richmond*
Minor Family. Papers (Mss1M6663c2837).

WORLD WIDE WEB
Ritland, John. "The Civil War History of John Ritland" (http://www.iowa-counties.com/civilwar/ritland/rcw.3.html), 28 July 2003.

PRIVATE COLLECTIONS

Arberry, John J. Letters (Gary Canada Collection, Keller, Texas).

Fancher, James. Diary (Kevin Anderson Collection, Shreveport, Louisiana).

Holcombe, John and Amanda. Letters (John Wilson Collection, Playa del Rey, California).

Knight, Jonathan Thomas. Letters (Gary Canada Collection, Keller, Texas).

Shelton, W. W. Letters (Gary Canada Collection, Keller, Texas).

Steele, E. Papers (Wanda Cuniff Collection, Nacogdoches, Texas).


MANUSCRIPT GOVERNMENT DOCUMENTS


*National Archives, Washington, D.C.*

Compiled Service Records of Confederate Soldiers Who Served in Organizations from the State of Texas (War Department Collection of Confederate Records, Record Group 109, Microfilm M323).

Confederate States Army Casualties. Lists and Narrative Reports, 1861–1865 (War Department Collection of Confederate Records, Record Group 109, Microfilm M836).

Eighth Census of the United States, 1860 (Records of the Bureau of the Census, Record Group 29, Microfilm M653, T1134).

Inspection Reports and Related Records Received by the Inspection Branch in the Confederate Adjutant and Inspector General's Office (War Department Collection of Confederate Records, Record Group 109, Microfilm M935).

Letters and Telegrams Received. Records of the Department of Texas and the Trans-Mississippi Department. Records of Military Commands (War Department Collection of Confederate Records, Record Group 109).

Letters Sent. District of West Louisiana, 2 vols. (chap. II, vols. 75–6). Records of the Department of Texas and the Trans-Mississippi Department. Records of Military Commands (War Department Collection of Confederate Records, Record Group 109).

Letters Sent. Trans-Mississippi Department, 4 vols. (chap. II, vols. 70–2, 73½). Records of the Department of Texas and the Trans-Mississippi Department. Records of Military Commands (War Department Collection of Confederate Records, Record Group 109).

Letters Sent by Lt. Col. G[abriel]. H. Hill, Commander of the Confederate Ordnance Works at Tyler, Texas, 1864–1865. Ordnance Records (War Department Collection of Confederate Records, Record Group 109, Microfilm M119).

Muster and Pay Rolls. Records Relating to Military Personnel. Records of the Adjutant and Inspector General's Department (War Department Collection of Confederate Records, Record Group 109).

Post, Department and Army Returns. Rosters and Lists. Records of Military Commands (War Department Collection of Confederate Records, Record Group 109).

"Rebels: List of Prisoners Captured at Fort De Russy, La." Baton Rouge List #1, Louisiana Station Rolls (War Department Collection of Confederate Records, Record Group 109).

U.S. Army Generals' Reports of Civil War Service, 1864–1887 (Records of the Adjutant General's Office, 1780s–1917, Record Group 94, Microfilm Film M1098).

*Texas State Library and Archives Commission, Austin, Texas*
Confederate Pension Applications (Records of the Comptroller of Public Accounts, Record Group 304).
County Real and Personal Property Tax Rolls, 1858–62. Ad Valorem Tax Division (Records of the Comptroller of Public Accounts, Record Group 304).

PUBLISHED GOVERNMENT DOCUMENTS
Gregory, H. F., et al. *A Civil War Military Site Survey: Natchitoches Parish and Environs.* Baton Rouge: Division of Archaeology, Office of Cultural Development, State of Louisiana, 1984.
Hewett, Janet B., Noah Andre Trudeau, and Bryce A. Suderow, eds. *Supplement to the Official Records of the Union and Confederate Armies.* 100 vols. Wilmington, N.C.: Broadfoot, 1994–2001.
Navy Department. *Official Records of the Union and Confederate Navies in the War of the Rebellion.* 31 vols. Washington: Government Printing Office, 1894–1922.
U.S. Bureau of the Census. *Agriculture of the United States in 1860; Compiled from the Original Returns of the Eighth Census.* Washington: Government Printing Office, 1864.
U.S. Bureau of the Census. *Population of the United States in 1860; Compiled from the Original Returns of the Eighth Census.* Washington: Government Printing Office, 1864.
U.S. Senate. *Senate Executive Documents.* 38th Cong., 1st sess., no. 53, pp. 22–3.
War Department. *The War of the Rebellion: A Compilation of the Official Records of the Union and Confederate Armies.* 128 vols. Washington: Government Printing Office, 1880–1901.

NEWSPAPERS AND OTHER PERIODICALS
*(Austin) Tri-Weekly State Gazette,* 1862–1865
*Burlington (Iowa) Weekly Hawk-Eye,* 1863
*Charleston (S.C.) Mercury,* 1862–1865
*De Bow's Review of the Southern and Western States,* 1862–1865
*Fort DeRussy (La.) News,* 1999
*Fort Worth Star-Telegram,* 1994
*(Galveston) Texas Christian Advocate,* 1862–1863
*Galveston Tri-Weekly News,* 1863–1864
*Galveston Weekly News,* 1863–1864
*Harper's Weekly,* 1863–1864
*Houston Tri-Weekly Telegraph,* 1862–1865
*Keokuk (Iowa) Daily Gate City,* 1863
*(Marshall) Texas Republican,* 1862
*New Orleans Times Picayune,* 1863–1864

*New York Daily Tribune,* 1863–1864
*New York Herald,* 1863
*New York Times,* 1863–1864
*Shreveport Semi-Weekly News,* 1863
*Shreveport Weekly News,* 1863
*Tyler Reporter,* 1862
*Washington National Tribune,* 1905, 1916
*(Washington) National Tribune,* 1863
*Washington Post,* 1893

BOOKS

Anderson, John Q., ed. *Brokenburn: The Journal of Kate Stone, 1861–1868.* Baton Rouge: Louisiana State Univ. Press, 1955.

————, ed. *A Texas Surgeon in the C.S.A.* Tuscaloosa, Ala.: Confederate, 1957.

Bearss, Edwin C., ed. *A Louisiana Confederate: Diary of Felix Pierre Poché,* translated by Eugenie Watson Somdal. Natchitoches: Louisiana Studies Institute, Northwestern State University, 1972.

Beecher, Harris H. *Record of the 114th Regiment, N.Y.S.V.: Where it Went, What it Saw, and What it Did.* Norwich, N.Y.: J. F. Hubbard, Jr., 1866.

Bentley, W[illiam]. H. *History of the 77th Illinois Volunteer Infantry, Sept. 2, 1862–July 10, 1865.* Peoria, Ill.: Edward Hine, Printer, 1883.

Bergeron, Arthur W., Jr., ed. *The Civil War Reminiscences of Major Silas T. Grisamore, C.S.A.* Baton Rouge: Louisiana State Univ. Press, 1993.

Blessington, Joseph Palmer. *The Campaigns of Walker's Texas Division.* Introductions by Norman D. Brown and T. Michael Parrish. 1875. Reprint, Austin, Tex.: State House Press, 1994.

Boggs, William R. *Military Reminiscences of Gen. William R. Boggs, C.S.A.* Edited by William K. Boyd. Durham, N.C.: Seeman Printery, 1913.

Bragg, Junius Newport. *Letters of a Confederate Surgeon, 1861–1865.* Edited by Mrs. T. J. Gaughan. Camden, Ark.: Hurley, 1960.

Brown, Leonard. *American Patriotism; or, Memoirs of "common men."* Des Moines, Iowa: Redhead and Wellslager, 1869.

Brown, Norman D., ed. *Journey to Pleasant Hill: The Civil War Letters of Captain Elijah P. Petty, Walker's Texas Division, C.S.A.* San Antonio: Institute of Texan Cultures, 1982.

Bryner, Cloyd. *Bugle Echoes: The Story of the Illinois 47th.* Springfield, Ill.: Phillips Bros., 1905.

Calhoun, Theodore. *The Life Story of Theodore Calhoun: A Native Texan, Born in 1837 at Fort Crockett, Houston County, Texas.* Austin, Tex.: self-published, 1930.

Clark, Orton S. *The One Hundred and Sixteenth Regiment of New York State Volunteers.* Buffalo, N.Y.: Matthews and Warren, 1868.

Connor, Seymour V., ed. *Dear America: Some Letters of Orange Cicero and Mary America (Aikin) Connor.* Austin, Tex.: Jenkins, 1971.

Davis, Nicholas A. *Chaplain Davis and Hood's Texas Brigade*. Edited by Donald E. Everett. 1863. Reprint, San Antonio: Principia Press, 1962.

[Debray, Xavier B.] *A Sketch of the History of DeBray's 26th Regiment of Texas Cavalry*. Austin. Tex.: E. von Boeckman, 1884.

Ewer, James K. *The Third Massachusetts Cavalry in the War for the Union*. Maplewood, Mass.: Historical Committee of the Regimental Assn., 1903.

Flinn, Frank M. *Campaigning With Banks in Louisiana, '63 and '64, and With Sheridan in the Shenandoah Valley in '64 and '65*. Lynn, Mass.: Thos. P. Nichols, 1887.

Forrest, Douglas French. *Odyssey in Gray: A Diary of Confederate Service, 1863–1865*. Edited by William N. Still Jr. Richmond: Virginia State Library, 1979.

Fremantle, Arthur James Lyon. *The Fremantle Diary: Being the Journal of Lieutenant Colonel James Arthur Lyon Fremantle, Coldstream Guards, on his Three Months in the Southern States*. Edited by Walter Lord. Boston: Little, Brown, 1954.

Gould, John M. *History of the First-Tenth-Twenty-ninth Maine Regiment*. Portland, Me.: Stephen Berry, 1871.

Grant, Ulysses S. *Personal Memoirs of U.S. Grant*. Edited by E. B. Long. Introduced by William S. McFeely. 1885. Reprint, New York: Da Capo Press, 1982.

Gravis, Peter W. *Twenty-Five Years on the Outside Row of the Northwest Conference: Autobiography of Rev. Peter W. Gravis*. 1892. Reprint, Brownwood, Tex.: Cross Timbers Press, 1966.

Harding, George C. *The Miscellaneous Writings of George C. Harding*. Indianapolis: Carlon and Hollenbeck, 1882.

Hatch, Carl E., ed. *Dearest Susie: A Civil War Infantryman's Letters to His Sweetheart*. New York: Exposition Press, 1971.

Heartsill, W[illiam]. W. *Fourteen Hundred and 91 Days in the Confederate Army*. Edited by Bell Irvin Wiley. 1867. Reprint, Wilmington, N.C.: Broadfoot, 1992.

*History of the Forty-Sixth Regiment Indiana Volunteer Infantry, September, 1861–September, 1865*. [Logansport, Ind.]: Wilson, Humphreys, 1888.

Hoffman, Wickham. *Camp, Court and Siege: A Narrative of Personal Adventure and Observation during Two Wars*. New York: Harper and Brothers, 1877.

Irwin, Richard B. *History of the Nineteenth Army Corps*. New York: G. P. Putnam's Sons, 1892.

Jackson, Joseph Orville, ed. *"Some of the Boys . . .": The Civil War Letters of Isaac Jackson, 1862–1865*. Carbondale: Southern Illinois Univ. Press, 1960.

Johansson, M. Jane, ed. *Widows by the Thousand: The Civil War Letters of Theophilus and Harriet Perry, 1862–1864*. Fayetteville: Univ. of Arkansas Press, 2000.

Johnson, Robert Underwood, and Clarence Clough Buel, eds. *Battles and Leaders of the Civil War*. 4 vols. New York: Century, 1887–88.

Kakuske, Louis F. *A Civil War Drama: The Adventures of a Union Soldier in Southern Imprisonment*. Translated by Herbert P. Kakuske. New York: Carlton Press, 1970.

Kallgren, Beverly Hayes, and James L. Crouthamel, eds. *"Dear Friend Anna": The Civil War Letters of a Common Soldier from Maine*. Orono: Univ. of Maine Press, 1992.

Knox, Thomas W. *Camp-Fire and Cotton-Field: Southern Adventure in Time of War.* New York: Blelock, 1865.

Lothrop, Charles H. *A History of the First Regiment Iowa Cavalry Veteran Volunteers, from Its Organization in 1861 to Its Muster Out of the United States Service in 1866.* Lyons, Iowa: Beers and Eaton, 1890.

Lufkin, Edwin B. *History of the Thirteenth Maine Regiment from Its Organization in 1861 to Its Muster-Out in 1865.* Bridgton, Me.: H. A. Shorey and Son, 1898.

Maberry, Robert, Jr. *Texas Flags.* College Station: Texas A&M Univ. Press, 2001.

Marshall, T. B. *History of the Eighty-Third Ohio Volunteer Infantry: The Greyhound Regiment.* Cincinnati: Eighty-Third Ohio Volunteer Infantry Assn., 1912.

Masterson, Ralph, ed. *Sketches from the Life of Dr. Horace Bishop.* San Angelo, Tex.: n.p., 1933.

Moore, Frank, ed. *The Rebellion Record: A Diary of American Events.* . . . 12 vols. New York: G. P. Putnam, 1861–63 (vols. 1–6); New York: D. Van Nostrand, 1864–68 (vols. 7–12).

Noel, Theophilus. *Autobiography and Reminiscences of Theophilus Noel.* Chicago: Theo. Noel Co., 1904.

Norris, L. David, ed. *With the 18th Texas Infantry: The Autobiography of Wilburn Hill King.* Hillsboro, Tex.: Hill College Press, 1996.

Nott, Charles C. *Sketches in Prison Camps: A Continuation of Sketches of the War.* 3rd ed. New York: Anson D. F. Randolph, 1865.

Pellet, Elias P. *History of the 114th Regiment, New York State Volunteers.* Norwich, N.Y.: Telegraph and Chronicle Power Press Print, 1866.

Poe, Clarence, ed. *True Tales of the South at War: How Soldiers Fought and Families Lived, 1861–1865.* Chapel Hill: Univ. of North Carolina Press, 1961.

Porter, David D. *Incidents and Anecdotes of the Civil War.* New York: D. Appleton, 1885.

Putnam, George Haven. *Memories of My Youth, 1844–1865.* New York: G. P. Putnam's Sons, 1914.

Rose, Victor M. *Ross' Texas Brigade, Being a Narrative of Events Connected with Its Service in the Late War Between the States.* Louisville, Ky.: Courier-Journal Book and Job Rooms, 1881.

Scott, John. *Story of the Thirty Second Iowa Infantry Volunteers.* Nevada, Iowa: self-published, 1896.

Scott, Reuben B. *The History of the 67th Regiment Indiana Infantry Volunteers.* Bedford, Ind.: Herald Book and Job Print, 1892.

Sears, Cyrus. *Paper of Cyrus Sears, Read Before the Ohio Commandery of the Loyal Legion, October 7th 1908.* Columbus, Ohio: F. J. Heer Printing, 1909.

Selfridge, Thomas O., Jr. *What Finer Tradition: The Memoirs of Thomas O. Selfridge, Jr., Rear Admiral, U.S.N.* Introduced by William N. Still Jr. Columbia: Univ. of South Carolina Press, 1987.

Shelton, Perry Wayne, comp., and Shelly Morrison, ed. *Personal Civil War Letters of General Lawrence Sullivan Ross, with Other Letters.* Austin, Tex.: Shelly and Richard Morrison, 1994.

Simon, John Y., ed. *The Papers of Ulysses S. Grant*. 24 vols. to date. Carbondale, Ill.: Southern Illinois Univ. Press, 1967–.

Smith, Walter George. *Life and Letters of Thomas Kilby Smith, Brevet Major-General, United States Volunteers, 1820–1887*. New York: G. P. Putnam's Sons, 1898.

Sperry, A. F. *History of the 33d Iowa Infantry Volunteer Regiment, 1863–6*. Edited by Gregory J. W. Urwin and Cathy Kunzinger Urwin. 1866. Reprint, Fayetteville: Univ. of Arkansas Press, 1999.

Stanyan, John M. *A History of the Eighth Regiment of New Hampshire Volunteers*. Concord, N.H.: Ira C. Evans, Printer, 1892.

Stuart, A. A. *Iowa Colonels and Regiments: Being a History of Iowa Regiments in the War of the Rebellion*. Des Moines, Iowa: Mills, 1865.

Taylor, Richard. *Destruction and Reconstruction: Personal Experiences of the Late War*. Introduced by T. Michael Parrish. 1879. Reprint, New York: Da Capo Press, 1995.

Terrell, W. H. H., comp. *Indiana in the War of the Rebellion: Report of the Adjutant General*. 1869. Reprint, [Indianapolis]: Indiana Historical Society, 1960.

Turnbo, Silas Claborn. *History of the Twenty-Seventh Arkansas Confederate Infantry*. Edited by Desmond Walls Allen. Conway, Ark.: Arkansas Research, 1988.

[Walton, William Martin]. *An Epitome of My Life: Civil War Reminiscences of Major Buck Walton*. Austin, Tex.: Waterloo Press, 1965.

Whitcomb, Caroline E., comp. *History of the Second Massachusetts Battery (Nims' Battery) of Light Artillery, 1861–1865*. Concord, N.H.: Rumford Press, 1912.

Winschel, Terrence J., ed. *The Civil War Diary of a Common Soldier: William Wiley of the 77th Illinois Infantry*. Baton Rouge: Louisiana State Univ. Press, 2001.

Woods, J. T. *Services of the Ninety-Sixth Ohio Volunteers*. Toledo, Ohio: Blade Printing and Paper Co., 1874.

Yeary, Mamie, comp. *Reminiscences of the Boys in Gray, 1861–1865*. 1912. Reprint, Dayton, Ohio: Morningside Books, 1986.

ARTICLES AND BOOK CHAPTERS

Barkley, A. J. "The Battle of Pleasant Hill, Louisiana: Recollections of a Private Soldier." *Annals of Iowa*, 3rd series, 3 (April 1897): 23–31.

Barr, Alwyn, ed. "The Battle of Bayou Bourbeau, November 3, 1863: Colonel Oran M. Roberts' Report." *Louisiana History* 6 (winter 1965): 83–91.

"The Battle of Mansfield." *Southern Bivouac* 3 (April 1885): 412–4.

Baylor, G. W. "'Mister, Here's Your Mule.'" *Confederate Veteran* 14 (October 1906): 463.

Bee, Hamilton P. "Battle of Pleasant Hill—An Error Corrected." *Southern Historical Society Papers* 8 (April 1880): 184–6.

Benson, S. F. "The Battle of Pleasant Hill, Louisiana." *Annals of Iowa*, 3rd series, 7 (October 1906): 481–504.

Bonner, T. R. "Sketches of the Campaign of 1864." *The Land We Love* 5 (October 1868): 459–66; and 6 (November 1868): 7–12.

Byrd, William. "The Capture of Fort De Russy, La." *The Land We Love* 6 (January 1869): 185–7.

Cheek, T. F. "T. F. Cheek Letters." In *Confederate Reminiscences and Letters, 1861–1865.* 17 vols. to date. 2:139–44 and 6:195–8. Atlanta, Ga.: United Daughters of the Confederacy, 1995–.

Childers, Henry H. "Reminiscences of the Battle of Pleasant Hill." *Annals of Iowa,* 3rd series, 7 (October 1906): 505–16.

Cutrer, Thomas W., ed. "'Bully for Flournoy's Regiment, We Are Some Punkins, You'll Bet': The Civil War Letters of Virgil Sullivan Rabb, Captain, Company 'I,' Sixteenth Texas Infantry, C.S.A." *Military History of the Southwest,* Part One, 19 (fall 1989): 161–90; and Part Two, 20 (spring 1990): 61–96.

————, ed. "'An Experience in Soldier's Life': The Civil War Letters of Volney Ellis, Adjutant, Twelfth Texas Infantry, Walker's Texas Division, C.S.A." *Military History of the Southwest* 22 (fall 1992): 109–72.

"Destruction of Simmsport." In *The Rebellion Record: A Diary of American Events . . . ,* edited by Frank Moore. 12 vols. 7:276. New York: G. P. Putnam, 1861–63 (vols. 1–6); New York: D. Van Nostrand, 1864–68 (vols. 7–12).

Douglas, H. T. "The Trans-Mississippi Department." *Confederate Veteran* 25 (April 1917): 153–4.

Durst, Leon, ed. "A Confederate Texas Letter: Bruno Durst to Jet Black." *Southwestern Historical Quarterly* 57 (July 1953): 94–6.

Edwards, G. G. "Fight at Milliken's Bend, Miss. [*sic*]" In *The Rebellion Record: A Diary of American Events . . . ,* edited by Frank Moore. 12 vols. 7:12–5. New York: G. P. Putnam, 1861–63 (vols. 1–6); New York: D. Van Nostrand, 1864–68 (vols. 7–12).

Erickson, Edgar L., ed. "With Grant at Vicksburg: From the Civil War Diary of Captain Charles E. Wilcox." *Journal of the Illinois State Historical Society* 30 (January 1938): 441–503.

Fairbanks, Henry N. "The Red River Expedition of 1864." In *War Papers: Read Before the Commandery of the State of Maine, Military Order of the Loyal Legion of the United States.* 4 vols. 1:181–90. 1898–1915. Reprint, Wilmington, N.C.: Broadfoot, 1992.

Furness, William Eliot. "The Negro As a Soldier." In *Military Essays and Recollections: Papers Read before the Commandery of the State of Illinois, Military Order of the Loyal Legion of the United States.* 457–87. Chicago: A. C. McClurg, 1894.

Glover, Robert W., ed. "The War Letters of a Texas Conscript in Arkansas." *Arkansas Historical Quarterly* 20 (winter 1961): 355–87.

Gordon, S. C. "Reminiscences of the Civil War from a Surgeon's Point of View." In *War Papers Read Before the Commandery of the State of Maine, Military Order of the Loyal Legion of the United States.* 4 vols. 4:129–44. Portland, Me.: Thurston Print, 1898.

Grant, Ulysses S. "The Vicksburg Campaign." In *Battles and Leaders of the Civil War,* edited by Robert Underwood Johnson and Clarence Clough Buel. 4 vols. 3:493–539. New York: Century, 1887–88.

Hall, Charles B. "Notes of the Red River Campaign of 1864." In *War Papers: Read Before the Commandery of the State of Maine, Military Order of the Loyal Legion of the United States.* 4 vols. 4:264–81. 1898–1915. Reprint, Wilmington, N.C.: Broadfoot, 1992.

Hanrahan, George, ed. "An Iowa Private in the Civil War." *Palimpsest* 58 (November–December 1977): 182–91.

Harrison, Jon, ed. "The Confederate Letters of John Simmons." *Chronicles of Smith County, Texas* 14 (summer 1975): 25–57.

Homans, John. "The Red River Expedition." In *Papers of the Military Historical Society of Massachusetts.* 13 vols. 8:65–98. Boston: Military Historical Society of Massachusetts, 1895–1913.

Irwin, Richard B. "The Red River Campaign." In *Battles and Leaders of the Civil War,* edited by Robert Underwood Johnson and Clarence Clough Buel. 4 vols. 4:345–62. New York: Century, 1887–88.

Johansson, Jane Harris, and David H. Johansson, eds. "Two 'Lost' Battle Reports: Horace Randal's and Joseph L. Brent's Reports of the Battles of Mansfield and Pleasant Hill, 8 and 9 April 1864." *Military History of the West* 23 (fall 1993): 169–80.

Lackner, Edgar E., ed. "Civil War Diaries of Edwin F. Stanton, U.S.A., and William Quensell, C.S.A.: 'Yank and Reb' under One Cover." *East Texas Historical Journal* 18, no. 2 (1980): 25–59.

Lale, Max S., ed. "For Lack of a Nail." *East Tennessee Historical Journal* 30, no. 1 (1992): 38.

———. "A Letter from Leonard Randal to His Son." *East Texas Historical Journal* 23, no. 2 (1985): 47–8.

[Logan, George William]. "Official Report of Colonel George William Logan." *Southern Historical Society Papers* 11 (November 1883): 497–501.

Marten, James, ed. "On the Road with Thomas H. Duval: A Texas Unionist's Travel Diary, 1863." *Journal of Confederate History* 6, no. 1 (1990): 76–93.

Moneyhon, Carl H., ed. "Life in Confederate Arkansas: The Diary of Virginia Davis Gray, 1863–1865, Part I." *Arkansas Historical Quarterly* 42 (spring 1983): 47–85; and Part II, 42 (summer 1983): 134–69.

Potts, Gregg, and Kevin Hardy Jr., eds. "Letters of a Union Chaplain at Mansfield, 1864." *North Louisiana Historical Association Journal* 16 (spring and summer 1985): 69–77.

Power, Sally P., ed. "A Vermonter's Account of the Red River Campaign." *Louisiana History* 40 (summer 1999): 355–64.

Rea, Ralph R., ed. "Diary of Private John P. Wright, U.S.A, 1864–1865." *Arkansas Historical Quarterly* 16 (autumn 1957): 304–18.

"Red River Expedition." In *The Rebellion Record: A Diary of American Events . . . ,* edited by Frank Moore. 12 vols. 8:517–67. New York: G. P. Putnam, 1861–63 (vols. 1–6); New York: D. Van Nostrand, 1864–68 (vols. 7–12).

Selfridge, Thomas O. "The Navy in the Red River." In *Battles and Leaders of the Civil War,* edited by Robert Underwood Johnson and Clarence Clough Buel. 4 vols. 4:362–6. New York: Century, 1887–88.

Shaw, William T. "The Battle of Pleasant Hill." *Annals of Iowa,* 3rd series, 3 (April–July 1898): 401–23.

Smith, E. Kirby. "The Defense of the Red River." In *Battles and Leaders of the Civil War,* edited by Robert Underwood Johnson and Clarence Clough Buel. 4 vols. 4:369–74. New York: Century, 1887–88.

Smith, Rebecca W., and Marion Mullins, eds. "The Diary of H. C. Medford, Confederate Soldier, 1864." *Southwestern Historical Quarterly* 34 (October 1930): 106–40; and 34 (January 1931): 203–30.

Soley, James Russell. "Naval Operations in the Vicksburg Campaign." In *Battles and Leaders of the Civil War,* edited by Robert Underwood Johnson and Clarence Clough Buel. 4 vols. 3:551–70. New York: Century, 1887–88.

White, Lonnie J., ed. "A Bluecoat's Account of the Camden Expedition." *Arkansas Historical Quarterly* 24 (spring 1965): 82–9.

Williams, E. Cort. "Recollections of the Red River Expedition." In *Sketches of War History, 1861–1865: Papers Read before the Ohio Commandery of the Military Order of the Loyal Legion of the United States, 1886–1888.* 8 vols. 2:96–120. Cincinnati, Ohio: Robert Clarke, 1888–1908.

Wooster, Ralph A., ed. "With the Confederate Cavalry in the West: The Civil War Experiences of Isaac Dunbar Affleck." *Southwestern Historical Quarterly* 83 (July 1979): 1–28.

## SECONDARY SOURCES

### BOOKS

Albaugh, William A. *Tyler, Texas, C.S.A.* Harrisburg, Pa.: Stackpole Press, 1958.

Allardice, Bruce S. *More Generals in Gray.* Baton Rouge: Louisiana State Univ. Press, 1995.

Anderson, Charles G. *Confederate General William Read "Dirty Neck Bill" Scurry (1821–1864).* Snyder, Tex.: Charles G. Anderson, 1999.

Arceneaux, William. *Acadian General: Alfred Mouton and the Civil War.* 2nd ed. Lafayette: Center for Louisiana Studies, University of Southwestern Louisiana, 1981.

Ayers, Edward L., and John C. Willis, eds. *The Edge of the South: Life in Nineteenth-Century Virginia.* Charlottesville: Univ. Press of Virginia, 1991.

Bailey, Anne J. *Between the Enemy and Texas: Parsons's Texas Cavalry in the Civil War.* Fort Worth: Texas Christian Univ. Press, 1989.

Barber, Patsy K. *Historic Cotile.* [Alexandria, La.]: Baptist Message Press, 1967.

Barr, Alwyn. *Polignac's Texas Brigade.* 1964. Reprint, College Station: Texas A&M Univ. Press, 1998.

Bauer, K. Jack. *Zachary Taylor: Soldier, Planter, Statesman of the Old Southwest.* Baton Rouge: Louisiana State Univ. Press, 1985.

Bearss, Edwin Cole. *The Campaign for Vicksburg.* 3 vols. Dayton, Ohio: Morningside, 1985–86.

———. *Steele's Retreat from Camden and the Battle of Jenkins' Ferry.* Little Rock: Arkansas Civil War Centennial Commission, 1967.

Belisle, John G. *History of Sabine Parish, Louisiana.* [Many, La.]: Sabine Banner Press, 1912.

*Biographical Directory of the American Congress, 1774–1996.* Alexandria, Va.: CQ Staff Directories, 1997.

*A Biographical History of Eminent and Self-Made Men of the State of Indiana.* 2 vols. Cincinnati, Ohio: Western Biographical, 1880.

Blair, William. *Virginia's Private War: Feeding Body and Soul in the Confederacy, 1861–1865.* New York: Oxford Univ. Press, 1998.

Boatner, Mark Mayo. *The Civil War Dictionary.* Rev. ed. New York: David McKay, 1988.

Bollet, Alfred Jay. *Civil War Medicine: Challenges and Triumphs.* Tucson, Ariz.: Galen Press, 2002.

Buenger, Walter L. *Secession and the Union in Texas.* Austin: Univ. of Texas Press, 1984.

Campbell, Randolph B. *An Empire for Slavery: The Peculiar Institution in Texas.* Baton Rouge: Louisiana State Univ. Press, 1989.

————. *A Southern Community in Crisis: Harrison County, Texas, 1850–1880.* Austin: Texas State Historical Assn., 1983.

Campbell, Randolph B., and Richard G. Lowe. *Wealth and Power in Antebellum Texas.* College Station: Texas A&M Univ. Press, 1977.

Capers, Gerald M. *Stephen A. Douglas: Defender of the Union.* Boston: Little, Brown, 1959.

Censer, Jane Turner. *North Carolina Planters and Their Children, 1800–1860.* Baton Rouge: Louisiana State Univ. Press, 1984.

Clinton, Catherine. *The Plantation Mistress: Women's World in the Old South.* New York: Pantheon Books, 1982.

Coates, Earl J., and Dean S. Thomas. *An Introduction to Civil War Small Arms.* Gettysburg, Pa.: Thomas Publications, 1990.

Connelly, Thomas Lawrence. *Army of the Heartland: The Army of Tennessee, 1861–1862.* Baton Rouge: Louisiana State Univ. Press, 1967.

Cooling, Benjamin Franklin. *Forts Henry and Donelson: The Key to the Confederate Heartland.* Knoxville: Univ. of Tennessee Press, 1987.

Cunningham, H. H. *Doctors in Gray: The Confederate Medical Service.* Baton Rouge: Louisiana State Univ. Press, 1958.

Current, Richard N., ed. *Encyclopedia of the Confederacy.* 4 vols. New York: Simon and Schuster, 1993.

Cutrer, Thomas W. *Ben McCulloch and the Frontier Military Tradition.* Chapel Hill: Univ. of North Carolina Press, 1993.

Daddysman, James W. *The Matamoros Trade: Confederate Commerce, Diplomacy, and Intrigue.* Newark, Del.: Univ. of Delaware Press, 1984.

Davis, William C., ed. *The Confederate General.* 6 vols. Harrisburg, Pa.: National Historical Society, 1991.

Dyer, Frederick H. *A Compendium of the War of the Rebellion: Compiled and Arranged from Official Records of the Federal and Confederate Armies, Reports of the Adjutant Generals of the Several States, the Army Registers, and Other Reliable Documents and Sources.* 2 vols. 1908. Reprint, Dayton, Ohio: Broadfoot Publishing Co. and Morningside Press, 1994.

Edmonds, David C. *Yankee Autumn in Acadiana: A Narrative of the Great Texas Overland Expedition through Southwestern Louisiana, October–December, 1863.* Lafayette, La.: Acadiana Press, 1979.

Evans, Bruce A. *A Primer of Civil War Medicine: Non-Surgical Medical Practice during the Civil War Years.* [Knoxville, Tenn.]: Bruce A. Evans, 1996.

Foote, Shelby. *The Civil War: A Narrative.* 3 vols. New York: Random House, 1958–74.

Fox, William F. *Regimental Losses in the American Civil War, 1861–1865.* Albany, N.Y.: Albany, 1889.

Freeman, Douglas Southall. *Lee's Lieutenants: A Study in Command.* 3 vols. New York: Charles Scribner's Sons, 1942–44.

Gallagher, Gary W. *The Confederate War.* Cambridge, Mass.: Harvard Univ. Press, 1997.

Glatthaar, Joseph T. *Forged in Battle: The Civil War Alliance of Black Soldiers and White Officers.* New York: Free Press, 1990.

Grimsley, Mark. *The Hard Hand of War: Union Military Policy Toward Southern Civilians, 1861–1865.* New York: Cambridge Univ. Press, 1995.

Hale, Douglas. *The Third Texas Cavalry in the Civil War.* Norman: Univ. of Oklahoma Press, 1993.

Harris, J. William. *Plain Folk and Gentry in a Slave Society: White Liberty and Black Slavery in Augusta's Hinterlands.* Middletown, Conn.: Wesleyan Univ. Press, 1985.

Hearn, Chester G. *Admiral David Dixon Porter: The Civil War Years.* Annapolis, Md.: Naval Institute Press, 1996.

Hendrickson, Kenneth E., Jr. *The Chief Executives of Texas: From Stephen F. Austin to John B. Connally, Jr.* College Station: Texas A&M Univ. Press, 1995.

Holder, Anne Thiele. *Tennessee to Texas: Francis Richardson Tannehill, 1825–1864.* Austin, Tex.: Pemberton Press, 1966.

Hollandsworth, James G., Jr. *Pretense of Glory: The Life of General Nathaniel P. Banks.* Baton Rouge: Louisiana State Univ. Press, 1998.

Huffstodt, Jim. *Hard Dying Men: The Story of General W. H. L. Wallace, General T. E. G. Ransom, and Their "Old Eleventh" Illinois Infantry in the American Civil War (1861–1865).* Bowie, Md.: Heritage Books, 1991.

Jimerson, Randall C. *The Private Civil War: Popular Thought during the Sectional Conflict.* Baton Rouge: Louisiana State Univ. Press, 1988.

Johansson, M. Jane. *Peculiar Honor: A History of the 28th Texas Cavalry, 1862–1865.* Fayetteville: Univ. of Arkansas Press, 1998.

Johnson, Ludwell H. *Red River Campaign: Politics and Cotton in the Civil War.* 1958. Reprint, Kent, Ohio: Kent State Univ. Press, 1993.

Kerby, Robert L. *Kirby Smith's Confederacy: The Trans-Mississippi South, 1863–1865.* New York: Columbia Univ. Press, 1972.

Kinard, Jeff. *Lafayette of the South: Prince Camille de Polignac and the American Civil War.* College Station: Texas A&M Univ. Press, 2001.

Lewis, Jan. *The Pursuit of Happiness: Family and Values in Jefferson's Virginia.* New York: Cambridge Univ. Press, 1983.

Logue, Larry M. *To Appomattox and Beyond: The Civil War Soldier in War and Peace.* Chicago: Ivan R. Dee, 1996.

Long, E. B. *The Civil War Day by Day: An Almanac, 1861–1865.* Garden City, N.Y.: Doubleday, 1971.

Lowe, Richard. *The Texas Overland Expedition of 1863*. 1996. Reprint, Abilene, Tex.: Mc-Whiney Foundation Press, 1998.

Lowe, Richard G., and Randolph B. Campbell. *Planters and Plain Folk: Agriculture in Antebellum Texas*. Dallas, Tex.: Southern Methodist Univ. Press, 1987.

Lowry, Thomas P. *The Story the Soldiers Wouldn't Tell: Sex in the Civil War*. [Mechanicsburg, Pa.]: Stackpole Books, 1994.

McGowen, Stanley S. *Horse Sweat and Powder Smoke: The First Texas Cavalry in the Civil War*. College Station: Texas A&M Univ. Press, 1999.

McPherson, James M. *Battle Cry of Freedom: The Civil War Era*. New York: Oxford Univ. Press, 1988.

———. *For Cause and Comrades: Why Men Fought in the Civil War*. New York: Oxford Univ. Press, 1997.

———. *Ordeal by Fire: The Civil War and Reconstruction*. 2nd ed. New York: McGraw-Hill, 1992.

———. *What They Fought For, 1861–1865*. Baton Rouge: Louisiana State Univ. Press, 1994.

Mathews, Mitford M., ed. *A Dictionary of Americanisms on Historical Principles*. Chicago: Univ. of Chicago Press, 1956.

Miller, Randall M., Harry S. Stout, and Charles Reagan Wilson, eds. *Religion and the American Civil War*. New York: Oxford Univ. Press, 1998.

Mitchell, Reid. *Civil War Soldiers*. New York: Viking, 1988.

Moore, Albert Burton. *Conscription and Conflict in the Confederacy*. New York: Macmillan, 1924.

Nichols, James L. *Confederate Engineers*. Tuscaloosa, Ala.: Confederate, 1957.

———. *The Confederate Quartermaster in the Trans-Mississippi*. Austin: Univ. of Texas Press, 1964.

Nunn, W. C., ed. *Ten Texans in Gray*. Hillsboro, Tex.: Hill Junior College Press, 1968.

Oates, Stephen B. *Confederate Cavalry West of the River*. Austin: Univ. of Texas Press, 1961.

Owsley, Frank Lawrence. *King Cotton Diplomacy: Foreign Relations of the Confederate States of America*. Chicago: Univ. of Chicago Press, 1931.

Parks, Joseph H. *General Edmund Kirby Smith, C.S.A.* Baton Rouge: Louisiana State Univ. Press, 1954.

Parrish, T. Michael. *Richard Taylor: Soldier Prince of Dixie*. Chapel Hill: Univ. of North Carolina Press, 1992.

Peebles, Ruth. *There Never Were Such Men Before: The Civil War Soldiers and Veterans of Polk County, Texas, 1861–1865*. Livingston, Tex.: Polk County Historical Commission, 1987.

Perkins, John D. *Daniel's Battery: The 9th Texas Field Battery*. Hillsboro, Tex.: Hill College Press, 1998.

Quarles, Benjamin. *The Negro in the Civil War*. 2nd ed. Boston: Little, Brown, 1969.

Reed, Rowena. *Combined Operations in the Civil War*. Annapolis, Md.: Naval Institute Press, 1978.

Reynolds, Donald E. *Editors Make War: Southern Newspapers in the Secession Crisis*. Nashville: Vanderbilt Univ. Press, 1970.

Robertson, James I., Jr. *Soldiers Blue and Gray*. Columbia: Univ. of South Carolina Press, 1988.

Sears, Stephen W. *Landscape Turned Red: The Battle of Antietam*. New Haven, Conn.: Ticknor and Fields, 1983.

Shattuck, Gardiner H., Jr. *A Shield and Hiding Place: The Religious Life of the Civil War Armies*. Macon, Ga.: Mercer Univ. Press, 1987.

Shea, William L., and Earl J. Hess. *Pea Ridge: Civil War Campaign in the West*. Chapel Hill: Univ. of North Carolina Press, 1992.

Sifakis, Stewart. *Compendium of the Confederate Armies: Texas*. New York: Facts on File, 1995.

Silverstone, Paul H. *Warships of the Civil War Navies*. Annapolis, Md.: Naval Institute Press, 1989.

Simpson, Brooks D. *Ulysses S. Grant: Triumph over Adversity, 1822–1865*. Boston: Houghton Mifflin, 2000.

Simpson, Harold B. *Hood's Texas Brigade: Lee's Grenadier Guard*. Waco, Tex.: Texian Press, 1970.

Smith, David Paul. *Frontier Defense in the Civil War: Texas' Rangers and Rebels*. College Station: Texas A&M Univ. Press, 1992.

Smith, Thomas T. *The Old Army in Texas: A Research Guide to the U.S. Army in Nineteenth-Century Texas*. Austin: Texas State Historical Assn., 2000.

Steiner, Paul E. *Disease in the Civil War: Natural Biological Warfare in 1861–1865*. Springfield, Ill.: Charles C. Thomas, 1968.

Stouffer, Samuel A., et al. *Studies in Social Psychology in World War II*. 4 vols. Princeton: Princeton Univ. Press, 1949–50.

Sumrall, Alan K. *Battle Flags of Texans in the Confederacy*. Austin, Tex.: Eakin Press, 1995.

Trudeau, Noah Andre. *Like Men of War: Black Troops in the Civil War, 1862–1865*. Boston: Little, Brown, 1998.

Tyler, Ron, et al., eds. *The New Handbook of Texas*. 6 vols. Austin: Texas State Historical Assn., 1996.

Vinovskis, Maris A., ed. *Toward a Social History of the Civil War: Exploratory Essays*. New York: Cambridge Univ. Press, 1990.

Warner, Ezra J. *Generals in Blue: Lives of the Union Commanders*. Baton Rouge: Louisiana State Univ. Press, 1964.

———. *Generals in Gray: Lives of the Confederate Commanders*. Baton Rouge: Louisiana State Univ. Press, 1959.

Weddle, Robert S. *Plow-Horse Cavalry: The Caney Creek Boys of the Thirty-Fourth Texas*. Austin, Tex.: Madrona Press, 1974.

Wiley, Bell Irvin. *The Life of Johnny Reb: The Common Soldier of the Confederacy*. Indianapolis: Bobbs-Merrill, 1943.

Winschel, Terry J. *Vicksburg: Fall of the Confederate Gibraltar*. Abilene, Tex.: McWhiney Foundation Press, 1999.

Winters, John D. *The Civil War in Louisiana*. Baton Rouge: Louisiana State Univ. Press, 1963.

Wooster, Ralph A. *Texas and Texans in the Civil War*. Austin, Tex.: Eakin Press, 1995.

Wright, Marcus J., comp. *Texas in the War, 1861–1865*. Edited by Harold B. Simpson. Hillsboro, Tex.: Hill Junior College Press, 1965.

Wyatt-Brown, Bertram. *Southern Honor: Ethics and Behavior in the Old South*. New York: Oxford Univ. Press, 1982.

Yearns, W. Buck, ed. *The Confederate Governors*. Athens: Univ. of Georgia Press, 1985.

ARTICLES AND BOOK CHAPTERS

Bailey, Anne J. "A Texas Cavalry Raid: Reaction to Black Soldiers and Contrabands." *Civil War History* 35 (June 1989): 138–52.

———. "Was There a Massacre at Poison Spring?" *Military History of the Southwest* 20 (fall 1990): 157–68.

Baker, Robin E., and Dale Baum. "The Texas Voter and the Crisis of the Union, 1859–1861." *Journal of Southern History* 53 (August 1987): 395–420.

Barr, Alwyn. "Sabine Pass, September 1863." *Texas Military History* 2, no. 1 (1962): 17–22.

———. "Texan Losses in the Red River Campaign, 1864." *Texas Military History* 3 (summer 1963): 103–10.

Bearss, Edwin C. "The Story of Fort Beauregard, Part I." *Louisiana Studies* 3 (winter 1964): 330–84; and Part II, 4 (spring 1965): 3–40.

Berwanger, Eugene H. "Union and Confederate Reaction to French Threats Against Texas." *Journal of Confederate History* 7, no. 1 (1991): 97–111.

Bollet, Alfred Jay. "Scurvy and Chronic Diarrhea in Civil War Troops: Were They Both Nutritional Deficiency Syndromes?" *Journal of the History of Medicine and Allied Sciences* 47 (January 1992): 49–67.

Buza, Melinda S. " 'Pledges of Our Love': Friendship, Love, and Marriage among the Virginia Gentry, 1800–1825." In *The Edge of the South: Life in Nineteenth-Century Virginia*, edited by Edward L. Ayers and John C. Willis. 9–36. Charlottesville: Univ. Press of Virginia, 1991.

Cimprich, John, and Robert C. Mainfort, Jr. "The Fort Pillow Massacre: A Statistical Note." *Journal of American History* 76 (December 1989): 830–7.

Clampitt, Brad. "Camp Groce, Texas: A Confederate Prison." *Southwestern Historical Quarterly* 104 (January 2001): 365–84.

Crawford, Martin. "Confederate Volunteering and Enlistment in Ashe County, North Carolina, 1861–1862." *Civil War History* 37 (March 1991): 29–50.

Damico, John Kelly. "Confederate Soldiers Take Matters into Their Own Hands: The End of the Civil War in North Louisiana." *Louisiana History* 39 (spring 1998): 189–205.

[Davis, Mrs. Walter Gray]. "Hall, Henry Gerard: Lieut. Colonel, 1833–1873." In *Who's Who of the Confederacy: A Symposium by the Members of the Albert Sidney Johnston Chapter No. 2060, United Daughters of the Confederacy*, composited by Susan Merle Dotson, 79–87. San Antonio, Tex.: Naylor, 1966.

Edmonds, David C. "Surrender on the Bourbeux: Honorable Defeat or Incompetency under Fire?" *Louisiana History* 18 (winter 1977): 63–86.

Figg, Laurann, and Jane Farrell-Beck. "Amputation in the Civil War: Physical and Social Dimensions." *Journal of the History of Medicine and Allied Sciences* 48 (October 1993): 454–75.

Fitzhugh, Lester N. "Texas Forces in the Red River Campaign, March–May, 1864." *Texas Military History* 3 (spring 1963): 15–22.

Gentry, Judith F. "White Gold: The Confederate Government and Cotton in Louisiana." *Louisiana History* 33 (spring 1992): 229–40.

Green, Michael Robert. "'. . . So Illy Provided . . .': Events Leading to the Creation of the Texas Military Board." *Military History of Texas and the Southwest* 10, no. 2 (1972): 115–25.

Hale, Douglas. "The Third Texas Cavalry: A Socioeconomic Profile of a Confederate Regiment." *Military History of the Southwest* 19 (spring 1989): 1–26.

Hackemer, Kurt. "The Other Union Ironclad: The USS *Galena* and the Critical Summer of 1862." *Civil War History* 40 (September 1994): 226–47.

———. "Strategic Dilemma: Civil-Military Friction and the Texas Coastal Campaign of 1863." *Military History of the West* 26 (fall 1996): 187–214.

Hallock, Judith Lee. "'Lethal and Debilitating': The Southern Disease Environment as a Factor in Confederate Defeat." *Journal of Confederate History* 7, no. 1 (1991): 51–61.

Heidler, Jeanne T. "'Embarrassing Situation': David E. Twiggs and the Surrender of United States Forces in Texas, 1861." *Military History of the Southwest* 21 (fall 1991): 157–72.

Hess, Earl J. "The 12th Missouri Infantry: A Socio-Military Profile of a Union Regiment." *Missouri Historical Review* 76 (October 1981): 53–77.

Hollandsworth, James G., Jr. "The Execution of White Officers from Black Units by Confederate Forces during the Civil War." *Louisiana History* 35 (fall 1994): 475–89.

Johnson, Ludwell H. "The Red River Campaign, 11 March–20 May 1864." In *The Civil War Battlefield Guide,* edited by Frances H. Kennedy, 163–6. Boston: Houghton Mifflin, 1990.

Joiner, Gary D., and Charles E. Vetter. "The Union Naval Expedition on the Red River, March 12–May 22, 1864." *Civil War Regiments* 4, no. 2 (1994): 26–67.

Kiper, Richard L. "John Alexander McClernand and the Arkansas Post Campaign." *Arkansas Historical Quarterly* 56 (spring 1997): 56–79.

Kiple, Kenneth F., and Virginia H. Kiple. "Black Tongue and Black Men: Pellagra and Slavery in the Antebellum South." *Journal of Southern History* 43 (August 1977): 411–28.

Larison, Tinsie. "Edward Clark." In *Ten Texans in Gray,* edited by W. C. Nunn, 18–35. Hillsboro, Tex.: Hill Junior College Press, 1968.

Lutz, Eusibia. "Liendo: The Biography of a House." *Southwest Review* 16 (January 1931): 190–9.

McKaughan, Joshua. "'Few Were the Hearts . . . that did not Swell with Devotion': Community and Confederate Service in Rowan County, North Carolina, 1861–1862." *North Carolina Historical Review* 73 (April 1996): 156–83.

Madaus, Howard Michael, and Robert D. Needham. "Unit Colors of the Trans-Mississippi Confederacy." *Military Collector and Historian* 41 (1989): 123–41, 172–82; and Part II, 42 (1990): 16–21.

Marten, James. "Fatherhood in the Confederacy: Southern Soldiers and Their Children." *Journal of Southern History* 63 (May 1997): 269–92.

Michot, Stephen S. "In Relief of Port Hudson: Richard Taylor's 1863 Lafourche Offensive." *Military History of the West* 23 (fall 1993): 103–34.

Mitchell, Reid. "Christian Soldiers? Perfecting the Confederacy." In *Religion and the American Civil War,* edited by Randall M. Miller, Harry S. Stout, and Charles Reagan Wilson, 297–309. New York: Oxford Univ. Press, 1998.

Moore, Waldo W. "The Defense of Shreveport—The Confederacy's Last Redoubt." *Military Affairs* 17 (summer 1953): 72–82.

Muir, Andrew Forest. "Dick Dowling and Sabine Pass." *Civil War History* 4 (December 1958): 399–428.

Mullins, Michael A. "The Fremont Rifles: The 37th Illinois at Pea Ridge and Prairie Grove." *Civil War Regiments* 1, no. 1 (1990): 42–68.

Oates, Stephen B. "Texas under the Secessionists." *Southwestern Historical Quarterly* 67 (October 1963): 167–212.

Pecquet, Gary M. "Money in the Trans-Mississippi Confederacy and the Currency Reform Act of 1864." *Explorations in Economic History* 24 (April 1987): 218–43.

Perkins, John. "The Titus Hunters: Company D, 11th Texas Infantry Regiment, Walker's Texas Division." *East Texas Historical Journal* 35 (spring 1997): 17–29.

Pruitt, Francelle. "'We've Got to Fight or Die': Early Texas Reaction to the Confederate Draft, 1862." *East Texas Historical Journal* 36, no. 1 (1998): 3–17.

Richards, Ira Don. "The Battle of Jenkins' Ferry." *Arkansas Historical Quarterly* 20 (spring 1961): 3–16.

Roebuck, Field. "The Camp Nelson Confederate Cemetery: A Tribute to Confederate Heroes." *Confederate Veteran* 40 (November–December 1992): 22–6.

Scheiber, Harry N. "The Pay of Troops and Confederate Morale in the Trans-Mississippi West." *Arkansas Historical Quarterly* 18 (winter 1959): 350–65.

Shea, William L. "The Confederate Defeat at Cache River." *Arkansas Historical Quarterly* 52 (summer 1993): 129–55.

Smith, Thomas T. "Blitzkrieg: The Myth of Blitz." *Infantry* 80 (July–August 1990): 28–30.

Sutherland, Daniel E. "Sideshow No Longer: A Historiographical Review of the Guerrilla War." *Civil War History* 46 (March 2000): 5–23.

Touchstone, Samuel J. "Camp Magruder and General Thomas J. Churchill's Civil War Camp." *North Louisiana Historical Association Journal* 24 (winter 1993): 40–1.

Tyler, Ronnie C. "Cotton on the Border, 1861–1865." *Southwestern Historical Quarterly* 73 (April 1970): 456–77.

Tyson, Carl Newton. "Texas: Men for War; Cotton for Economy." *Journal of the West* 14 (January 1975): 130–48.

Urwin, Gregory J. W. "'We Cannot Treat Negroes . . . as Prisoners of War': Racial Atrocities and Reprisals in Civil War Arkansas." *Civil War History* 42 (September 1996): 193–210.

Watson, Samuel J. "Religion and Combat Motivation in the Confederate Armies." *Journal of Military History* 58 (January 1994): 29–55.

Weitz, Mark A. "Drill, Training, and the Combat Performance of the Civil War Soldier: Dispelling the Myth of the Poor Soldier, Great Fighter." *Journal of Military History* 62 (April 1998): 263–89.

Whittington, G. P. "Rapides Parish, Louisiana—A History," 10th installment. *Louisiana Historical Quarterly* 18 (January 1935): 5–39.

Winschel, Terrence J. "To Rescue Gibraltar: John Walker's Texas Division and Its Expedition to Relieve Fortress Vicksburg." *Civil War Regiments* 3, no. 3 (1993): 33–58.

———. "Walker's Texas Division: Milliken's Bend." *Civil War Regiments* 3, no. 3 (1993): 90–1.

Wooster, Ralph A., and Robert Wooster. "'Rarin' for a Fight': Texans in the Confederate Army." *Southwestern Historical Quarterly* 84 (April 1981): 387–426.

THESES AND DISSERTATIONS

Clampitt, Bradley Ray. "The Break-Up of the Confederate Trans-Mississippi Army, 1865." M.A. thesis, University of North Texas, 2001.

Felgar, Robert P. "Texas in the War for Southern Independence, 1861–1865." Ph.D. diss., University of Texas, 1935.

Hamaker, Blake Richard. "Making a Good Soldier: A Historical and Quantitative Study of the 15th Texas Infantry, C.S.A." M.A. thesis, University of North Texas, 1998.

Owens, Jeffrey Alan. "The Civil War in Tensas Parish, Louisiana: Community History." M.A. thesis, University of Texas at Tyler, 1990.

Parker, Scott Dennis. "'The Best Stuff Which the State Affords': A Portrait of the Fourteenth Texas Infantry in the Civil War, 1862–1865." M.A. thesis, University of North Texas, 1998.

Reid, Thomas R. "The Spartan Band: A History of Burnett's 13th Texas Cavalry Regiment, 1862–1865." M.A. thesis, Lamar University, 2001.

Smith, David P. "In Defense of Texas: The Life of Henry E. McCulloch." M.A. thesis, Stephen F. Austin State University, 1975.

Snyder, Perry Anderson. "Shreveport, Louisiana, during the Civil War and Reconstruction." Ph.D. diss., Florida State University, 1979.

Townsend, Stephen Andrew. "The Rio Grande Expedition, 1863–1865." Ph.D. diss., University of North Texas, 2001.

# INDEX